Intranational macroeconomics

Historically, the study of international trade and finance has focused on the movements of goods and capital between nations. But as countries are becoming more integrated, the macroeconomic role of national borders is diminished. The approach that researchers have recently adopted to further our understanding of how economic interactions between nations will evolve as national borders decline in importance is to analyze economic interactions within a country (i.e., "intranational macroeconomics"). This book brings the intranational macroeconomics literature into clearer focus by collecting the strands of research into a common thread. Each chapter attempts to answer the following two questions: First, what contributions do national borders make to our understanding of macroeconomics? Second, how will these contributions change as the world becomes more integrated?

Gregory D. Hess is the Robert S. Danforth–Ben E. Lewis Professor of Economics at Oberlin College. He previously taught at the Universities of Kansas and Cambridge and St. Johns College, Cambridge, and held visiting appointments at Carnegie Mellon University's Graduate School of Industrial Administration and the London Business School. Professor Hess also served as economist on the Federal Reserve Board in Washington, D.C., and as a visiting scholar at the Federal Reserve Banks of Kansas City and Cleveland. Professor Hess has published articles in numerous academic journals, including the *Journal of International Economics*, the *Journal of Monetary Economics*, and the *American Economic Review*.

Eric van Wincoop is Senior Economist in the international research function of the Federal Reserve Bank of New York. He has also taught at Boston University and held visiting appointments at Kyoto University, the University of Stockholm, the Federal Reserve Bank of Minneapolis, and the Gasparini Institute of Economic Research in Milan. Dr. van Wincoop has published articles in leading journals such as the *Journal of International Economics*, the *Journal of Monetary Economics*, the *International Economic Review*, and the *European Economic Review*. In September 1998, he won the Hicks-Tinbergen Medal (jointly with Laura Bottazzi and Paolo Pesenti) from the European Economic Association for the best article published in the *European Economic Review* in the previous two years.

Intranational macroeconomics

Edited by

GREGORY D. HESS   ERIC VAN WINCOOP
Oberlin College   *Federal Reserve Bank of New York*

CAMBRIDGE
UNIVERSITY PRESS

CAMBRIDGE UNIVERSITY PRESS
Cambridge, New York, Melbourne, Madrid, Cape Town,
Singapore, São Paulo, Delhi, Tokyo, Mexico City

Cambridge University Press
The Edinburgh Building, Cambridge CB2 8RU, UK

Published in the United States of America by Cambridge University Press, New York

www.cambridge.org
Information on this title: www.cambridge.org/9781107403796

First published 2000
First paperback edition 2011

A catalogue record for this publication is available from the British Library

Library of Congress Cataloging in Publication Data

Intranational macroeconomics / edited by Gregory D. Hess, Eric van Wincoop.
p. cm.
A collection of 12 papers discussed at a conference "associated with the book during
the summer of 1998" and hosted by the Federal Reserve Bank of New York.
Includes bibliographical references and index.
ISBN 0-521-66163-3
1. International economic integration. 2. Macroeconomics. 3. Business cycles.
4. Economic policy. I. Hess, Gregory D. II. van Wincoop, Eric.
HF1418.5 .I59 2000
339 - dc21 99-049059

ISBN 978-0-521-66163-8 Hardback
ISBN 978-1-107-40379-6 Paperback

Contents

Acknowledgments

We thank the Federal Reserve Bank of New York for hosting a conference associated with the book during the summer of 1998, and the Center for European Integration (ZEI) as a financial contributor to the conference. We are also indebted to the following discussants during the conference for their effort and insight: David Backus, Marianne Baxter, Richard Clarida, Donald Davis, Marco Del Negro, Atish Ghosh, Michael Klein, Prakash Loungani, Cara Lown, Kei-Mu Yi, and Oved Yosha. We thank Elizabeth Lewis for making the conference run smoothly. We finally would like to thank our wives, Lora and Emily, for their unconditional support.

Introduction

Globalization has become a modern-day buzzword. Daily events remind us of the interconnectedness of economies on a global scale. Over the last several years, we have seen emerging market crises spread throughout the world. We have seen stock markets fluctuate together across the globe. When a foreign economy experiences a downturn, the first question we ask is "when and how much will this affect our domestic economy?" We no longer live in a world where we can safely ignore the potential spillovers from a far away crisis.

There is little doubt that this globalization is directly associated with nations becoming more integrated. Over the last few decades, barriers both to the trade in goods and capital have been lowered. Partly this is the result of the development of new technologies. International trade in goods and assets has been facilitated by the decline in the costs of transportation and communication, the latter due to cheaper computer and telephone networks. However, a reduction of policy-imposed restrictions, through deregulation and liberalization, has also played a fundamental role in the rise of globalism. Capital controls have been significantly reduced over the past three decades. This process began with the demise of the Bretton Woods system as it was no longer necessary to impose capital controls to defend the fixed exchange rate parities. It has continued throughout the 1990s as emerging markets have significantly increased access of foreign investors to their markets and as EU countries eliminated remaining controls by January 1993 as part of the single European market.

We have also seen a reduction in trade barriers. Across the globe, tariff and nontariff barriers have declined. New trade unions, such as the North American Free Trade Agreement (NAFTA) in North America and MERCOSUR in South America, have developed as well. Since the completion of the single market in Europe in January 1993, there has been free movement of goods within the European Community. Border formalities in Europe have been abolished. The adoption of a single currency in the Euro zone since January 1999 is expected to reduce barriers to trade in goods and capital further.

1

Where will this process eventually lead us? Geographic borders have an independent impact on an economy only to the extent that economic policies and political institutions differ across borders. As these differences blur, national borders will become less meaningful. An approach that has recently been adopted by researchers to better understand how economic interactions *between* countries will evolve as national borders decline in importance is to analyze economic interactions across regions *within* a country, whose economies are already highly integrated. The aim of this book is to unify the various contributions to this literature and to elevate it to the level of a new field, which we refer to as *intranational macroeconomics*.

Policy-imposed barriers to the flow of goods, capital, labor, and knowledge across intranational borders are generally quite small. Tariffs, trade quotas, capital controls, and immigration laws do not apply to intranational borders. Regions within a country share a common currency, tax system, legal foundation, accounting system, and language. They provide, therefore, a proper benchmark for understanding macroeconomic relationships within an economically integrated geographic area.

In this light, intranational macroeconomics provides important insight into international macroeconomics. First, it reveals important aspects of the likely implications for trade, growth, business cycles, and capital flows of increased integration among countries. Second, it also informs us about the limitations of economic integration. For example, to the extent that investors' portfolios are biased toward local firms even within a country, it suggests that the international home bias is unlikely to vanish, even when countries become perfectly integrated. Third, insights from intranational macroeconomics can provide guidance toward developing better international macroeconomic models. For example, it can shed light on which barriers are important and the extent to which they are specific to international borders.

The purpose of this book is to bring the intranational macroeconomics literature into clearer focus by weaving the various strands of research into a common thread. To date, the majority of the intranational literature has evolved along independent lines: some researchers work on growth, some on risk sharing, some on relative prices, and still others on labor migration. For the literature to advance toward a deeper understanding of the macroeconomics of borders, however, we feel that a unified collection is in order. Moreover, by collecting this research into one volume, we hope that a wider audience can be educated about the scope of intranational macroeconomic research to date. Most chapters provide an overview of current research in each of the various areas.

Three broad sets of themes have received considerable attention in the intranational macroeconomics literature. First, what do we know about the extent of goods and capital market integration at the intranational level as compared to the international level? Second, what are the implications for business cycles and growth of the higher degree of intranational integration? Finally, what are the policy lessons at the national and international level that can be drawn from intranational evidence? Chapters 1 to 6 deal with the first question; Chapters 7 to 9, with the second; and Chapters 10 to 12, with the final question. Because the three questions are closely interrelated, some chapters will naturally touch on each of them.

The first four chapters consider different measures of capital market integration. Even though international capital markets have become more integrated over time, even today there remains extensive evidence suggesting a low degree of international capital mobility. First, there is a home (i.e., domestic) bias in both stock and bond portfolios. Even investors in small countries invest most of their portfolio in domestic assets, which is at odds with the diversification of risk. Second, national saving and investment are highly correlated, both across countries and over time in individual countries. This suggests that most of an increase in domestic saving is directed toward financing a rise in domestic investment. Third, cross-country consumption correlations are on average even lower than cross-country output correlations, suggesting a low degree of risk sharing across countries. Finally, many authors have documented excess sensitivity of national consumption growth to expected income growth, suggesting that international credit markets are not well integrated.

An important conclusion that can be drawn from the first four chapters is that the extent of capital market integration is higher at the intranational level than the international level. In Chapter 1, Eric van Wincoop surveys the intranational saving-investment literature. The correlation between saving and investment is generally much lower at the intranational level. In order to draw conclusions about the degree of capital mobility, it is important to control for factors that affect the correlation even under perfect capital mobility. This is examined using data for Japanese prefectures and OECD countries. It is found that the correlation remains lower for the prefectures than the countries.

In Chapter 2, Mario Crucini and Gregory Hess use consumption and output data to estimate a simple model of risk sharing. Using data for Canadian provinces, U.S. states, Japanese prefectures, and OECD countries, they find that a much larger fraction of consumers share risk across regions within a country than across countries. Not surprisingly, because regions within countries have already diversified a large fraction of their risk, they find that the potential welfare gains from additional risk sharing are smaller among regions within countries than among countries themselves.

In Chapter 3, Bent Sørensen and Oved Yosha use tests of excess sensitivity to explore the extent of intranational and international credit integration. They argue that the well-documented excess sensitivity of consumption growth to expected income growth at the country level does not necessarily imply a lack of international credit market integration to the extent that country income growth is correlated with movements in the global interest rate. They therefore control for global effects by subtracting OECD consumption and income growth. Similarly, they obtain an estimate of the extent of intranational credit market integration for the United States and Canada after subtracting national growth rates from state and province growth rates. Their results show substantially higher intranational credit market integration than international credit market integration.

Nonetheless, even though there is substantial evidence that intranational capital markets are better integrated than international ones, there is also evidence that intranational capital markets are not perfectly integrated. In Chapter 4, Gur Huberman surveys evidence documenting that there is also an intranational portfolio home bias. For instance, he reports that pension investments are significantly biased toward stock of the employer's company. He also documents substantial geographic bias in the ownership of claims on Regional Bell Operating Companies. Even the portfolios of money market fund managers are biased toward local firms. This evidence suggests that the home bias in stock and bond portfolios is unlikely to dissipate fully as fuller international capital market integration proceeds. Another piece of evidence that intranational capital markets are not perfectly integrated can be found in Chapter 2, where Crucini and Hess find that in the United States and Japan the correlation between regional and national consumption is less than the correlation between regional and national output.

Similar conclusions can be reached with regards to labor and goods market integration. Although it is well known that labor is more mobile across regions within a country than across countries, documented in Chapter 8 by Antonio Fatás, he also demonstrates that even within countries there are often substantial barriers to labor mobility. In particular, labor is less mobile across regions within European countries than across U.S. states. Migration across European regions has even dropped in spite of larger unemployment disparities.

Evidence on goods market integration is presented in Chapters 5 and 6. In Chapter 5, Charles Engel and John Rogers also document a higher degree of goods market integration at the intranational level. They use evidence on relative prices. One might expect that prices of similar goods move closer together when regions are more integrated. Using disaggregated price data for U.S. states and Canadian provinces, Engel and Rogers find that the relative prices of goods are much more volatile across countries than within, even after controlling for distance. Exchange rate volatility does not fully account for this volatility disparity. In Chapter 6 Holger Wolf surveys evidence on the extent of intranational trade. The key finding in the literature is that, after controlling for distance and other geographic variables, trade between Canadian provinces is about 10 times larger than between Canadian provinces and U.S. states. Although this suggests a higher degree of goods market integration within countries than across, possibly as the result of hard to measure trade barriers, Wolf also documents a substantial intranational home bias. Controlling for distance and scale, he finds that trade is more than three times as high within a state than across states. This evidence suggests that the home bias in trade may not completely go away even when countries become perfectly integrated.

Turning now to the second main theme of the literature, there are many reasons to expect both business cycles and long-term growth patterns to depend on the extent of integration among regions. First, as argued in Chapter 7 by Paul Evans, a higher degree of factor market and goods market integration can be expected to lead to more rapid convergence of per capita incomes toward parallel balanced growth paths. Second, one would expect more-persistent growth differentials among regions with a high degree of labor mobility as workers continue to relocate toward the most attractive regions. Third, one may expect less volatile business cycles among regions with a high degree of labor mobility as adjustment to regional shocks takes place through migration. Finally, one would expect business cycles to have a larger common component across regions when they are more integrated. There is evidence that more trade leads to a stronger comovement of business cycles. A higher degree of monetary and fiscal policy coordination, particularly in the form of a single currency or federal fiscal policy, could also lead to a larger common component of business cycle volatility across regions.

The evidence presented in Chapters 7 to 9 is consistent with these views. In Chapter 7, Paul Evans finds rapid convergence of the per capita growth rates of the 48 contiguous U.S. states to parallel balanced growth paths. At the same time, he finds that convergence among a broad set of countries is either slow or nonexistent. He argues that a key issue in understanding this phenomena is the higher degree of labor mobility across U.S. states than across countries

In Chapter 8, Antonio Fatás identifies a number of empirical regularities based on a comparison of the labor market data for U.S. states to that of countries within the European Union (EU). For example, he finds much larger differences in employment growth rates in U.S. states than in EU countries. Moreover, these differences are highly persistent within the United States – states with high growth rates from 1961 to 1975 generally also had high growth rates from 1975 to 1990. There is no such relationship among EU countries. With regards to business cycle adjustments, Fatás shows that in the United States most of the adjustment to regional labor demand shocks takes place through migration, whereas among European countries most of the adjustment takes place through unemployment and changes in labor market participation. The latter are often supported through the welfare system and can be viewed as a form a hidden unemployment.

In Chapter 9, Todd Clark and Kwanho Shin study the sources of business cycles for both U.S. states and European countries. They decompose shocks to disaggregate industry growth rates, at the state and European country level, into common, regional (state or country), industry-specific, and idiosyncratic shocks. They find that common shocks are more important for the U.S. states than for European countries. Moreover, country-specific shocks in Europe are more important than state-specific shocks in the United States. These findings are consistent with the view that states are more integrated than countries and U.S. states experience more common policy shocks (monetary and fiscal) than European countries.

An important question is what policy lessons at the national and international level can be drawn for countries that are in the process of increased integration with other countries. In Chapter 10 Maurice Obstfeld and Giovanni Peri review the intranational empirical evidence and draw from it important policy implications for European countries in the context of monetary integration. They start from the point of view that European countries are unlikely to become more integrated than regions within those countries are already. In comparison to the U.S. states, they find that for regions within Germany, Italy, and the United Kingdom, there is less labor migration, more reliance on interregional transfer payments in the adjustment process to overcome adverse shocks, and relatively slow adjustment to regional labor demand shocks. Because relative prices have not operated as an important adjustment mechanism in the past, neither for regions of European countries nor for U.S. states, they suggest that members of the European Monetary Union (EMU) may find it hard to resist expansion of its centralized fiscal functions in the direction of intercountry stabilization transfers. They weigh the advantages and disadvantages of expanding such centralized transfer programs and consider other alternatives, such as exercising more flexibility in national fiscal policies, undertaking internal restructuring, and having governments operate as risk-sharing intermediaries for its residents through capital markets that trade claims on a broad measure of output.

Again with the view that we can draw lessons for EMU from the experience of existing currency unions that simply consist of one country, in Chapter 11 Jürgen von Hagen reviews the available evidence on the extent of risk sharing through centralized fiscal policy within existing currency unions (countries) and discusses advantages, drawbacks, and limitations of such centralized transfer schemes. Even though the evidence shows that intranational risk sharing through the fiscal system is significant in most countries, there is substantial variation across countries in the extent of insurance provided, with risk sharing being rather modest in the United States. There is no clear evidence that intranational risk sharing is larger in unitary than in federal states. von Hagen distinguishes between the stabilization and risk-sharing roles of such transfer schemes and discusses limitations to the size of centralized transfer schemes as a result of moral hazard and political economy constraints. He also considers the implications of such centralized fiscal transfer schemes for the effectiveness of monetary policy of a currency union.

The last chapter, by Sandra Hanson McPherson and Chris Waller, examines the intranational role of monetary policy. They address to what extent and through which channels a common monetary policy affects regions of a currency union differently. The authors use data on U.S. states to address the question. The answer has obvious implications for both U.S. monetary policy and that of the European Monetary Union. The authors argue that when financial markets of a currency union are not well integrated, the common monetary policy can have different effects on different regions within the union. This depends particularly on the importance of small banks and firms, which are not well integrated in national financial markets. They present evidence showing that there is a causal link from the amount of lending by banks in a state to the economic performance of the state. This finding suggests that, even within the United States, financial markets are not perfectly integrated, consistent with some of the evidence discussed earlier. Moreover, it implies that a common monetary policy can impact different regions of the currency union differently, which depends among other things on the size of banks and firms in a region.

PART I

Financial and goods market integration

CHAPTER 1

*Intra*national versus *inter*national saving-investment comovements*

Eric van Wincoop[†]

1.1 Introduction

On the surface, international capital markets appear to be highly integrated. Cross-border transactions in equity and bonds, virtually zero in 1970, were 152% of GDP in the United States in 1996, and 435% of GDP in Italy in the same year. Among the major industrialized countries, covered interest rate differentials have vanished, and stock indices have become closely interconnected. With most barriers to capital flows removed, arbitrage across markets is easily accomplished through high-speed media. Emerging markets that have opened the floodgates to international capital markets have experienced large inflows, followed by sharp reversals, which have significantly impacted their economies.

But in a longer-term sense, the extent of international financial integration remains quite limited even today. Tesar and Werner (1998) report that at the end of 1996 the fraction of the equity portfolio invested abroad by domestic residents was 10% for the United States, 11% for Canada, 18% for Germany, and 22% for the United Kingdom. Although these numbers increased a bit from a decade ago, it shows that investors are still primarily investing at home. Other evidence corroborates that the extent of diversification, or risk sharing, is very limited across countries. The correlation of consumption across countries is lower than that of income, exactly the opposite of what one would expect with substantial risk sharing.[1] Long-term consumption growth uncertainty is about as large as long-term income growth uncertainty.[2]

* I thank Marianne Baxter and participants at the Intranational Macroeconomics conference at the Federal Reserve Bank of New York for useful comments and suggestions. The views expressed are those of the author and do not necessarily reflect the position of the Federal Reserve Bank of New York or the Federal Reserve System.
† Mailing address: International Research Function, Federal Reserve Bank of New York, 33 Liberty St., New York, NY 10045. E-mail: *eric.vanwincoop@ny.frb.org*.
[1] See Backus, Kehoe, and Kydland (1992).
[2] See Athanasoulis and van Wincoop (2000).

A final piece of evidence concerning the low degree of long-run international financial integration is the Feldstein-Horioka finding that countries with high saving rates also tend to be countries with high investment rates. The original Feldstein and Horioka (1980) study was based on 1960s and 1970s data, but the strong cross-sectional relationship still holds today. It is consistent with the lack of portfolio diversification. However, the current consensus is that little information can be extracted from saving-investment comovements about the extent of international capital mobility. It has for example been argued that countries with high population or technology growth rates can be expected to have both high saving and investment rates, independent of the degree of capital mobility. Similarly, positive time-series correlations between saving and investment rates can be attributed to business cycles, which affect saving and investment in the same direction, even when there are no barriers to capital mobility.

This chapter will shed light on evidence from national saving and investment rates by comparing it to the *intra*national evidence. Regions within a country are already highly integrated, so that the intranational evidence may provide a good benchmark for interpreting the international data. We will look at both time-series and cross-sectional relationships between saving and investment rates, comparing national and intranational data. In addition, we will control for common factors, which can be expected to affect both saving and investment rates, even in the absence of barriers to capital mobility.

The chapter is organized as follows. In Section 1.2, we review the existing literature on the relationship between intranational saving and investment rates. In Section 1.3, we take a closer look at the Japanese prefectural data and compare the evidence to that for OECD countries. We will control for factors that are believed to affect both saving and investment rates even when financial markets are perfectly integrated. Although the evidence suggests that intranational financial markets are highly integrated, at the international level we find that there are still substantial barriers to long-term capital mobility, as reflected in the cross-sectional evidence. Section 1.4 interprets the findings and discusses modeling implications. The final section concludes.

1.2   Review of the literature

Bayoumi (1997), Bayoumi and Rose (1993), Dekle (1996), Iwamoto and van Wincoop (2000), Sinn (1992), Thomas (1993), and Yamori (1995) compute the comovement between saving and investment for Japanese, U.S., U.K., and Canadian regions. These papers differ in the type of saving-investment relationship considered, and the definition and measurement of saving and investment. In this section, we will first review the findings from that literature and then discuss some issues concerning the definition and computation of intranational saving and investment rates.

Table 1.1. *Estimates of the comovement between regional saving and investment rates*

Author(s)	Country	Statistical method	Sample	Estimate of comovement
Bayoumi and Rose (1993)	United Kingdom	Panel regression	1971–1975	−0.48 (0.16)
			1976–1980	0.24 (0.21)
			1981–1985	0.01 (0.14)
	United Kingdom	Cross-sectional regression	1971–1975	−0.99 (0.53)
			1976–1980	0.54 (0.80)
			1981–1985	0.03 (0.33)
Thomas (1993)	United Kingdom	Panel regression	1971–1987	−0.56 (0.13)
	Canada	Panel regression	1961–1989	−0.10 (0.02)
Bayoumi (1997)	Canada	Cross-sectional regression	1961–1993	−0.07 (0.08)
Dekle (1996)	Japan	Cross-sectional regression	1975–1988	−0.36 (0.08)
			1975–1979	−0.44 (0.11)
			1980–1984	−0.32 (0.09)
			1985–1988	−0.24 (0.05)
Sinn (1992)	United States	Cross-sectional regression	1957	−0.12 (0.08)
			1953	−0.06 (0.08)
Iwamoto and van Wincoop (2000)	Japan	Cross-sectional correlation	1975–1980	0.30 (0.15)
			1980–1985	0.47 (0.10)
			1985–1990	0.43 (0.10)
		Time-series correlation	1975–1990	0.31 (0.04)

Note: The table provides a summary of estimates in the literature of the comovement between regional saving and investment rates. Four measures of comovement, reported in the third column, have been used: (i) an estimate of β from the panel regression $(I/Y)_{it} = \alpha + \beta(S/Y)_{it}$, (ii) an estimate of β from the cross-sectional regression $(I/Y)_i = \alpha + \beta(S/Y)_i$, (iii) the cross-sectional correlation, and (iv) the average time-series correlation. Standard errors associated with the estimated comovement are reported in brackets in the last column. With regards to the regression estimates, only Thomas (1993) instruments the saving rate. Thomas (1993) estimates a panel, but because he includes annual time dummies, the result can be interpreted as the average 1-year cross-sectional regression estimate for his sample.

Table 1.1 summarizes the results from the literature. The estimated relationship between intranational saving and investment rates is shown in the last column. It depends on the measure of comovement used, which is shown in the third column. Four measures are commonly used in the literature: (i) the estimate β from a panel regression $(I/Y)_{it} = \alpha + \beta(S/Y)_{it}$, (ii) the estimate β from a cross-sectional regression $(I/Y)_i = \alpha + \beta(S/Y)_i$, where the saving and investment rates are usually time averages, (iii) a cross-sectional correlation, and (iv) the average time-series correlation.

With the exception of the results of Iwamoto and van Wincoop (2000), estimates of the comovement between saving and investment rates are either insignificantly different from zero or significant and negative. Again with the exception of Iwamoto and van Wincoop (2000), most of the point estimates are negative. These results stand in sharp contrast to that for countries. In the Feldstein-Horioka cross-sectional regression $(I/Y)_i = \alpha + \beta(S/Y)_i$ for 16 OECD countries, β was found to be approximately 0.9 for each of four 5-year periods. The last subperiod was 1970–1974. Obstfeld (1995) finds that this coefficient has dropped a bit over time but is still 0.64 (s.e. = 0.09) for the period 1986–1990. This is based on a larger sample of 22 countries.

One possibility is that the lower correlation between saving and investment rates across regions is simply the result of measurement error. All papers in this literature do indeed face significant measurement problems. Bayoumi and Rose (1993) do not have data on regional investment. They use data for specific industries, which exclude one quarter to half (depending on the region) of private sector investment. Sinn (1992) used U.S. data based on a study by Romans (1965). Household and corporate saving are computed in an indirect way by adding over all possible forms of saving. Investment is based on data for eight different industries. As noted by Sinn (1992) himself, the low coefficient on the saving variable he finds might very well be a result of measurement error due to the intricacy of Romans' calculations. Thomas (1993) finds total saving by adding up over household, corporate, and general government saving. No data on corporate saving are available, so that national retained earnings is attributed to the regions based on data on gross profits. Private and government investment are computed by aggregating over respectively a limited number of industries and types of government investment. For the UK government, consumption refers to categories only adding up to 60% of the total.

It is remarkable though that most of these papers find a *negative* comovement between aggregate saving and investment. This is hard to attribute to measurement error. Because the types of measurement error in saving and investment rates appear to be unrelated, it should not bias the covariance between saving and investment rates. It leads to an upward bias in the standard deviations of saving and investment rates and, therefore, a downward bias in the absolute value of the correlation or the coefficient of a panel or cross-sectional regression. But it cannot explain the negative comovements.

In contrast, Iwamoto and van Wincoop (2000) find a positive and significant comovement between regional saving and investment rates. The difference stems not from measurement problems but from the definition of regional saving and investment rates. In Iwamoto and van Wincoop (2000), regional saving is the sum of saving by all residents and institutions of a region. These are households, firms, and local governments. Similarly, regional investment is the sum of all physical investment by firms and the local government in a region.

Bayoumi and Rose (1993) define regional saving as GDP − C, where C is private consumption. They use an estimate of private investment. The other papers define regional saving as GNP − C − G, where G is general government consumption, and define regional investment as the sum of private and general government investment. This adds to saving and investment of a region's residents (households, firms, and local governments) an arbitrary measure of saving and investment by the central government. A central government's saving in a region is defined as tax revenue from the region, minus transfers to the region, minus central government consumption spending in the region, minus some allocation of net interest payments to the region. With this definition, a change in transfers from the central government to the region's residents, holding constant consumption by the region's residents, has no effect on regional saving. It has offsetting effects on central government saving and that by regional residents.

The advantage of defining saving as that by the residents of a region is that it is consistent with the definition of national saving, which is that by the residents of a country. It is natural to define a region or country by the residents that reside in it. With this definition, regional saving minus investment is the net capital outflow from a region. It is indeed these capital flows across regions that we are interested in. Obstfeld (1995) also criticized the general government definition of saving and investment when he argued that net transfers from the central government should be included in a region's income. For a given level of consumption by the region's residents, it reduces the need to borrow from other regions.

Figure 1.1 illustrates why these two different measures of regional saving and investment lead to such different results. It shows Japanese regional government saving and investment, as a fraction of regional GDP, averaged over the period 1985–90. The upper panel defines the government as the sum of all local governments: the prefectural government and governments of cities, towns, villages, and wards. The lower panel is based on the general government concept, adding local and central government saving and investment, where central government saving in the region is as defined above. It also includes social security payments minus benefits. The figure shows a remarkable difference between these two measures. There is a strong positive relationship between local government saving and investment rates, with a correlation of 0.98. At the same time, there is a negative relationship between general government saving and investment rates, with a correlation of −0.84.

The difference is a result of the central government's transfer policy, combined with the different definitions of regional government. Local governments of the less wealthy regions receive the largest transfers from the central government, both for consumption and investment purposes. Of the cross-regional variation in total central government transfers, 61% is accounted for by cross-regional variation in per capita GDP. Under the general government definition, these transfers are not counted as part of the region's government income. But because the money is spent by the local government, both for consumption and

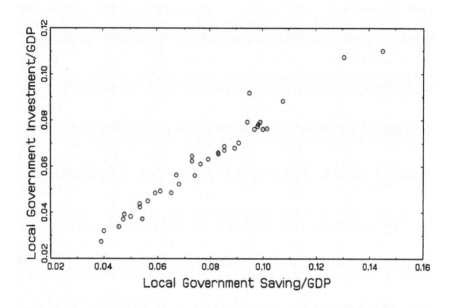

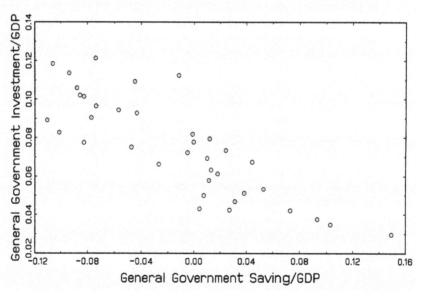

Figure 1.1. Japanese regional government saving and investment (% of GDP, average 1985–1990).

investment purposes, general government saving tends to be low and investment high in regions with relatively large transfers from the central government. This accounts for the negative relationship seen in the bottom panel of Figure 1.1.[3] When using the local government definition, the transfer is counted as regional government income. To the extent that it is intended for investment purposes, it therefore raises both local government saving and investment, accounting for the positive relationship in the upper panel.

Figure 1.2 illustrates the effect of these different definitions of regional government on the cross-sectional relationship between total regional saving and investment rates, again averaged over 1985–90. Because of the strong positive relationship between local government saving and investment, there is a positive cross-sectional correlation of 0.4 between total saving and investment when the regional government is defined as the sum of local governments. But there is a negative correlation of −0.49 between aggregate saving and investment rates when the general government definition is used. This is consistent with the negative comovements found by Dekle (1996) and Yamori (1995) for Japanese regions when using the general government concept and by Thomas (1993) for UK and Canadian regions.

1.3   OECD versus Japanese prefectural data: A closer look

We will now take a closer look at the Japanese regional data and compare them to those for a set of 15 OECD countries. In this section, we define Japanese regional saving and investment as that by all the residents in the region (households, firms, and local governments), using the dataset developed by Iwamoto and van Wincoop (2000). After a brief discussion of the data, we will first look at the relationship between raw saving and investment rates and subsequently at the comovement between saving and investment rates after controlling for common factors that are expected to lead to a positive correlation even when financial markets are perfectly integrated.

1.3.1   The data

The sample period is 1975–1990 for both the Japanese regional data and the OECD data. The OECD data are from the United Nations National Accounts

---

[3] The fact that general government saving is negative or near zero in most of the regions can be explained as follows. Total general government saving, aggregated over all regions, is positive, even larger than general government investment in most years. Through the central government there are large transfers from large wealthy regions (around Tokyo, Aichi, and Osaka) to smaller less wealthy regions. Because transfers are not counted as income, but consumption from the transfers does reduce the general government saving measure, the few large wealthy regions have the biggest general government saving rates, whereas the smaller regions have negative general government saving rates.

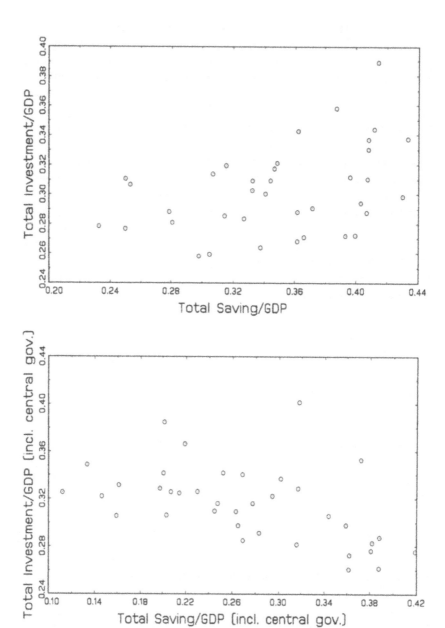

Figure 1.2. Japanese regional saving/GDP and investment/GDP (average 1985–1990).

Statistics. Here we will only provide some general information about the dataset constructed by Iwamoto and van Wincoop (2000) for Japanese regions. Details can be found in that paper. The main data sources used are the Annual Report on Prefectural Accounts and the Annual Statistical Report on Local Government Finance. The Annual Report on Prefectural Accounts reports regional GDP and GNP, as well as the breakdown into expenditure and factor income components. The disadvantage is that it uses a general government concept. That is why the second data source is used to construct local government saving and investment. Both data sources are used to obtain estimates of private saving and investment (by households and firms).

There are 47 prefectures. Prefectures across which there is extensive commuting are aggregated. This is done mainly because of the way taxation is measured. Income taxes are withheld at the location where the work is performed, which is not necessarily where the person resides. As a result, prefectures like Tokyo have an unusually high ratio of taxation relative to GNP. Another factor adding to this is that some Tokyo companies have employees in surrounding prefectures, but withhold taxes in Tokyo. Three regions with significant commuting are identified: one around Tokyo (Saitama, Chiba, Tokyo, Kanagawa prefectures), one around Osaka (Shiga, Kyoto, Osaka, Nara, Wakayama prefectures), and one around Aichi (Gifu, Aichi, Mie prefectures). This reduces the dataset from 47 prefectures to 37 regions.

Iwamoto and van Wincoop also correct for a problem with regards to the measurement of retained earnings, which has been pointed out by Obstfeld (1986). He argues that corporate retained earnings should be counted as income of the country that holds the claims. This problem is likely to be more serious for the measurement of intranational saving because investors are better diversified across regions within a country than across countries in the world. Retained earnings should be reallocated across the regions based on their relative claims, which we approximate by the region's share of national GDP. Although the moments reported later for Japanese regions are based on this corrected saving measure, we find that the results are very similar without this adjustment.

1.3.2   Raw saving and investment rates

Table 1.2 compares results on the comovement between saving and investment rates for Japanese regions and OECD countries. The same four different measures of comovement as discussed in Section 1.2 are reported. One or more of these is generally reported in the literature on saving-investment comovements. The original Feldstein and Horioka (1980) paper reports results based on cross-sectional regressions of the investment rate on the saving rate. The open economy real business cycle literature has focused primarily on time-series

Table 1.2. *Comovement between saving and investment rates: Japanese regions versus OECD countries*

	Sample	Japanese regions	OECD countries
1. Panel regression: β from $I_{it} = \alpha + \beta S_{it}$	1970–90	0.31 (0.03)	0.75 (0.04)
2. Cross-sectional regression: β from $I_t = \alpha + \beta S_t$	1975–80	0.21 (0.13)	1.06 (0.14)
	1980–85	0.32 (0.11)	0.75 (0.04)
	1985–90	0.21 (0.08)	0.62 (0.11)
3. Cross-sectional correlation	1975–80	0.26 (0.15)	0.90 (0.04)
	1980–85	0.43 (0.10)	0.84 (0.09)
	1985–90	0.40 (0.11)	0.85 (0.08)
4. Average time-series correlation	1975–90	0.31 (0.04)	0.56 (0.04)

correlations.[4] As seen in Table 1.1, several of the papers in the intranational literature use results from a panel regression of the investment rate on the saving rate. This combines cross-sectional and time-series aspects.

It is clear from Table 1.1 that there is a stronger positive comovement between saving and investment rates for OECD countries than for Japanese regions, no matter which measure is used. When saving and investment rates are averages from 1985 to 1990, the estimate of β in the original Feldstein-Horioka cross-sectional regression $I_i = \alpha + \beta S_i$ is 0.21 for Japanese regions versus 0.62 for OECD countries. Similarly, the cross-sectional correlation is 0.4 for Japanese regions versus 0.85 for OECD countries. The coefficient β of the Feldstein-Horioka regression has dropped over time for OECD countries, whereas there is no trend at the level of regions. This drop at the country level has been reported by several authors (e.g., Feldstein and Bacchetta 1991; Obstfeld 1995) and is often interpreted as evidence of increased capital mobility across countries. However, it is rather arbitrary to regress investment on saving. When saving is regressed on investment, the coefficient actually rises over time. A more "neutral" approach is to compute the correlation, which has not changed much over time.

---

[4] See, for example, Backus et al. (1992), Baxter and Crucini (1993, 1995), Cardia (1991), Finn (1990), and Mendoza (1991, 1995).

Figures 1.3 through 1.5 further illustrate the differences between Japanese regions and OECD countries. Figure 1.3 shows the average saving and investment rates over the period 1985–90. For countries, they are almost on a 45-degree line. Countries like Japan with a high saving rate also have a high investment rate. Countries like the United States with a low saving rate also have a low investment rate. The lower panel of the figure shows that there is not a strong positive relationship for Japanese regions. As was argued above, to the extent that there is a weak positive relationship it is mainly because of the high correlation between local government saving and investment rates. We will control for that in Section 1.3.3.

Figure 1.4 shows the cumulative distribution of net capital flows (saving minus investment), divided by GDP and averaged over 1985–90. On average capital outflows from Japanese regions are larger than from OECD countries because Japan as a whole had a substantial current account surplus. What is more relevant is the variation of capital flows across regions and countries. The intranational flows vary from −6.1% of GDP to 13.2% of GDP, whereas the international flows vary from −4.9% to 3.9% of GDP. The much larger variation in the size of intranational capital flows is consistent with the weaker relationship between saving and investment rates.

Figure 1.5 shows the time-series correlation between saving and investment rates and relates it to the size of countries and regions. Size is measured by 1990 GDP in dollars. One might argue that the higher average correlation at the country level is due to size. When saving rises in a large country, it can lower world interest rates and therefore raise investment. This argument may apply to the United States, which indeed has a large time-series correlation of 0.78. But beyond the United States, there does not exist a positive relationship between country size and time-series correlations. Small countries like Greece, Sweden, Finland, Austria, and Iceland all have time-series correlations above 0.75. For Japanese regions, the time-series correlations vary from −0.71 to 0.96. The largest region, around Tokyo, actually has the lowest correlation: −0.71.

1.3.3   Controlling for common factors

So far we have not drawn any conclusions about the degree of capital mobility from the reported "stylized facts" on saving–investment comovements. One needs to be careful in doing so because a high correlation between saving and investment rates is in theory perfectly consistent with a high degree of capital mobility. For example, saving and investment tend to both rise during a business cycle upturn, whether financial markets are highly integrated or not. Our aim in this section is to control for such common factors, which lead to a comovement between saving and investment rates irrespective of the extent of international

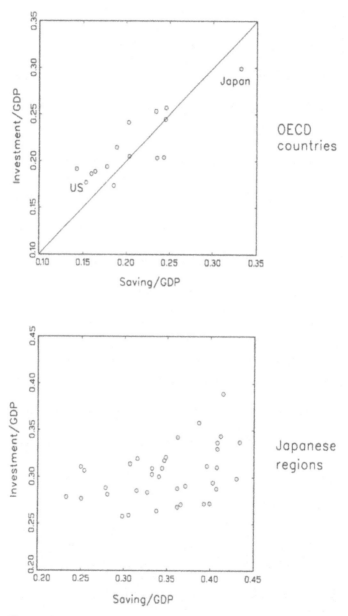

Figure 1.3. Average saving and investment rates (1985–1990).

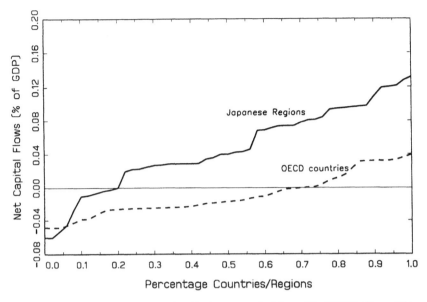

Figure 1.4. Cumulative distribution net capital flows (% of GDP). *Notes*: This figure shows the percentage of countries and regions whose average net capital outflow (% of GDP) over the period 1985–1990 is below a certain level (cumulative distribution).

(or intranational) financial integration. We will consider separately the time-series and cross-sectional correlations.

1.3.3.1 Time-series correlation

One definition of perfect financial integration is that financial markets are complete in the Arrow-Debreu sense. With perfect risk sharing, there is no need to trade assets after some initial date because at the initial date there is already trade on all possible future contingencies. Therefore capital flows are zero. The capital account (and current account) can only differ from zero as a result of revaluation of existing claims. Baxter and Crucini (1993) indeed find that a model with financial market completeness implies a high time-series correlation between saving and investment rates. This casts doubt on conclusions that the high saving–investment correlation for countries is a reflection of a low degree of capital mobility. It is exactly what you would expect under financial market completeness.

There is good reason to believe that neither international nor intranational financial markets are complete. First, if there were even a tiny transaction cost associated with new transactions and markets were complete, trade in all future contingencies would take place once, after which there would be no further

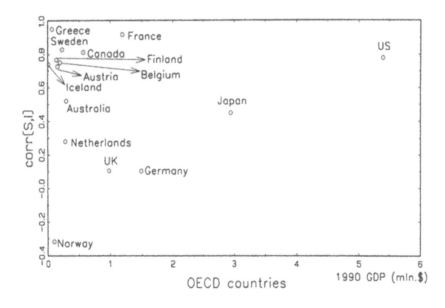

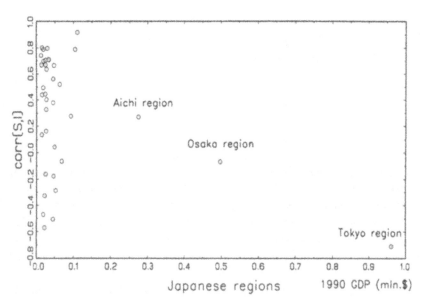

Figure 1.5. Size and corr(S, I).

trade. The enormous size of trade in financial assets across and within countries indicates that financial markets are not complete. Second, what would clearly be the most important international financial markets, claims on the present discounted value of an index on national income, do not exist.[5] Stocks and corporate bonds are claims on corporate profits, which are only about 3% of GDP in the United States. Third, models with complete financial markets imply that the consumption correlation should be significantly higher than the income correlation. This is exactly the opposite of what has been found in international data. van Wincoop (1995) finds that even for Japanese prefectures the average correlation across prefectures of Hodrick Prescott-filtered consumption is only 0.43, the same as the GDP correlation. Finally, the low correlation between saving and investment at the intranational level is inconsistent with financial market completeness (see earlier discussion).

Even though financial markets may not be complete in the Arrow-Debreu sense, here we will entertain a narrower definition of financial integration. Financial markets across countries are said to be well integrated when the demand of the assets of a particular country depends, apart from the expected return, on the global supply of funds. Given global saving, saving by residents of the particular country should not matter. In other words, there should not be a "home bias."[6] When that is the case, the price of equity issued by companies in the country, and therefore investment, depends on factors that determine the global supply of funds, which we will summarize by the vector g, and factors that determine the productivity (or profitability) of capital in that country. These are again global factors g and a set of country-specific factors, which are in deviation from their global counterpart. Saving in the same country also depends on global and country-specific factors. The global factors g affect saving directly and indirectly through the global interest rate. One can always organize the country-specific factors that affect saving and the productivity of capital in a country as a set of uncorrelated vectors v, w, z, whereby v and w affect the productivity of capital, and v and z affect saving. Therefore, $I = I(g, v, w)$ and $S = S(g, v, z)$.

In such a world with integrated financial markets, saving and investment can be correlated as a result of global shocks and country-specific shocks to v that affect both the productivity of capital and saving. After controlling for such common factors g and v, saving and investment should be uncorrelated.

---

[5] Shiller (1993) advocates these markets. See the discussion in Athanasoulis, Shiller, and van Wincoop (1999) for a discussion of why these markets have not developed yet.

[6] This does not imply that markets are complete because traded assets do not need to span the market. We also abstract from the possibility that there may be a home bias because the return on non-traded assets is less correlated with the return on home assets than the return on foreign assets. Both Baxter and Jermann (1997) and Bottazzi, Pesenti, and van Wincoop (1996) find little evidence to support that.

This is not the case when financial markets are not fully integrated. When residents have a bias toward their own country's assets, a shock to z that raises the country's saving, but not global saving, will lead to an increase in demand for the country's capital, and therefore an increase in equity prices and investment.

Because global shocks affect each country identically, when financial markets are integrated, saving in deviation from global saving depends on v and w, whereas investment in deviation from global investment depends on v and z. After controlling for v, country-specific saving and investment rates should then be uncorrelated.

A similar approach applies to regions within a country. Financial markets across regions within a country are said to be well integrated when demand for the assets of a particular region depends, apart from its expected return, on total supply of funds to the national capital market. We call this the national supply of funds. In the absence of international capital markets, it is simply national saving. When international financial markets are perfectly integrated, it is global saving. In general, the national supply of funds will depend on both national and global factors, which we summarize by the factor n. Given the national supply of funds, saving by the residents of a particular region should not matter. Following a reasoning similar to that discussed earlier, we can write investment and saving as $I = I(n, v, w)$ and $S = S(n, v, z)$, where n is a vector of national and global factors, whereas v, w, and z are uncorrelated region-specific factors (in deviation from their national counterpart). Because shocks to n affect all regions identically, saving in deviation from national saving depends on v and w, whereas investment in deviation from national investment depends on v and z. After controlling for the common region-specific factors v, region-specific saving and investment rates should be uncorrelated.

In implementing this, we include in the vector v a measure y of the business cycle and a vector F of fiscal variables. A business cycle upturn is expected to raise investment as the profitability of investment increases, whereas at the same time saving rises as the boom is anticipated to be temporary and agents smooth consumption over time. Baxter and Crucini (1995), Cardia (1991), Finn (1990), and Mendoza (1991, 1995) have all illustrated in the context of open economy real business cycle models that temporary output shocks can lead to a high time-series correlation between saving and investment rates. Fiscal policy can similarly affect both saving and investment rates. For example, an increase in government consumption, financed by a rise in future taxes, should lower both saving and investment. Another possibility, suggested by Summers (1988), Tobin (1983) and Westphal (1983), is that the government targets the current account through its fiscal policy. We estimate the following equations for both

OECD countries and Japanese regions

$$S_{it} = \alpha_i + \alpha_y y_{it} + \alpha_F F_{it} + \epsilon_{it}^S \tag{1}$$

$$I_{it} = \beta_i + \beta_y y_{it} + \beta_F F_{it} + \epsilon_{it}^I \tag{2}$$

For OECD countries, S_{it} and I_{it} are saving and investment in deviation from their global counterparts.[7] For Japanese regions, they are in deviation from their national counterpart. α_i and β_i are country (or region) fixed effects. The other coefficients are assumed to be identical across countries (or regions). We compute the country-specific business cycle y as HP(100) filtered GDP minus HP(100) filtered global GDP. The region-specific business cycle variable is HP(100) filtered regional GDP minus HP(100) filtered national GDP. We use three fiscal variables: the tax rate,[8] government consumption rate, and government investment rate, all in deviation from their global (or Japanese national) counterpart.

In estimating (1) and (2), we need to take into account that the right-hand-side variables are endogenous. An increase in investment can lead to an upswing in the business cycle. Similarly, fiscal policy may respond to changes in private saving and investment. We therefore estimate (1) and (2) with two-stage least squares. As instruments we use one-period lagged right-hand-side variables and country or region fixed effects. We have also considered two-year lagged instruments, which leads to similar results.

corr $(\epsilon_{it}^S, \epsilon_{it}^I)$ is the correlation between saving and investment rates after controlling for business cycles, fiscal policy, and national (or global) shocks. It should be zero when financial markets are integrated. The upper part of Table 1.3 shows the results of this exercise. For Japanese regions, the time-series correlation becomes insignificantly different from zero: -0.01 with a standard error of 0.04. For OECD countries it drops to 0.28 with a standard error of 0.05. Although this is still significantly positive, it is not large, which suggests that financial markets of both countries and Japanese regions are highly integrated.

For the Japanese prefectures, the average correlation of 0.31 between the unadjusted regional saving and investment rates can be almost entirely attributed to national shocks. The correlation between region-specific saving and investment rates (after subtracting their national counterparts) is 0.04.

For OECD countries, both global and country-specific shocks contribute to the positive correlation of 0.56 between saving and investment rates. The correlation between country-specific saving and investment rates (after subtracting

---

[7] Global is defined as the sum of the countries in the sample.

[8] We use a net measure of taxes, equal to actual tax revenue minus subsidies and other transfers to the private sector.

Table 1.3. corr(S, I) *after controlling for common factors*

	Japanese regions	OECD countries
	Time-series correlation	
Raw data	0.31	0.56
	(0.04)	(0.04)
Control for common factors	−0.01	0.28
	(0.04)	(0.05)
	Cross-sectional correlation	
Raw data	0.40	0.85
	(0.11)	(0.08)
Control for		
growth, fisc, y_{1990}	0.25	0.76
	(0.18)	(0.13)
growth	0.51	0.83
	(0.12)	(0.09)
fisc	0.17	0.76
	(0.15)	(0.12)
y_{1990}	0.35	0.87
	(0.13)	(0.07)

global averages) is 0.44. It drops further to 0.28 after we also control for country-specific fiscal policy and business cycles. The regression results for OECD countries are:

$$S_{it} = \alpha_i + 0.33\tau_{it} - 1.03I_{it}^g - 1.11G_{it} - 0.05y_{it} + \epsilon_{it}^S$$
$$\phantom{S_{it} = \alpha_i + } (0.09) \quad (0.23) \quad (0.09) \quad (0.09)$$

$$I_{it} = \beta_i + 0.27\tau_{it} + 1.22I_{it}^g - 0.78G_{it} + 0.45y_{it} + \epsilon_{it}^I$$
$$\phantom{I_{it} = \beta_i + } (0.09) \quad (0.25) \quad (0.10) \quad (0.10)$$

where τ_{it}, I_{it}^g, and G_{it} are the tax rate, government investment rate, and government consumption rate, respectively. Standard errors are in parentheses. The most important variable in accounting for the positive comovement between country-specific saving and investment rates is government consumption, which has a strong negative effect on both saving and investment. The positive coefficient on the tax rate in the investment equation is counterintuitive, but it can be attributed to multicollinearity. A balanced budget increase in both taxes and government consumption leads to a drop in both saving and investment. Controlling for fiscal policy, the business cycle does not play a role in accounting for the positive correlation between country-specific saving and investment rates.

Although the coefficient of the investment rate on the business cycle is positive and significant, saving is not significantly affected by the business cycle once we control for fiscal policy.[9]

Because there is a weak trend in the fiscal variables of some countries and prefectures, we have also estimated the regressions after extracting an HP(100) filter from the fiscal variables, just as was done to compute the business cycle. The results are virtually identical to those in Table 1.3.

1.3.3.2 Cross-sectional correlation

Even though national and global shocks can contribute to a positive time-series correlation for Japanese regions, they cannot contribute to a positive cross-sectional correlation. By definition, they affect all regions identically. Similarly, global shocks cannot account for the cross-sectional correlation between national saving and investment. But the region-specific (or country-specific) elements of the vector v can account for a positive cross-sectional correlation under perfect financial integration. We will estimate regressions

$$I_i = \alpha_I + \beta_I v_i + \epsilon_I \tag{3}$$

$$S_i - \alpha_S + \beta_S v_i + \epsilon_S \tag{4}$$

where I and S are the average saving and investment rates over the period 1985–1990, and v is a vector of region-specific (or country-specific) variables that affect both saving and investment.

The literature suggests the following variables in the vector v: the labor force growth rate, the productivity growth rate, the distribution of wealth, and fiscal variables. Obstfeld (1986) illustrates in an overlapping generations model that countries with high growth rates are expected to have both high saving and investment rates. Summers (1988) has argued the importance of initial wealth as a contributor to the cross-sectional correlation between saving and investment. We will measure it by 1990 per capita GDP in dollars. Fiscal policy may also play a role. As discussed earlier, the government may target the current account through its fiscal policy. We saw in Section 1.2 that, for Japanese regions, fiscal policy in the form of central government transfers plays a role in accounting for the cross-sectional correlation. We control for two fiscal variables. For OECD countries, these are the average tax rate and government investment rate during 1985–1990. For Japanese regions, they are the average government tax rate and transfers from the central government to the local government as a fraction of the region's GDP.[10]

---

[9] The coefficient of saving on the business cycle is positive when we do not instrument right-hand-side variables, but it remains insignificant even then.

[10] Additionally controlling for government consumption rates has little effect.

Table 1.3 shows the cross-sectional correlation between saving and investment rates after controlling for these factors (the correlation between ϵ_I and ϵ_S). *growth* stands for the two growth variables, whereas *fisc* stand for the two fiscal variables. When controlling for all five variables, the correlation of saving and investment across Japanese prefectures drops to 0.25 and is insignificantly different from zero. For countries, it remains high, at 0.76 with a standard error of 0.13. The table also shows the results of controlling separately for growth variables, fiscal variables, and 1990 GDP. Controlling for growth leaves the correlation practically unchanged for countries and even raises it for regions. Controlling for fiscal policy alone reduces the correlation to 0.17 for Japanese regions. This confirms that most of the moderately positive relationship between prefectural saving and investment rates is a result of fiscal policy. For OECD countries, the correlation remains a high 0.76 after controlling for fiscal policy.

It is sometimes argued that the correlation between saving and investment rates can be accounted for by a lack of goods market integration.[11] In the absence of purchasing power parity, real interest rates are not necessarily equalized across countries, even when financial markets are perfectly integrated. But, as argued by Obstfeld (1995), in order for this argument to be applicable to cross-sectional data one currency must be continuously appreciating in real terms against another currency. Otherwise, real interest differentials would still vanish in the long run. Continuous real appreciation can be the result of different productivity growth rates across countries. But as shown earlier, the high cross-sectional correlation for OECD countries does not go away when we control for productivity growth differentials. It is therefore unlikely that a lack of goods markets integration can account for the cross-sectional relationships.

1.4   Interpretation of the evidence

Both cross-sectional and time-series results point to a high degree of capital mobility across regions within Japan. For countries, the conclusion is different for the cross-sectional evidence (low degree of capital mobility) than time-series evidence (high degree of capital mobility). In this section, we will first develop an interpretation for the country evidence, arguing that there is a higher degree of short-run capital mobility than long-run capital mobility across countries. After that, we briefly discuss the key barriers to international capital mobility, which are less important at the intranational level. We discuss in the context of a rudimentary model why such barriers can lead to a closer saving-investment comovement in the long run than the short run.

[11] See Frankel (1986, 1993).

1.4.1 Interpretation of the country evidence

In order to interpret the cross-country results, it is useful to first consider what factors contribute to the cross-sectional variation in the investment rate. Let r be the after-tax return on capital that investors demand. With τ the effective tax rate, the cost of capital is $r/(1-\tau)+\delta$, where δ is the rate of depreciation. The capital income share is $\alpha = (r/(1-\tau)+\delta)K/Y$, where K is capital and Y is total output. In the steady state, $I/K = \delta + g$, where I is investment and g is the steady-state growth rate. Therefore the steady-state investment rate is

$$\frac{I}{Y} = \frac{\alpha(\delta + g)}{r/(1-\tau)+\delta} \tag{5}$$

In order to obtain cross-sectional variation in the investment rate, there must be cross-sectional variation in either g, τ, α, δ, or r. We have already seen that cross-sectional variation in g and τ does not account for the cross-sectional correlation between saving and investment rates. Similarly, we find that when controlling for the capital share α, the cross-sectional correlation between saving and investment rates over the 1985–1990 period remains 0.86.[12] We do not have evidence about differences in the rate of depreciation across countries, but it seems doubtful that this accounts for much of the large cross-sectional variation in investment and saving rates that we observe.

It is therefore natural to conclude that there is a lack of capital mobility across countries in a long-run sense. Equation (5) shows that the only other factor that can account for cross-sectional variation in the steady-state investment rate is differences across countries in the rate of return r that investors demand. The cross-country variation in r must also be correlated with the cross-country variation in saving in order to explain the high cross-country correlation between saving and investment rates. That implies imperfect capital mobility in a long-run sense. Under perfect capital mobility, the cost of capital depends only on the global supply of funds. Conditional on that, domestic saving should not matter.

This is not necessarily inconsistent with the time-series evidence, which is associated with higher frequency fluctuations in saving and investment rates. As discussed in Section 1.1, capital moves swiftly across countries that have opened up their borders to foreign capital. Interest rate differentials are arbitraged away in a matter of seconds. The daily volume of transactions in equity, bonds, and foreign exchange markets is enormous. A country can easily absorb a temporary current account imbalance through international borrowing and lending. But, at the same time, the extent of international portfolio diversification is

---

[12] The capital share is defined as one minus the labor share, where the labor share is computed as the ratio of employee compensation to GDP, using OECD National Accounts data. The cross-sectional correlation between investment and the labor share is 0.23, whereas that between saving and the labor share is 0.08. Marrinan (1989) obtains a similar result.

quite limited. It is important to make a distinction between stocks and flows. It is quite possible for the stock of assets to be heavily biased toward domestic securities, while marginal changes in the stock remain very responsive to international conditions. This distinction can account for the difference between cross-country and time-series evidence. Capital appears to be more mobile across countries in the short run than the long run.

1.4.2   Barriers to capital mobility

Some of the key barriers to international capital mobility are asymmetric information, exchange rate uncertainty and contract enforcement problems. Brennan and Cao (1997), Gehrig (1993), and Zhou (1998) illustrate at a theoretical level the effect of asymmetric information on the home bias in portfolios. Because asymmetric information is closely related to language, cultural, and regulatory barriers, it is likely to be less relevant for regions within a country. The second barrier, exchange rate uncertainty, is not relevant at all for regions within a country. Bacchetta and van Wincoop (1998, 2000) show in the context of two-country general equilibrium models that exchange rate uncertainty reduces net capital flows and present some preliminary evidence consistent with that. Contract enforcement problems are also more severe at the international level, particularly because there is no international bankruptcy court. Lane (1997) finds that, among low and middle income countries, there is a positive relationship between income and external debt, which he interprets as an indication that higher income weakens contract enforcement problems. Alvarez and Jermann (1997) and Kehoe and Perri (1998) show that contract enforcement constraints have substantial macroeconomic implications in comparison to complete financial markets without such constraints.

1.4.3   Long run versus short run

All these barriers have one aspect in common: domestic and foreign securities become imperfect substitutes, with a preference for domestic securities. In order to see that this can have a stronger long-run than short-run effect on saving–investment comovements, consistent with the evidence, we will consider a very rudimentary small open economy model. This is not an explicit model of any of the barriers listed previously, but it does capture, exogenously, the home bias aspect of these barriers. We assume that claims to the capital stock are only held by domestic residents, an extreme form of home bias, and that there is free trade in a riskless international bond. The interest rate of the bond is exogenous from the point of view of the small open economy. For simplicity, we assume that it is constant, equal to r. The risk premium on domestic capital, and therefore the return on domestic capital that investors demand, is assumed to depend positively on the fraction of wealth invested in domestic capital:

$$r = f(K/(K + B)) \qquad f'(\cdot) > 0 \tag{6}$$

where B is net bond holdings. Firms set the expected marginal product of capital equal to $r + \delta$. Assuming a simple production function $y = \theta K^{\alpha}$, we have

$$\alpha \theta K^{\alpha-1} = r + \delta \tag{7}$$

In a slight abuse of notation, from now on θ is the expected productivity parameter. These two equations imply that $K = k(B, \theta)$, with $\partial k/\partial B > 0$ and $\partial k/\partial \theta > 0$.

Domestic saving is a function of the state of the world and a parameter m. In this model, B is the only state variable.[13] Therefore

$$S = S(B, m) \tag{8}$$

where, without loss of generality, we assume that $\partial S/\partial m > 0$. m can be associated with a wide range of factors, such as demographics, intertemporal preference shocks, and financial innovations that facilitate saving. The form of the saving function depends on the utility function from which it is derived. We will not need to be specific about the exact form of the saving function. Finally, the capital stock and bonds accumulate according to

$$\dot{K} = -\delta K + I \tag{9}$$

$$\dot{B} = S - I \tag{10}$$

These last three equations, plus $K = k(B, \theta)$, imply the following differential equation for bonds (assuming a constant θ):

$$\dot{B} = \frac{S(B, m) - \delta k(\theta, B)}{1 + \partial k/\partial B} \tag{11}$$

We assume that $\partial S/\partial B < 0$, so that the level of bonds does not explode.[14] Therefore in steady state $S = I$.

From $K = k(B, \theta)$ and the steady-state equation $\delta K = S(B, m)$, it is easily verified that the steady-state capital stock depends positively on m. From (7), it then follows that a larger m leads to a lower steady-state expected return on capital, a higher capital output ratio, and a higher investment rate I/Y. Because $S = I$ in the steady state, it also leads to a higher saving rate. It can be similarly

---

[13] The capital stock is not a state variable because we have assumed zero adjustment costs associated with domestic investment. Therefore the capital stock adjusts instantaneously after a shock.

[14] This is a sufficient condition, not a necessary condition.

illustrated that cross-sectional variation in θ leads to perfectly correlated cross-sectional variation in steady-state investment and saving rates.

It is easy to understand why investment rises in response to an increase in saving. If the higher saving is channeled entirely into increased bond holdings, it reduces the return on capital that investors demand. The risk premium on capital becomes smaller. This raises the investment rate. From a slightly different perspective, at a given expected return on capital, and therefore a given allocation of wealth across the two assets, the demand for capital rises as total saving rises.

Even though saving and investment are equal in the steady state (in the long run), the model allows for large short-term current account volatility. Saving and investment do not necessarily move closely together in the short run. Taken literally, in response to a rise in θ, the increase in investment is infinite in the model. Because saving depends on a state variable B, it does not change immediately. Therefore there will be an immediate infinite net capital inflow (per unit of time). Even with adjustment costs to capital accumulation, so that the investment boom is finite, there can be a large current account deterioration immediately following the shock. In the presence of adjustment cost to capital accumulation, it can also be expected that in the short run an increase in saving will be channeled primarily into holdings of foreign bonds.

1.5   Conclusion

We have reviewed the intranational saving–investment literature in order to provide a benchmark to put the international evidence in perspective. Although saving and investment at the intranational level have not been measured according to a uniform definition in the literature, the conclusion is always the same: there is a much stronger relationship between national than intranational saving and investment rates. In order to say something about the degree of capital mobility, it is important to control for common factors, which can be expected to affect both saving and investment rates even when there are no barriers to capital flows. We find that both time-series and cross-sectional correlations between saving and investment rates of Japanese regions are close to zero after controlling for such factors, suggesting a high degree of financial integration among regions within Japan. At the level of OECD countries, we find that the time-series correlation is very small after controlling for global, business cycle, and fiscal shocks, but the high cross-sectional correlation cannot easily be attributed to common factors.

The evidence for OECD countries is of interest by itself, but it becomes even more meaningful when compared to the intranational evidence. It suggests that there are primarily barriers to long-term capital mobility across countries. We have discussed a variety of candidates (assymetric information, exchange rate uncertainty, and contract enforcement problems), all of which are more important across countries than across regions within a country.

References

Alvarez, F., and U. J. Jermann. 1997. "Asset Pricing When Risksharing Is Limited by Default." Working Paper. Wharton School.

Athanasoulis, S., and E. van Wincoop. 2000. "Growth Uncertainty and Risksharing." *Journal of Monetary Economics*, forthcoming.

Athanasoulis, S., R. Shiller, and E. van Wincoop. 1999. Macro markets and financial security. *Economic Policy Review* 5(1): 21–40.

Bacchetta, P., and E. van Wincoop. 1998. "Does Exchange Rate Stability Increase Trade and Capital Flows?" Working Paper 6704. NBER.

Bacchetta, P., and E. van Wincoop. 2000. Trade in nominal assets and net international capital flows. *Journal of International Money and Finance* 19: 55–72.

Backus, D. K., P. J. Kehoe, and F. E. Kydland. 1992. International real business cycles. *Journal of Political Economy* 100: 745–75.

Baxter, M., and M. Crucini. 1993. Explaining saving-investment correlations. *American Economic Review* 83(3): 416–36.

Baxter, M., and M. Crucini. 1995. Business cycles and the asset structure of foreign trade. *International Economic Review* 36(4): 821–54.

Baxter, M., and U. J. Jermann. 1997. The international diversification puzzle is worse than you think. *American Economic Review* 87(1): 170–80.

Bayoumi, T. 1997. *Financial Integration and Real Activity*. Ann Arbor: University of Michigan Press.

Bayoumi, T., and A. K. Rose. 1993. Domestic savings and intra-national capital flows. *European Economic Review* 37: 1197–202.

Bottazzi, L., P. Pesenti, and E. van Wincoop. 1996. Wages, profits, and the international portfolio puzzle. *European Economic Review* 40(2): 219–54.

Brennan, M. J., and H. H. Cao. 1997. International portfolio investment flows. *Journal of Finance* 52(5): 1851–80.

Cardia, E. 1991. The dynamics of a small open economy in response to monetary, fiscal, and productivity shocks. *Journal of Monetary Economics* 28: 411–34.

Dekle, R. 1996. Saving-investment associations and capital mobility: On the evidence from Japanese regional data. *Journal of International Economics* 41: 53–72.

Feldstein, M., and P. Bacchetta. 1991. "National Saving and International Investment," in D. Bernheim and J. Shoven, eds., *National Saving and Economic Performance*, Chicago: University of Chicago Press.

Feldstein, M., and C. Horioka. 1980. Domestic saving and international capital flows. *Economic Journal* 90: 314–29.

Finn, M. G. 1990. On saving and investment in a small open economy. *Journal of International Economics* 29: 1–21.

Frankel, J. A. 1986. "International Capital Mobility and Crowding-Out in the US Economy: Imperfect Integration of Financial Markets or of Goods Markets?," in R. W. Hafer, ed., *How Open Is the US Economy?* Lexington, MA: Heath.

Frankel, J. A. 1993. "Quantifying International Capital Mobility in the 1980s," in J. Frankel, ed., *On Exchange Rates*. Cambridge, MA: MIT Press.

Gehrig, T. P. 1993. An information based explanation of the domestic bias in international equity investment. *Scandinavian Journal of Economics* 95(1): 97–109.

Iwamoto, Y., and E. van Wincoop. 2000. Do Borders Matter? Evidence from Japanese Intranational Capital Flows. *International Economic Review* 41(1): 241–69.

Kehoe, P., and F. Perri. 1998. "International Business Cycles with Endogenous Market Incompleteness." Working Paper. Federal Reserve Bank of Minneapolis.

Lane, P. R. 1997. "Empirical Perspectives on Long-Term External Debt." Working paper. Columbia University.

Marrinan, J. 1989. "The Effects of Fiscal Policy on Saving and Investment in an Open Economy." Ph.D. Thesis. University of Minnesota.

Mendoza, E. G. 1991. Real business cycles in a small open economy. *American Economic Review* 81(4): 797–818.

Mendoza, E. G. 1995. The terms of trade, the real exchange rate and economic fluctuations. *International Economic Review* 36(1): 101–38.

Obstfeld, M. 1986. Capital mobility in the world economy: Theory and measurement. *Carnegie Rochester Conference Series on Public Policy* 24: 55–104.

Obstfeld, M. 1995. "International Capital Mobility in the 1990s," in Kenen, P. B., ed., *Understanding Interdependence: The Macroeconomics of the Open Economy*. Princeton, NJ: Princeton University Press.

Romans, J. T. 1965. *Capital Exports and Growth among US Regions*. Middletown: Wesleyan University Press.

Shiller, R. J. 1993. *Macro Markets. Creating Institutions for Managing Society's Largest Economic Risks*. Oxford: Clarendon Press.

Sinn, S. 1992. Saving-investment correlations and capital mobility: On the evidence from annual data. *Economic Journal* 102: 1162–70.

Summers, L. 1988. "Tax Policy and International Competitiveness," in J. Frenkel, ed., *International Aspects of Fiscal Policy*. Chicago: University of Chicago Press.

Tesar, L. L., and I. Werner. 1998. The internationalization of the securities market since the 1987 crash. *Brookings Papers on Financial Services*, The Brookings Institution.

Thomas, A. H. 1993. "Saving, Investment and the Regional Current Account: An Analysis of Canadian, British and German Regions." Working Paper 93/62. IMF.

Tobin, J. 1983. Comment on "domestic saving and international capital movements in the long and the short run," by M. Feldstein. *European Economic Review* 21: 153–6.

van Wincoop, E. 1995. Regional risksharing. *European Economic Review* 37: 1545–67.

Westphal, U. 1983. Comment on "domestic saving and international capital movements in the long and the short run," by M. Feldstein. *European Economic Review* 21: 153–6.

Yamori, N. 1995. The relationship between domestic saving and investment: The Feldstein-Horioka test using Japanese regional data. *Economics Letters* 48: 361–6.

Zhou, C. 1998. Dynamic portfolio choice and asset pricing with differential information. *Journal of Economic Dynamics and Control* 22: 1027–51.

CHAPTER 2

International and intranational
risk sharing*

Mario J. Crucini[†] *and Gregory D. Hess*[‡]

2.1   Introduction

According to the theory of aggregate risk sharing, if individual households have
access to a complete market for financial assets then they can, by pooling their
risk, insure fully against the idiosyncratic uncertainty in their resources. (See,
among others, Townsend 1987; Altug and Miller 1990; Cochrane 1991; Mace
1991.) In such an environment, theory predicts that marginal utility is perfectly
correlated across agents. Under quite general assumptions, the theory also predicts that household changes in consumption should move one-for-one with
aggregate changes in consumption absent idiosyncratic fluctuations in preferences or measurement error. Importantly, differences in consumption changes
across households should not be correlated with changes in a household's
resources.[1]

Recently, dynamic general equilibrium macroeconomic models have been
extended to the open economy to study the international comovement of aggregate variables. The first generation of these models was quite successful in
explaining two aspects of the data: a countercyclical trade balance (Backus,
Kehoe, and Kydland 1992) and a high correlation between savings and investment despite perfect capital mobility (Baxter and Crucini 1993). One startling
rejection of one of the model's predictions, identified by Backus et al. (1992),
spawned a large literature as to whether and by how much countries share

* We thank Marco del Negro and Eric van Wincoop for extremely helpful comments.

[†] Mailing address: Department of Economics, Vanderbilt University, Nashville, TN. E-mail: *Mario.
J.Crucini@Vanderbilt.edu.*
[‡] Mailing address: Department of Economics, Oberlin College, Oberlin, OH. E-mail: *gregory.
hess@oberlin.edu.*

[1] This risk sharing can take place through formal market institutions or through less formal ones
that may apply to families or rural villages. Risk sharing within families has been explored by
Hayashi, Altonji, and Kotlikoff (1996) and at the village level by Townsend (1995).

risk.[2] These authors rejected the theory that they point to for the following reason. In a two-country standard dynamic general equilibrium model where only exogenous productivity shocks drive fluctuations in output, since individuals in each country can share risk internationally and thereby diversify their nation specific risk, the cross-country correlation of consumption is predicted to be much higher than the cross-country correlation of output or productivity shocks. In the data, however, they find that the opposite is true, and they labeled this phenomena the *quantity anomaly*.

More recently, Obstfeld (1994) studied the cross correlations of consumption and output growth rates between an individual country and the rest of the world as well as among OECD countries. He reported that, although the cross correlation of consumption growth rates have risen since 1973, they are always lower than those for output. Bayoumi and McDonald (1995) found, using consumption- and income-based tests, that only Japanese consumption was fully integrated with the rest of the world. See also Canova and Ravn (1996) and Hess and Shin (1997) for recent international evidence for the OECD. Lewis (1996) found that consumption growth had a smaller common component in countries that imposed capital controls compared to countries that did not, suggesting that some risk sharing is taking place at least among countries that do not explicitly restrict international capital mobility.

In order to better understand the reasons why economic regions such as countries may only share risk incompletely, researchers have attempted to reexamine this important issue across economic regions within a country. So-called intranational evidence provides a natural experiment for understanding international puzzles because regions within a country have reduced barriers to trade in goods and assets while also sharing a common currency and legal framework. Therefore, by using within-country data, we can help to identify whether the lack of consumption risk sharing pointed to by Backus et al. is due to international factors (e.g., capital restrictions) and exchange rate uncertainty or is merely a matter of geography independent of national boundaries. The intranational approach to risk sharing has been used by Atkeson and Bayoumi (1993), Asdrubali, Sorensen, and Yosha (1996), Crucini (1999), Hess and Shin (1997, 1998a,b), and Athanasoulis and van Wincoop (1998) to explore the quantity anomaly within regions and states of the United States. Bayoumi and McDonald (1995), Bayoumi and Klein (1995), and Crucini (1999) also analyze the quantity anomaly for Canadian provinces, whereas van Wincoop (1995) examines Japanese regions. Collectively, these studies suggest that the quantity anomaly may be reversed in the case of the Canadian provinces but remains in force for the Japan prefectures (marginally) and for the U.S. states.

---

[2] The second major discrepancy between theory and data that these authors point out is that the terms of trade are dramatically more volatile in the data than the models suggest. The relationship between intranational and international price movements is discussed in Chapter 5 by Engel and Rogers and in Hess and Shin (1997, 1998a).

The goal of this survey paper is to reexamine consumption risk sharing, within and between countries, using a number of datasets from recently published papers. We provide empirical findings using the following datasets: for the United States – Asdrubali et al. (1996); for Canada – Crucini (1999); for Japan – van Wincoop (1995); and for the OECD – Hess and Shin (1997). These datasets are discussed in more detail in Section 2.3.1.

We examine three important issues in the risk-sharing literature. First, in Section 2.3.2 we establish a comprehensive set of stylized facts for intranational and international risk sharing. Second, in Section 2.3.3, following the work of Crucini (1999), we estimate an econometric model, which helps us to pin down the extent of risk sharing. This is an important step given that a simple rejection of perfect risk sharing based on stylized facts does not by itself help researchers to uncover the extent to which risk is not being shared. Finally, because the ultimate reason for risk sharing is to reduce risk and thereby enhance expected welfare, in Section 2.3.4 we present calculations for the welfare implications of risk sharing and the welfare implications of regional business cycles.

2.2   Risk-sharing theory

In this section, we derive testable implications of risk pooling across regions from two models. The first is an endowment economy with complete Arrow–Debreu markets analogous to that studied by Mace (1991). The second model follows Crucini (1999), allowing for intertemporal smoothing at a constant real interest rate but varying degrees of risk pooling across regions. Many of the qualitative predictions of these models hold up in more elaborate production economies such as in Backus et al. (1992) and Baxter and Crucini (1995).

2.2.1   Complete risk sharing

In this section, we derive testable implications from a model in which risk is shared across R individuals, each a representative agent for her region of residence, taken to be either a country (international risk sharing) or a region within a country (intranational risk sharing). This model closely follows the Arrow–Debreu complete markets model studied by Mace (1991). Each region i is assumed to consist of a representative household. Uncertainty is summarized by the state variable s_τ, $\tau = 1, 2, \ldots, S$ that takes on S different values in each time t. The term $\pi_t(s_\tau)$ captures the probability of state s_τ occurring at t with $\sum_{\tau=1}^{S} \pi_t(s_\tau) = 1$. Expected lifetime utility of the representative household in each country or region is given by

$$\sum_{t=0}^{\infty} \beta^t \sum_{\tau}^{S} \pi_t(s_\tau) U(c_{it}(s_\tau), b_{it}(s_\tau)) \tag{1}$$

where $c_{it}(s_\tau)$ is consumption for the representative household in region i at time

t when the state is s_τ, and $0 < \beta < 1$ is the subjective discount factor, assumed to be the same across households. $b_{it}(s_\tau)$ is an exogenous preference shock to region i, given the state of nature. Each region i receives the endowment of $y_{it}(s_\tau)$ at time t under state (s_τ) so that the feasibility constraint for this economy is $\sum_{i=1}^{R} y_{it}(s_\tau) = \sum_{i=1}^{R} c_{it}(s_\tau)$.

Suppose that risk is shared completely across all R regions. Then the resulting allocation is obtained by the following Lagrangian problem solved by the social planner at each time t:

$$\mathcal{L} = \sum_{i=1}^{R} \omega_i \sum_{t=0}^{\infty} \beta^t \sum_{\tau}^{S} \pi_t(s_\tau) U(c_{it}(s_\tau), b_{it}(s_\tau))$$

$$+ \mu_t(s_\tau) \left[\sum_{i=1}^{R} y_{it}(s_\tau) - \sum_{i=1}^{R} c_{it}(s_\tau) \right] \qquad (2)$$

where the μ's are the Lagrangian multipliers. The planner assigns time-invariant weights ω_i such that $0 < \omega_i < 1$ and $\sum_{i=1}^{R} \omega_i = 1$. The first-order conditions are

$$\hat{\mu}_t(s_\tau) = \omega_i U_c(c_{it}(s_\tau), b_{it}(s_\tau)) \qquad i = 1, \ldots, R \qquad (3)$$

where $\hat{\mu}_t(s_\tau) \equiv \mu_t(s_\tau)/\beta^t \pi_t$ and μ_t is the Lagrange multiplier associated with the aggregate feasibility constraint. To understand the implications of the theory, notice that the left-hand-side of (3) is only a function of time and the aggregate state and, hence, is the same for all regions. This multiplier is the current shadow value of an extra unit of resources at time t, given state s_τ.

To understand the broader empirical predictions of the model, assume that the representative individual has the following constant relative risk aversion (CRRA) utility function:

$$U(c_{it}(s_\tau), b_{it}(s_\tau)) = \exp((1 - \gamma) b_{it}) \left(\frac{1}{1 - \gamma} \right) (c_{it})^{(1-\gamma)}, \qquad \gamma > 0$$

where γ is the coefficient of constant relative risk aversion. The first-order condition for consumption of individual i can then be simplified by taking logs, aggregating, and first differencing so that household consumption behaves according to

$$\Delta \log(c_{it}) = \Delta \log(c_t^a) + \left(\frac{1 - \gamma}{\gamma} \right) \Delta(b_{it} - b_t^a), \qquad i = 1, \ldots, R \qquad (4)$$

where $b_t^a = (1/T) \sum_{i=1}^{R} b_{it}$, and $\log(c_t^a) = (1/R) \sum_{i=1}^{R} \log(c_{it})$. Hence for CRRA utility, changes in consumption of each individual move one-for-one with the change in average consumption holding fixed the preference shock. To note, with exponential (CARA) utility, the relationship holds in levels rather than log-levels – (see Mace 1991).

Under perfect risk sharing, consumption growth should move one-for-one across regions, ceteris paribus. Of course, exogenous shocks to preferences could drive regional changes in consumption as well as measurement error even with perfect risk sharing. Importantly though, under complete regional risk sharing, the differences in consumption changes across regions should be unrelated to their individual resources as the benevolent social planner is assumed to share resources across all regions. This simple intuition has led to the following important empirical proposition for testing regional risk sharing (both within and across countries).

Proposition 1

- *Let the observed change in consumption growth, $\Delta \log(c_{it})$, be the sum of true consumption growth, $\Delta \log(c_{it})^*$, measurement error, $\epsilon_{it} \sim N(0, \sigma_\epsilon^2)$, and an idiosyncratic preference shock, $v_{it} \sim N(0, \sigma_v^2)$; namely, $\Delta \log(c_{it}) = \Delta \log(c_{it})^* + \epsilon_{it} + v_{it}$.*
- *Let the observed change in income growth, $\Delta \log(y_{it})$, be the sum of true income growth, $\Delta \log(y_{it})^*$, and measurement error, $\eta_{it} \sim N(0, \sigma_\eta^2)$, such that $\Delta \log(y_{it}) = \Delta \log(y_{it})^* + \eta_{it}$.*
- *Assume that observed consumption growth and income growth have variances that are constant across regions and time, $\sigma_{\Delta \log(c)}^2$ and $\sigma_{\Delta \log(y)}^2$, respectively.*

The theory of perfect risk sharing predicts that true consumption growth should be more correlated across countries than true income growth:

$$\text{corr}(\Delta \log(c_{it})^*, \Delta \log(c_{jt})^*) > \text{corr}(\Delta \log(y_{it})^*, \Delta \log(y_{jt})^*)$$

$$i \neq j \quad (5)$$

In the presence of measurement error and idiosyncratic preference shocks, support for this prediction can be inferred from observed correlations if the volatilities of measurement error and preference shocks satisfy

$$\frac{\text{corr}(\Delta \log(c_{it}), \Delta \log(c_{jt}))}{\text{corr}(\Delta \log(y_{it}), \Delta \log(y_{jt}))} > \frac{[1 - \{(\sigma_\epsilon^2 + \sigma_v^2)/\sigma_c^2)\}]}{[1 - (\sigma_\eta^2/\sigma_y^2)]} \quad i \neq j \quad (6)$$

The major thrust of Proposition 1, that consumption should be more correlated across countries than output, is the fundamental prediction from the theory that was posed by Backus et al. (1992). This is stated in expression (5). However, because measurement error and preference shocks can affect the observed correlations, expression (6) clarifies how "cleanly" measured consumption growth must be relative to income growth – the right-hand-side – in order for any observed ratio of cross correlations in consumption and income – the left-hand side – to provide evidence of (5). Notice that the right-hand-side numerator of (6) is the ratio of the true volatility of consumption to its observed volatility. This ratio will rise if there is more measurement error (σ_ϵ^2) in consumption, or if preference shocks become larger (σ_v^2). This expression also indicates why it is so difficult to determine whether measurement error or preference shocks are behind the finding of the low cross correlation of observed consumption because they both enter symmetrically. Similarly, the right-hand-side denominator of (6) is the ratio of the true volatility of income to its observed volatility. This ratio will rise if there is more measurement error in income (σ_η^2).

The role of preference shocks and measurement error in interpreting consumption and income correlations to assess the theory of complete risk sharing has been explored in a number of papers. In a two-country model with tradable and nontradable goods, Stockman and Tesar (1995) find that by introducing taste shocks, which are 85% as large as productivity shocks, the model is more consistent with data. However, the trade balance is no longer countercyclical in their model. Moreover, using exogenous taste shocks in addition to exogenous, large, and persistent productivity shocks does not appear to leave much room for theory to explain open economy fluctuations. Devereux, Gregory, and Smith (1992) show that when preferences are nonseparable between consumption and leisure, leisure operates like a nontradable good, and low cross-country consumption correlations can result. The formalization of the role of measurement error is discussed in Hess and Shin (1998a).

2.2.2   Incomplete risk sharing

Models that feature less than complete risk sharing are actually the rule, rather than the exception, in international macroeconomics. The most obvious example is the workhorse small open economy model with the marginal rate of substitution equated to the world real interest rate (often assumed to be constant) while the opportunity set changes over time, possibly due to changes in income, productivity, government spending, or taxes. In this simple model, because we assume that there is only one asset rather than a more complete set of financial instruments (e.g., equity markets for domestic and foreign securities), consumption growth will contain both aggregate and idiosyncratic components even in the absence of taste shocks or measurement error.

Based on this insight, Baxter and Crucini (1995) demonstrate that the observed deviations from complete risk sharing will be larger the more persistent are the output shocks that each nation (or region) faces. Using an open economy model with a risk-free bond as the only asset (i.e., incomplete markets), they show that the more persistent are each country's shocks, the less cross-correlated consumption will be. The intuition is that highly persistent shocks with incomplete markets will make the shadow value of each country's resources (i.e., their permanent incomes) diverge more so that, in turn, consumption will have a smaller common component.

In an attempt to gauge the extent or scope of risk sharing, Crucini (1999) and Hess and Shin (1998b) consider specific environments of incomplete risk sharing. We follow Crucini's (1999) methodology because, using regional level data, it nests the Mace (1991) consumption specification with minimal modification. Specifically, agents have access to borrowing and/or lending opportunities at a fixed interest rate, r, that allows them to shift resources across time periods. The fraction of their stochastic income stream that the representative agent in each region chooses to pool in turn determines the flow of income that is available for intertemporal smoothing. Proposition 2 describes the assumptions and the resulting consumption function.

Proposition 2

- *If the representative agent in each region only pools a fraction, λ, of their income with the remaining fraction, $(1 - \lambda)$, of their income not pooled; and*
- *If agents are able to borrow or lend at a risk free rate $r = \beta^{-1} - 1$ to smooth their consumption paths according to the permanent income hypothesis; and*
- *If there are no region specific preference shocks.*

Then consumption changes by region will approximately follow the process:[3]

$$\Delta \log(c_{it}) = \lambda \Delta \log \left(c_t^a \right) + (1 - \lambda)(1 - \beta)$$

$$\times \sum_{k=0}^{\infty} \beta^k [E_t \log(y_{it+k}) - E_{t-1} \log(y_{it+k})] \tag{7}$$

The interpretation of this equation is straightforward using permanent income reasoning. Agents change consumption one-for-one with changes in permanent income, which is a λ-weighted average of changes in their own permanent income, and changes in the permanent income of others engaged in the risk-sharing arrangement. At one extreme, if regions completely share risk, then $\lambda = 1$, and consumption changes move one-for-one with the aggregate consumption change. At the other extreme, if regions do not share risk at all, then $\lambda = 0$, and each region's consumption change will be driven by the revisions in their own permanent income. We utilize a variant of this specification in the next section to estimate the extent of risk sharing across regions using the various panel datasets.

---

[3] See Crucini (1999) for the derivation.

2.2.3   Welfare implications

Finally, although Propositions 1 and 2 are helpful in understanding the degree of risk sharing across regions, an essential question concerns the potential welfare benefits from risk sharing. This question is fundamental to placing the earlier results in perspective. If the potential gains from risk sharing are small, then results suggesting that there is only limited risk sharing observed would be of less interest because the implied loss in welfare would be insignificant.

In an influential study on the costs of business cycles, Lucas (1987) asked, what fraction of a constant stream of consumption would a representative agent be willing to pay to avoid fluctuations in consumption that are associated with the business cycle? Adopting a CRRA utility function: $U(c_{it}) = (1/(1 - \gamma))(c_{it})^{(1-\gamma)}$, he demonstrated that the welfare cost of consumption variability is equal to $g(\sigma_z^2) \approx \frac{1}{2}\gamma\sigma_z^2$, where σ_z^2 is a measure of the variability of consumption measured as the variance of an i.i.d. shock around a deterministic trend. He calculated the welfare losses to be less than one tenth of a percentage point of consumption, assuming consumption growth was trend stationary, even with very low rates of intertemporal substitution (i.e., very high values for constant relative risk aversion).

Lucas's approach has been criticized for only allowing temporary shocks to consumption's level rather than permanent ones as well (e.g., see Cole and Obstfeld 1991; van Wincoop 1994).[4] van Wincoop (1994) demonstrated that if consumption growth were a random walk, as the simple permanent income hypothesis would suggest, then the gain measured in terms of the percent change in welfare associated with the complete elimination of consumption variability is $-0.5 \cdot \gamma \cdot \sigma_{\Delta \log(c)}^2/(r - \bar{\mu})$, where $r = (\beta^{-1} - 1) + \gamma\bar{\mu}$ is the risk-free rate, $\bar{\mu} = \mu - (\gamma/2)\sigma_{\Delta \log(c)}^2$ is the economy's risk-adjusted growth rate, and μ is the economy's expected growth rate.

These welfare exercises provide the basis for a useful benchmark for the extent of risk sharing faced by individuals within the context of a representative agent economy. Following the specification of welfare gains embodied in van Wincoop (1994), we wish to understand the potential gain over an infinite horizon from sharing risk across regions and the cost of regional business cycles based on a utility-derived calculation in the spirit of Lucas (1987). These issues have already been examined in a number of other papers. At the international level, Cole and Obstfeld (1991) found only small gains from international risk sharing (0.2% of output per year), comparable to those found by Lucas for the cost of U.S. business cycles. Using a more general setup, van Wincoop (1994) found much larger benefits from international risk sharing: 1.8–5.6% welfare

---

[4] van Wincoop (1994, 1998) also demonstrates that the issue of the correct underlying statistical model for the shocks to output (i.e., the underlying risk that each region wishes to diversify) and the specification of preferences can dramatically affect the calculations for the extent of potential gains from risk sharing. See also Dolmas (1998) on this last point.

gains were still obtainable. More recently, for U.S. states, Athanasoulis and van Wincoop (1998) calculate the permanent increase in income associated with a welfare improvement by which all regional output risk is shared. They find that over a 5- and 15-year horizon, the welfare gain is 0.7 and 1.4%, respectively.

2.3   Results

This section is subdivided into four subsections. The first describes the datasets from published studies that we used in our study. The second provides descriptive statistics of this data, while the third provides estimates of the extent of risk sharing across regions. The fourth subsection provides estimates of the welfare gains from exhausting the as yet unexploited gains from regional risk sharing.

2.3.1   The data

In this subsection we describe the international and intranational datasets we use to test our propositions on risk sharing. These datasets have been used in recently published studies and cover a range of countries (OECD) as well as regions within Canada, the United States, and Japan. The usefulness of using these alternative datasets is that we can reexplore the extent to which regions share risk in a common framework and better gauge the robustness of currently published findings.

The Canadian income and consumption data is from Crucini (1999). The original source is the Provincial Economic Accounts published by Statistics Canada. The income data are gross domestic product, whereas the consumption data are total consumption of goods (both durables and nondurables) and services by the private sector. Provincial deflators for final demand are used to deflate both gross domestic product and consumption. The Canadian panel contains data for the 10 provinces and a Canadian aggregate. The sample period is from 1971 to 1991.

For the United States, we use the state level income and consumption data from Asdrubali et al. (1996). The income measure for the United States is also gross domestic product, but the consumption data are based on retail sales. The original source of the output data is the Bureau of Economic Anaylsis (see Beemiller and Dunbar 1993 for details). The consumption data are from the Survey on Buying Power published by Sales Management. Asdrubali et al. gross-up the original consumption data by the difference between national consumption and retail sales measure (both durables and nondurables). State and local government consumption are added to this figure to arrive at state consumption. The U.S. aggregate consumer price index (CPI) is used to convert the data to constant dollar terms.[5] The panel includes all 50 states plus the District of Columbia. The sample period is from 1963 to 1990.

---

[5] See Del Negro (1998) for issues in constructing state-level CPI indices from city-level reports.

The Japanese data, from van Wincoop (1995), includes gross domestic product and total private consumption (for nondurables plus durables) for 47 prefectures. The main source of the data is the Annual Report on Prefectural Accounts produced by the Economic Planning Agency. Gross domestic product deflators are available for each prefecture, but consumption deflators are available at a more aggregative level (10 districts). The sample period is from 1975 to 1990.

Finally, the income and consumption data employed by Hess and Shin (1997) is used for the international dimension of our study. The original source is the World Data CD-ROM 1995, produced by the World Bank. Output is nominal gross domestic product divided by the gross domestic product deflator. Consumption is private consumption of goods (both durables and nondurables) and services, also deflated by the gross domestic product deflator. Even though Hess and Shin (1998a) found for U.S. states and regions that the inclusion of durable goods raises the cross correlation of consumption as well as its time-series volatility, we do not further explore this issue in this paper due to data availability.

2.3.2   Descriptive statistics

We begin with a few simple descriptive statistics. The raw data have been transformed to real per capita terms, and we use the log-differences of the variables in what follows. To ensure maximal comparability across panels, we used the following sample periods in our subsequent analysis: Canada, 1972–91; Japan, 1975–90; United States, 1972–90; and OECD countries, 1972–90.

To get at the issue of regional comovement we compute two cross-regional correlations. The first is the correlation of regional consumption or income growth with *aggregate* consumption or income growth. The second is the correlation of regional income or consumption growth with a *reference* region. We compute an aggregate national variable for the Japanese prefectures and U.S. states by taking a sum of the real levels of domestic product (or consumption) across regions. The aggregate is then transformed to real per capita growth using the same transformation applied to the regional data. The Canadian provincial data include a Canadian aggregate, so we use this construct for Canada. Note that the regional data and national aggregates are not reconciled with national income and product accounts, so these aggregates can differ somewhat from the OECD data for Canada, Japan, and the United States. The second measure of regional comovement is the correlation of the growth rate in each region with a reference region. We chose Ontario, Tokyo, Ohio, and the United States as our reference regions for the Canadian, Japanese, U.S., and OECD panels, respectively. Table 2.1 reports these regional comovement measures averaged across all regions in the panel along with the panel averages of the standard deviation of regional consumption and output and the cross correlation of regional consumption with regional output.

Table 2.1. *Properties of output and consumption across panel datasets*

Panel	Standard deviation		Correlation of output and consumption	Correlation with aggregate		Correlation with reference region	
	Output	Cons.		Output	Cons.	Output	Cons.
Canada	4.67	2.26	0.64	0.63	0.80	0.57	0.75
Japan	2.28	2.00	0.30	0.56	0.52	0.27	0.42
United States	4.60	5.63	0.53	0.74	0.63	0.73	0.59
OECD	2.30	2.35	0.69			0.44	0.37

Notes: Each cell reports the average moments across all regions within the panel. The first two columns present the average standard deviations. Column three reports the contemporaneous correlation between output and consumption. Columns four and five report the average cross–correlations of output and consumption, respectively. The final two columns report the average regional–reference correlations for output and consumption, respectively. The reference regions are: Ontario, Tokyo, Ohio, United States for the four panels, respectively.

Beginning with the standard deviation of output, we see similar values of 2.28% and 2.30% for the Japanese prefectures and OECD countries, whereas both the U.S. states and Canadian provinces have much larger, but comparable, standard deviations: 4.60% and 4.67%, respectively. Turning to the volatility of consumption, the United States is the clear outlier with an average standard deviation of consumption equal to 5.63% per year compared to less than 2.5% for the other panels. Recall that the U.S. consumption data differs from the other panel data in that it is measured by retail sales as opposed to actual consumption. The greater volatility of retail sales is consistent with the finding in Hess and Shin (1998a) that for aggregate U.S. data, total retails sales is about 10% more volatile than total consumption of durable and nondurable goods. Moreover, the volatility of the consumption measure falls if one includes only the retail sales of nondurable goods, which is available only for 19 states since 1978.[6] We are at a loss to explain the differences in output volatility across the panels.

The third column of Table 2.1 reports the cyclicality of regional consumption as measured by its contemporaneous correlation with regional output. Consumption is procyclical with respect to regional economic activity in all cases, though the magnitudes differ. The average correlation of consumption and output growth across the OECD is 0.69, quite close to the values of 0.64 for the Canadian provinces, and 0.53 for the U.S. states. The typical Japanese prefecture, however, has a consumption–output correlation of only 0.30.

---

[6] Hess and Shin (1998a) exclusively analyze these states and find that, even though the volatility of nondurables is much lower than that for durables, the cross-regional correlation is much lower for nondurables than it is for durables. They report that nondurable retail sales are approximately one-quarter less volatile than total retail sales. Because nondurable consumption data for regions and countries is generally not available, we do not explore this issue further in this chapter.

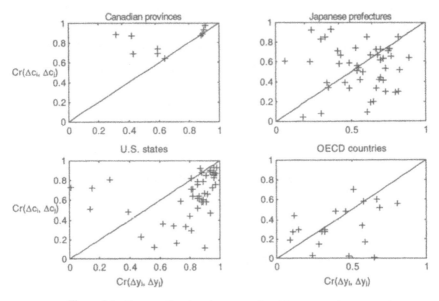

Figure 2.1. Cross-national and cross-regional income and consumption correlations.

The comovement across regions for both output and consumption are presented in the final four columns of Table 2.1. We first discuss the comovement of regional output and consumption with their aggregate counterparts, which are reported in columns four and five. We see that the output comovement is highest across the U.S. states, averaging 0.74, and lowest across the Japanese prefectures, where the correlation averages 0.56. Given that we are only using about 15 years of data, these differences are not statistically significant. The consumption comovements are more distinct across panels and do not line up with the income comovement patterns. Canadian provincial consumption growth is very highly correlated, averaging 0.80, whereas the average correlation of the Japanese prefectures with the aggregate is only 0.52.

Figure 2.1 presents the full set of bilateral comparisons with the correlation of consumption growth of each pair (a region and the aggregate) plotted against the corresponding correlation of income growth. According to the theory of aggregate risk sharing (see Proposition 1), the data points should lie about the 45-degree line. We see that consumption correlations lie uniformly above income correlations in the Canadian panel (all points lie on or above the 45-degree line), whereas for the United States and the OECD countries income correlations often exceed consumption correlations (the majority of points lie below the 45-degree line). The Japanese prefectures give a more ambiguous picture.

The correlation patterns using the reference regions in the final two columns of Table 2.1 typically yield lower cross-regional correlations, which is what one would expect given that the aggregate contains the regional variable by construction. Tokyo was chosen based on its economic size and appears more idiosyncratic than Ontario, Ohio, or the United States. In terms of the *quantity anomaly* pointed to by Backus et al. (1992), we see that the average correlation of output with aggregate or reference output is distinctly higher than the average correlation of consumption with aggregate or reference consumption for the OECD and U.S. cases, but the reverse is true of the Canadian provinces. The ranking of the correlations for the Japanese prefectures (at least based on averages across regions) is unclear because the relative ranking of the magnitudes of the correlations switches depending on whether the aggregate or reference region is used in constructing the correlation.

From expression (6), we can calculate how large must be the magnitude of measurement error and preference shocks in order for the true correlation of consumption to be greater than that for output. If we assume that output is measured without error (i.e., $\sigma_\eta^2 = 0$), then consumption growth would have to be approximately 15% noise and preference shocks $[1.0 - (0.63/0.74)]$ in order to make the true correlation of consumption equal to that for output across states within the United States for durable plus nondurable goods. Hess and Shin (1998a) report that measurement error and preference shocks would have to be over fifty percent of measured consumption for only nondurable goods.

An additional factor to consider in the analysis of cross correlations of consumption and output is that we would expect to observe comovement in consumption and income across countries even in the absence of international trade and financial market linkages to the extent that technological changes and policy changes move in a synchronous fashion. An initial attempt to consider the simultaneity in the data proceeds as follows. Let z_{it} be either regional consumption or regional income growth, and let z_t^a be either the growth rate for the aggregate variable or the reference variable in the panel. We then estimate the following regression as a time series for each individual region within the panel:

$$z_{it} = \alpha_i + \beta_i z_t^a + \epsilon_{it} \tag{8}$$

We refer to the ratio of the explained sum of squares to total sum of squares from Equation (8) as the common component and the remainder (unexplained variation) as the idiosyncratic component.[7] Table 2.2 reports the results, again averaging across the regions in each panel.

Consistent with the earlier findings reported in Table 2.1, the states within the United States have (on average) an exceptionally strong common component in output, and a smaller common component in consumption. For both panels A and B, this relative ranking of common output versus common consumption component is shared with the OECD countries but reversed for Canadian regions. Once again, for Japan, the relative rankings are ambiguous.

---

[7] See Del Negro (1998) for a much more sophisticated decomposition into common and idiosyncratic components based on factor analysis.

Table 2.2. *Variance decompostion: Simple projection*

Panel	Output		Consumption	
	Common	Region-specific	Common	Region-specific
Panel A: Projection on aggregate variable				
Canada	0.44	0.56	0.65	0.35
Japan	0.35	0.65	0.32	0.68
United States	0.65	0.35	0.45	0.55
OECD				
Panel B: Projection on reference variable				
Canada	0.37	0.63	0.59	0.41
Japan	0.12	0.88	0.24	0.76
United States	0.64	0.36	0.39	0.61
OECD	0.25	0.75	0.19	0.81

Notes: Estimation results for Equation (8) averaged across regions within each panel. Common (idiosyncratic) refers to the explained (unexplained) sum of squares.

Figure 2.2 presents the full complement of consumption–income correlations between each region and the aggregate using raw and common component adjusted data. The x-coordinates are raw correlations of income growth and consumption growth within each region or country, whereas the y-coordinates are correlations of income and consumption after removing a common component. After controlling for possible common movements in income and consumption across regions, we see a decrease in the income and consumption comovements within countries as compared to across OECD countries (i.e., the within-country correlation pairs generally lie below the 45-degree line for Canada, Japan, and the United States, whereas the across-country correlation pairs for the OECD lie nearly on the 45-degree line. However, even within regions and after the adjustment, the correlations tend to be strongly positive.

2.3.3   Risk-sharing specification

We extend the results of estimating the risk-sharing specification to the regional Japanese data to see if Crucini's (1999) conclusion that the extent of risk sharing is greater within than across countries based on data for the U.S. states and Canadian provinces compared to the G-7 is also true of Japanese prefectures. However, we also employ different data and countries in the estimation process for the U.S. regions and country-level data as a robustness check (the results for the Canadian provinces are taken directly from Crucini 1999).

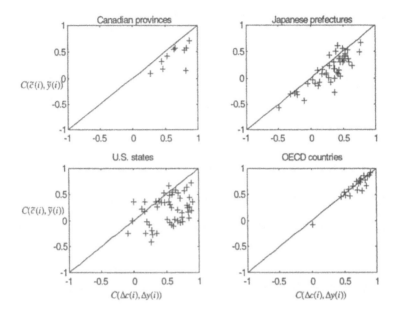

Figure 2.2. Consumption–income correlations within regions and countries.

The U.S. data employed by Crucini (1999) differs in a number of respects from the data employed by Asdrubali et al. (1996), which we now use. Crucini (1999) deflates consumption by the aggregate U.S. deflator for nondurable goods and services and uses state personal income as the income measure deflates by the aggregate U.S. GNP deflator. Asdrubali et al. deflate both consumption and income by the aggregate U.S. consumer price index and their income measure is gross domestic product. The last difference between the estimation conducted here and in Crucini (1999) is that we include 21 OECD countries as opposed to only the G-7.

To estimate the incomplete risk-sharing Equation (7) from Crucini (1999), we need to make an assumption as to the process for the log of permanent income. Accordingly, we assume that innovations to the log of permanent income are reasonably proxied by the change in income (i.e., annual income is close to a random walk).[8] We estimate the following equation separately, region-by-region as a time series, for each region in the panel:

$$\Delta \log(c_{it}) = \alpha_i + \lambda_i \Delta \log \left(c_t^a\right) + (1 - \lambda_i)\Delta \log(y_{it}) + u_{it} \qquad (9)$$

where the variables are now in logarithms and the variable $\Delta \log(c_t^a)$ is a simple average of the consumption growth rates of all the regions in the panel. The

---

[8] Crucini (1999) examines the robustness of this assumption and finds that the risk-sharing parameter estimates are somewhat sensitive to the estimated process of regional income.

Table 2.3. *Risk-sharing parameter estimates*

Panel	Mean statistics			Number of regions for which a 95% confidence interval encompasses a risk-sharing parameter equal to			
	$\hat{\lambda}$	se($\hat{\lambda}$)	R^2	$\hat{\lambda} = 1$	$1 > \hat{\lambda} > 0$	$\hat{\lambda} = 0$	$\hat{\lambda} = 0$ or 1
Canada	0.88	0.08	0.75	6	4	0	0
Japan	0.93	0.24	0.39	41	1	2	3
United States	0.81	0.32	0.50	29	6	4	12
OECD	0.40	0.19	0.50	3	10	7	1

Notes: Parameter estimates of Equation (9), where the equation is estimated for each region in the panel as a time series and the average estimate of λ, standard error of λ (denoted se), and R^2, are reported in the first three columns. The last four columns report information associated with the distribution of the estimated λ's.

error term is interpreted as a combination of measurement error and/or taste shocks, the latter of which would have to be uncorrelated with the determinants of aggregate consumption or regional permanent income.

The estimation results for Equation (9) are reported in Table 2.3. The first three columns report, for each panel, the average estimated value for λ, the average standard error of the estimate for λ, and the average R^2, respectively. The final four columns of the table give an indication of the distribution of the estimates of λ within each panel, which may be more informative than simply the statistical mean. We see that the risk-sharing parameters average more than 0.8 across the Canadian provinces, U.S. states, and Japanese prefectures, compared to about one half this magnitude for the OECD countries. These results reaffirm Crucini's (1999) findings that the degree of risk sharing is higher across regions within countries than across industrialized countries, although it is less than perfect in all cases. The complete risk-sharing model cannot be rejected in 6 of 10 provinces, 29 of 51 states, and 41 of 47 Japanese prefectures.[9] In contrast, the null can be rejected in all but 3 of the 21 OECD countries. The results for Japan are even stronger than for the United States in the sense that, although both have a similar number of economic regions, a significant number (12) of the states have risk-sharing parameter estimates with 95% confidence intervals overlapping both 0 and 1; Japan has only one such region.

The estimated risk-sharing parameters for the United States and the Japanese prefectures appear somewhat in contrast to what the simple correlation patterns of consumption suggest about the extent of risk sharing across regions. It appears likely that measurement error in consumption (and/or taste shocks) are

---

[9] The finding that a large proportion of U.S. states do not perfectly share risk accords well with Hess and Shin (1998a) in their results for only 19 states with consumption measured by the retail sales of nondurables.

partly responsible for the differences because these components of regional consumption variance would be cast into the residual term in the regression equation (assuming they are uncorrelated with regional income).[10] Alternatively, specification error in the construction of the revision of permanent income $(1 - \beta) \sum_{k=0}^{\infty} \beta^k [E_t y_{it+k} - E_{t-1} y_{it+k}] = \Delta \log(y_{it})$ under the random walk assumption will lower the contribution from the region-specific component and increase the contribution from the unexplained component. Measurement error in the construction of regional income data will also lower the region-specific component. Finally, further specification error could be due to the presence of a fraction of consumers who neither share risk nor consume out of permanent income, but rather consume according to a "rule of thumb" such that consumption deviates from permanent income considerations.

In a complementary study, Hess and Shin (1998b), using household food consumption data for the United States from the Panel Study for Income Dynamics, estimate a regression equation similar to (9). They estimated the fraction of risk that is shared within regions, within industries, and across regions and industries (i.e., aggregate). Importantly, rather than using income data to proxy regional and/or industry changes in permanent income, they use, according to the theory, constructed consumption changes by region and industry for this purpose. They report that only about 45% of risk is shared across regions and industries, whereas the remainder is shared within regions and industries.

2.3.4   Welfare gains

We explore the welfare implications of regional and national fluctuations in consumption in this section. Adopting a CRRA utility function, $U(c_{it}) = (1/(1 - \gamma))(c_{it})^{(1-\gamma)}$, we follow the approach taken by van Wincoop (1994), assuming consumption is a random walk. This leads to an increase in the welfare implications of fluctuations relative to what Lucas (1987) found since he assumed consumption reverted to a deterministic trend. As discussed in Section 2.3 the formula for a welfare gain associated with a drop in the standard deviation of consumption growth by $d\sigma^2_{\Delta c}$ is

$$-0.5 \gamma d\sigma^2_{\Delta c}/(r - \bar{\mu}) \tag{10}$$

where $\bar{\mu} = \mu - (0.5\gamma\sigma^2_{\Delta c})$ is the risk adjusted growth rate and $r = (\beta^{-1} - 1) + (\gamma \cdot \bar{\mu})$. We set $\gamma = 4$, $\bar{\mu} = 0.017$, and $\beta = 0.99$, which are the same values used by van Wincoop (1994), except for the coefficient of relative risk aversion (he used unity). The implied level of r is 7.8%.

To calculate the welfare gain from removing the remaining region-specific variability of consumption growth, we need a good measure of the latter. Fortunately, the incomplete risk-sharing specification, Equation (9) provides a theoretically appealing variance decomposition of consumption growth that relates

---

[10] This view is also emphasized by Sorensen and Yosha (1998).

Table 2.4. *Welfare gains from removing region-specific consumption growth variability* ($\gamma = 4$)

Panel	Statistic	Region PI	Covariance	Unexplained	Total
Canada	Highest quintile	0.32	0.56	0.64	1.52
	Average	0.15	0.34	0.46	0.94
	Lowest quintile	0.12	0.27	0.12	0.50
Japan	Highest quintile	0.47	−0.36	2.00	2.12
	Average	0.15	−0.06	0.85	0.94
	Lowest quintile	0.04	−0.04	0.35	0.35
United States	Highest quintile	2.18	0.48	9.71	12.37
	Average	1.01	0.25	5.73	6.99
	Lowest quintile	0.68	−2.62	3.71	1.78
OECD	Highest quintile	1.55	0.00	1.50	3.06
	Average	0.74	0.13	0.65	1.52
	Lowest quintile	0.09	0.04	0.30	0.44

Notes: From regression (9), we decompose the region-specific variability of consumption, $\text{var}(\Delta \log(c_{it})) - \hat{\lambda}_i^2 \text{var}(\Delta \log(c_t^a))$, into three components: $((1 - \hat{\lambda}_i)^2 \text{var}(\Delta \log(y_{it})), 2\hat{\lambda}_i(1 - \hat{\lambda}_i)^2 \text{cov}(\Delta \log(c_t^a), \Delta \log(y_{it}))$, and the variance of the residual, $\sigma_{u_i}^2$, respectively. The columns headed by "Regional PI", "Covariance", and "Unexplained" are calculated as $-0.5 \cdot \gamma \cdot d\sigma_{\Delta c}^2/(r - \bar{\mu})$ multiplied by these three terms. The final column, denoted "Total", reports the sum of the three components. Because we have λ_i for each separate region or country, we report the mean, highest, and lowest quartile welfare changes.

to the portfolio choices implied by the estimated risk-sharing parameters. Using Equation (9), we apportion the variability of regional consumption into a common part, $(\hat{\lambda}_i^2 \text{var}(\Delta \log(c_t^a))$; a part related to variation in regional income, $((1 - \hat{\lambda}_i)^2 \text{var}(\Delta \log(y_{it}))$; the covariance between the two, $2\hat{\lambda}_i(1 - \hat{\lambda}_i)^2 \text{cov}(\Delta \log(c_t^a), \Delta \log(y_{it}))$; and an unexplained part which is just the variance of the regression residual $(\sigma_{u_i}^2)$. Importantly, the final three components can be summed to obtain that part of consumption variability that is not accounted for by aggregate consumption movements [i.e., regional consumption growth net of the volatility of shared consumption growth, $\text{var}(\Delta \log(c_{it})) - \hat{\lambda}_i^2 \text{var}(\Delta \log(c_t^a))$]; hence, we will focus on these terms in our welfare calculations.

Table 2.4 reports the welfare results using the variance decomposition implied by the risk-sharing regression. Specifically we ask how much agents in each region would be willing to give up in terms of average consumption to eliminate the variance of regional consumption growth that is not accounted for by movements in average consumption. The first component we identify is the welfare gain from removing the variance associate with regional income growth variation (see column denoted "Regional PI"). The second term in the calculation, in the welfare (gain), is proportional to the covariation between regional income growth and aggregate consumption (see column denoted "Covariance"), and the final welfare gain is from the variance of the residual (see column denoted "Unexplained").[11] The final column, denoted "Total", reports the sum of the three components. The total should be interpreted as an upper bound on the welfare gains because it includes the regression residual.[12]

Each column of Table 2.4 reports the welfare implications (in percentages of steady-state consumption) of moving each of these variances to zero. Due to the fact that we have regions that are heterogeneous with respect to their risk sharing parameters (λ_i) and underlying variances of permanent income, we calculate the welfare measures separately for each region and then report the mean welfare cost (across all regions in a panel) and the mean welfare cost for the quintile with the highest or lowest total welfare benefit from eliminating consumption risk not already shared.

Three things should be noted in comparing our results with Lucas's. First, he considered only the welfare gains from removing aggregate consumption variability, whereas we make our calculations for removing region-specific consumption variability after conditioning on aggregate consumption. Second, we assume that the fluctuations to consumption's level are permanent, whereas Lucas assumed that fluctuations to consumption were i.i.d. around a deterministic trend. Most importantly, however, Lucas was interested in the reduction of consumption variability brought about by a reduction in output variability. To be consistent with Lucas, the increased welfare brought about by the removal of the regional output cycle would be presented under the column "Regional PI" in Table 2.4. In contrast, the risk-sharing literature emphasizes the reduction in idiosyncratic consumption variability. This is related to the final column of Table 2.4 presented under the header "Total" as in this case we have controlled regional consumption only for aggregate consumption.[13]

The results in Table 2.4 suggest that the average Canadian and Japanese regions would be willing to give up about 1% of consumption to eliminate their total regional risk in consumption. The estimate rises to about 1.5% for the mean OECD nation. The mean U.S. state would be willing to pay 7% of consumption,

[11] The columns headed by "Regional PI", "Covariance", and "Unexplained" are calculated as $-0.5 \cdot \gamma \cdot d\sigma_{\Delta c}^2/(r - \bar{\mu})$ multiplied by $((1 - \hat{\lambda}_i)^2 \mathrm{var}(\Delta \log(y_{it}))$, $2\hat{\lambda}_i(1 - \hat{\lambda}_i)^2 \mathrm{cov}(\Delta \log(c_t^a)$, $\Delta \log(y_{it}))$, and the variance of the residual, (σ_{ui}^2), respectively.

[12] In effect, when using the first column to compute welfare changes, we are assuming that all the residual variance is diversifiable risk when in reality it is some unknown combination of regional permanent income variation (that is not captured by regional income growth), taste shocks, and measurement error. The number does take into account risk already shared however because the variance attributable to aggregate consumption growth is excluded from the calculation.

[13] The welfare calculations when $\lambda = 1$ is imposed provides slightly higher values than those reported in Table 2.4 because those reported in the table are calculated based on estimates of λ that minimize the unexplained sum of squares.

though almost all this (5.73%) is attributable to the error term in the estimated risk-sharing regression. Some of this might well be captured by a more carefully specified permanent income process but some is also likely measurement error, in which case it should not be included as a potential welfare-improving change.

Focusing on the variance that is attributed to regional income variation, the welfare measures are quite modest for the average Canadian and Japanese region and exactly equal to one another at 0.15%. However, there is a greater variance of welfare benefits cross-sectionally in Japan than in Canada, with the highest quintile prepared to give up about 0.5% of consumption compared to only 0.32% for the top quintile among the Canadian provinces.

Turning to the U.S. states, we see comparable welfare implications of regional income variability to what is observed internationally. The large possible gains in the OECD are easy to understand because they have a low risk-sharing parameter, which gives regional income movements a larger influence in regional consumption variability. The larger possible gains in the U.S. case suggest that even though risk-sharing is more extensive, in the sense of pooling of resources, the benefits to additional pooling are greater because state-level income is more variable than national income. The puzzle that remains is why more risk sharing does not take place in the United States if the costs of doing so are comparable to what exists in Canada and Japan. We discuss some possibilities in our concluding section.

2.4   Conclusions

In this survey, we provide evidence that even though both intranational and international risk sharing are imperfect, the data suggests that there is more of the former than of the latter. We did not discuss, however, the channels by which this intranational risk sharing has taken place. While using different methodologies, though the same data sources for U.S. states, Asdrubali et al. (1996), Del Negro (1998) and Athanasoulis and van Wincoop (1998) measured the extent of risk sharing that takes place through financial markets via assets and through fiscal policy tax and transfer schemes as well as the component of risk that is left unshared.[14] The range of estimates is

---

[14] The methodologies they employ differ quite substantially. Asdrubali, Sorensen, and Yosha (1996) implement their idea of 'smoothing' to calculate the percentage of a shock that is smoothed through capital markets (income smoothing), savings adjustment (consumption smoothing), the federal tax-transfer system, and the remainder is left unsmoothed. Del Negro (1997) uses factor analysis to decompose output and income fluctuations and then relates these to consumption growth. Athanasoulis and van Wincoop (1998) base their calculations on a 26-year horizon that distinguishes between risk shared through financial markets and those through fiscal net transfers.

remarkably similar. Approximately 10–20% of shocks to gross state product are shared through fiscal tax-transfers, approximately 45–60% of risk sharing is achieved though financial markets, and 25–35% is left "unsmoothed" or unshared.

The fact that we observe incomplete risk sharing across geographic regions has also led researchers to uncover the source of this incompleteness. One approach is that, due to private information or merely preference, individuals simply prefer to hold local assets even within a country. Coval and Moskowitz (1997) and Huberman (1997) find strong evidence of a local preference for equities based on portfolio decisions both for fund managers and individuals. Alternatively, some shocks to resources may be hard to diversify. A good candidate for these types of shocks are those that affect human capital which may be embodied in the industry that individuals are attached to. Using state-level data for the United States, Sorensen and Yosha (1997) explore the basis of industry-related movement in resources. Using family-level evidence, Hess and Shin (1998b) find that industry-related movements in resources are not perfectly shared across regions. We anticipate that future work in the area of risk sharing will attempt to further our understanding of how market incompleteness manifests itself both within and across countries. The issue of whether unexplained idiosyncratic fluctuations in measured consumption are better interpreted as measurement error or preference shocks also requires additional research.

References

Altug, S., and R. Miller. 1990. Household choices in equilibrium. *Econometrica*, 82: 1177–98.

Asdrubali, P., B. E. Sorensen, and O. Yosha. 1996. Channels of interstate risksharing: United States 1963–1990. *Quarterly Journal of Economics* 111: 1081–110.

Athanasoulis, S., and E. van Wincoop. 1998. "Risksharing Within the United States: What Have Financial Markets and Fiscal Federalism Accomplished?" Research Paper 9808. Federal Reserve Bank of New York.

Atkeson, A., and T. Bayoumi. 1993. Do private capital markets insure regional risk? Evidence from the United States and Europe. *Open Economies Review*, 4: 303–24.

Backus, D. K., P. J. Kehoe, and F. E. Kydland. 1992. International real business cycles. *Journal of Political Economy* 84: 84–103.

Bayoumi, T., and M. Klein. 1995. "A Provincial View of Capital Mobility." Working Paper Number 5115. National Bureau of Economic Research.

Bayoumi, T., and R. McDonald. 1995. Consumption, income and international capital market integration. *IMF Staff Papers* 42: 552–76.

Baxter, M., and M. Crucini. 1993. Explaining saving/investment correlations. *American Economic Review* 83: 416–36.

Baxter, M., and M. J. Crucini. 1995. Business cycles and the asset market structure of foreign trade. *International Economic Review* 36: 821–54.

Beemiller, R., and A. Dunbar. 1993. Gross state product, 1977–90. *Survey of Current Business* 73: 28–49.

Canova, F., and M. Ravn. 1996. International consumption risk sharing. *International Economic Review* 37: 573–601.

Cochrane, J. H. 1991. A simple test of consumption insurance. *Journal of Political Economy* 99: 957–76.

Cole, H., and M. Obstfeld. 1991. Commodity trade and international risk sharing: How much do financial markets matter? *Journal of Monetary Economics* 28: 3–24.

Coval, J. D., and T. Moskowitz. 1997. "Home Bias at Home: Local Equity Preferences in Domestic Portfolios." Mimeo. University of Michigan Business School.

Crucini, M. J. 1999. On international and national dimensions of risk sharing. *Review of Economics and Statistics* 81: 73–84.

Del Negro, M. 1998. "Aggregate Risksharing Across US States." Mimeo.

Devereux, M., A. Gregory, and G. Smith. 1992. Realistic cross country consumption correlations in a two country, equilibrium, business cycle model. *Journal of International Money and Finance* 11: 3 16.

Dolmas, J. 1998. Risk preferences and the welfare cost of business cycles. *Review of Economic Dynamics* 1: 646–76.

Hayashi, F., J. Altonji, and L. Kotlikoff. 1996. Risk sharing between and within families. *Econometrica* 64: 261–94.

Hess, G. D., and K. Shin. 1997. International and intranational business cycles. *Oxford Review of Economic Policy* 13: 93–109.

Hess, G. D., and K. Shin. 1998a. Intranational business cycles in the United States. *Journal of International Economics* 44: 289–313.

Hess, G., and K. Shin. 1998b. "Risk Sharing by Households Within and Across Regions and Industries." Mimeo. University of Kansas.

Huberman, G. 1997. "Familiarity Breeds Investment." Mimeo. Columbia Business School.

Lewis, K. 1996. What can explain the apparent lack of international consumption risk sharing. *Journal of Political Economy* 104: 267–97.

Lucas, R. E., Jr. (1987). *Models of Business Cycles*. Oxford, United Kingdom: Basil Blackwell.

Mace, B. 1991. Full insurance in the presence of aggregate uncertainty. *Journal of Political Economy* 99: 928–56.

Obstfeld, M. 1994. "Are Industrial-Country Consumption Risks Globally Diversified?," in L. Leiderman and A. Razin, eds., *Capital Mobility: the Impact on Consumption, Investment and Growth*. Cambridge, U.K.: Cambridge University Press.

Sorensen, B., and O. Yosha. 1997. "Income and Consumption Smoothing Among U.S. States: Regions or Clubs." Mimeo.

Sorensen, B., and O. Yosha. 1998. International risk sharing and european monetary unification. *Journal of International Economics*, forthcoming.

Stockman, A., and L. Tesar. 1995. Tastes and technology in a two-country model of the business cycle: Explaining international comovements. *American Economic Review* 85: 168–85.

Townsend, R. M. 1987. "Arrow–Debreu Programs as Microeconomic Foundations of Macroeconomics," in T. Bewley, ed., *Advances in Economic Theory: Fifth World Congress*, vol. 2, pp. 379–428. New York: Cambridge University Press.

Townsend, R. 1995. Consumption insurance: An evaluation of risk-bearing systems in low-income countries. *Journal of Economic Perspectives* 9: 83–102.

van Wincoop, E. 1994. Welfare gains from international risksharing. *Journal of Monetary Economics* 34: 175–200.

van Wincoop, E. 1995. Regional risksharing. *European Economic Review* 37: 1545–67.

van Wincoop, E. 1998. How big are the potential gains from international risksharing? *Journal of International Economics*, forthcoming.

CHAPTER 3

Intranational and international credit market integration: Evidence from regional income and consumption patterns*

Bent E. Sørensen[†] and Oved Yosha[‡]

3.1 Introduction

Intranational macroeconomics, namely, interrelations among regions within countries, can shed new light on questions in "traditional" macroeconomics and international macroeconomics. A recent study by Beaudry and van Wincoop (1996) focuses on issues related to consumption and saving. They use a panel of U.S. state-level data to provide better estimates of the intertemporal elasticity of substitution in consumption than those obtained from aggregate U.S. time-series data (Hall 1988). Other studies have been done by Bayoumi and Klein (1997) who study interprovince and international capital market integration, using Canadian province-level data, and Ostergaard, Sørensen, and Yosha (1998), who investigate excess sensitivity (Hall 1978) and excess smoothness (Campbell and Deaton 1989; West 1988) in consumption, using U.S. state-level personal disposable income and consumption data. This literature is surveyed in the next section.[1]

Here, we study intertemporal income and consumption patterns of regions within countries and countries within the OECD in order to: (1) evaluate the degree of integration of these countries in the world credit market; and (2) compare the degree of credit market integration of regions within countries with the degree of international credit market integration.

The degree of integration in the world credit market of a group of regions or countries is of relevance for whether the group constitutes an Optimal Currency Area (Mundell 1961). If there is much integration among the regions, but the

* We thank Maria Luengo-Prado for superb research assistance and Greg Hess, Michael Klein, and Eric van Wincoop for helpful comments.
† Mailing address: Economic Research Department, Federal Reserve Bank of Kansas City, 925 Grand Blvd., Kansas City, MO, 64198. E-mail: *Bent. E. Sorensen@kc.frb.org.*
‡ Mailing address: Berglas School of Economics, Tel Aviv University, Tel Aviv 69978. E-mail: *yosha@post.tau.ac.il.*
[1] Another related paper is Bayoumi and Rose (1993) who investigate intranational saving-investment correlations (Feldstein and Horioka 1980) using British regional data.

group as a whole is not well integrated with the outside world, then these regions should have their own common currency. Mundell's criteria for identifying Optimal Currency Areas include capital and labor mobility. Labor mobility among U.S. states was studied by Blanchard and Katz (1992); capital mobility among U.S. states, in the sense of income smoothing via cross-state ownership of productive assets, was studied by Asdrubali, Sørensen, and Yosha (1996) and Hess and Shin (1998) and is further studied in Chapter 2; income insurance for U.S. states through the fiscal policy of a central authority was studied by von Hagen (1992), who also provides a detailed survey of related literature in this volume. Here, we focus on credit market integration, namely the extent of ex-post adjustments of consumption in response to *uninsured* shocks to disposable income.

We want to emphasize the difference between capital market integration in the sense of cross-country ownership of productive assets that provides (ex-ante) income insurance to countries (an issue we do not address in this paper) and credit market integration that enables countries to smooth consumption (ex-post) in response to (uninsured) income shocks (e.g., through international borrowing and lending). Credit market integration refers to the functioning of financial intermediaries and to all institutions and contractual arrangements that facilitate the adjustment of consumption to the optimal level in the face of shocks to income. Examples that come to mind are trade credit arrangements, contract enforcement procedures, and (lack of) transaction costs in general.

Country-level (regional-level) consumption patterns cannot be expected to correspond well to Hall's (1978) permanent income hypothesis (PIH) model if credit markets are not well integrated between countries (regions). A second reason why country-level or regional-level consumption smoothing may not be well described by Hall's fixed-interest PIH model is that countries and regions may face upward sloping interest schedules. This effect is likely to be more pronounced for very large countries.[2]

In our analysis, we use a log-linear variant of the PIH model suggested by Hall (1978). An implication of the PIH is that the correlation of changes in consumption with lagged changes in income should be low (zero if the interest rate is constant); see Section 3.3 for details. We refer to a nonzero correlation of consumption changes with lagged income changes as excess sensitivity (Deaton 1992), and we use the estimated amount of excess sensitivity as a measure of deviations from the assumptions of the PIH. We assume that the PIH would give a good approximation to the intertemporal consumption-smoothing behavior of the representative consumer of each region, if each region could freely borrow and lend from other regions and countries at a fixed

---

[2] If international credit markets are integrated, the world interest rate will adjust to global supply and demand. Small countries may face upward sloping demand interest schedules if their demand for credit is highly correlated with the world demand for credit.

interest rate. Excess sensitivity of regional-level consumption may then have three explanations: (1) credit markets are not integrated between regions within countries; (2) credit markets are not integrated between countries, preventing countries from smoothing shocks that are common to regions within these countries; or (3) world interest rates respond to global demand and supply.

Consider first our analysis using (within-country) regional-level data. Our approach builds on the distinction between aggregate income shocks that hit an entire country and idiosyncratic region-specific income shocks. To smooth idiosyncratic shocks, regions can simply borrow and lend among themselves without need to transact on the world market. If the interregional credit market operates well, goods will flow across regions, smoothing consumption in all the regions.[3] Notice that because shocks are idiosyncratic, they sum to zero across regions in any given period. Therefore, in this benchmark model, aggregate demand and supply are unaffected by the idiosyncratic shocks and hence the equilibrium interregional interest rate is also unaffected. By contrast, to smooth aggregate shocks to income, the regions must transact (individually or as a country) on the world credit market in order to induce international flows of goods. To do so, at an exogenously given interest rate, the country must be well integrated in the world credit market *and* be "small" in the sense that, by borrowing and lending internationally, it does not affect the world interest rate.

If regions within countries are relatively well integrated, there should be little or no sensitivity of idiosyncratic regional consumption to lagged idiosyncratic regional income (i.e., controlling for country-level shocks). We can therefore examine if regional credit markets are well integrated by estimating the amount of excess sensitivity of region-specific consumption to region-specific income. If, furthermore, the country is well integrated in the world credit market and faces a constant interest rate, the same should be true for aggregate income and consumption and, therefore, also for total (nonidiosyncratic) regional income and consumption. Testing if the coefficient in a regression, without controlling for country-level shocks, is identical to the coefficient in a regression where aggregate shocks are controlled for provides a test of whether the country can be considered "a small open economy."[4] [Note that these regressions do not utilize (nominal or real) interest rates.] The conclusion of our empirical analysis

---

[3] The actual direction of goods flows will depend on the stochastic properties of the income process (the degree of persistence of the income shocks).

[4] This idea is related to the literature on the intertemporal approach to the current account (Sachs 1981; Ghosh 1995; Glick and Rogoff 1995; Obstfeld and Rogoff 1995; Razin 1995), and in particular to Bayoumi and Klein (1997). We provide a more detailed discussion later. Also related are studies by Jappelli and Pagano (1989) and Bacchetta and Gerlach (1997), who use excess sensitivity of consumption as a measure of credit market imperfections within countries. Another related literature, that we do not survey, is concerned with the extent to which national borders matter for trade (see, e.g., McCallum 1995; Engel and Rogers 1996; Helliwell 1996).

using regional-level data is that interregional credit markets are well integrated, but countries display significant excess sensitivity of consumption, probably due to imperfect international credit markets or an endogenous world interest rate. [This agrees with the conclusion of Ostergaard et al. (1998) for the United States.]

Next, we apply this empirical strategy to a group of OECD countries, treating each country in the group as a "region." We take as given that regions within each country are relatively well integrated (our regional-level regressions do not provide strong evidence against this assumption) and focus on the degree of (intercountry) integration of the countries that compose the group. If OECD credit markets are well integrated, we should expect to find: (1) little (or no) excess sensitivity of consumption in regressions where aggregate (OECD-wide) fluctuations are controlled for and (2) considerable excess sensitivity in regressions where aggregate fluctuations are not controlled for, due to the endogeneity of the OECD-wide interest rate. Suppose we do not find different degrees of excess sensitivity in such OECD country-level regressions with and without controlling for OECD-wide shocks, but we do find different degrees of excess sensitivity in regional-level regressions with and without controlling for nationwide shocks. We would interpret this as evidence that country-level excess sensitivity is caused by national borders restricting the operation of international credit markets.

Indeed, the analysis for the sample of OECD countries shows significant excess sensitivity both when aggregate (OECD-wide) fluctuations are and are not controlled for, suggesting that international credit markets are not, on average, well integrated. As mentioned earlier, we obtain very different results for U.S. states and Canadian provinces. The United States and Canada are very large, yet credit markets within these countries are highly integrated. Therefore, geographical distance cannot be the only explanation for the less-than-perfect credit market integration among OECD countries. The excess sensitivity found in country-level data is thus likely to be caused by national borders constituting barriers to credit market integration.

3.2   Intranational and international consumption smoothing: A survey

Beaudry and van Wincoop (1996) stress the importance of obtaining good estimates of the intertemporal elasticity of substitution in consumption (e.g., for policy evaluations). They demonstrate empirically that such estimates are hard to generate with U.S. aggregate-level data. Estimating an Euler equation obtained from the optimization of a U.S. representative consumer with constant elasticity of substitution utility and using aggregate U.S. income and consumption data and various instruments for the (time-varying) interest rate, they obtain statistically significant estimates of the intertemporal elasticity of substitution in consumption but strongly reject the model in virtually all the specifications. When rule-of-thumb consumers (who consume their current income) are incorporated in the model, as in Campbell and Mankiw (1990, 1991), the model is not rejected, but the estimates of the intertemporal elasticity of substitution in consumption are no longer statistically significant.

They then estimate the model (including rule-of-thumb consumers) using U.S. state-level data. The model is not rejected, and the estimates of the intertemporal elasticity of substitution in consumption are statistically significant and economically meaningful, averaging at about unity. The common wisdom that, despite the prediction of plausible theoretical models, consumption is insensitive to the interest rate may be unfounded. Perhaps aggregate macroeconomic time-series data are not sufficiently informative for studying this issue.

To further illustrate the effect of interest rates on consumption and saving decisions, Beaudry and van Wincoop estimate the common time component in their panel dataset and showed that this common time component tracks the expected (3-month Treasury-bill) interest rate quite closely. They do not, however, pursue the issue, leaving open the question of what drives this correlation. Because in their analysis the interest rate process is exogenous, their framework is not well suited for explaining what drives the positive correlation of aggregate consumption and the U.S.-wide interest rate.

Ostergaard et al. (1998) consider the potential endogeneity of the U.S.-wide interest rate. Because the United States is *not* a small open economy [unlike the assumption implicitly made in most of the empirical literature on the PIH following Hall (1978)], the nationwide interest rate must respond to supply and demand pressures. Ostergaard et al. stress that aggregate constraints in the goods market can affect the nationwide interest rate. Suppose, for example, that the United States is hit by a positive aggregate income shock. If the impact on permanent income is larger than the current income shock,[5] there will be an even greater positive shock to desired consumption, in anticipation of further positive shocks to income.[6] In a fully integrated and frictionless world, U.S. consumers would borrow internationally, and aggregate net imports would increase instantaneously in response to the increased consumption demand. In reality, aggregate imports cannot adjust quickly, so the increased demand for credit creates upward pressure on the U.S.-wide interest rate that rises to

---

[5] This result is found in most studies and is a consequence of persistence of shocks to income; see Campbell and Mankiw (1987) for a thorough study. They demonstrate that the result is not fully robust to the time-series specification of the income process; but our logic will carry through as long as current income shocks cause desired current consumption changes that are not of the same size as the income shocks.

[6] See Campbell and Deaton (1989) and West (1988). We are, of course, aware of the excess smoothness of consumption phenomena documented by these authors, who find that consumption does not respond sufficiently to persistent shocks to income. We, nevertheless, regard the PIH as the natural benchmark model.

equilibrate aggregate demand and supply.[7] Thus, aggregate constraints in the goods market generate a positive relation between aggregate fluctuations in consumption and the U.S.-wide interest rate.[8]

Ostergaard et al. (1998) study the empirical implications of this reasoning for the excess sensitivity of current consumption to lagged income – a well-documented regularity in the data that has generated much theoretical and empirical work (see Deaton 1992 for a survey). If aggregate constraints are indeed important, the PIH may nevertheless be a good model for describing the reaction of consumption to *idiosyncratic* shocks to income in individual states, where idiosyncratic (state-specific) income shocks are defined as the deviations of state per capita income from the U.S. average per capita income.

Suppose that the net imports of a state within the United States can adjust more rapidly than the net imports of the United States as a whole. Then, if a positive idiosyncratic income shock hits a state in some year, there will be a large increase in idiosyncratic demand for consumption in that state because idiosyncratic income shocks are highly persistent.[9] This state-specific demand may be satisfied quickly (relative to total U.S. demand) by moving goods from other states without affecting the U.S.-wide interest rate because, in any given year, the sum across states of state-specific shocks is zero by definition.

To test this logic Ostergaard et al. remove the aggregate U.S.-wide component in U.S. state-level disposable income and consumption and perform excess sensitivity tests, finding that idiosyncratic consumption exhibits substantially less excess sensitivity to lagged idiosyncratic disposable income than if the aggregate component is not controlled for. They interpret this as evidence that excess sensitivity of consumption in aggregate U.S. data is driven to a large extent by U.S.-wide effects because, in the aggregate, U.S. net imports and investment do not adjust quickly to fluctuations in consumption demand. Further, ordering states by the persistence of income shocks, they find that removal of the aggregate component from the state-level data reduces excess sensitivity for all states by the same amount and that the excess sensitivity of consumption is greater in states with more persistent income shocks.[10]

---

[7] For example, an increased demand for goods in the United States will typically be reflected in higher prices and upward pressure on the interest rate because production runs abroad (and in the United States) cannot be adjusted instantaneously.

[8] This argument was first raised in theoretical work by Michener (1984) and Christiano (1987).

[9] Ostergaard et al. (1998) report that the average persistence of shocks to state-level per capita disposable income of U.S. states is very similar to the persistence of the per capita aggregate U.S. disposable income.

[10] Ostergaard et al. (1998) also study whether state-specific disposable income and consumption exhibit excess smoothness, in the sense of Campbell and Deaton (1989) and West (1988), namely, whether current state-specific consumption is sufficiently sensitive to current state-specific income. Because excess smoothness is less directly related to the empirical tests in this paper, we do not pursue this issue further.

Bayoumi and Klein's (1997) analysis is cast in different terms – along the lines of the intertemporal approach to the current account[11] – but is conceptually related to the preceding ideas. Bayoumi and Klein allow for different degrees of integration of a region with the other regions in the country, and with the rest of the world. They develop a model of intertemporal optimization by individual regions that choose consumption paths C_{it} taking as given $(Y - G - I)_{it}$, the regionally produced output net of the (exogenously given) investment and government expenditures in that region (where i is an index of regions).[12] They express the Euler equation for each region in terms of its trade balance. The equation is estimated allowing for a fraction of consumers (in the region) who are integrated in world markets, whereas the remaining consumers are integrated only in the interregional market within the country. Using Canadian province-level data, they find that the trade balance of Canadian provinces responds more strongly (at the yearly frequency) to deviations of provincial output from aggregate Canadian output than to deviations of provincial output from world output. They interpret this as evidence that Canadian provinces are more integrated among themselves than with the rest of the world.

We want to suggest a somewhat different interpretation of their results. Bayoumi and Klein regress the current trade balance of a region, $(X - M)_{it}$, on its current output, $(Y - G - I)_{it}$, controlling for national and world output. Because $X - M = Y - G - I - C$, such a regression is equivalent to a regression of $(Y - G - I - C)_{it}$ on $(Y - G - I)_{it}$, which yields a regression coefficient equal to one minus the coefficient in the regression of C_{it} on $(Y - G - I)_{it}$. Conceptually, this is precisely the test for perfect risk sharing performed by Obstfeld (1994) for OECD countries and by Cochrane (1991), Mace (1991), and Townsend (1994) using microdata.[13] Bayoumi and Klein are, therefore, testing for perfect capital market integration in the sense of perfect risk sharing, "bunching" (ex-ante) income smoothing via cross-ownership of productive assets, (ex-ante) income smoothing through central government fiscal policy, and (ex-post) consumption smoothing through saving behavior, including borrowing and lending on intranational and international credit markets.[14] By contrast, Ostergaard et al. (1998) focus only on the third channel of smoothing,

---

[11] See the references in footnote 4.

[12] For conciseness, we refer to $Y - G - I$ as regional output.

[13] There are, of course, differences in implementation. Obstfeld (1994) runs time-series regressions of consumption on Gross Domestic Product, Mace (1991) regresses individual consumption on individual income and aggregate consumption, cross-sectionally controlling for demographic variables, whereas Cochrane (1991) regresses individual consumption on variables that are correlated with shocks to income such as unemployment or health status.

[14] Asdrubali et al. (1996) demonstrate how the total amount of risk sharing can be decomposed into these levels of smoothing.

assuming that consumers take as given their disposable income, which includes after-tax labor income as well as asset income.

3.3   Empirical design

Consider a country composed of regions indexed by i. Let the period t disposable income of region i be exogenously given and denoted Y_{it}, and let the period t consumption of region i be C_{it}. Assume that regional consumption is determined by a representative consumer maximizing an isoelastic utility function with the intertemporal elasticity of substitution given by a parameter γ. Subject to a log-linear approximation and assuming that r_t – the countrywide interest rate on savings made at t – is known with certainty at t, state i's consumption follows the process

$$\Delta \log C_{it} = \alpha_i + \gamma r_{t-1} + e_{it} \tag{1}$$

where $E_{t-1} e_{it} = 0$; for details, consult Deaton (1992, p. 64). That is, a higher interest rate on savings made at $t - 1$ enhances saving at $t - 1$ and, other things kept equal, raises the growth rate of consumption from $t - 1$ to t.

If the country is a "small open economy," r_t is the world interest rate, which is independent of shocks to the income of the country or any of its regions. Therefore, for any region i, the covariance of r_{t-1} and $\Delta Y_{i,t-1}$ is zero, and a regression of $\Delta \log C_{it}$ on $\Delta \log Y_{i,t-1}$ will give a coefficient of zero. A test of this is, of course, the excess sensitivity test proposed by Hall (1978), who assumed that the interest rate is exogenous and time invariant.

If the country is not a "small open economy," the equilibrium interest rate in the country, r_t, will depend on shocks to the income of the country. A positive and persistent aggregate shock to the country's income in period $t - 1$ will induce all its regions to increase their demand for current (period $t - 1$) consumption by more than the rise in current income. Because, by assumption, the country is not a "small open economy," there will be upward pressure on r_{t-1}, and the covariance of r_{t-1} and $\Delta Y_{i,t-1}$ will be positive. Therefore, a regression of $\Delta \log C_{it}$ on $\Delta \log Y_{i,t-1}$ will give a positive coefficient.

If time dummy variables ("time-fixed effects") are included in the regression, then, assuming that interregional credit markets operate without frictions, the regression should not exhibit excess sensitivity (namely, will give a zero coefficient) because the interest rate effect is common to all regions and will be absorbed into the time dummies. Excess sensitivity in the regression with time-fixed effects, therefore, indicates that regional credit markets are not well integrated.[15] We interpret the difference in the amount of excess sensitivity in

---

[15] Of course, the regression with time dummies may still display excess sensitivity due to failure of the log-linear model to represent regional consumption behavior adequately [Deaton (1992) lists many reasons why this may occur].

region-level regressions with and without time-fixed effects as a measure of the extent to which a country can be considered fully integrated in the world credit market and able to borrow and lend at a fixed world interest rate.

We estimate analogous regressions for a sample of OECD countries, treating each country as a "region." Allowing for time-fixed effects in such regressions has the interpretation of controlling for the potential endogeneity of the OECD-wide interest rate, which is certain to vary in response to OECD-wide income shocks caused by the large size of the OECD. If intercountry (and interregional) credit markets operate well, we should expect little or no excess sensitivity of country-level idiosyncratic consumption to lagged country-level idiosyncratic income (i.e., when OECD-wide income shocks are controlled for). We interpret the difference in the amount of excess sensitivity in country-level regressions with and without time-fixed effects as a measure of the extent to which the OECD-wide interest rate is constant.

3.4   Empirical results

We report empirical results for Canadian provinces, U.S. states, and a group of OECD countries for which suitable data are available. For Canada, we use various measures of consumption; for the United States, we only have state-level retail sales as a proxy for state-level consumption; and for OECD countries, we use total private consumption data. Canadian income and consumption data are available from Statistics Canada. The income data for the United States are from the Bureau of Economic Analysis, whereas state-level retail sales data were obtained from Sales and Marketing Management. The OECD data are from the OECD National Accounts Vol. II, and our measure of disposable income of a country is net national income minus corporate saving minus direct taxes.

Denote province i's per capita disposable income and consumption by Y_{it} and C_{it}, and aggregate Canadian per capita disposable income and consumption by Y_t and C_t. For each province, we performed augmented Dickey-Fuller tests for a unit root in disposable income, in province-specific disposable income ($Y_{it} - Y_t$), in consumption (C_{it}), measured either by retail sales, by non- and semidurable consumption and services, or by total consumption, and in province-specific consumption ($C_{it} - C_t$), finding no evidence against unit roots in either series. Similar results were found for U.S. states by Ostergaard et al. (1998). Country-level disposable income and consumption are well known to display unit root or near unit root behavior. We, consequently, perform our analysis using first-differenced data. We find that the Canadian provincial disposable income series follow stochastic processes that are roughly similar to those of U.S. state-level disposable income series [i.e., they approximately follow AR(1) processes in first differences with a small, but significant, positive coefficient on lagged income].[16]

We report results for three models. Model 1 is a regression of province-level consumption on province-level disposable income:

$$\Delta \log C_{it} = \alpha_i + b \, \Delta \log Y_{i,t-1} + \epsilon_{it} \tag{2}$$

where ϵ_{it} is an i.i.d. mean zero error term. The parameter b is our measure of excess sensitivity (of consumption to lagged income). In order to estimate the amount of excess sensitivity using province-specific income and consumption, we follow Ostergaard et al. (1998) and estimate Model 2:

$$\Delta(\log C_{it} - \log C_t) = \alpha_i + b \, \Delta(\log Y_{i,t-1} - \log Y_{t-1}) + \epsilon_{it} \tag{3}$$

We further estimate Model 3:

$$\Delta \log C_{it} = \alpha_i + v_t + b \, \Delta \log Y_{i,t-1} + \epsilon_{it} \tag{4}$$

where v_t is a time-fixed effect. Equations (3) and (4) provide alternative ways of controlling for aggregate effects (which would yield the same results if all provinces were of equal size). We report results of both models as a robustness check. To further examine the sensitivity of the results to minor changes in specification, we also estimate the three models using the variables in levels rather than in logs.

In Tables 3.1 and 3.2, we display our main empirical results for Canada, as well as results for the United States and a group of ten OECD countries. The results in Table 3.1 are for logarithmic data, whereas the results in Table 3.2 are for the data in levels. In Table 3.2, the retail sales and nondurable consumption data have been scaled by the ratios of aggregate (nationwide) retail sales and nondurable consumption to aggregate consumption in order that the size of the coefficients for the three alternative consumption measures be comparable.

The results for the United States are consistent with the interpretation that the excess sensitivity in state-level consumption is explained to a large extent by the lack of integration of the U.S. economy as a whole in the world credit market or by an endogenous world interest rate. For the log-variables, we find an excess sensitivity coefficient of 0.37 for state-level income and consumption, but the size of the coefficient drops to only 0.13 when we control for aggregate consumption and income. (The results for the United States are not sensitive to whether the variables enter in levels or in logarithms; indeed the U.S. results in Table 3.2 are almost identical to those reported in Table 3.1.) Ostergaard

---

[16] Detailed tables reporting unit root tests and coefficients for AR(1) and AR(2) models for first-differenced consumption and disposable income (as such, and with the aggregate subtracted) are available from the authors upon request.

Table 3.1. *Sensitivity of regional level consumption to lagged income (Logarithmic data)*

	United States	Canada			OECD
	(1) Retail sales	(2) Retail sales	(3) Nondurable	(4) Total cons.	(5) Total cons.
Model 1:					
b	0.37	0.29	0.16	0.19	0.25
	(0.025)	(0.035)	(0.019)	(0.023)	(0.030)
Model 2:					
b	0.13	0.16	0.03	0.08	0.20
	(0.035)	(0.043)	(0.022)	(0.023)	(0.032)
Model 3:					
b	0.13	0.17	0.04	0.07	0.18
	(0.034)	(0.040)	(0.019)	(0.021)	(0.033)

Notes: Standard errors in parentheses. C_{it} and C_t denote region i and aggregate (United States/Canada/OECD) year t per capita personal consumption, measured as retail sales, non- and semidurable consumption and services ("Nondurable"), or total consumption. Y_{it} and Y_t similarly are regional and total per capita disposable income, respectively. Sample period: United States 1963–93; Canada 1961–96; OECD 1960–93.
OECD: Australia, Austria, Canada, Finland, Greece, Japan, Switzerland, United Kingdom, United States, West Germany.
Model 1: $\Delta \log C_{it} = \alpha_i + b \, \Delta \log Y_{i,t-1} + \epsilon_{it}$.
Model 2: $\Delta(\log C_{it} - \log C_t) = \alpha_i + b \, \Delta(\log Y_{i,t-1} - \log Y_{t-1}) + \epsilon_{it}$.
Model 3: $\Delta \log C_{it} = \alpha_i + v_t + b \, \Delta \log Y_{i,t-1} + \epsilon_{it}$.

et al. (1998) argued that this indicates that consumption functions, derived under the assumption of a fixed interest rate, ignore important general equilibrium effects on the intertemporal allocation of consumption, and – as explained in the previous section – this can be interpreted as empirical evidence that the United States is not a "small open economy."

In columns 2–4 of Tables 3.1 and 3.2, we show estimates of the excess sensitivity parameter for Canada, using retail sales, nondurable consumption, and total consumption, respectively. Our preferred measure of consumption is nondurable consumption. Retail sales are included for comparison with the United States (where we had to resort to retail sales), and total consumption is included for comparison with OECD countries because this is the measure of consumption that was available for the countries in our sample.

The size of the excess sensitivity coefficient varies with the choice of the consumption measure. With idiosyncratic consumption and income, the results in Table 3.1 (logarithmic data) indicate a level of excess sensitivity similar to that found for the United States. Canadian consumption shows less excess sensitivity when nationwide income shocks are controlled for, as was the case for

Table 3.2. *Sensitivity of regional level consumption to lagged income (Data in levels)*

	United States	Canada			OECD
	(1)	(2)	(3)	(4)	(5)
	Retail sales	Retail sales	Nondurable	Total cons.	Total cons.
Model 1:					
b	0.37	0.22	0.10	0.12	0.17
	(0.026)	(0.035)	(0.018)	(0.022)	(0.028)
Model 2:					
b	0.17	0.18	0.04	0.09	0.17
	(0.036)	(0.041)	(0.022)	(0.021)	(0.031)
Model 3:					
b	0.16	0.19	0.03	0.07	0.16
	(0.035)	(0.039)	(0.017)	(0.019)	(0.032)

Notes: Standard errors in parentheses. C_{it} and C_t denote region i and aggregate (United States/Canada/OECD) year t per capita personal consumption, measured as retail sales, non- and semidurable consumption and services ("Nondurable"), or total consumption. Y_{it} and Y_t similarly are regional and total per capita disposable income, respectively. Sample period: United States, 1963–93; Canada 1961–96; OECD 1960–93.
OECD: Australia, Austria, Canada, Finland, Greece, Japan, Switzerland, United Kingdom, United States, West Germany.
Model 1: $\Delta C_{it} = \alpha_i + b\,\Delta Y_{i,t-1} + \epsilon_{it}$.
Model 2: $\Delta(C_{it} - C_t) = \alpha_i + b\,\Delta(Y_{i,t-1} - Y_{t-1}) + \epsilon_{it}$.
Model 3: $\Delta C_{it} = \alpha_i + v_t + b\,\Delta Y_{i,t-1} + \epsilon_{it}$.
The results for the United States for Models 1 and 2 are from Ostergaard et al. (1998).

the United States. This is a very robust finding that does not depend on the precise consumption measure used or whether the data are log-transformed (although the difference is less spectacular for income and consumption in levels – Table 3.2). It is interesting that there is no evidence of excess sensitivity of nondurable consumption for Canada when nationwide variables are controlled for. (Column 3, Models 2 and 3 in both tables.) The findings of Ostergaard et al. (1998), that excess sensitivity of the consumption of U.S. states is partly explained by aggregate constraints, are therefore not limited to the United States.

The results of Tables 3.1 and 3.2 show that the decline in excess sensitivity, when controlling for aggregate income shocks, is larger in the United States than in Canada. In the United States, the excess sensitivity coefficient declines by about 0.20 in both tables, when the aggregate is controlled for, whereas the corresponding decline for Canada is smaller. The United States is obviously a very large country, and we find it unlikely that it, being a world financial center, faces more restricted access to international credit markets than Canada. We, therefore, interpret the larger decline in excess sensitivity when aggregate U.S. consumption and income are controlled for, as an indication that aggregate U.S. borrowing and lending activities affect the world interest rate more strongly due to the larger size of the U.S. economy.

Summarizing, both countries exhibit excess sensitivity in consumption, but the amount of excess sensitivity is much smaller when aggregate effects are controlled for. The difference is more pronounced for the United States than for Canada, a much smaller country. Furthermore, focusing on the regressions with nondurable consumption (for which we only have data for Canada), we find very little excess sensitivity of consumption in Models 2 and 3. Thus, there is virtually no evidence against the PIH model for idiosyncratic regional income and (nondurable) consumption data, and our findings indicate that neither the United States nor Canada is a "small open economy."

We turn to the group of OECD countries. We estimate the following equations (which are country-level analogs of Models 1–3).

$$\Delta \log C_{ct} = \alpha_c + \delta \, \Delta \log Y_{c,t-1} + \epsilon_{ct} \tag{5}$$

where ϵ_{ct} is an i.i.d. mean zero error term and δ is a measure of country-level excess sensitivity. The country-level version of Model 2 is

$$\Delta(\log C_{ct} - \log C_{gt}) = \alpha_c + \delta \, \Delta(\log Y_{c,t-1} - \log Y_{g,t-1}) + \epsilon_{ct} \tag{6}$$

where the subscript g denotes a "global" (OECD-wide) per capita variable and subscript c denotes a country-level variable. We further estimate a country-level version of Model 3:

$$\Delta \log C_{ct} = \alpha_c + v_t + \delta \, \Delta \log Y_{c,t-1} + \epsilon_{ct} \tag{7}$$

We see – in column 5, first row of both tables – that this group of 10 countries exhibits significant excess sensitivity of consumption (in line with most studies in the literature). We further find that excess sensitivity is *not* lower for idiosyncratic income and consumption (see the second and third rows of column 5), than for total country income and consumption. (The coefficient point estimate is slightly lower in Table 3.1 but not in Table 3.2.) Thus, individual OECD countries do not seem to be better integrated in international credit markets than the OECD as a whole. Because the regressions (6) and (7) control for OECD-wide shocks (and therefore are immune to endogenous world interest rate effects), this indicates that country-level excess sensitivity is caused to a large extent by border effects that restrict the operation of international credit markets.

As a final test, we combine Equations (3) and (6) and estimate the regression jointly for U.S. states and Canadian provinces:

$$\Delta(\log C_{it} - \log C_{gt}) = \alpha_i + \delta \, \Delta(\log Y_{c,t-1} - \log Y_{g,t-1})$$
$$+ b \, \Delta(\log Y_{i,t-1} - \log Y_{c,t-1}) + \epsilon_{it} \tag{8}$$

The first regressor is the deviation of U.S./Canadian per capita income from OECD per capita income, and the second regressor is the deviation of the per capita income of each U.S. state and Canadian province from the per capita income of the respective country. This regression "nests" the regional and country-level regressions. If excess sensitivity is caused by border effects, one might expect to find a larger estimate of δ than of b. This is exactly what we find – the point estimates (standard errors) of δ and b are 0.40 (0.04) and 0.14 (0.03). The standard errors leave no doubt that the estimates are significantly different from each other. Furthermore, the estimated coefficients are robust to minor changes in the specification. We interpret this as further evidence that national borders matter for credit market integration.

3.5   Conclusion

We have surveyed studies on consumption that use intranational macrolevel data. The number of articles is still small, reflecting the fact that this area of research is in its infancy. We pointed out the relation between the study by Ostergaard et al. (1998), which focuses on consumption, and the literature on the "intertemporal approach to the current account," and we provided new results using data for Canadian provinces and OECD country-level data. The results show that the qualitative findings of Ostergaard et al. (1998) carry over to another important federation – Canada – and are robust to various measures of consumption. A contribution of this article is the application of these ideas to the measurement of international credit market integration. Our results are consistent with interregional credit markets in the United States and Canada being highly integrated and with credit markets *not* being well integrated across national borders.

References

Asdrubali, P., B. E. Sørensen, and O. Yosha. 1996. Channels of interstate risk sharing: United States 1963–90. *Quarterly Journal of Economics* 111: 1081–110.

Bacchetta, P., and S. Gerlach. 1997. Consumption and credit constraints: International evidence. *Journal of Monetary Economics* 40: 207–38.

Bayoumi, T., and M. W. Klein. 1997. A provincial view of economic integration. *IMF Staff Papers* 44: 534–556.

Bayoumi, T., and A. Rose. 1993. Domestic savings and intra-national capital flows. *European Economic Review* 37: 1197–202.

Beaudry, P., and E. van Wincoop. 1996. The intertemporal elasticity of substitution: An exploration using a US panel of state data. *Economica* 63: 495–515.

Blanchard, O., and L. Katz. 1992. Regional evolutions. *Brookings Papers on Economic Activity* I: 1–75.

Campbell, J. Y., and A. Deaton. 1989. Why is consumption so smooth? *Review of Economic Studies* 56: 357–73.

Campbell, J. Y., and N. G. Mankiw. 1987. Are output fluctuations transitory? *Quarterly Journal of Economics* 102: 857–80.

Campbell, J. Y., and N. G. Mankiw. 1990. Permanent income, current income, and consumption. *Journal of Business and Economic Statistics* 8: 265–79.

Campbell, J. Y., and N. G. Mankiw. 1991. The response of consumption to income: A cross-country investigation. *European Economic Review* 35: 723–67.

Christiano, L. J. 1987. Why is consumption less volatile than income. *Federal Reserve Bank of Minneapolis Quarterly Review* 11: 1–20.

Cochrane, J. H. 1991. A simple test of consumption insurance. *Journal of Political Economy* 99: 957–76.

Deaton, A. 1992. *Understanding Consumption.* New York: Oxford University Press.

Engel, C., and J. Rogers. 1996. How wide is the border? *American Economic Review* 86: 1112–25.

Feldstein, M., and C. Horioka. 1980. Domestic savings and international capital flows. *Economic Journal* 90: 314–29.

Ghosh, A. 1995. Capital mobility amongst the major industrialized countries: Too little or too much? *Economic Journal* 105: 107–28.

Glick, R., and K. Rogoff. 1995. Global versus country-specific productivity shocks and the current account. *Journal of Monetary Economics* 35: 159–92.

Hall, R. E. 1978. Stochastic implications of the life cycle-permanent income hypothesis: Theory and evidence. *Journal of Political Economy* 86: 971–87.

Hall, R. E. 1988. Intertemporal substitution in consumption. *Journal of Political Economy* 96: 339–57.

Helliwell, J. 1996. Do national borders matter for Quebec's trade? *Canadian Journal of Economics* 29: 507–22.

Hess, G., and K. Shin. 1998. Intranational business cycles in the United States. *Journal of International Economics* 44: 289–313.

Jappelli, T., and M. Pagano. 1989. Consumption and capital market imperfections: An international comparison. *American Economic Review* 79: 1088–105.

Mace, B. J. 1991. Full insurance in the presence of aggregate uncertainty. *Journal of Political Economy* 99: 928–56.

McCallum, J. 1995. National borders matter: Canada–US regional trade patterns. *American Economic Review* 85: 615–23.

Michener, R. 1984. Permanent income in general equilibrium. *Journal of Monetary Economics* 13: 297–305.

Mundell, R. 1961. A theory of optimum currency areas. *American Economic Review* 51: 657–65.

Obstfeld, M. 1994. "Are Industrial-Country Consumption Risks Globally Diversified?," in L. Leiderman and A. Razin, eds., *Capital Mobility: The Impact on Consumption, Investment, and Growth.* New York: Cambridge University Press.

Obstfeld, M., and K. Rogoff. 1995. "The Intertemporal Approach to the Current Account," in G. Grossman and K. Rogoff, eds., *Handbook of International Economics.* Amsterdam: North Holland.

Ostergaard, C., B. E. Sørensen, and O. Yosha. 1998. "Permanent Income, Consumption, and Aggregate Constraints: Evidence from US States." Working Paper. Brown University and Tel Aviv University.

Razin, A. 1995. "The Dynamic Optimization Approach to the Current Account: Theory and Evidence," in P. Kenen, ed., *Understanding Interdependence: The Macroeconomics of the Open Economy.* Princeton, NJ: Princeton University Press.

Sachs, J. 1981. The current account and macroeconomic adjustment in the 1970s. *Brookings Papers on Economic Activity* 1: 201–68.

Townsend, R. 1994. Risk and insurance in village India. *Econometrica* 62: 539–91.

West, K. 1988. The insensitivity of consumption to news about income. *Journal of Monetary Economics* 21: 17–33.

von Hagen, J. 1992. "Fiscal Arrangements in a Monetary Union: Evidence from the US," in D. Fair and C. de Boissieu, eds., *Fiscal Policy, Taxation, and the Financial System in an Increasingly Integrated Europe*. Boston: Kluwer.

CHAPTER 4

Home bias in equity markets: International and intranational evidence*

Gur Huberman[†]

4.1   Introduction

The original models of portfolio selection and asset pricing recognize no national borders, transaction costs, or taxes. Moreover, they assume that investors have homogenous expectations. The two main implications of these early models are that the market portfolio is mean-variance efficient and that every investor's portfolio consists of two funds common to all investors.

Weaknesses of the simplifying assumptions used to establish the original models were recognized early on. Some assets trade very differently from securities (real estate, especially residential, is the first that comes to mind), and other assets are not tradable at all (human capital is a prominent example). We need go no further to attribute the empirical failure of two fund separation to the heterogeneity of individuals' opportunity sets. Differential information and experience, and therefore heterogeneous beliefs can also explain why investors' holdings fail to conform to the two-fund prediction.

Merton (1973) and Breeden (1979) go beyond the original models and analyze the dynamics of consumption, savings, and portfolio choice within an equilibrium setting. In this model, individuals invest to transfer wealth over time and across states of nature as defined by the marginal utility of consumption.

Even though the initial work was not explicitly concerned with cross-border investments, its implications were quite clear: as long as transactions costs are sufficiently small, investors should diversify internationally. Empirically, people seem to ignore this intuitively appealing recommendation. Aggregate data suggest that people concentrate their equity investments in their home countries (i.e., most investors are subject to the home country bias).

* I am grateful to David Backus, Gregory Hess, Eric van Wincoop, and Zhenyu Wang for useful comments and conversations.
† Columbia University. Mailing address: Columbia Business School, Columbia University, New York, NY. E-mail: *gh16@columbia.edu.*

Economists tried to explain the home country bias as a by-product of market frictions (i.e., transaction costs, institutional restrictions, or taxes), asymmetric information, or within models of consumption and investment which recognize that countries' consumption patterns differ. These attempts seem to have failed, as reported in a recent survey by Lewis (1998).

A variety of phenomena resemble the home country bias but are divorced from the international context. Among them are employees' preference to hold their employer's stock, the tendencies of holders of equity of the Regional Bell Operating Companies to hold the stock of the company that serves them, the bias of mutual fund managers to hold stocks of geographically closer firms, and the approximately $500 million invested in Texas municipal bond funds. (There is no state income tax in Texas.)

Building on Huberman (1997), this paper will survey these phenomena and will explore the thread common to them all, namely familiarity. We will first discuss the arguments supporting international diversification and contrast them with the French-Poterba (1991) calculations on possible inference from the lack of international equity diversification. We will then critically present two of the main potential explanations for the home country bias, leaving the third – information asymmetry – until after we survey the intranational evidence. Following the presentation of the intranational evidence, we discuss asymmetric information and familiarity as potential explanations of the home country bias, concluding with a few open issues.

4.2   Why diversify internationally?

Modern portfolio theory begins with Markowitz (1952, 1959), who studies the portfolio selection of a mean-variance optimizer. This investor has a probability distribution about uncertain security returns and chooses his portfolio weights according to his tradeoff between expected portfolio return and its variance. Sharpe (1964), Lintner (1965a,b), and Mossin (1965) derive the capital asset pricing model (CAPM) – the equilibrium implications of all investors behaving according to the Markowitz prescription while having homogenous expectations and equal access to all investment opportunities and facing no transaction costs or taxes. In the CAPM, all investors split their money between the safe asset and a unique portfolio of risky assets, the market portfolio.

Grubel (1968), Levy and Sarnat (1970), and Solnik (1974) apply the insight of the CAPM in the international arena. Even though it is clear that under the CAPM assumptions, one should hold a portfolio of international stocks, these authors set out to estimate the benefits of international diversification. Estimation of the benefits, however, requires the estimation of the assumed homogenous beliefs, or at least of the first two moments of the returns distributions.

To this end, historical returns are used to estimate the first two moments of the current returns distribution. Unfortunately, the available history is too short, and conditions have changed over time. Therefore, the estimators, especially of expected returns, are not reliable. Moreover, the optimization over the set of feasible portfolios that leads to the mean-variance frontier is likely to result in exaggerated benefits to diversification because it relies excessively on the unreliable estimators.

Jorion (1985) provides a critique of the classical estimation techniques, applies a Bayesian approach to assess the benefits of international diversification, and concludes that they are likely to accrue mostly from risk reduction. Glassman and Riddick (1996) explore additional methodological problems. Shawky, Kuemzel, and Mikhail (1997) survey the literature on the benefits from international diversification.

Why countries' equity investments should be mostly domestic is not explained by classical portfolio theory, regardless of the difficulty in the precise estimation of the benefits to international diversification. French and Poterba (1991) offer a novel method to appreciate the problem by interpreting the magnitude of the home country bias in the context of the CAPM.

4.3   The international home bias: The French-Poterba calculations

French and Poterba (1991) consider an investment universe consisting of equity indices of six countries – the United States, Japan, the United Kingdom, France, Germany, and Canada – from the perspective of investors in three countries – the United States, Japan, and the United Kingdom. They estimate that these investors hold 93, 98, and 82% of their equity investments, respectively, in their home countries. More recently Tesar and Werner (1998) estimate that equity investors in the United States, Japan, and the United Kingdom allocate 10, 5, and 24%, respectively, to foreign stocks.

French and Poterba observe that they can reliably estimate a variance–covariance matrix of the returns on the six indices, but not the vector of their expected returns. French and Poterba consider a hypothetical mean-variance optimizing investor, and address the following question: given the variance–covariance matrix and an international asset allocation equal to the aggregate allocation of investors in the particular country, what is the implied vector of expected returns? They compute the expected returns vectors from the perspective of the U.S., Japanese, and UK investors.

French and Poterba compare the imputed expected returns across investors, and for each investor, across countries. Each investor is most optimistic about his own country's equity returns. The expected return on U.S. equities is 5.5% in the eyes of U.S. investors, compared with 3.1 and 4.4% in the eyes of

Japanese and U.K. investors, respectively. The expected return on Japanese equities is 6.6% in the eyes of Japanese investors, compared with 3.2 and 3.8% in the eyes of U.S. and U.K. investors, respectively. Interestingly, the most egregious numbers come form the investors who display the weakest home bias, the U.K. investors. In their eyes, the expected returns on their equities is 9.6%, compared with 4.5 and 3.8% in the eyes of U.S. and Japanese investors, respectively.

4.4 Potential explanations: Cross-border transaction costs and hedging needs

Three categories of potential explanations of the home country bias have emerged: institutional barriers to cross-border investments, systematic differences in hedging needs, and systematic differences in perceived returns distribution. Numerous papers entertained and soundly rejected the first two explanations. We cover them briefly here and then consider the third approach at greater length.

Barriers to cross-border investments include outright capital controls, taxes, and higher transactions costs associated with international investments. But these seem to pose no material challenge to cross-border investments among the developed countries. Indeed, Tesar and Werner (1995) write: "the high transactions rate on foreign investments suggests that investors frequently adjust the composition and size of their international portfolios, even though much of this activity has little impact on net investment positions .... [This observation] suggests that high transaction costs associated with trading foreign securities cannot be the reason for the observed reluctance of investors to diversify their positions internationally."

Different hedging needs may arise because residents of different countries consume bundles that are subject to different stochastic inflation rates, or because they produce and consume different nontraded goods, or because they own assets which do not trade. Cooper and Kaplanis (1994) examine the first possibility, and reject it. Indeed, for each of their sample's eight developed countries, they reject the joint hypothesis that the representative investor is risk averse and that the domestic stock market's return is positively correlated with the domestic inflation rate. So if investors tilt their portfolio toward domestic holdings, they must be risk loving!

Pesenti and van Wincoop (2000) examine the role of nontraded goods and conclude, "we find that accounting for nontradables leads to only a small bias towards domestic assets. The bias is no larger than 27%, and probably much smaller than that."

The impact of nontraded assets on hedging demands depends on the correlation between their returns and those of the domestic and international securities, and on whether the investor is long or short the nontraded assets. For instance, if the investor owns nontraded assets and their returns are negatively correlated with the domestic equity market's return, he should tilt his portfolio toward domestic holdings. Baxter and Jermann (1997) argue persuasively that the single most important nontraded asset is human capital and that returns to human capital are highly correlated with the returns to the domestic stock market. Indeed, Baxter and Jermann typical investors from four countries – Japan, Germany, the United Kingdom and the United States – who wish to allocate their portfolios among equity indices of these markets. Optimally, each investor should *short* a substantial fraction of his national market portfolio!

Uppal (1992) surveys the theoretical and empirical literature on taxes, institutional barriers to international equity investing and hedging domestic inflation as motivations for the home country bias, and concludes, "it is unlikely that these three factors are significant enough to explain the degree of the bias in portfolios that is observed empirically."

Before we relate the home country bias to systematic differences in perceived returns, we consider additional, *intranational*, evidence. This evidence sheds new light on the home country bias, strengthening the case for differences in perceived returns as the explanation for the puzzle.

4.5   Intranational evidence

4.5.1   The experiment with the RBOCs

One explanation of the home country bias is that people prefer to invest in the familiar. People root for the home team and feel comfortable putting their money with a business that is visible to them. Paucity of international diversification is only one of the implications of this tendency to invest in the familiar.

This explanation is consistent with a variety of observations, which we describe next. It falls outside the traditional expected utility paradigm. In fact, it does not even specify whether the bias for the familiar stems from the investor's utility function or from his beliefs. Nonetheless, the explanation is testable.

To test this behavioral theory, consider the geographic distribution of the seven Regional Bell Operating Companies (RBOCs) in the fourth quarter of 1996. Each RBOC has been the major provider of local telephone service in its region since the 1984 divestiture of AT&T. The behavioral theory implies that a disproportionate number of an RBOC's customers tend to hold a disproportionate number of shares of that RBOC and invest a disproportionate amount of money in their local RBOC. (For more details, see Huberman 1997.)

Empirically, we address the following questions.

1   Do more state's residents hold shares in the RBOC that serves that state than in other RBOCs?

Yes, in every state but Montana, more people hold shares of the local RBOC than of any other RBOC. On average, the local RBOC has more than twice as many accounts as the average number of accounts for the out-of-state RBOCs and 63% more accounts than the next most popularly held RBOC.

2   For each state, compare the proportion of its RBOC's shareholders (relative to the total number of people holding that RBOC's shares) with the similar proportion for the other RBOCs. Is the local RBOC's proportion higher than that of the other RBOCs?

In every state, the fraction of the local RBOC account holders exceeds that of the highest fraction among the other RBOCs. On average, the fraction of the local RBOC is 82% higher than that of the next RBOC.

3   For each state, compare the fraction of its RBOC's outstanding equity with the fraction of the outstanding equity of the out-of-state RBOCs held by the state's residents. Is a larger fraction of an RBOC's equity held by the people it serves?

In all 48 states, the average fraction of equity of out-of-state RBOCs is smaller than the fraction of the local RBOC equity that is held locally. On average, the fraction of RBOC equity held locally is 2.76 higher than the average fraction of the out-of-state RBOCs' equity held in that state.

For 19 out of the 48 states, the fraction of the local RBOC equity held locally is larger than the fraction of any other RBOC's equity held in that state. On average, the ratio of the fraction of the local RBOC's equity held locally to that of the highest fraction of an out-of-state RBOC's equity is 2.40.

4   Compare the aggregate dollar value of a state's residents' investment in the local RBOC with that of their investments in the out-of-state RBOCs. Is the investment in the local RBOC higher?

For 26 out of the 48 states, more money is invested in the local RBOC than in any other RBOC. On average, the amount invested in the local RBOC is 1.84 times higher than the amount invested in the next most heavily invested RBOC.

5   For each state, compare the typical dollar value of a shareholder's investment in the local RBOC with that of the out-of-state RBOCs. Are they similar?

The average account size for the local RBOC is $13,817 – higher than $8,869, the average account size for out-of-state RBOCs when we exclude BellSouth from the sample, or $9,576, the average if we include BellSouth. This comparison suggests that investors who hold shares of the local RBOC because it is the local RBOC tend to buy more than a token number of shares in the local RBOC.

6   Estimate the excess dollar amount invested in the local RBOC (relative to the out-of-state RBOCs) and divide it by the excess number of account holders to derive an estimate of the account size of investors who hold shares in the local RBOC just because it is the local RBOC. Is it substantial, and how does it compare with the typical account size of an RBOC holder?

The average estimated account size of the people who hold shares in the local RBOC just because it is the local RBOC is $23,968. The population-weighted average is $21,182. The median estimate is $25,056. These numbers are much larger than typical RBOC account sizes, suggesting that an RBOC customer is not only more likely to invest in his local telephone company but also likely to invest much more money in the local telephone company than in other Bell companies.

The RBOCs are among the most widely held stocks in the United States. There are hundreds of thousands of shareholders of the RBOCs. The typical account size is worth about $16,000, which seems like a lot of money considering that $21,300 was the 1995 median value of direct and indirect stock ownership for the 66.7% of families in the $50,000–100,000 annual income bracket that held stocks (see Kennickel, Starr-McCluer, and Sunden 1997).

The comparison between the typical investment in an RBOC and the typical equity exposure of a family in the $50,000–100,000 income bracket suggests that many stockholders are underdiversified. In fact, the New York Stock Exchange (1995) reports that the median (mean) number of stocks held directly by shareholders is 2 (5.3) – surely an indication of highly concentrated portfolios.

4.5.2   Investment in the employer's stock

Sadly, investment in the familiar extends to workers who choose to invest some – perhaps all – of their retirement money in their employers' stocks.

Since 1993 defined contribution pension plans [401(k)] must have at least three investment options: a broad-based equity fund, a bond fund, and a money market fund. Frequently, these plans also allow workers to invest in company stock. Employers may – and do – offer incentives to workers to have the company stock in their retirement accounts: employers make matching contributions to retirement accounts in the form of company stock. Sometimes the matching contributions are higher if the employee chooses to invest his or her retirement funds in the company stock.

Schultz (1996) reports the results of a 1996 survey of 246 of the largest American companies, which was conducted by the Institute of Management and Administration. (These employers have 10.6 million defined contribution plan participants.) The survey found that employer stock accounted for $133 billion of the total $318 billion in the defined contribution plans surveyed (i.e., 42% of the total)!

Williams (1997) reports that as of September 1996, 32.3% of the total assets among the top 1,000 corporate-defined contribution plans were in employer stock, and 62.3% of the $732 billion in these defined contribution plans were in stocks. This fraction is lower than that provided by the Institute of Management and Administration, but it is too large to be consistent with reasonable diversification.

In some cases, workers prefer to buy the company stock instead of investing in the other options available in their pension plan. In other cases, the preference for the company stock is induced by a matching contribution of the employer. And in yet other cases, the company contributes its own stock to the plan, without offering the workers any choice in the matter.

Business Week (1997) reports, "in some companies, even when employees have the choice of other investment options, they tend to go for what they know. Look at Abbott Labs. Until January, 1996, employees had no choice: All of the 401(k) money went into company stock. Then the company added four investment choices and the chance to reallocate. Today, 68% of the employees' regular investment still goes toward stock and the total plan remains 90% invested in Abbott shares."

Employers have two mutually enforcing reasons for putting their workers' retirement money into the company's stock: one, this makes employees identify more strongly with the company and thereby become better workers; and two, workers actually like to see their retirement money invested in the company's stock and don't particularly mind forgoing even the opportunity to allocate their retirement money away from the company's stock.

4.5.3   The John Hancock survey

The John Hancock-Gallup survey sheds further and consistent light on the issues discussed here (Driscoll, Malcolm, Sirull, and Slotter 1995). The survey compiled the responses of 803 randomly selected individuals whose employers offered a 401(k), savings, thrift, or profit sharing plan with a choice of funds in which to invest. To qualify, these workers had to be currently contributing to the considered retirement plan.

About half the respondents worked for employers with more than 1,000 employees, a quarter had employers with 200 to 1,000 employees, and another quarter had fewer than 200 employees. The respondents' average annual salary was $53,460. Of the respondents, 12% had annual salaries of under $25,000, 53% had an annual salary between $25,000 and $55,000, and 30% had an annual salary of $55,000 or more. (The numbers do not add up to 100% because some people would not answer this question.) On the whole, then, the respondents were typical investors in 401(k) plans.

The results most relevant to our study are as follows:

1 On average, survey participants have saved $39,130 in the plan and $35,200 outside the plan; 41% of the participants invest in their employers' stock.

2 Participants were asked to rate their familiarity with different types of investment. On a scale of 1 (do not know anything) to 5 (very familiar), they rated their own company's stock highest, at 3.4. Lower-rated types of investment were money market funds (3.3), stock funds (3.1), government/treasury funds (3.0), bond funds (2.9), etc.

3 Participants were asked to rate the risk level associated with different investment types on a scale of 1 (meaning no risk) to 5 (high risk). International/global funds were rated 3.8, stock funds were rated 3.5, and company stock was rated 3.2.

4 Of the participants, 93% said that they were more likely to contribute to a familiar investment option.

5 Of the participants who have non-plan savings, 70% invest in safe short-term liquid investments (57% of the 70% are in bank accounts and 9% are in money market funds). The remaining 30% save in stock funds (13%); individual stocks (9%); bond funds, nonresidence real estate and individual bonds (3% in each category).

The third item is the most revealing: Respondents found their employers' stocks safer than diversified equity funds, domestic or international!

4.5.4   Additional evidence

A person who looks for examples of investment in the familiar will find many. We mention four.

Coval and Moskowitz (1997a) report that the typical portfolio of a U.S. money manager consists of stocks of firms that are located 100 miles closer to the manager's office than the average U.S. firm. The bias toward investing locally increases with firm leverage and decreases with firm size but seems unrelated to the money manager's size.

Following the 1994 takeover of Gerber Products by Sandoz, *The New York Times* reported from Fremont, Michigan, that "hundreds of local residents – including descendants of those farmers who first invested in the cooperative that became Gerber Products – are figuring out how to reinvest anywhere from the hundreds to tens of millions of dollars they will receive from the Gerber stock." Fremont had 3,900 residents. Gerber directly accounted for 40% of local taxes and employed about 1,300 people according to *The New York Times* (Feder, 1994). Although Fremont's shareholders of Gerber were very lucky, their portfolio selection was far from wise.

The Wall Street Journal (Deogun, 1997) provides another example, reporting that at least $23 billion of Coca Cola stock, or 16%, is held in Georgia, most of it in metropolitan Atlanta, and to many shareholders, selling is anathema. (Coke's headquarters are in Atlanta.)

The existence of Texas municipal bonds mutual funds is another anecdote consistent with the familiarity hypothesis and difficult to explain otherwise. Residents of a state who wish to pay no federal or state income tax on their interest income and would like to enjoy the benefits of diversification, acquire shares in municipal bond funds that specialize in bonds issued in that state. About $500 million are invested in Texas-based municipal bond funds. Texas, however, has no state income tax!

Finally, returning to the international arena, recall that Tesar and Werner (1995) write, "observations on the portfolio choices of Canadian and US investors suggest that to the extent investors do invest in foreign securities, their investment decisions do not reflect pure diversification motives. Instead, geographic proximity seems to be an important ingredient in the international portfolio allocation decision."

4.6 Asymmetric information, perceived returns, and familiarity as explanations

Having reviewed the intranational evidence pertaining to the home country bias, we turn now to its cognitive and emotive explanations. Asymmetric information-based explanations are cognitive. Explanations that link portfolio choices to preference unrelated to investments are emotive. These categories are not mutually exclusive, and so far the evidence is consistent with both. We survey that evidence as well as the relevant theoretical work.

4.6.1 Comparing expectations of American and German subjects

Kilka and Weber (1997) directly elicit expectations about returns of American and German stocks from American and German business school students. The expectations were both about individual stocks and two leading stock indices – the Dow Jones and the DAX. Subjects were asked to assess their competence to form beliefs about the equities in question and then to provide a rough probability distribution of the future three months returns of these equities.

The U.S. subjects felt that they were more competent to construct return distributions of U.S. stocks and the Dow than of German stocks and the DAX, and vice versa for the German subjects.

In general, the elicited returns distributions were more dispersed the less competent a subject felt about his ability to form such a distribution: German (U.S.) subjects had higher dispersions for U.S. (German) than for German (U.S.) equities and, within each country, higher dispersions for the equities about which they felt less competent to judge. (The exceptions were the two indices, where the average dispersion of the returns distributions in the eyes of both U.S. and German subjects were similar for the two indices.)

An analogous result holds for the expected returns. For individual stocks, imputed expected return was higher the more competent the subject felt about his ability to form a return probability distribution. (Again, the indices provided the exceptions. The German subjects' average expected returns of the two indices were virtually the same, as were the U.S. subjects' average expected returns of the two indices. The difference in outcomes for the indices and the individual stocks is unsettling and calls for further investigation.)

Weber and Kilka's results for individual stocks suggest that familiarity, or perceived competence, tends to narrow the spread of return distributions and increase its expected value. The latter is consistent with the French-Poterba calculations, but the former undermines their methodology!

French and Poterba's starting point is the estimation of the variance-covariance matrix of the six national equity indices from historical returns. The procedure produces statistically reliable estimates, but investors may have in mind different matrices of the returns' second moments. Weber and Kilka show that investors tended to perceive the domestic market as less volatile than foreign markets. If so, mean-variance optimizing investors will increase the weight of their domestic holdings beyond French and Poterba's prescription.

More important, the results suggest that people simply *like* stock with which they are familiar. Familiarity (or "competence," in the language of the questionnaire) is positively correlated with higher expected returns and lower risk. (Recall that the latter finding also appears, in a different form, in the John Hancock survey.)

Do investors really form probability distributions when choosing portfolio weights? Kilka and Weber *ask* subjects to provide probability-relevant points of the return distributions and *interpret* the answers in terms of imputed probability distributions. But what if the language of probability distribution is alien to many investors?

It is likely that most investors do not form return probability distributions, and their portfolios reflect various biases such as the bias toward the familiar. Nonetheless, it may still be the case that the marginal investors are shrewd mean-variance optimizers, and that therefore risk return tradeoffs are consistent with the predictions of the CAPM. But the evidence favoring the CAPM is weak at best.

Another possibility is that the marginal investors solve a form of the Consumption CAPM. But if not all investors solve that problem, aggregate consumption data cannot help in assessing the empirical validity of the Consumption CAPM, or the equity premium puzzle.

4.6.2 Asymmetric information and buy-and-hold equity indexation to counter inferiority of information

Asymmetric information is sometimes offered as an explanation of the home country bias. Brennan and Cao (1997), Gehrig (1993), and Zhou (1998) analyze models of rational expectations, competitive equilibria of markets with agents who are asymmetrically informed about the future values of risky assets. They assume that each country has one risky asset, and that domestic investors have more accurate signals about their market's value in the future than do foreigners. With various additional assumptions, these authors show that investors are likely to hold a disproportionate amount of the domestic asset.

The models' basic assumption – that domestic investors can predict the return of their market better than foreigners – is empirically implausible, especially when it comes to the world's developed economies. The ability to predict the direction of a whole market relative to the world is probably more unusual and requires skills that go well beyond superior knowledge of the domestic market.

It may be natural and tempting to ascribe the local bias to superiority of information or, equivalently, to interpret the bias against investing in distant equities as a measure of protection against inferior information. However, this argument is superficial: the distant and presumably ignorant investor can buy an *index* of the equities about which he recognizes that he knows very little. This strategy will assure him of exposure to the return and risk of these stocks, but will not result in underperformance.

Another argument that casts doubt on a naive asymmetric information-based hypothesis is that superior information is usually short-lived, and the long-term investor who buys and holds a diversified portfolio of risky assets will be rewarded for his risk exposure but will not be penalized for trading with people who can predict the fortunes of these risky assets better than he.

Finally, any model of investors who earn superior returns on their superior information must contend with the question of who is on the other side of the informed traders' trades. Rational individuals who recognize their informational inferiority may choose to avoid trading; they may elect to be buy-and-hold index investors when it comes to the securities about which they feel they know little. But then, how will those with information be rewarded for the information they possess?

Although superficially appealing, the asymmetric information approach currently still lacks a solid theoretical foundation. The empirical evidence favoring the asymmetric information hypothesis is not yet sweeping either.

Coval and Moskowitz (1997b) estimate quarterly returns on the local and distant portions of money managers' portfolios between September 30, 1980, and December 31, 1994, and document that the local portions outperform the distant portions by about 0.2% monthly. The outperformance weakens over the sample period, and its magnitude and statistical significance are sensitive to the authors' choice of risk adjustment. Unfortunately, Coval and Moskowitz do not report the overall performance of the funds; therefore, it is difficult to assess the impact of their local tilt.

Froot, O'Connell, and Seasholes (1998) explore the behavior of daily international portfolio flows into and out of 46 countries in 1994–98. Among other results, they "find little support for the Brennan and Cao (1997) hypothesis that emerging market inflows are the result of a cumulative informational disadvantage on the part of international investors about local country conditions. The common factor of inflows within a region seems to positively predict prices and to move contemporaneously with prices. On the other hand, the country-specific factor of flows has little price impact and predicts future returns poorly."

Frankel and Schmukler (1996) consider the three U.S.-based closed-end funds that invest in Mexican equities. They document that changes in the net asset value of these funds lead changes in their share prices and suggest that the evidence demonstrates that domestic and foreign investors have divergent expectations, possibly based on asymmetric information.

4.6.3   What is familiarity?

Familiarity may represent information available to the investor, but not yet to the market. It may represent the investor's illusion that he has superior information. It may represent an investor's belief that she *will* have superior information – perhaps she will be among the first to hear of bad news, and therefore will be able to get out in time. Thus, familiarity as information ranges from the investor actually possessing superior information, to the investor thinking that he currently has superior information, to the investor thinking that she will have superior information at some important point in the future.

People are better informed about the familiar than the unfamiliar – this is almost the defining property of the familiar! But being better informed means spotting as many "sell" opportunities as "buy." In fact, even having the illusion of superior information – now or in the future – should not, by itself, bias one's position to buy a security, if one follows a standard portfolio selection procedure.

The evidence suggests that people favor the familiar, so even if they have superior information – or just think they do – people do not use such information within a standard portfolio selection procedure. It is difficult to interpret their behavior as optimal, even if they are better informed, or think that they are better informed.

Alternatively, we can think of familiarity as comfort. People just prefer to deal with what they know or think they know, rather than with the unknown. Heath and Tversky (1991) show that people's attitudes toward risky bets depend not only on monetary risk-reward tradeoffs but also on the subjects' self-assessed competence, which can be interpreted as comfort level. However, the results of Heath and Tversky do not explain why people tend to bet on familiar stocks by buying, rather than selling, them. The experimental results of Kilka and Weber (1997) suggest that people look more favorably on familiar stocks – they associate higher expected returns and lower risks with them.

Preference for the familiar and distaste for and fear of the unfamiliar are familiar phenomena with wide-ranging manifestations. One example is people's support for local causes such as sports teams and charities. Race- and gender-based discrimination reflect less innocuous aspects of such a preference. And many wars and interethnic violent conflicts may be the most pernicious outbreaks of the distaste for the alien.

4.7   Concluding remarks

This paper summarizes evidence that investors' portfolio choices deviate systematically from the prescription of portfolio theory: they tend to overweigh the familiar while forgoing some diversification. The explanations of this behavior range from those based on information asymmetries to those based on fundamental properties of human decision making under uncertainty.

Although the tendency to invest in the familiar is well documented, we still lack a deep understanding of the reason for it. Moreover, we do not know how it fits into a traditional model of risk-return tradeoff. Additional questions it raises include: what are the policy implications if people fail to diversify their retirement investments? What are the asset-pricing implications of this systematic deviation from the traditional prescription for portfolio construction?

References

Baxter, M., and U. J. Jermann. 1997. The international diversification puzzle is worse than you think. *American Economic Review* 87(1): 170–80.

Breeden, D. T. 1979. An intertemporal asset pricing model with stochastic consumption and investment opportunities. *Journal of Financial Economics* 7: 265–95.

Brennan, M. J., and H. H. Cao. 1997. International portfolio investment flows, *Journal of Finance* 52: 1851–80.

Business Week. "The Cream of the Crop in Pensions, Too," May 19, 1997.

Cooper, I., and E. Kaplanis. 1994. Home bias in equity portfolios, inflation hedging, and international capital market equilibrium. *Review of Financial Studies* 7: 45–60.

Coval, J. D., and T. J. Moskowitz. 1997a. "Home Bias at Home: Local Equity Preference in Domestic Portfolios." Working Paper. UCLA.

Coval, Joshua D., and Tobias J. Moskowitz. 1997b. "The Georgraphy of Investment: Are There Gains to Investing Locally?" Working Paper. UCLA.

Deogun, N. 1997. "The Legacy: Roberto Goizueta Led Coca-Cola Stock Surge, and Its Home Prospers." *Wall Street Journal* October 20.

Driscoll, K., J. Malcolm, M. Sirull, and P. Slotter. 1995. "1995 Gallup Survey of Defined Contribution Plan Participants." Paper issued by John Hancock Financial Services.

Feder, B. J. 1994. "Gerber's Hometown Ready to Welcome Sandoz." *New York Times,* August 2, page D1.

Frankel, J. A., and S. L. Schmukler. 1996. Country fund discounts and the Mexican crisis of December 1994: Did local residents turn pessimistic before international investors? *Open Economics Review* 7: 511–34.

French, K. R., and J. M. Poterba. 1991. Investor diversification and international equity markets. *American Economic Review* 81: 222–26.

Froot, K. A., P. G. J. O'Connell, and M. Seasholes. 1998. "The Portfolio Flows of International Investors, I." Working Paper 6687. NBER.

Gehrig, T. P. 1993. An information based explanation of the domestic bias in international equity investment. *The Scandinavian Journal of Economics* 21: 97–109.

Glassman, D. A., and L. A. Riddick. 1996. Why empirical international portfolio models fail: Evidence that model misspecification creates home asset bias. *Journal of International Money and Finance* 15: 275–312.

Grubel, H. G., 1968. Internationally diversified portfolios. *American Economic Review* 58: 1299–314.

Huberman, G. 1997. "Familiarity Breeds Investment." Working Paper. Columbia University.

Jorion, P. 1985. International portfolio diversification with estimation risk. *Journal of Business* 58: 259–78.

Kennickel, A. B., M. Starr-McCluer, and A. E. Sunden. 1997. Family finances in the U.S.: Recent evidence from the survey of consumer finances. *Federal Reserve Bulletin,* January: 1–24.

Kilka, M., and M. Weber. 1997. "Home Bias in International Stock Returns Expectations." Working Paper. University of Mannheim.

Levy, H., and M. Sarnat, 1970. International diversification of investment portfolios. *American Economic Review* 60: 668–75.

Lewis, K. K. 1998. "International Home Bias in International Finance and Business Cycles." Working Paper 6351. NBER.

Lintner, J. 1965a. The valuation of risky assets and the selection of risky investments in stock portfolios and capital budgets. *Review of Economics and Statistics* 47: 13–37.

Lintner, J. 1965b. Security prices, risk and maximal gains from diversification. *Journal of Finance* 20: 587–615.

Markowitz, H. 1952. Portfolio selection. *Journal of Finance* 7: 77–91.

Markowitz, H. 1959. *Portfolio Selection: Efficient Diversification of Investments*. New York: Wiley and Sons.

Merton, R. C. 1973. Intertemporal capital asset pricing model. *Econometrica* 41: 867–87.

Mossin, J. 1965. Equilibrium in a capital asset market. *Econometrica* 35: 768–83.

New York Stock Exchange. 1995. *Shareownership 1995*.

Pesenti, P., and E. van Wincoop. 2000. "Can nontradables generate substantial home bias?" *Journal of Money, Credit and Banking*, forthcoming.

Sharpe, William F. 1964. Capital asset prices: A theory of market equilibrium under conditions of risk. *Journal of Finance* 19: 425–42.

Shawky, H. A., R. Kuemzel, and A. D. Mikhail. 1997. International portfolio diversification: A synthesis and an update. *International Financial Markets, Institutions, and Money* 7: 303–27.

Schultz, E. E. 1996. Workers put too much in their employer's stock. *Wall Street Journal*, September 13.

Solnik, B. H. 1974. Why not diversify internationally rather than domestically? *Financial Analyst Journal* 30: 91–135.

Tesar, L. L., and I. M. Weber. 1995. Home bias and high turnover. *Journal of International Money and Finance* 14: 467–92.

Tesar, L. L., and I. M. Weber. 1998. The internationalization of security markets since the 1987 crash. *Brookings Papers on Financial Services*.

Uppal, R. 1992. The economic determinants of the home country bias in investors' portfolios: A survey. *Journal of International Financial Management and Accounting* 4: 171–89.

Williams, F. 1997. Equities top 62% of 401(k) assets. *Pensions and Investments*, January 20.

Zhou, C. 1998. Dynamic portfolio choice and asset pricing with differential information. *Journal of Economic Dynamics and Control* 22: 1027–51.

CHAPTER 5

Relative price volatility: What role does the border play?*

Charles Engel[†] and John H. Rogers[‡]

Popular accounts of the international economy stress the increased "globaliza-tion" of economic activity. The press and other media highlight the increased openness of goods markets and capital markets across borders, and the bur-geoning volume of trade flows and international capital flows. Although there is little doubt that markets are opening worldwide, academic work has begun to focus more on the amount of market segmentation, particularly in goods markets. One strand of the literature (exemplified by Krugman 1991) stresses the role of geography in determining international trade flows. This new line of research finds its ancestry in the "gravity" model of trade.[1] A related area of research stresses that segmentation of goods markets internationally allows mo-nopolistic firms to price discriminate across national markets. Krugman (1987) presents some of the early theoretical analysis, which has been bolstered by a wealth of empirical evidence.[2]

Empirical work stemming from study of the gravity model has used the volume of trade flows between two locations as a measure of integration be-tween those locations.[3] When there are few impediments to trade, either im-posed by policy, culture, or geography, then goods should flow freely between countries, cities, or provinces. Our contention, however, is that trade flows are

* We thank Richard Clarida for his useful comments. The views expressed in this paper are those of the authors and do not necessarily reflect those of the Board of Governors or the Federal Reserve System. Engel's work on this project was funded in part by a National Science Foundation grant to the National Bureau of Economic Research.

† University of Washington and NBER. Mailing address: Department of Economics, University of Washington, Seattle WA. E-mail: *cmengel@u.washington.edu.*
‡ Mailing address: Board of Governors of the Federal Reserve System, Washington, DC. E-mail: *john.h.rojers@frb.gov.*

[1] See, for example, Pöyhönen (1963), Pullianen (1963) or Linneman (1966). Helliwell (1998) traced the lineage of this area of research.
[2] See Goldberg and Knetter (1997) for an excellent survey of the literature.
[3] Recent empirical studies of the gravity model include Bergstrand (1985, 1989), Frankel and Wei (1994), Frankel, Stein, and Wei (1994), McCallum (1995), and Helliwell (1996).

a problematic measure of the degree of market integration. Traditional trade theory that assumes no impediments to trade still predicts that the volume of trade flows between two regions depends on such things as factor endowments or the degree to which economies of scale are exploited. The absence of costs to trading does not imply that there will be an unlimited, or even necessarily a large volume of trade. So, to use the volume of trade flows as a measure of how openness has changed over time, we must carefully monitor other determinants of trade flows to ascertain whether the change in trade volumes can be attributed to changes in integration or other factors.

Our approach to measuring market integration is to examine prices of goods and services. A fundamental proposition of economic theory is that, in the absence of transactions costs, identical goods must sell for the same price. A comprehensive measure of how well two markets are integrated is how closely prices move together in those markets. Prices will fail to equalize when there are barriers to the free movement of goods. These barriers might be natural barriers, such as the geographic distance between regions emphasized by the gravity literature. But there may be other barriers that are man-made. Tariffs and other formal trade barriers lead to inequality of consumer prices between locations, as do informal trade barriers. These latter include, for example, marketing agreements, or tradition, which tend to leave foreign goods on an unequal footing with domestically produced goods in the consumer market.

Here we extend our earlier research, particularly Engel and Rogers (1996), that investigates the relative importance of these types of barriers to market integration. We examine the behavior of prices of 14 categories of consumer goods and services among 14 cities in the United States and 10 provinces in Canada. We ask why the price of a particular category of goods in one location fluctuates relative to the price of similar goods in a different location. We relate a measure of this volatility to various explanatory variables, including the distance between the pair of locations, a dummy variable for whether the locations are in different countries, and a variable meant to capture different labor market conditions in the two locations.

Related work investigates market integration by looking at the adjustment of goods prices. A series of papers by Engel and Rogers separately (Engel 1993, 1999; Rogers and Jenkins 1995) documents the idea that markets are very poorly integrated if final goods prices are the benchmark. Failures of the law of one price account for the vast majority of real exchange rate movements in the short run and longer for industrialized countries. Another co-authored paper (Engel and Rogers 1998) looks at the behavior of a number of categories of goods over a large sample of countries. Relative to Engel and Rogers (1996), the later paper uses data from more locations – 23 countries and 8 North American cities – but fewer goods – only eight categories. We find that relative price volatility (the volatility of prices of similar goods across locations) is a function primarily of exchange rate volatility and distance. Other similar work includes that of Wei and Parsley (1995), who find that the speed of convergence to purchasing power parity (PPP) also depends on the distance between locations.[4]

Two recent contributions examine the convergence of prices within the United States. Parsley and Wei (1996) find that the speed of convergence of prices of goods sold in cities within the United States is lower the more distant the city pairs. Nonetheless, convergence tends to be much faster than is found in international price data, suggesting that national borders somehow affect the speed of convergence. O'Connell and Wei (1997) model prices as a nonlinear process in which the speed of adjustment is greater when relative prices lie outside of some band. This model, which fares well empirically, is meant to capture the effect of transportation costs. Goods arbitrage will not occur when prices across locations are close, even if they are not equal. But, when they diverge greatly, market forces act more rapidly to cause prices to converge.

Our work on international and intranational pricing can be considered the complement of the recent work on trade flows within and between countries. McCallum (1995), Helliwell (1996), Wei (1996), and Wolf (1997) all find that the volume of trade between countries is significantly less than the volume of trade within countries, taking into account other determinants of trade volumes such as distance and size of the trading unit.

Here, we are particularly interested in the effect of the U.S.–Canadian free trade agreement on the volatility of these relative prices. Using estimates from a gravity model, Helliwell (1998) finds that the bias in trade between Canadian provinces (relative to trade between provinces and U.S. states) fell significantly after the free trade agreement. If indeed trade restrictions were a chief obstacle to market integration, then we should see prices moving more closely together after the free trade agreement than before. So, we investigate how prices behave before January 1990, when the free trade agreement went into effect, compared with how they behave afterwards.

Our basic empirical results show that even though distance is a significant deterrent to market integration, national borders impose a much more important barrier. But, trade barriers do not seem to explain the border effect. As in Engel and Rogers (1996), we conclude that there are likely two significant reasons why the border matters so much. First, to the degree that any two markets are segmented, there is opportunity for pricing to market. If, in addition, there is nominal price stickiness and prices are set in the consumers' currencies, then Canadian and U.S. prices can diverge greatly in the short run when the nominal exchange rate fluctuates. However, this nominal price-stickiness effect does not account for all the border effect. We posit that there are national markets for

---

[4] Engel, Hendrickson, and Rogers (1997) find no such bias in a panel study involving eight cities from four countries on two continents.

consumer goods, established by tradition, by national distribution networks, and by national marketing campaigns. These national markets would lead to deviations in U.S. and Canadian prices even in the absence of nominal price stickiness.

One issue that needs to be addressed up front is our use of consumer prices for some goods and services that are traditionally classified as "nontraded." In the model of Engel and Rogers (1996), all consumer goods have a nontraded component. This nontraded component comes from location-specific costs of marketing and distribution services and other local services. It is probably not useful to classify goods simply as traded and nontraded. There is a continuum depending on the degree of input of local services. So, there are at least two determinants of how closely linked consumer markets are between locations: the degree of the barriers to shipment of the traded goods component and the size of the nontraded component in any consumer good. But, also, as we discuss in Engel and Rogers (1996), there is a third determinant. Even if the nontraded service accounts for a large fraction of the cost of the good, the costs of these services are not necessarily independent across locations. For example, in a two-factor two-sector model of international trade, if one good is traded and one factor is traded, then factor prices for both factors will be equalized across locations. In turn, the price of nontraded goods is equalized across countries.[5]

A fourth factor that determines whether prices equalize is the degree of monopoly mark-up. In standard models of price discrimination, in regions where the elasticity of demand is lower, the mark-up will be higher. This is the avenue highlighted by much of the work on pricing to market.

Following Engel and Rogers (1996), we can write the price of some good in location i as

$$p_i = \mu_i w_i^{\gamma} q_i^{1-\gamma}$$

where μ_i is the mark-up, w_i is the cost of the nontraded service, q_i is the price of the traded component, and γ is the share of the nontraded component in total costs.

So, we can write:

$$\ln(p_i) - \ln(p_j) = \ln(\mu_i/\mu_j) + \gamma \ln(w_i/w_j) + (1 - \gamma)\ln(q_i/q_j)$$

Assuming each of the components on the right-hand side is independent of the others, we have the variance of the relative price given by

$$\text{Var}(\ln(p_i) - \ln(p_j)) = \text{Var}(\ln(\mu_i/\mu_j)) + \gamma^2 \text{Var}((\ln(w_i/w_j)))$$

$$+ (1 - \gamma)^2 \text{Var}(\ln(q_i/q_j))$$

So, the variance of the relative price increases as the variance of the relative

[5] For example, the model of Engel and Kletzer (1989) has this structure.

mark-ups increases, as the variance of the relative costs of the nontraded service increases, and as the variance of the relative price of the traded good increases. The latter variance is not zero because of transportation costs and other barriers to shipment of traded goods. Then, assuming

$$\text{Var}((\ln(w_i/w_j)) > \text{Var}(\ln(q_i/q_j))$$

the variance of the relative price of the final product also increases as the share of the nontraded component increases.

In our empirical work that follows, we find that the presence of a national border separating two locations is a significant determinant of the variance of the relative price of the final product. There is not an obvious link between the fact that our data contain prices on many nontraded goods and the presence of the border effect. Most hypotheses of why goods are not traded imply that goods are not traded across distant locations, whether or not there is a national border between the locations. So, for example, if transportation costs are high, then the good might not be traded between cities or provinces that are far apart. But, it is not clear why the national border should matter. The border effect cannot be easily explained by simply noting that some of the goods in our sample are nontraded. What is required is an explanation of why goods are more nontraded across national borders than among locations within a country. That is, why are international markets more segmented than intranational markets, taking into account distance?

5.1   Econometric model and data

5.1.1   Model specification

Let q_{ij} be the log of the relative price of some good between locations i and j. We model this price as following a stationary sixth-order autoregressive process, with 12 monthly seasonals.[6] We take the standard deviation of the 12-month ahead forecast as the dependent variable to be explained by factors such as the distance between location i and j and a dummy variable for whether the locations are in the same country or in a different country.

In practice, we find qualitatively essentially the same results whether we use the standard deviation of the 12-month forecast error from the stationary model or the standard deviation of the first-difference of q_{ij}.[7] This may seem surprising at first. We certainly expect q_{ij} to be a stationary variable. There is probably no plausible economic theory that would suggest that q_{ij} could have a unit root.

---

[6] For prices that are measured bimonthly, we assume an AR(4) with six seasonal dummies.

[7] We actually use two-month differences because some of our data are bimonthly.

But in practice, even if q_{ij} is stationary, it is so persistent that there is very little evidence of convergence for any of the price series. So, for most of the regressions we estimate, we use the standard deviation of the first-difference of q_{ij} as the dependent variable because it enhances the reproducibility of our findings.

Let $V(q_{ij})$ be one of the measures of volatility of q_{ij} described earlier. Our basic regressions are of the form

$$V(q_{ij}) = \beta_1 d_{ij} + \beta_2 B_{ij} + \sum_{k=1}^{m} \lambda_k D_k \tag{1}$$

Here, d_{ij} is the log of the distance between locations i and j; B_{ij} is a dummy variable that takes on the value of one if locations i and j are in different countries, and D_k are dummy variables for each location, which take on a value of one for D_i and D_j and a value of zero for all other locations. We expect to find $\beta_1 > 0$ and $\beta_2 > 0$.

For each good, there are 251 city pairs. We consider the standard deviation of, for example, New York–Los Angeles prices to be a separate observation from the New York–Chicago and Chicago–Los Angeles observations. In general, if there are $G + 1$ cities, then there are only G independent relative prices. Yet we calculate $G(G + 1)/2$ standard deviations.[8] It is helpful to think of our estimation as a two-step procedure in which we estimate a model for the levels of relative prices in the first step and then estimate a model for the covariance matrix of those relative prices in the second step.

Consider the model in which we take the standard deviation of the first difference of q_{ij}. Define $\varepsilon_{ij,t} = q_{ij,t} - q_{ij,t-1}$. Pick one location as the reference, and call it location 0. We can consider the $\varepsilon_{i0,t}$ as the first-differences of the G independent prices. The other $\varepsilon_{ij,t}$ are related to $\varepsilon_{i0,t}$ by $\varepsilon_{ij,t} = \varepsilon_{i0,t} - \varepsilon_{j0,t}$.

Equation (1), however, can be thought of as a model that estimates the elements of the covariance matrix of the $\varepsilon_{i0,t}$. Let $\text{Var}(\varepsilon_{ij})$ be the variance of $\varepsilon_{ij,t}$. Then

$$\text{Var}(\varepsilon_{ij}) = \text{Var}(\varepsilon_{i0}) + \text{Var}(\varepsilon_{j0}) - 2 \cdot \text{Cov}(\varepsilon_{i0}, \varepsilon_{j0})$$

where Cov refers to the covariance. It follows that

$$\text{Cov}(\varepsilon_{i0}, \varepsilon_{j0}) = \tfrac{1}{2}(\text{Var}(\varepsilon_{i0}) + \text{Var}(\varepsilon_{j0}) - \text{Var}(\varepsilon_{ij}))$$

So, all of the covariances, $\text{Cov}(\varepsilon_{i0}, \varepsilon_{j0})$, can be obtained from estimates of the variances of the relative prices. Thus, estimates of the $G(G + 1)/2$ elements of the covariance matrix of $\varepsilon_{i0,t}$ can be obtained from estimates of the $G(G+1)/2$

---

[8] Actually, we calculate fewer standard deviations because we do not attempt to measure the standard deviation of the prices from U.S. cities measured in even-numbered months relative to those measured in odd-numbered months.

variances of $\varepsilon_{ij,t}$. Equation (1), then, can be considered a model that provides estimates of the elements of the covariance matrix of $\varepsilon_{i0,t}$.

In words, if Chicago is the base location, even after we calculate the variance of the Chicago–New York and the Chicago–Los Angeles relative prices, we are still interested in the variance of the New York–Los Angeles relative price because this variance is needed to calculate the covariance of the Chicago–New York and the Chicago–Los Angeles relative prices. So the New York–Los Angeles relative price is not redundant.

In one set of regressions, rather than using a measure of the volatility of q_{ij} as the dependent variable, we use the correlation of the logs of p_i and p_j [where, recall, $q_{ij} \equiv \ln(p_i) - \ln(p_j)$]. Let each of these nominal prices share a common nominal shock and independent idiosyncratic shocks:

$$\Delta \ln(p_{it}) = u_{it} + v_t$$

$$\Delta \ln(p_{jt}) = u_{jt} + v_t$$

Noting that $\varepsilon_{ij,t} = u_{it} - u_{jt}$, then $\text{Var}(\varepsilon_{ij}) = \text{Var}(u_i) + \text{Var}(u_j)$. But, the correlation of $\Delta \ln(p_{it})$ and $\Delta \ln(p_{jt})$ can be written as

$$\left(1 + \frac{\text{Var}(u_i)}{\text{Var}(v)}\right)^{-1/2} \left(1 + \frac{\text{Var}(u_j)}{\text{Var}(v)}\right)^{-1/2}$$

So, the correlation measure scales the variance of the independent idiosyncratic shocks by the variance of the common nominal shock. As the idiosyncratic shocks increase in variance relative to the common shock, the correlation declines.

For this specification, we estimate the model:

$$\text{corr}(p_i, p_j) = \alpha_1 d_{ij} + \alpha_2 B_{ij} + \sum_{k=1}^{m} \theta_k D_k \tag{2}$$

where the right-hand side variables are defined as in Equation (1). We now expect to find $\alpha_1 < 0$ and $\alpha_2 < 0$.

5.1.2   Data

Table 5.1 displays the 14 categories of goods for which we have data. The data are disaggregated into these categories because that is the most disaggregated data that is publicly available for U.S. cities. The Canadian subindexes that are reported do not match exactly with U.S. indexes, so we construct subindexes for Canadian categories from even more disaggregated data. The data are monthly for each of the ten Canadian provinces, and for four U.S. cities – New York, Los Angeles, Chicago, and Philadelphia. We have bimonthly data for ten other U.S.

Table 5.1. *Categories of goods in disaggregated consumer price indices and locations used*

Good	United States	Canada
1	Food at home	Food purchased from stores
2	Food away from home	Food purchased from restaurants
3	Alcoholic beverages	Alcoholic beverages
4	Shelter	Shelter
5	Fuel and other utilities	Water, fuel, and electricity
6	Household furnishings and operations	Housing operations and furnishings
7	Men's and boys' apparel	$0.8058 \times$ (men's clothing) $+ 0.1942 \times$ (children's clothing)
8	Women's and girls' apparel	$0.8355 \times$ (women's clothing) $+ 0.1645 \times$ (children's clothing)
9	Footwear	Footwear
10	Private transportation	Private transportation
11	Public transportation	Public transportation
12	Medical care	Health care
13	Personal care	Personal care
14	Entertainment	$0.8567 \times$ (recreation) $+ 0.1433$(reading material)

Notes: The U.S. cities in the sample are: Baltimore, Boston, Chicago, Dallas, Detroit, Houston, Los Angeles, Miami, New York, Philadelphia, Pittsburgh, San Francisco, St. Louis, and Washington, DC. The Canadian provinces are Newfoundland, Prince Edward Island, Nova Scotia, New Brunswick, Quebec, Ontario, Manitoba, Saskatchewan, Alberta, and British Columbia.

cities. For five of these cities the data are measured in odd-numbered months, and the others in even-numbered months.

The data are monthly from September 1978 to December 1997. These data are similar to the data we used in Engel and Rogers (1996). The categories of consumer prices are identical. The data in that paper started in September 1978 and ended in December 1994. The data are for the same 14 U.S. cities. Our earlier paper had data on consumer prices for nine Canadian cities, but Statistics Canada ceased publishing disaggregated price data by city at the end of 1994. So, in the present paper, we use price data by Canadian province.

Distance between U.S. cities is calculated using the great circle distance. For Canadian provinces, we measure great circle distances from the largest city of each province.[9]

[9] Newfoundland–St. John's; Prince Edward Island–Charlottetown; Nova Scotia–Halifax; New Brunswick–St. John; Quebec–Montreal; Ontario–Toronto; Manitoba–Winnepeg; Saskatoon–Regina; Alberta–Calgary; British Columbia–Vancouver.

Table 5.2A. *Summary statistics – Three different measures of Law of One Price (LOP) deviations, full sample*

Good	SD(Δp_{jk})			Corr($\Delta p_j, \Delta p_k$)			SD(P_{jk})		
	U-U	C-C	U-C	U-U	C-C	U-C	U-U	C-C	U-C
All	0.83	0.52	1.80	0.54	0.65	0.35	1.35	1.08	1.85
1	1.42	1.68	2.48	0.46	0.47	0.30	1.99	2.48	4.71
2	1.23	0.95	2.03	0.19	0.58	0.15	2.13	1.78	4.53
3	1.80	1.50	2.51	0.29	0.49	0.15	2.85	2.56	4.87
4	2.02	0.84	2.40	0.27	0.51	0.13	3.41	2.03	4.96
5	5.03	2.86	5.18	0.30	0.36	0.07	4.96	4.89	7.04
6	2.08	0.98	2.32	0.11	0.33	0.12	2.86	1.47	4.39
7	5.41	2.34	5.05	0.28	0.39	0.13	5.59	2.47	6.23
8	9.15	2.58	8.60	0.44	0.42	0.25	9.23	2.59	9.31
9	6.31	2.66	5.27	0.16	0.40	0.18	7.81	3.18	7.58
10	1.12	1.56	2.50	0.77	0.52	0.30	1.77	2.32	4.97
11	4.62	1.82	6.55	0.37	0.93	0.07	7.45	2.55	9.21
12	1.29	1.73	2.37	0.21	0.48	0.12	2.23	3.42	5.13
13	2.60	1.16	2.67	0.03	0.43	0.07	4.10	1.87	5.35
14	2.00	0.84	2.35	0.08	0.68	0.04	2.97	1.13	4.45
Pooled (1–14)	3.29	1.68	3.73	0.32	0.51	0.16	4.24	2.48	5.91

Notes: Entries in each column give the mean values across all intercity combinations within the United States (labeled U-U), within Canada (C-C), and across the U.S.-Canadian border (U-C), respectively. In column (1), the measure of volatility is the standard deviation of the relative price series. Column (2) gives the average correlation between the price in city j and city k. In both cases, prices are measured as two-month differences. In column (3), the measure of volatility is the standard deviation of the 12-month ahead forecast error of the relative price, based on a sixth-order univariate autoregression. The sample period is September 1978 to December 1997. (*) The average distance between cities is 1070 miles for the intra-U.S. pairs, 1343 miles for the intra-Canada pairs, and 1428 miles for the cross-border pairs. The standard deviation of the two-month log-difference in the nominal exchange rate is 1.57.

Table 5.2 presents some summary statistics for each of the 14 categories of goods, as well as for the overall CPI (labeled "All"). The first set of statistics is for the standard deviation of the first difference of the relative prices.[10] The statistics are reported for all within-U.S. city pairs, for all within-Canada province pairs, and for all U.S. city–Canadian province pairs. In all but three cases, the standard deviation for the cross-border location

[10] The standard deviations are multiplied by 100.

pairs is greater than for either of the within-country pairs. We will investigate whether this arises because cross-border locations are, on average, farther apart or whether the border itself contributes to this standard deviation. The three exceptions, in which the largest standard deviation is for U.S. city pairs, are the three clothing categories – men's and boys' apparel, women's and girls' apparel, and footwear. It may be notable that only a small fraction of the goods sold in these categories is produced either in the United States or Canada. Finally, we note from Table 5.2A that in all but three cases, the smallest standard deviation is for within-Canada province pairs. This tendency for volatility to be lower in Canada may reflect greater integration of local markets within Canada, or it may reflect some sort of difference in how prices are constructed in Canada versus the U.S. We will take account of this in our regressions in Section 5.2.

The second set of statistics reported in Table 5.2A is the correlation coefficients of prices for U.S. city pairs, Canadian province pairs, and cross-border location pairs. Here we note a pattern similar to that found with the standard deviation measures. The cross-border pairs appear to be the least integrated, as evidenced by their lower correlations. In this case, the correlations are lowest for cross-border pairs for all categories except footwear, household furnishings and operations, and personal care.

The third set of statistics reported in Table 5.2A is the standard deviation of the 12-month forecast error from the model described at the beginning of Section 5.1.1. Here we note that for all goods except women's and girls' clothing, the standard deviation is largest for the location pairs that lie on opposite sides of the U.S.–Canadian border. For all goods except private transportation and medical care, the intra-Canadian relative prices are the least volatile.

Table 5.2B report standard deviations of the first differences of relative prices for three subperiods: 1978–89, 1990–3 and 1994–7. The earlier subperiod is prior to the U.S.–Canadian free trade agreement. That agreement went into effect in January 1990. Allowing a few years for adjustment, the 1994–7 period represents a time span in which there were fewer formal trade restrictions than in the 1980s. If it is formal trade restrictions that lead to less market integration across the national border, then we would expect to see that national borders matter less in the 1994–7 period than in the 1978–89 period. In fact, we note very little difference. As reported in the last row, taking all 14 goods together, the standard deviation falls from 3.63% to 3.54% from 1978–89 to 1994–7. The standard deviation is higher in the earlier period for 7 of the goods, but higher in the latter period for the other 7.

Table 5.2B. *Summary statistics – Relative price variability over three subperiods*

Good	SD(Δp_{jk}), 1978–89			SD(Δp_{jk}), 1990–3			SD(Δp_{jk}), 1994–7		
	U-U	C-C	U-C	U-U	C-C	U-C	U-U	C-C	U-C
All	0.92	0.52	1.82	0.70	0.55	1.89	0.61	0.45	1.65
1	1.29	1.65	2.42	1.63	1.75	2.68	1.55	1.61	2.39
2	1.46	0.97	2.00	0.71	0.88	2.31	0.70	0.77	1.70
3	1.76	1.73	2.61	1.92	1.13	2.40	1.70	1.01	2.21
4	2.44	0.88	2.68	1.26	0.85	2.13	0.99	0.65	1.72
5	4.80	2.81	5.06	5.11	2.90	5.38	5.28	2.69	5.05
6	1.90	1.00	2.23	2.28	0.95	2.47	2.32	0.91	2.37
7	4.83	1.86	4.48	5.92	2.61	5.88	5.85	2.79	5.06
8	8.31	1.75	7.86	9.89	2.65	9.51	9.74	3.56	8.58
9	5.83	2.05	4.76	7.22	2.93	5.90	6.77	3.66	5.82
10	1.08	1.62	2.61	1.19	1.63	2.63	1.14	1.20	2.03
11	4.20	1.97	6.75	4.99	1.37	5.74	5.22	1.59	6.46
12	1.40	2.14	2.60	1.17	0.80	2.03	0.98	0.68	1.81
13	2.42	1.08	2.51	2.87	1.31	2.95	2.76	1.19	2.71
14	1.98	0.77	2.31	2.05	0.80	2.29	1.86	0.94	2.46
Pooled (1–14)	3.12	1.59	3.63	3.44	1.61	3.88	3.26	1.62	3.54

Notes: Entries in each column give the mean values across all intercity combinations within the United States (labeled U-U), within Canada (C-C), and across the U.S.-Canadian border (U-C), respectively. These three columns repeat the calculation of column (1) Table 5.2A, over the subperiods September 1978 to December 1989, January 1990 to December 1993, and January 1994 to December 1997, respectively. The standard deviation of the two-month log-difference in the nominal exchange rate is 1.56, 1.62, and 1.51 for the 1978–89, 1990–3, and 1994–7 subperiods, respectively.

5.2   Basic regression results

Table 5.3 reports three versions of estimates of Equation (1) and one version of Equation (2). The first set of estimates attempts to replicate the estimates in Engel and Rogers (1996). It uses the same time period. We note that in this paper, Canadian price data is by province, whereas in the 1996 paper it was by city. In this first set of estimates, the dependent variable is the standard deviation of the two-month differences in the relative price between pairs of locations. The sample period in this regression is identical to the 1996 paper: September 1978 to December 1994.

The second specification is a version of Equation (2). The dependent variable is the correlation of the first-difference of p_i and p_j for locations i and j. The sample period is September 1978 to December 1994, so the second specification differs from the first only in the definition of the dependent variable.

Table 5.3. *Updating the main regression of Engel-Rogers (1996)*

Good	Specification 1 Log distance	Specification 1 Border	Specification 2 Log distance	Specification 2 Border	Specification 3 Log distance	Specification 3 Border	Specification 4 Log distance	Specification 4 Border
All	4.47	1.13	−4.00	−0.27	4.02	1.11	11.4	2.84
	(0.73)	(0.008)	(0.68)	(0.008)	(0.68)	(0.007)	(3.03)	(0.04)
1	6.68	0.88	−4.86	−0.16	6.72	0.86	9.22	2.48
	(1.55)	(0.018)	(0.85)	(0.008)	(1.62)	(0.016)	(2.96)	(0.04)
2	2.10	0.98	−1.03	−0.27	1.95	0.94	7.60	2.70
	(1.54)	(0.014)	(0.86)	(0.010)	(1.32)	(0.012)	(2.97)	(0.04)
3	2.52	0.89	0.05	−0.26	2.15	0.87	0.81	2.30
	(1.89)	(0.022)	(0.91)	(0.10)	(1.86)	(0.020)	(3.98)	(0.06)
4	10.6	0.96	−5.94	−0.27	9.75	0.93	31.1	2.34
	(1.89)	(0.020)	(1.06)	(0.013)	(1.75)	(0.018)	(5.71)	(0.07)
5	37.4	1.20	−10.1	−0.27	34.1	1.11	55.1	1.99
	(7.57)	(0.082)	(2.01)	(0.020)	(7.90)	(0.079)	(6.95)	(0.09)
6	−2.61	0.83	−0.38	−0.13	−1.20	0.79	−1.59	2.40
	(1.48)	(0.014)	(0.83)	(0.011)	(1.29)	(0.014)	(3.26)	(0.04)
7	3.97	1.28	−1.99	−0.27	4.19	1.10	6.76	2.36
	(4.33)	(0.048)	(1.46)	(0.017)	(3.87)	(0.046)	(4.35)	(0.07)
8	3.34	2.89	−2.08	−0.24	6.44	2.58	18.7	3.39
	(11.0)	(0.152)	(1.13)	(0.016)	(9.74)	(0.137)	(10.1)	(0.12)
9	3.19	0.76	−1.60	−0.09	−0.98	0.69	−5.18	2.07
	(5.14)	(0.056)	(1.11)	(0.011)	(4.50)	(0.049)	(6.38)	(0.08)
10	12.8	1.18	−4.60	−0.39	12.3	1.11	15.8	2.89
	(1.67)	(0.017)	(0.93)	(0.009)	(1.51)	(0.015)	(2.88)	(0.04)
11	15.4	3.19	−0.44	−0.54	17.7	3.15	−0.99	3.81
	(5.29)	(0.090)	(0.92)	(0.011)	(5.22)	(0.086)	(8.81)	(0.11)
12	−2.31	0.90	1.55	−0.26	−2.00	0.87	−0.88	2.52
	(1.81)	(0.023)	(1.23)	(0.015)	(1.64)	(0.021)	(6.34)	(0.07)
13	−0.17	0.77	−0.95	−0.18	0.65	0.74	−1.94	2.49
	(1.86)	(0.018)	(1.09)	(0.011)	(1.70)	(0.017)	(5.60)	(0.056)
14	3.53	0.91	−2.14	−0.28	4.14	0.92	6.77	2.57
	(1.29)	(0.017)	(0.89)	(0.012)	(1.43)	(0.017)	(3.79)	(0.042)
1–14	6.88	1.26	−2.60	−0.26	6.84	1.19	10.1	2.59
	(3.41)	(0.041)	(0.48)	(0.006)	(3.22)	(0.039)	(3.99)	(0.049)

Notes: All regressions contain a dummy for each of the 24 individual locations, in addition to the variables listed in the cell. Heteroscedasticity-consistent standard errors are reported in parentheses. There are 251 observations in each regression. Coefficients and standard errors on log distance are multiplied by 100. In specification 1, the dependent variable is the standard deviation of the two-month difference in the relative price. Standard deviations are computed over the sample period September 1978 to December 1994, as in Engel and Rogers (1996). In Specification 2, the dependent variable is the correlation between ΔP_{ij} and ΔP_{ik}, the two-month change in the price of good i in cities j and k, respectively. Correlations are computed over the sample period September 1978 to December 1994. Specification 3 is analogous to specification 1, but computes standard deviations over the extended sample period September 1978 to December 1997. In specification 4, the dependent variable is the standard deviation of the time-series of 12-month ahead forecast errors of the relative price, based on a sixth-order univariate autoregression estimated beginning in March 1979 and ending in December 1996.

The third specification is identical to the first, except that the model is estimated for an updated data set: September 1978 to December 1997.

The fourth specification is estimated on the same sample as the third, but the dependent variable is the standard deviation of the 12-month ahead forecast error from the AR(6) model with seasonal dummy variables.

All four specifications qualitatively tell almost identical stories. First, we focus on the common elements of the four specifications. Then we briefly mention some minor differences. Note that Table 5.3 only reports the coefficient estimates for the distance and border dummy variables and not the individual location dummy variables.

1   The final row of Table 5.3 reports regression results for a regression that pools data for all 14 goods. For all specifications, distance between locations is statistically significant and of the correct sign. Apparently distance explains part of the segmentation of markets.

2   In the pooled regressions, the border dummy variable is highly significant and of the correct sign for all specifications. Even taking into account distance, U.S.–Canadian location pairs are less integrated than city pairs within the United States or province pairs within Canada.

3   The first 15 rows report the results for regressions for the overall CPI and each of the 14 individual goods. In every single regression, the border coefficient is significant and of the expected sign.

4   Distance is usually of the expected sign and significant. But, for some goods this tends not to be true. For example, distance is always statistically insignificant (and sometimes of the wrong sign) for alcoholic beverages, household furnishings and operations, men's and boys' clothing, footwear; medical care, and personal care. Distance is always significant and of the correct sign for food at home, shelter, fuel and other utilities, private transportation, and entertainment.

5   There is no apparent relationship between the "tradability" of the good and the size of either the distance or border coefficients.

These regression results tend to confirm those in Engel and Rogers (1996). One slight difference is that, in the regressions for individual goods, the distance variable is less frequently significant and of the correct sign. This is probably because, in the current study, the data for Canada is provincial, as opposed to city, data. Measuring distance between provinces in Canada, or between provinces in Canada and cities in the United States is more ambiguous than calculations of distances between cities in the earlier study.

We note that there is virtually no difference between specifications 1 and 3 – the specification corresponding to the Engel and Rogers (1996) sample period

(September 1978 to December 1994) and the updated sample (September 1978 to December 1997).

We also note in the three specifications that use the standard deviation as a measure of volatility (specifications 1, 3 and 4), the ratio of the coefficient on log of distance and the border is about the same. This suggests that the influence of the border (relative to distance) does not depend on the specification or the sample period.

Now we turn to the minor differences across the four specifications. Distance is significant using the 12-month forecast errors, but for no other specification, for food away from home. Distance is significant in specifications 2 and 4 (but not 1 and 3) for women's and girls' apparel.

As we noted in our earlier paper, the border coefficient is not only highly statistically significant but also very large in economic terms. To see this, note that the average distance between a pair of locations in our sample is around 1,200 miles. So, the average effect of distance on the standard deviation is $0.0684 \cdot \ln(1,200) = 0.485$. The effect of crossing the border is 1.19, which is more than twice the effect of the average distance. The estimated coefficient on the border (in the pooled regression) in this paper for the two-month changes in relative prices is almost identical to the estimate in Engel and Rogers (1996). However, the estimated coefficient on the log of distance is about two thirds the estimate in our earlier paper. We hypothesize that this arises because our earlier paper had data on Canadian city prices, for which distance can be precisely measured, whereas this paper uses price data by Canadian province for which distance measures are necessarily cruder.

5.3   What explains the large border effect?

In this section we investigate possible explanations for the large border effect. Our first candidate hypothesis is that the border matters because of formal trade restrictions. Helliwell (1998) cited evidence that, for trade flows, the border effect declines noticeably in the 1990s. He attributed this to the implementation of the U.S.–Canadian free trade agreement in the early part of the decade.

Table 5.4 presents regressions over subperiods 1978–89, 1990–3, and 1994–7. Of particular interest is comparison of the first column, which is for the period prior to the free trade agreement, to the last column, which is for a period in which the free trade agreement is in effect and sufficient time has passed for the economies to adjust to the new laws. The first thing that we note from the pooled regression results is that the coefficient on the border dummy drops by about 20% in the two subperiods: 1.23 in the early period and 1.00 in the later period.

If we look by good, the border coefficient does drop for 11 of the 14 goods from the earlier to the later period. The decline is generally small, but it is

Table 5.4. *Analysis of the subperiods*

	Pre-FTA (1978–89)		1990–3		1994–7	
Good	Log distance	Border	Log distance	Border	Log distance	Border
All	5.10	1.07	2.74	1.24	−0.04	1.13
	(1.00)	(0.01)	(1.11)	(0.01)	(0.99)	(0.01)
1	6.04	0.87	9.31	0.94	8.48	0.70
	(1.52)	(0.02)	(3.13)	(0.04)	(4.06)	(0.03)
2	2.82	0.77	−0.37	1.59	−0.12	0.99
	(1.78)	(0.02)	(1.99)	(0.02)	(1.38)	(0.02)
3	4.05	0.88	0.73	0.86	−3.09	0.79
	(1.95)	(0.03)	(3.61)	(0.03)	(3.08)	(0.03)
4	11.9	0.96	6.21	1.01	1.03	0.92
	(2.38)	(0.02)	(1.77)	(0.02)	(1.50)	(0.02)
5	43.7	1.20	35.9	1.13	17.1	0.76
	(7.78)	(0.08)	(12.1)	(0.12)	(13.2)	(0.09)
6	−2.42	0.77	−0.75	0.88	1.57	0.73
	(4.71)	(0.02)	(2.80)	(0.03)	(3.06)	(0.03)
7	−2.43	1.10	12.9	1.50	5.35	0.69
	(4.71)	(0.05)	(7.79)	(0.09)	(7.41)	(0.09)
8	−2.89	2.72	10.7	3.09	14.8	1.78
	(12.3)	(0.17)	(16.4)	(0.20)	(12.1)	(0.15)
9	2.00	0.80	5.47	0.67	−10.9	0.38
	(5.05)	(0.06)	(8.91)	(0.09)	(6.51)	(0.09)
10	12.2	1.20	16.9	1.12	9.32	0.82
	(1.59)	(0.02)	(3.02)	(0.03)	(2.31)	(0.02)
11	14.6	3.58	14.1	2.41	20.6	2.57
	(6.36)	(0.11)	(6.03)	(0.09)	(9.91)	(0.11)
12	−0.85	0.83	−6.44	1.10	−1.15	0.97
	(1.93)	(0.02)	(1.94)	(0.03)	(1.32)	(0.01)
13	−1.56	0.72	2.10	0.83	6.84	0.62
	(3.19)	(0.02)	(2.92)	(0.04)	(3.35)	(0.04)
14	1.72	0.88	6.34	0.89	7.15	1.10
	(1.58)	(0.02)	(2.51)	(0.03)	(3.47)	(0.04)
1–14	6.35	1.23	8.08	1.29	4.99	1.00
	(3.53)	(0.04)	(4.12)	(0.05)	(3.30)	(0.04)

Notes: These regressions replicate those of column 1 in Table 5.3, over the subperiods September 1978 to December 1989, January 1990 to December 1993, and January 1994 to December 1997, respectively.

statistically significant. The largest decline occurs for the clothing items – men's and boys' clothing, women's and girls' clothing, and footwear – as well as for private transportation, public transportation, and fuel and other utilities.

Helliwell (1998) notes that the effect of distance on trade is shrinking over time. So, if we want to measure the effect of the border on market integration, we should compare it to the effect of distance on integration. By this measure, the border is no more important in the 1994–7 subperiod than in the pre-free trade agreement period. Looking at the pooled regression, the border coefficient falls by about 20%, and the coefficient on distance falls from 6.35 to 4.99 (and is not statistically significant). In the 1990s, it appears that the effects of both distance and the border in segmenting markets have fallen about equally.

So, following Helliwell's logic, the decline of the border effect in the 1990s is probably not caused by the free trade agreement according to our regressions. The border effect has declined, and the size of the border effect has declined in proportion to the decline of the distance effect. Markets are becoming more integrated, perhaps because of improvements in the efficiency of transportation of goods, or communications, or marketing. But, the removal of trade barriers cannot explain the simultaneous diminution in the importance of both the border and distance effects.

Because the removal of trade barriers does not do much to diminish the border effect, we turn to other possible explanations in Table 5.5. One possibility is that labor markets may be more homogeneous within countries. As we noted in Section 5.1, the variability of the relative price between two locations will depend on the variability of the relative price of nontraded services, which we approximate with relative wages between locations. We investigate this hypothesis by including the standard deviation of the relative wage into our regression (1) to see if it reduces the explanatory power of the border dummy.

The results of those regressions (which add the standard deviation of the relative wage as an explanatory variable to specification 3 from Table 5.3) are reported in the first column of Table 5.5. According to our theory, the relative price volatility ought to increase when the relative wage volatility is greater. But, in the pooled regression, we actually find the opposite result – the relative wage variable has a negative sign (though it is statistically insignificant). It does not change the border coefficient at all and has a very minor effect on the distance coefficient. In the regressions for the individual goods, the relative wage variable is generally insignificant and has the wrong sign for 7 of the 14 goods.

When we construct the price of a good for a U.S. city relative to a Canadian province, the prices are converted into a common currency using the U.S. dollar–Canadian dollar exchange rate. One possible explanation for the large border

Table 5.5. *Assessing the importance of the border*

	Specification 1			Specification 2	
Good	Log distance	Border	SD of real wage	Log distance	Border
All	4.07	1.11	−0.24	7.86	0.71
	(0.73)	(.007)	(0.45)	(2.97)	(.036)
1	5.14	0.84	7.34	8.96	0.29
	(1.36)	(.015)	(1.18)	(1.48)	(.015)
2	1.95	0.94	−0.02	3.80	0.20
	(1.40)	(.013)	(1.40)	(1.26)	(.010)
3	1.64	0.86	2.36	3.54	0.40
	(1.98)	(.020)	(1.23)	(1.99)	(.017)
4	9.97	0.93	−1.05	6.37	0.22
	(1.85)	(.018)	(1.28)	(1.07)	(.013)
5	34.4	1.12	−2.05	32.2	0.74
	(8.50)	(.080)	(5.86)	(7.40)	(.077)
6	−1.98	0.78	3.64	1.56	0.17
	(1.31)	(.014)	(1.73)	(1.09)	(.013)
7	6.54	1.14	−9.65	5.66	0.91
	(4.03)	(.048)	(2.61)	(3.69)	(.043)
8	10.7	2.64	−17.6	11.2	2.53
	(10.3)	(.142)	(6.33)	(8.85)	(.122)
9	−1.31	0.69	1.51	0.83	0.44
	(4.77)	(.050)	(3.02)	(4.36)	(.051)
10	11.2	1.09	4.73	9.31	0.36
	(1.50)	(.016)	(0.93)	(1.22)	(.013)
11	15.3	3.11	11.0	19.6	2.86
	(5.61)	(.094)	(6.28)	(4.98)	(.085)
12	−2.10	0.87	0.46	0.13	0.27
	(1.69)	(.022)	(1.23)	(1.17)	(.015)
13	1.11	0.74	−2.13	1.55	0.20
	(1.88)	(.017)	(1.18)	(1.60)	(.016)
14	4.16	0.92	−0.06	5.29	0.35
	(1.51)	(.017)	(1.11)	(1.38)	(.016)
1–14	6.91	1.19	−0.29	7.86	0.71
	(3.26)	(.041)	(3.50)	(3.03)	(.038)

Notes: All regressions contain a dummy for each of the 23 individual cities, in addition to the variables listed in the cell. Heteroscedasticity-consistent standard errors are reported in parentheses. There are 251 observations in each regression. Coefficients and standard errors on log distance and the wage variable are multiplied by 100. Specification 1 adds to specification 3 of Table 5.3 the standard deviation of the two-month change in real wages. In specification 2, the dependent variable is the standard deviation of the two-month change in the relative real price, estimated over the full sample.

coefficient is nominal price stickiness. Specifically, suppose that U.S. prices tend to be sticky in U.S. dollar terms, and Canadian prices are sticky in Canadian dollar terms. The exchange rate is much more volatile than goods prices. So, when we examine cross-border prices, we should expect a lot of volatility – the goods prices, in their own currencies, do not move much but the exchange rate does. Relative prices for location pairs within a country – either the United States or Canada – of course do not involve an exchange rate, and so are likely to be fairly stable because the prices are sticky in their own currencies. So, the cross-border prices may exhibit high volatility because they contain the volatile exchange rate, while within-country prices do not.

We would like to find out whether the exchange rate volatility accounts for all the border effect. One way to get at this is to construct cross-border relative prices that do not involve the exchange rate. We would not want to take the Canadian price of a good in Ontario, for example, relative to the U.S. dollar price of a good in New York, because that relative price would then be in units of Canadian dollars per U.S. dollars, whereas all the within-country prices would be unit-free.

Instead, we first express the prices of all goods in a particular location relative to the overall price index of that location. For example, we take food at home (good 1) in Ontario relative to the overall consumer price index (CPI) in Ontario. We can then compare this relative price to a similar price in a different location, such as the price of food at home in New York relative to the overall CPI in New York. By constructing relative prices such as this, we can compare prices across all locations without using nominal exchange rates. If the sticky-price cum volatile-nominal-exchange-rate explanation accounted for all the border effect, then the border coefficient should not be significant in a regression such as Equation (1) with relative prices constructed in this way.

We present the coefficient estimates from such regressions in the second panel of Table 5.5. The coefficient estimates from this regression are not directly comparable to any previous regressions because the dependent variable is constructed differently. But, the notable point about these regressions is that the border coefficients are still highly significant for the pooled data and for every good. Apparently we cannot explain the market segmentation between the U.S. and Canada solely on the basis of sticky nominal prices.

5.4   Conclusions

Using the metric of price dispersion, markets are segmented between the United States and Canada to a much greater extent than can be explained by the distance between the locations. It appears that formal trade restrictions do not explain the segmentation. Differences in labor costs also do not help explain the relative price dispersion across locations. Although there may be a role for sticky nominal prices in conjunction with a volatile nominal exchange rate, that avenue does not explain the entire border effect.

What is left? It appears that consumer markets are, to a great degree, national markets. Perhaps this is because distribution networks are organized nationally. Perhaps it is because marketing efforts are conducted on a national basis. Perhaps there are nontariff legal barriers to movement of goods between U.S. and Canadian markets. Perhaps tastes, shaped by custom and advertising, are differentiated across national borders.

It is a significant understatement to observe that prices are an important economic variable. At this stage, we do not have a clear understanding of what determines differences in prices across locations. This continues to be an important and rich area for research.

References

Bergstrand, J. 1985. The gravity equation in international trade: Some microeconomic foundations and empirical evidence. *Review of Economics and Statistics* 67: 474–81.

Bergstrand, J. 1989. The generalized gravity equation, monopolistic competition and the factor-proportions theory in international trade. *Review of Economics and Statistics* 71: 143–53.

Engel, C. 1993. Real exchange rates and relative prices: An empirical investigation. *Journal of Monetary Economics* 32: 35–50.

Engel, C. 1999. Accounting for U.S. Real Exchange Rate Changes. *Journal of Political Economy* 107: 507–38.

Engel, C., and K. M. Kletzer. 1989. Saving and investment in an open economy with non-traded goods. *International Economic Review* 30: 735–52.

Engel, C., M. K. Hendrickson, and J. H. Rogers. 1997. Intra-national, intra-continental, and intra-planetary PPP. *Journal of the Japanese and International Economies* 11: 480–501.

Engel, C., and J. H. Rogers. 1996. How wide is the border? *American Economic Review* 86: 1112–25.

Engel, C., and J. H. Rogers. 1998. "Regional Patterns in the Law of One Price: The Roles of Geography Versus Currencies," in J. A. Frankel, ed., *The Regionalization of the World Economy*. Chicago: University of Chicago Press.

Frankel, J., and S.-J. Wei. 1994. "Yen Bloc or Dollar Bloc? Exchange Rate Policies of the East-Asian Economies," in T. Ito and A. O. Krueger, eds., *Macroeconomic Linkage: Savings, Exchange Rates and Capital Flows*, pp. 295–333. Chicago: University of Chicago Press.

Frankel, J., E. Stein, and S.-J. Wei. 1994. Trading blocs and the Americas: The natural, the unnatural and the supernatural. *Journal of Development Economics* 47: 61–96.

Goldberg, P. K., and M. M. Knetter. 1997. Goods prices and exchange rates: What have we learned. *Journal of Economic Literature* 35: 1243–72.

Helliwell, J. 1996. Do national borders matter for Quebec's trade? *Canadian Journal of Economics* 29: 507–22.

Helliwell, J. 1998. "How Much Do National Borders Matter?" Washington, DC: Brookings Institution Press.

Krugman, P. 1987. "Pricing to Market When the Exchange Rate Changes," in S. W. Arndt and J. D. Richardson, eds., *Real-Financial Linkages Among Open Economies*, pp. 49–70. Cambridge, MA.: MIT Press.

Krugman, P. 1991. *Geography and Trade*. Cambridge, MA.: MIT Press.

Linneman, H. 1966. *An Econometric Study of International Trade Flows*. Amsterdam: North Holland.

McCallum, J. C. P. 1995. National borders matter: Canada-U.S. regional trade patterns. *American Economic Review* 85: 615–23.

O'Connell, P. J., and S.-J. Wei. 1997. "The Bigger They Are, the Harder They Fall: How Price Differences Across Cities Are Arbitraged." Working Paper 6089. National Bureau of Economic Research.

Parsley, D., and S.-J. Wei. 1996. Convergence to the law of one price without trade barriers or currency fluctuations. *Quarterly Journal of Economics* 111: 1211–36.

Pöyhönen, P. 1963. A tentative model for the volume of trade between countries. *Weltwirtschaftliches Archiv* 90.

Pulliainen, K. 1963. A world study: An econometric model of the pattern of the commodity flows of international trade in 1948–60. *Economiska Samfudets Tidskrift* 16: 78–91.

Rogers, J. H., and M. Jenkins. 1995. Haircuts or hysteresis? Sources of movements in real exchange rates. *Journal of International Economics* 38: 339–360.

Wei, S.-J. 1996. "Intra-national Versus Inter-national Trade." Working Paper 5531. National Bureau of Economic Research.

Wei, S.-J., and D. Parsley. 1995. "Purchasing Power Disparity During the Recent Floating Rate Period: Exchange Rate Volatility, Trade Barriers and Other Culprits." Working Paper 5032. National Bureau of Economic Research.

Wolf, H. 1997. "Patterns of Intra- and Inter-state Trade." Working Paper 5939. National Bureau of Economic Research.

CHAPTER 6

(Why) Do borders matter for trade?*

Holger C. Wolf[†]

> Another illusion which flow studies usually dispel is the belief that the econ-
> omy of any large nation or division of the world represents one large open
> market. The very fact that a large volume of traffic terminates over short dis-
> tances testifies to the omnipresent "friction of distance", to the realization of
> economies of scale at several locations, and to other location forces. Walter
> Isard (1960:127)

6.1   Introduction

Much of the empirical literature on international trade has long relied on the convenient fiction that countries can be treated as dimensionless points. Recently,
however, renewed attention has been devoted to understanding subnational trade
patterns. The new interest in *intranational* trade, exhibiting a strong overlap with
regional economics (Ohlin 1933; Hoover 1948; Isard 1960), is based on several
motivations.

First and foremost, the traditional selection of countries as the object of
study has scant theoretical foundation. Trade theory aims to explain the spatial location of production and the resulting trade between locations. There is
no particular reason why attention should be restricted to locations that are
separated by a political boundary.

From an empirical standpoint, the operational question is the relative variability in the relevant trade determinants (endowments, taste, tariff rates, etc.)
across alternative spatial units. No general pattern is likely to emerge. For some
issues, notably commercial policy, the focus on countries is clearly appropriate. In contrast, to understand the effects of spatial spillovers based on human

* The paper has benefited substantially from comments received by Donald Davis, Gregory Hess,
  Eric van Wincoop, and participants at the conference, as well as by comments on earlier related
  work by Russ Hillberry, Shang-Jin Wei, and John Helliwell.
† Georgetown University and NBER. Mailing address: ICC 5-58, Georgetown University, Washington, DC 20057. e-mail: *wolfh@gunet.georgetown.edu*.

contact and information sharing, cities or even blocks within cities are perhaps the most intuitive focus of study. Yet other issues, such as specialization based on skilled "immobile" labor may best be studied on the regional level.

The empirical merits of trade theories based on endowment differences likewise might best be examined on the subnational level (Ohlin 1933): differences in relative endowments between north and south Italy, or between southwest and northeast Germany may well be significantly larger than differences between Italy as a whole and Germany as a whole. Indeed, it is likely that the variation across areas typically decreases in the size of areas.[1]

The choice of an appropriate spatial unit for empirical trade studies is thus not a trivial issue, and it is unlikely that the same level of aggregation is ideal for all questions. The increasing attention paid to intranational exchange provides one promising avenue for a better understanding of trade patterns. Looking forward, the ongoing merger of regional economics and international trade into the "new economic geography" combining the insights of (primarily intranational) location theories and of (primarily international) trade theories promises an integrated theory of the location of production and usage (and, thus, of trade) across various spatial aggregations, replacing the increasingly unproductive split between "open" and "closed" economics.

The present essay focuses on a fundamental question raised by this merger: once relative spatial location is formally accounted for, does the portioning of geographic space into political space by borders still have relevance? Put differently, is knowledge of economic fundamentals (location, endowments, transportation networks, scale economies, etc.) about some set of locations sufficient to explain their trade patterns, or does, conditional on knowing these fundamentals, the information that some of these locations are separated by political borders allow for a better explanation of their trade patterns?

The same question has been asked before for a number of different transactions. In general, the answer has been resoundingly affirmative. Individuals hold (as yet) inexplicably large portions of their financial wealth in assets of their country of residence, bank lending is heavily concentrated on domestic borrowers, investments within a country are primarily undertaken by residents and financed through domestic financial institutions, intranational travel and communication far exceeds international travel and communication (even controlling for distance), prices differ more across borders than within borders (Engels and Rogers 1996), etc. A recently active literature asks the same question for trade: do countries, ceteris paribus, trade more with themselves than

---

[1] Increasing integration further muddies the waters. As commercial policies and monetary standards are increasingly shared among country groups (with the EU perhaps the clearest example), some standard trade questions related to commercial policy or monetary factors, such as the impact of trade policies or the effect of exchange rate uncertainty on trade, are perhaps better asked on the supranational level.

with other countries, that is, does there exist significant *home bias* in trade, or alternatively, significant *border effects*?

6.2   Methodology

Such border effects are by their nature only defined residually vis-à-vis a baseline model of "normal" trade. This creates a substantial hurdle for empirical work because, despite substantial progress, a consensus model of trade determination, far less an agreed upon empirical baseline specification, remains elusive. The home-bias literature by and large has avoided selecting one or the other of the competing model classes, instead opting for the theoretically less appealing but empirically powerful "gravity specification." The latter, dating back to the late nineteenth century, asserts that interactions between two locations decrease in the distance ("friction") between the location and increase in their mass (market size) (Ravenstein 1885, 1889; Hoover 1948; Stewart 1948; Zipf 1949; Cavanaugh 1950; Dodd 1950; Isard and Peck 1954; Beckerman 1956; Carrothers 1956; Harris 1957; Linneman 1969; Tinbergen 1962; Armington 1969a,b).

The gravity specification provides a useful benchmark (Rauch 1996b) for two reasons. First, almost any model producing specialization (and hence trade) will, with the addition of transportation costs that increase in distance, generate a negative dependence between distance and trade.[2] Furthermore, given specialization, most demand specifications imply that gross trade volumes increase in market size. As a consequence, the gravity specification is consistent with most of the major approaches to trade determination, including Heckscher-Ohlin-Samuelson (HOS), Armington expenditure share, and differentiated product models.[3]

Second, and equally important, the gravity specification boasts a remarkably good fit for trade regressions (and indeed for most spatially distributed activities from migration to travel to telephone calls).[4] In combination, compatibility with a wide range of models and good fit combine to yield an attractive baseline.

The loose term "gravity equation" comprises a number of alternative specifications linking a measure of bilateral trade between two markets to their joint market size and their distance. The most commonly used specification uses a

---

[2] On the role of transportation costs in trade, see Edwards (1970), Geraci and Prewo (1977), and Melvin (1985a,b).

[3] See Anderson (1979), Asilis and Rivera-Batiz (1994), Bergstrand (1985, 1989), Davis and Weinstein (1996), Deardorff (1998), Evenett and Keller (1998), Harrigan (1993, 1994).

[4] A sample of recent applications and surveys includes Bergstrand (1985, 1989), Deardorff (1984), Frankel and Wei (1993), Helpman (1987), Hummels and Levinsohn (1995), Rauch (1996a), Sanso, Cuairan, and Sanz (1993), and Wei (1996) among others. Virtually all studies find strong positive scale and strong negative distance effects.

log-log format[5]:

$$\text{Export}_{ij,t} = Y_i^{b_1} Y_j^{b_2} P_i^{c_1} P_j^{c_2} D_{ij}^{b_3} X_{i,j,t}^{\gamma} e^{u_{ijt}} \tag{1}$$

where $\text{Export}_{ij,t}$ denotes exports from state i to state j, Y denotes per capita GDP (measured commensurately with trade), P denotes population, and D_{ij} is the distance between the two states. X denotes a set of auxiliary variables differing across applications, which is further discussed later. Previous findings suggest that within countries (though not across countries) per capita gross domestic product (GDP) and population enter with equal sign (Helliwell 1998), allowing the use of total GDP.

Full compatibility of the gravity model with theoretical models of trade determination requires the inclusion of controls for the location of states i and j relative to all other states, or "remoteness."[6] Intuitively, the farther two states are located away from other states, the larger will be their volume of bilateral trade for a given bilateral distance. Remoteness for state i for exports from state i to state j is measured as the GDP weighted average distance between state i and all states except j:

$$R_{ij} = \sum_{k=1, k \neq j}^{48} \frac{D_{ik}}{\text{GDP}_k} \tag{2}$$

Remoteness is thus, intuitively, an increasing function of distance and a decreasing function of mass. In the regression, we expect a positive sign for the remoteness variables: for a given bilateral distance, greater distance from other states increases bilateral trade.

Within this framework, testing for border effects is relatively straightforward. If the dataset includes both inter- and intranational trade observations, a dummy defined equal to one for the latter observations picks out any border effect, the antilog of the coefficient measures its economic importance.

6.3   The state of the debate: Home bias exists

The gravity approach to home-bias measurement has been applied to two main datasets. McCallum (1995) uses the approach to examine trade of Canadian provinces with each other relative to their trade with U.S. states, finding, depending on specification, a home bias between 10 and 20. Put differently, according to these results, a Canadian province trades 20 times more with another

---

[5] Gaudry, Blum and McCallum (1996) and Sanso et al. (1993) examine the appropriateness of the log formulation versus linear and mixed alternatives. The optimal functional form is found to be quite close to the log formulation, and parameter differences between the optimal and the log formulation are second order.

[6] See Anderson (1979) and Deardorff (1995).

Canadian province than with a U.S. state that is of equal size and equidistant. In a series of papers, Helliwell (1996a,b, 1997a,b, 1998) and Helliwell and McCallum (1995) have extended this research in a number of directions, confirming a broad home bias of about factor 10.[7]

Moving beyond regressions, Helliwell (1998) provides a set of telling examples on the size of home bias. He notes that, on average, U.S. states have GDPs that are 2.8 times larger than average Canadian provinces (average state–province and province–province distances are quite similar) yet province–province trade flows exceed province–state flows by 3.3 times, yielding a crude estimate of home bias of 2.8 times 3.3 or about 10, the lower end of the regression estimates. As a specific example, he notes that Ontario is equidistant from British Columbia and California. Because California is 12 times larger than British Columbia, one might expect total trade between Ontario and California to be 12 times larger than total trade between Ontario and British Columbia (given the near unity scale elasticities). In fact, trade between Ontario and British Columbia is twice as large as trade between Ontario and California, yielding a rough border effect of more than 20, the upper end of the regression estimates.

Using an imaginative approach to construct intranational trade figures comparable to international statistics based on input–output tables, Wei (1996) examines intra- versus international trade for a group of OECD countries. The OECD dataset has been reexamined and expanded by Helliwell (1997a, 1998) and Nitsch (1997). Estimating the same specification for OECD and the Canadian data yields a comparable, though mostly slightly smaller, home bias for the OECD.

6.4   What are the causes of home bias?

In conjunction, the set of studies leave little doubt about the answer to the question: what are the causes of home bias? *Border effects are a sturdy feature of trade*. The natural next step is to ask what explains the home bias? The answer to this question is of some interest from a policy perspective. By itself, the border effect is solely a statement about trade *volume* and thus has no immediate welfare implications. To assess the latter, the causes of the border effect must be known.

One appealing explanation is provided by national trade barriers of various kinds. These include both deliberate trade policy instruments and barriers that are incidental, deriving from different national systems. The latter group is composed of exchange rate variability, multicurrency transaction costs, different standards and customs, different languages and legal systems, and the nodal structure of national infrastructure. All these factors arguably generate a jump in

---

[7] See also Messinger (1993) and Anderson and Smith (1997).

transaction costs for shipments crossing borders.[8] The jump requires additional compensatory gains from international compared to national trade, creating a nonlinearity in the trade-distance relation picked up by the home-bias dummy.

The trade-barrier explanation has substantial intuitive appeal. However, the *size* of the bias is troubling. Helliwell (1996a) reports intriguing evidence from a sample survey of economists, which reveals his estimate of 20 to be far above consensus estimates (Helliwell 1996). Definitionally, the border effect is the product of the barrier and the elasticity of trade with respect to the barrier. As Harrigan (1993) shows, at least measurable trade barriers for the OECD countries used in the home-bias studies are low. Furthermore, empirical estimates of price elasticities cluster about 0.5 to 1.0 for imports and about 1.25 to 2.5 for exports (Goldstein and Khan 1985), too low to explain border effects for the size of trade barriers found by Harrigan (1993). A full attribution of home-country bias to trade barriers thus requires very significant underestimation of either trade barriers (including indirect barriers) or trade elasticities in the previous literature.[9]

Looking forward, the next natural step in this direction is to examine how the border effect reacts to the inclusion of explicit measures of trade barriers as additional explanatory variables. To the best of my knowledge, there does not at present exist a study that squarely focuses on this issue and attempts to attribute the home bias to alternative trade barriers in a systematic fashion. However, a number of studies allow inferences about the explanatory power of some specific trade barriers for border effects. Wei (1996) examines whether exchange rate variability affect the home bias and finds only very moderate effects. Formal measures of trade restrictions do not seem to have been used to date, although common membership in a trade bloc seems to exert a positive effect on bilateral trade, and Helliwell (1998) finds that for the case of Canada–United States trade, home bias diminished somewhat after the free trade agreement (FTA) came into effect.

Trade barriers based on information asymmetries seem to hold more promise, even though evidence remains fragmentary. Among the results in the literature are positive dummies for common language and a quite robust correlation between international (but not intranational) migration and trade linkages[10] as well as intriguing results suggesting different trade patterns for information intensive goods.[11] These findings are consistent with informal stories suggesting the importance of contact and personal knowledge of customs and language

[8] Consistent with such cultural/linguistic barriers, border effects are also highly pronounced for social interactions, including telephone calls and visits.

[9] It might be the case, however, that *past* trade barriers, in conjunction with hysteresis in location, partially account for home bias (Eichengreen and Irwin 1996; Rauch 1993).

[10] See Egan and Mody (1992), Gould (1994), Head and Ries (1998), Helliwell (1997a).

[11] See Rauch (1996a), Evans (1997), Helliwell (1998), and Estin and Johansson (1994).

Table 6.1. *Average length of buyer–seller relationships (years)*

	Intranational	International	Ratio
United Kingdom	30	7.0	4.3
France	21	6.3	3.3
Sweden	24	14.6	1.6
Germany	15	12.3	1.2

Source: Egan and Mody (1992).

for establishing trade linkages. In turn, these might yield longer buyer–seller relationships within countries as compared to across countries (see Table 6.1).

To the extent that the quality of knowledge about a location increases in the proximity to that location (Gould and White 1974; Gould 1975) and exhibits a border effect, the spatial distribution of information might also have consequences for the spatial distribution of trade. Border effects on information are quite appealing: it would not seem unreasonable to suppose that the typical Canadian manager has more information about conditions in other Canadian provinces (if only because institutions are shared) than about an equidistant U.S. state.

Preferences for "home-country goods" provides a second, independent explanation for border effects: to the extent that consumers prefer products made "at home" to identical products made abroad, one would observe home bias among countries with substantial production overlap.[12] The view is somewhat difficult to test because it requires a definition of "home goods," which, given the increasing internationalization of production stages, is far from trivial. Assuming the classification problems can be resolved, one would expect consumer surveys to indicate such preferences. As far as could be established by a cursory literature search, there is some support for a home bias in preferences for a select group of "signature goods" such as cars and some beverages and foods; however, this preference does not seem to extend to more mundane items such as combs, pins, or shoelaces. Furthermore, even for the signature goods, one might suppose that the "home bias" to a significant extent reflects verifiable product differences.[13]

[12] See Neven, Norman, and Thisse (1991) and Roy and Viaene (1998).
[13] For example, pre-single market German law severely restricted permissible beer ingredients. To the degree that foreign beers contain additional ingredients, it becomes difficult to decide whether the preference of German beer drinkers for beer brewed in Germany reflects a preference for "German" beer regardless of its composition, or merely a preference for beer without additives regardless of the brewing location.

Furthermore, the bias may well go in the opposite direction, with consumer preferences tilted toward specific foreign products even in the absence of verifiable product differences (European bottled table water sold in the United States). Indeed, for developing countries, a general preference for foreign goods – again existing even if observable attributes of products are comparable – has long been discussed and has provided part of the rationale for tariff barriers.

A third explanation combines increasing returns and distance costs – defined broadly to include both transportation costs and other, notably, information related costs of overcoming distance (Ohlin 1933) – to obtain an endogenous home bias reflecting optimal location and production choices. A number of variants of this general idea predict home bias. For example, small taste differentials may cause domestic firms to specialize in variants best suited to domestic taste. More generally, depending on the tradeoff between production costs and transportation costs, production of goods may take place in multiple locations, with local consumers purchasing preferentially from local producers. Recent work by Evans (1997) is intriguing in this regard: reexamining home bias for different products, she finds the border effect to be least pronounced for differentiated goods. Figure 6.1 plots the average shipment distances for intra-U.S. trade by product points in the same direction with substantially longer shipment distances for finished differentiated products compared to intermediate and less differentiated products. The welfare implications of home bias in these cases is obviously more benign compared to home bias arising from governmental trade barriers.

This last explanation differs in an important aspect from its two rivals in being, to a significant degree, scalable. Thus to the extent that tastes differ between New York, Atlanta, and San Francisco, the presence of significant intranational transportation costs will lead to a matching location choice of producers on the subnational level and may thus explain home bias on the subnational as well as on the national level. Likewise, Evans' (1997) explanation could, in principle, hold on the intra- as well as on the international level. In contrast, it is much harder to extend the other two explanations downward.

For example, the U.S. Constitution contains strong protections against barriers to interstate commerce (with the notable exclusion of banking), making it difficult to apply a trade barrier argument to subnational units. In a like vein, exogenously given preferences for goods produced in the home region relative to identical goods produced in other regions (e.g., for Atlanta versus Dallas bottled Coke) appear a bit of a stretch. For one, the regional provenance of products is rarely known. For another, there does not seem to exist (or at least I could not unearth) evidence (for the United States) indicating that consumers systematically preferred products produced in their state of residence to identical products made in other states.

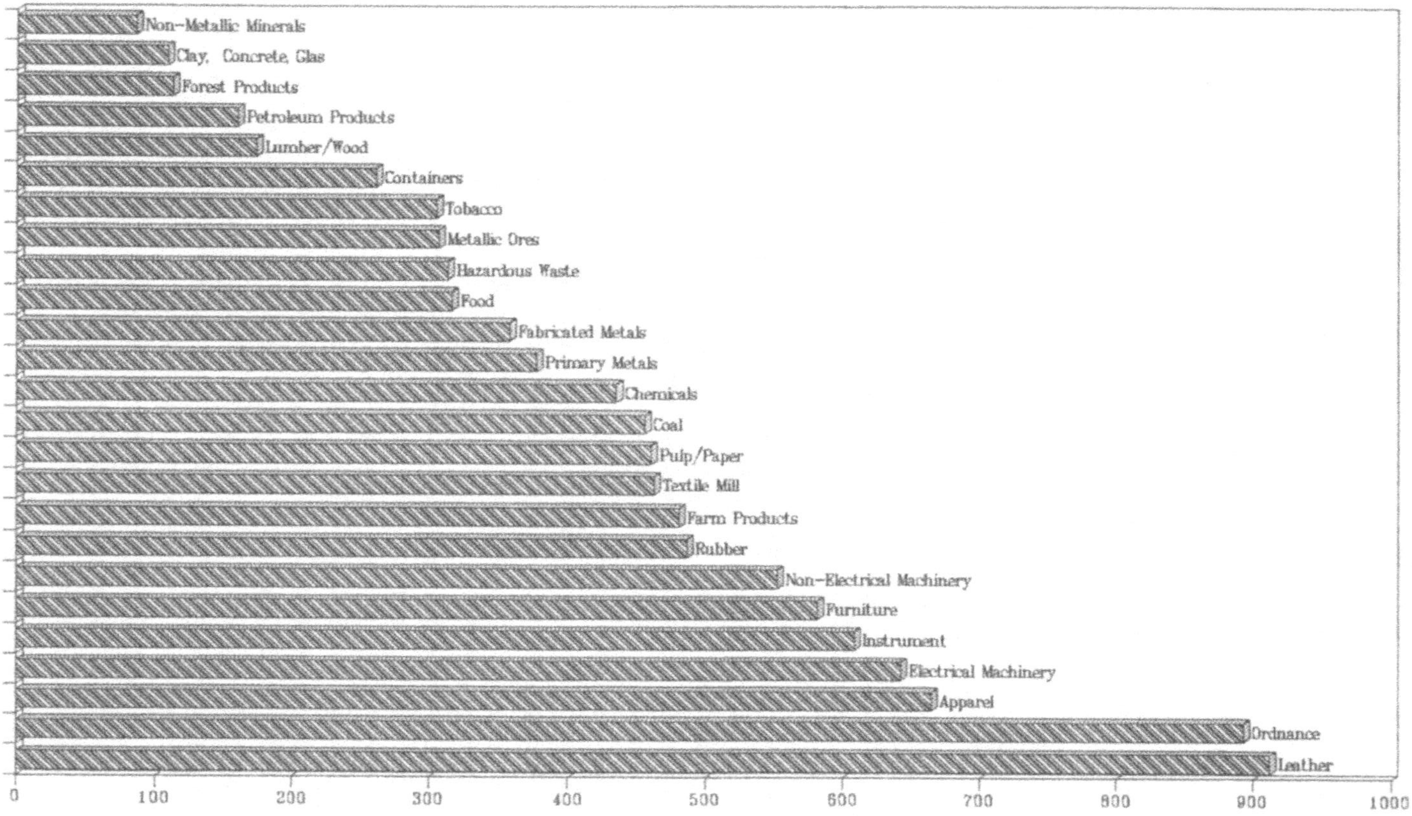

Figure 6.1. Average intra-U.S. shipment distance (miles).

6.5   A test: Does subnational home-bias exist?

The scalability of the endogenous location explanation allows a straightforward test of the sufficiency of the first two explanations: to the extent that trade barriers and preferences for "home goods" relative to identical foreign goods are the main driving cause of the observed border effects, we should not observe such border effects for subnational trade.

Such a test has until recently been difficult to perform due to the lack of data on intraregional versus interregional trade. For the United States, the Commodity Flow Survey (CFS) of 1993 however provides just such data. The establishment-based survey covers 9 transportation modes[14] and more than 20 sectors.[15] The sample excludes shipments from/to foreign sources/destinations, as well as shipments by farms, forestry, fisheries, construction, transportation, oil/gas extraction, government, households, and most services. Surveyed establishments were requested to list origin and destination addresses for four 2-week sample periods spaced over the year, along with value and weight, which were used to construct within state and across-state shipment flows. Trade is measured by the f.o.b. dollar value of shipments between and within states.

The CFS dataset can thus be readily used to replicate the standard modified gravity regressions on the subnational level. To do so, we define a state as adjacent to itself, so that the (NoBorder) dummy (defined as equal to one for intrastate shipments) measures the additional effect of the absence of a border given distance, size, remoteness, and adjacency. Interstate distance is measured as the distance between the largest city in each state. The measurement of intrastate distance remains rather unsettled in the literature, with most previous studies using a fraction (mostly one-fourth) of the smallest bilateral distance for a given state i as an estimate of the intrastate distance for state i. To achieve maximum comparability, we also use this measure. It should be noted, however, that the measure is far from ideal. Thus if central place theory is taken to the limit, and it is assumed that each state consists of a single city that trades with itself and with cities located in other states, the correct intrastate distance is zero. More generally, the higher the share of the largest production cluster in a state relative to state size, the lower the effective intrastate distance, a feature

---

[14] The transportation modes were rail, for-hire truck, private truck, air, inland water, deep-sea water, pipeline, U.S. Postal Service, and courier transportation.

[15] The sectors were mining (except mining services), food and kindred products, tobacco products, textile mill products, apparel, lumber and wood products, furniture, paper and allied products, printing and publishing (except services), chemicals, petroleum refining, rubber and miscellaneous plastics products, leather and leather products, stone, clay, glass and concrete products, primary metals industries, fabricated metals products, industrial and commercial machinery, computer equipment, electronic and other electrical equipment, transportation equipment, instruments, wholesale trade, catalog and mail order houses, motion pictures and video tape distribution, covered under SIC codes 10 (except 108), 12 (except 124), 14 (except 148), 20–26, 27 (except 279), 28–39, 50, 41, 596, and 782.

Table 6.2. *Gravity equation: Baseline results*

Dep. Variable	Export	Export	Export	Export
Technique:	OLS	OLS	OLS	OLS
Observations:	2137	2137	2137	2137
Add. Controls	No	Yes	Yes	Yes
	1	2	3	4
Constant	−0.39	−0.288	−0.241	−0.230
	(5.22)	(4.07)	(3.49)	(3.26)
$\ln(Y^1)$	0.717	0.626	0.689	0.702
	(47.57)	(34.85)	(37.30)	(37.37)
$\ln(Y^2)$	0.681	0.692	0.745	0.758
	(45.24)	(42.99)	(45.30)	(45.23)
$\ln(Distance)$	−1.367	−1.252	−1.440	−1.487
	(59.49)	(47.03)	(45.96)	(47.03)
Remote 1	−0.059	−1.141	−0.930	−0.844
	(0.54)	(7.26)	(6.03)	(5.36)
Remote 2	0.872	0.544	0.705	0.787
	(7.99)	(5.11)	(6.72)	(7.38)
NoBorder	1.173	1.237	1.232	
	(8.76)	(9.43)	(9.63)	
Adjacent		0.317	0.555	0.718
		(4.56)	(7.80)	(10.15)
Distance < 500 m			−0.733	−0.735
			(10.68)	(10.49)
R^2	0.865	0.883	0.889	0.884
Border effect	323%	344%	342%	

not captured by the one-quarter assumption. These problems appear, however, to be of a secondary nature, using half the distance between the largest and the second largest city in the state as the intrastate distance yields very similar results for the border effect.

The basic results are reported in Table 6.2. The top row provides additional information on the regression. "Add. Controls" denotes whether additional controls for joint location on the Pacific, the Atlantic, and the Great Lakes are included. These controls are generally insignificant and, to avoid cluttering the table, are not reported. The first column in Table 6.2 reports the results for the basic gravity model, a regression of the log of export on the logs of the two state GDPs, the log of distance between the two states, the two remoteness measures, and the dummy for intrastate trade. All parameters except home remoteness are highly significant and enter with the expected sign. The R^2 is, as usual in gravity regressions, quite high.[16] The key coefficient on the *NoBorder* dummy is highly positively significant and translates into factor 3.23: trade within a state is three times higher than would be expected based on distance and scale.

The second column adds the adjacency dummy. The interpretation of the home-state bias coefficient thus changes to the additional trade within a state controlling for the fact that such trade is between contiguous areas. The home bias is not affected by this addition, increasing slightly to factor 3.44. The adjacency dummy is positive and significant. The effect is familiar from previous studies looking at trade across national borders, yet it is puzzling in the present context. Even though, in the case of cross-border trade, additional costs associated with shipping via a third country or forced changes of transport modes may lead to higher trade between adjacent countries, the strong constitutional protections of interstate commerce render this explanation implausible for the case of U.S. states. The positive effect of adjacency may instead reflect the lack of "intervening opportunities" (Stouffer 1940). It is arguably reasonable to suspect that trade between Philadelphia and New Haven would be larger if New York City were not located between them. To a degree, the distance variable captures the effect as a greater bilateral distance between two states and is presumably positively correlated with the probability of an intervening opportunity. However, given that most states have at best a few dominating cities, and that states differ dramatically in size, the link between the bilateral distance between two states i and j and the probability of a commercial center being located in a state j between i and j is unlikely to be exact, the significance of the adjacency variable may thus reflect its proxy-function as dummy for the *absence* of an intervening opportunity.[17] The third column adds an additional dummy for distances of less than 500 miles to capture nonlinearities, and the fourth column drops the *NoBorder* dummy. The short distance proxy enters negative and does not affect the home-bias result.

How do these results compare with earlier studies? Although slightly different specifications and differences in dataset construction render an exact comparison of these results difficult, the regression results for this subnational dataset overall look quite similar to results obtained earlier by Helliwell, McCallum, Nitsch and Wei for datasets containing international and intranational trade

---

[16] The size of the R^2 does not merely reflect the presence of unscaled exports on the left-hand side and unscaled GDP on the right-hand side. Replicating the regression with the log of the ratio of exports to the product of state GDPs as the dependent variable also yields an R^2 of more than 0.8.

[17] A second explanation for a subset of observations is the presence of production clusters straddling state borders (e.g., the St. Louis/East St. Louis cluster straddling Missouri and Illinois and the Washington/Baltimore cluster straddling the District of Columbia and Maryland). To the degree that intracluster trade is quite heavy, the adjacency dummy may pick up the effect.

relations. The distance elasticity lies between the elasticities found for the Canadian-U.S. and the OECD dataset, with a range from 1 to 1.6. The scale elasticities are closer to the OECD results (around 0.7) than to the U.S.-Canadian results (around 1). Home bias is below the two alternative datasets (factor 3 rather than factor 10) but remains sizable. This suggests that national trade barriers provide a significant but incomplete explanation for the presence of border effects.

As discussed earlier, one attractive complementary explanation is endogenous location choice of producers, which provides a scalable explanation for border effects. The literature on location choice has identified a complex array of determinants including, among others, the local availability of nonmobile factors, transport costs for inputs and outputs, internal scale economies, and spillovers within and across industries.[18]

For the present purpose, two results from this literature are potentially informative. The first are pressures for production clusters across products, or production stages arising from simple transportation issues (the location of steel mills close to coal fields provides a classic example) or of other benefits of proximity as discussed by Marshall and taken up in the recent literature on economic geography (Krugman 1991a,b, inter alia). To the extent that different production stages are performed in separate corporate entities, one would thus observe a high degree of intracluster trade, which, given the typical location of clusters within states, would be picked up by the *NoBorder* dummy. A number of indirect pieces of evidence point in this direction. First, the weight-weighted average shipment distance for intrastate transactions is very short, ranging between 25 and 75 miles, and is almost uncorrelated with state size. Second, the proportion of all shipments transported over a distance of less than 100 miles has increased quite dramatically over the last three decades, consistent with intracluster trade combined with the trend toward outsourcing over this period. Although it would be unwarranted to view these snippets as strong empirical support for a cluster explanation of intranational home bias, they arguably provide motivation for a more rigorous examination.

Second, location choice of final producers may likewise produce home-state bias. To the extent that production costs, including the cost of obtaining inputs, do not differ significantly across locations, or that production cost differences across locations are dominated by transportation costs for final goods between locations, preference differences across otherwise similar locations will lead producers to specialize in the variety with the highest local demand. In the standard gravity regression, such specialization would, given location of most

---

[18] Weber (1909), Christaller (1966), Marshall (1920), Engländer (1926) and Lösch (1940) are among the classic works. Recent works include David and Rosenbloom (1990), Head, Ries, and Swenson (1995), inter alia.

large demand clusters (cities/counties) in a single state, again be picked up by the *NoBorder* dummy.

6.6 Conclusion

Do borders matter for trade, ceteris paribus? The question, addressed in a number of recent studies, can be answered affirmatively. Controlling for distance, size, adjacency, and common language, information about whether two locations are separated by a political border is useful for assessing their trade.

Looking forward, the next task of the literature will be to move beyond the documentation of home bias to a more rigorous examination of its causes. Extending the standard gravity model by explicit measures of trade barriers would be of obvious interest. To learn more about location choice as a cause of home bias, a sectoral disaggregation of home bias into intermediate and final products promises to shed some indirect light on the relative importance of production clusters (leading to home bias in intermediate goods) versus location close to final demand (leading to home bias in final goods), whereas a disaggregation into "commodities" and "network goods" might shed some light on the informational aspects of home bias (Evans 1997; Rauch 1996a; Helliwell 1998).

Such research will ultimately also allow a better appreciation of the welfare consequences of home bias. If "excessive" home trade reflects nothing more than optimal endogenous location choice reflecting tradeoffs between transportation and production costs (and thus a simple misspecification of the standard gravity model), little welfare consequences arise. If, on the other hand, home bias, at least on the national level, reflects trade barriers of some kind, welfare consequences may well be significant.

References

Andersen, J. 1979. A theoretical foundation for the gravity equation. *American Economic Review* 69: 106–16.

Anderson, M., and S. Smith. 1997. "Canadian Provinces in World Trade." Mimeo. Washington and Lee University, Lexington.

Armington, P. 1969a. A theory of demand for products distinguished by place of production. *IMF Staff Papers* 16(1): 159–78.

Armington, P. 1969b. The geographic pattern of trade and the effect of price changes. *IMF Staff Papers* 16(2): 179–99.

Asilis, C., and L. Rivera-Batiz. 1994. "Geography, Trade Patterns, and Economic Policy." Working paper 94/16. IMF.

Beckerman, W. 1956. Distance and the pattern of intra-European trade. *Review of Economics and Statistics* 38: 31–40.

Bergstrand, J. 1985. The gravity model in international trade. *Review of Economics and Statistics* 67: 474–81.

Bergstrand, J. 1989. Generalized gravity equation, monopolistic competition, and the factor-proportions theory in international trade. *Review of Economics and Statistics* 71: 143–53.

Carrothers, G. 1956. A historical review of the gravity and potential concepts of human interaction. *Journal of the American Institute of Planners* 22: 36–45.

Cavanaugh, J. 1950. Formulation, analysis and testing of the interactance hypothesis. *American Sociological Review* XV: 763–6.

Christaller, W. 1966. *Central Places in Western Germany*, Carlisle Baskin, trans. Englewood Cliffs, NJ: Prentice Hall.

David, P., and J. Rosenbloom. 1990. Marshallian factor externalities and the dynamics of industrial location. *Journal of Urban Economics* 28: 349–70.

Davis, D., and D. Weinstein. 1996. "Does Economic Geography Matter For International Specialization?" Working paper 5706. NBER.

Deardorff, A. 1984. "Testing Trade Theories and Predicting Trade Flows," in R. Jones and P. Kenen, eds., *Handbook of International Economics*, vol. 1, pp. 467–517. Amsterdam: Elsevier.

Deardorff, A. 1998. "Determinants of Bilateral Trade: Does Gravity Work in a Neoclassical World?," in J. Frankel, ed., *Regionalization of the World Economy*. Chicago: University of Chicago Press.

Dodd, S. 1950. The interactance hypothesis. *American Sociological Review* XV: 245–56.

Edwards. S. L. 1970. Transport cost in British industry. *Journal of Transport Economics and Policy* 4: 265–83.

Egan, M. L., and A. Mody. 1992. Buyer-seller links in export development. *World Development* 20: 321–34.

Eichengreen, B., and D. Irwin. 1996. "The Role of History in Bilateral Trade Flows." Working paper 1996. NBER.

Engels, C., and J. Rogers. 1996. How wide is the border? *American Economic Review* 86: 1112–25.

Engländer, O. 1926. Kritisches und Positives zu einer allgemeinen reinen Lehre vom Standort. *Zeitschrift fur Volkswirtschaft und Sozialpolitik* V (7–9).

Estin, L., and B. Johansson. 1994. Affinities and frictions of trade networks. *Annals of Regional Science* 28(3): 243–61.

Evans, C. 1998. "Do National Border Effects Matter?" Mimeo. Harvard University.

Evenett, S., and W. Keller. 1998. "On Theories Explaining the Success of the Gravity Equation." Working paper 6529. NBER.

Frankel, J., and S.-J. Wei. 1993. "Trade Blocs and Currency Blocs." Working paper 4335. NBER.

Gaudry, M., U. Blum, and J. McCallum. 1996. "A First Gross Measure of Unexploited Single Market Potential," in S. Urban, ed., *Europe's Challenges*. Wiesbaden: Gabler.

Geraci, V., and W. Prewo. 1977. Bilateral trade flows and transport costs. *Review of Economics and Statistics* 59: 67–74.

Goldstein, M., and M. Khan. 1985. "Income and Price Effects in Foreign Trade," in *Handbook of International Economics*. Amsterdam: North Holland.

Gould, D. 1994. Immigrant links to the home country. *Review of Economics and Statistics* 76(2): 302–16.

Gould, P. 1975. "People in Information Space," Lund Studies in Geography, Ser. B. No. 72. Lund.

Gould, P., and R. White. 1974. *Mental Maps*. Harmondsworth: Penguin Books.

Harrigan, J. 1993. OECD imports and trade barriers in 1993. *Journal of International Economics* 35: 91–111.

Harrigan, J. 1994. Scale economies and the volume of trade. *Review of Economics and Statistics* 76: 321–8.

Harris, S. 1957. *International and Interregional Economics*. New York: McGraw Hill.

Head, K., and J. Ries. 1998. Immigration and trade creation: Econometric evidence from Canada. *Canadian Journal of Economics* 31: 47–62.

Head, K., J. Ries, and D. Swenson. 1995. Agglomeration benefits and location choice. *Journal of International Economics* 38: 223–47.

Helliwell, J. 1996a. Convergence and migration among Canadian provinces. *Canadian Journal of Economics* 29: S324–30.

Helliwell, J. 1996b. Do national borders matter for Quebec's trade. *Canadian Journal of Economics* 29: 509–22.

Helliwell, J. 1997a. "National Borders, Trade and Migration." Working paper 6027. NBER.

Helliwell, J. 1997b. "Do Borders Matter For Social Capital." Working paper 5863. NBER.

Helliwell, J. 1998. "Comparing Interprovincial and Province-State Trade" (Chapter 2). Mimeo.

Helliwell, J., and J. McCallum. 1995. National borders still matter for trade. *Policy Options* 16: 44–8.

Helpman, E. 1987. Imperfect competition and international trade. *Journal of the Japanese and International Economies* 1: 62–81.

Hoover, E. M. 1948. *The Location of Economic Activity*. New York: Knopf.

Hummels, D., and J. Levinsohn. 1995. Monopolistic competition and international trade. *Quarterly Journal of Economics* 110(3): 799–836.

Isard, W. 1960. *Methods of Regional Analysis: An Introduction to Regional Science*. Cambridge, MA: MIT Press.

Isard, W., and M. Peck. 1954. Location theory and international and interregional trade theory. *Quarterly Journal of Economics* 68: 97–114.

Krugman, P. 1991a. *Geography and Trade*. Cambridge, MA: MIT Press.

Krugman, P. 1991b. Increasing returns and economic geography. *Journal of Political Economy* 99(3): 483–99.

Linneman, H. 1969. "Trade Flows and Geographical Distance, or the Importance of Being Neighbors," in H. C. Bos, ed., *Towards Balanced International Growth*, pp. 111–28. Amsterdam: North Holland.

Lösch, A. 1940. *Die räumliche Ordnung der Wirtschaft*. Jena.

Marshall, A. 1920. *Principles of Economics*, 8th ed. London: Macmillan.

McCallum, J. 1995. National borders matter: Canada-US regional trade patterns. *American Economic Review*; 85: 615–23.

Melvin, J. 1985a. The regional economic consequences of tariffs and domestic transport costs. *Canadian Journal of Economics*; 18: 237–57.

Melvin, J. 1985b. Domestic taste differences, transportation costs, and international trade. *Journal of International Economics*. 18: 65–82.

Messinger, H. 1993. Interprovincial trade flows of goods and services. *Canadian Economic Observer* 3: 8–14.

Neven, D., G. Norman, and J.-F. Thisse. 1991. Attitudes towards foreign products and international price competition. *Canadian Journal of Economics* 24: 1–11.

Nitsch, V. 1997. "National Borders and International Trade." Mimeo. Bankgesellschaft, Berlin.

Ohlin, B. 1933. *Interregional and International Trade.* Cambridge, MA: Harvard University Press.

Rauch, J. 1993. Does history matter only when it matters little? *Quarterly Journal of Economics* 108: 843–67.

Rauch, J. 1996a. "Networks Versus Markets in International Trade." Working paper 5617. NBER.

Rauch, J. 1996b. "Trade and Search." Working paper 5618. NBER.

Ravenstein, E. G. 1885. The laws of migration. *Journal of the Royal Statistical Society.* 48: 167–235.

Ravenstein, E. G. 1889. The laws of migration. *Journal of the Royal Statistical Society* 52: 241–305.

Roy, S., and J.-M. Viaene. 1998. Preferences, country bias, and international trade. *Review of International Economics* 6 (2): 204–19.

Sanso, M., R. Cuairan, and F. Sanz. 1993. Bilateral trade flows, the gravity equation, and functional form. *Review of Economics and Statistics* 75: 266–75.

Stewart, J. 1948. Demographic gravitation. *Sociometry* 11.

Stouffer, S. 1940. Intervening opportunities: A theory relating mobility to distances. *American Sociological Review* V: 845–67.

Tinbergen, J. 1962. *Shaping the World Economy.* New York: Twentieth Century Fund.

Weber, A. 1909. *Uber den Standort der Industrie.* Tübingen.

Wei, S.-J. 1996. "Intra-National Versus International Trade." Working paper 5531. NBER.

Zipf, G. 1949. *Human Behavior and the Principle of Least Effort.* Reading, MA: Addison-Wesley.

PART II

Business cycles and growth

CHAPTER 7

Income dynamics in regions and countries[*]

Paul Evans[†]

7.1   Introduction

My purpose in this chapter is to investigate the dynamics of per capita income
in the regions of a given country and, to a lesser extent, in the countries of the
world. A key question that I seek to answer is whether the per capita incomes
of the regions or countries tend to converge toward parallel balanced growth
paths. If an affirmative answer appears to be reasonable, I shall then seek to
estimate how rapidly this convergence takes place, how far apart the balanced
growth paths are, and what variables determine how high the balanced growth
paths are.

The plan of this chapter is as follows. Section 7.2 discusses the implications
of growth theory and the answers that the recent empirical growth literature
has provided to these questions. It also explains why these answers cannot
be given much credence. Section 7.3 argues that the income dynamics of the
regions of a country may be qualitatively different from those for the countries
of the world. In particular, per capita incomes could converge toward parallel
balanced growth paths for the former while diverging for the latter. Furthermore,
to the extent that labor mobility is quantitatively important across a collection
of regions within some country, convergence is likely to be much more rapid for
them than for countries of the world among which labor mobility is negligible.
Section 7.4 presents empirical results for the 48 contiguous U.S. states. It is
hoped that these results can indicate what one might expect to observe for
countries at some future date when factors are as mobile across countries as
they are now across the states. Section 7.5 compares these empirical findings
with some obtained for a sample of countries. Finally, Section 7.6 offers a few
conclusions.

[*] I thank Kei-Mu Yi, Gregory Hess, and Eric van Wincoop for helpful comments.
[†] Mailing address: Department of Economics, Ohio State University, Columbus, OH 43210;
E-mail: *evans21@osu.edu.*

131

Table 7.1. *Real per capita GDP for country groups in 1990 Geary-Khamis dollar*

Country group	1820	1870	1913	1950	1973	1992
Western Europe	1292	2110	3704	5123	12288	17384
Western Offshoots	1205	2440	5237	9255	16075	20850
Southern Europe	806	1111	1753	2025	6029	8273
Eastern Europe	750	1030	1557	2604	5742	4608
Latin America	715	800	1515	2614	4750	5294
Asia	550	580	742	727	1680	3239
Africa	450	480	575	792	1274	1318

Source: Table E-3 of Maddison (1995).

7.2   Review of the literature

Robert Solow (1956), David Cass (1965), and Tjalling Koopmans (1965) inter alios formulated neoclassical growth theories in which production functions are characterized by diminishing returns to labor and reproducible factors separately and constant returns to them jointly. As a result, their models predict that per capita income can grow in the long run only if exogenous technological improvement keeps the efficiency of labor growing. On the assumption that the efficiency of labor grows at a constant rate, per capita income converges to a unique balanced growth path in their models. In other words, if per capita income is below (above) its level on the balanced growth path, it grows more (less) rapidly than along the balanced growth path. Their models also predict that the height of the balanced growth path toward which per capita income converges is higher, the thriftier and less fertile are the inhabitants of the economy and the more productively they use their resources.

Applying this model to national economies is straightforward on the assumption that factors do not move across national frontiers and countries are identical except for their initial conditions. Given these strong assumptions, neoclassical growth theories predict that countries with high per capita incomes grow more slowly than countries with low per capita incomes. These predictions, however, are grossly inconsistent with the historical experience since 1820. According to Angus Maddison (1995, p. 22), the world's richest country in 1820 had three times the per capita income of the poorest country for which data are available. That ratio rose to 7 in 1870, 11 in 1913, 35 in 1950, 40 in 1973, and 72 in 1992. Table 7.1. reports his estimates of per capita income for seven country groups over the period 1820–1992, and Table 7.2. reports growth rates calculated from them. Before 1950, richer groups tended also to grow more rapidly. Only since 1950 has any tendency for rich countries to grow more slowly than poor countries been evident. Even that tendency is confined mostly to western and

Table 7.2. *Growth rates of real per capita GDP for country groups in percent per year*

Country Group	1820–1870	1870–1913	1913–1950	1950–1973	1973–1992
Western Europe	0.98	1.31	0.88	3.80	1.83
Western Offshoots	1.41	1.78	1.54	2.40	1.37
Southern Europe	0.64	1.06	0.39	4.74	1.67
Eastern Europe	0.79	0.97	1.38	3.44	−1.16
Latin America	0.22	1.49	1.47	2.60	0.57
Asia	0.11	0.57	−0.05	3.64	3.46
Africa	0.13	0.42	0.87	2.07	0.18

Source: Derived from data in Table 7.1.

southern Europe and Asia; Latin America and especially Africa have continued to lose ground in relative terms. For large samples of countries over the period since 1960, the correlation between growth rates and initial levels of per capita income is positive (see Barro 1997).

Maddison (p. 20) estimates that world per capita income grew 1.21% a year between 1820 and 1992. Growth that rapid is unprecedented in world history and prehistory (see Landes 1998). Indeed, growth in the previous 10,000 years could not have been even as high as 0.04% a year, Maddison's estimate for 1500–1820. The reason is that world per capita income would have had to start at only $10 a year in order to have grown to Maddison's estimate of $565 a year in 1500. Neoclassical growth theory has nothing useful to say about this enormous increase in the growth rate. Nor does it appear to explain why growth rates since 1820 have differed across groups of countries for long periods.

To overcome these shortcomings of neoclassical growth theory, Paul Romer (1986, 1990), Robert Lucas (1988), and Philippe Aghion and Peter Howitt (1992) inter alios formulated growth theories that endogenize the steady-state growth rate. Their models essentially replace the assumption of constant returns to all factors and diminishing returns to reproducible factors with the assumption of increasing returns to all factors and constant returns to reproducible factors. These theories, however, also proved to have counterfactual implications. In particular, they imply that growth rates should be highly persistent, rising or falling with investment rates, shares of employment in research and development, and the size and schooling of the population inter alia. In fact, growth rates of individual countries evidence little persistence notwithstanding the great persistence in their presumed determinants (see Easterly, Kremer, Pritchett, and Summers 1993; Jones 1995; Evans 1997a). As a result, a consensus has been emerging that theories of endogenous growth are useful primarily for understanding why the world as a whole and countries at the technological frontier can grow in the long run[1] (see Barro 1997, pp. ix–xii, 1–8). Properly used, neoclassical growth theory can then explain cross-country differences in per capita income. Using it properly, however, entails recognizing that technology only gradually diffuses across countries and that countries do differ in more than merely initial conditions. See Landes (1998) for a rich account of the many ways in which countries differ.

A large literature has used cross-country data in order to investigate the determinants of how high a given country's balanced growth path is and how rapidly it approaches this path. [Barro (1997) provides a useful review of this literature.] The basic econometric framework in this literature is the partial-adjustment model

$$Dy_c = \gamma + \eta\left(y_c^* - y_c^0\right), \qquad 0 < \eta < 1 \tag{1}$$

where Dy_c is the average growth rate of per capita income over some extended period of time for country c, y_c^* is the steady-state value of the logarithm of per capita income for country c at the beginning of the period, y_c^0 is its actual value, γ is the mean growth rate of the steady-state value of per capita income for the world as a whole and for each country, and η is the rate at which adjustment occurs. On the assumption that y_c^* is linearly related to a vector x_c of variables and an error term, Equation (1) then implies that

$$Dy_c = \alpha + \beta' x_c - \eta y_c^0 + \xi_c \tag{2}$$

where α is a parameter, β is a vector of parameters, and ξ_c is an error term that is supposed to have a zero mean and a constant variance and to be uncorrelated across countries. The parameter η measures the rate at which each country converges toward its balanced growth path, accounting not only for the accumulation of reproducible factors but also for the diffusion of technology across countries. Each entry of the parameter vector β equals the product of η and the effect of the corresponding entry of x_c on the height of country c's balanced growth path. Therefore, from knowledge of β and η, one can calculate the effect of x_c on the height of the balanced growth path and hence its unconditional effect on the logarithm of per capita income. Furthermore, one can calculate its predicted effect on the average growth rate Dy_c, conditional on a fixed initial value for per capita income. Unconditionally, however, x_c does not affect country c's growth rate, whose steady-state value γ is exogenous.

This literature reports highly significantly positive estimates of η, which imply convergence toward the balanced growth paths for per capita income of

---

[1] Narayana R. Kocherlakota and Kei-Mu Yi (1997) report evidence of endogenous growth for the United States and the United Kingdom. One interpretation of their finding is that during at least part of each country's sample period, it was the technological leader.

2 or 3% a year.[2] Furthermore, these balanced growth paths are estimated to be significantly higher, the more favorable the country's investment climate is, the more educated its population is, and the lower its fertility rate is. As a result, if Equation (2) were correctly specified, neoclassical growth theory would receive strong support as a theory of cross-country differences in per capita income.

Unfortunately, Equation (2) is likely to be misspecified in empirically important ways. Simultaneity is probably its worst problem. If $\eta > 0$, Equation (2) explains the unconditional level of y_c along its balanced growth path as well as the conditional growth rate over the period during which Dy_c is measured. As a result, the same simultaneity problem arises from fitting Equation (2) as would arise from regressing y_c^0 directly on x_c; namely, both are biased if per capita income affects any of the variables in x_c. It would be astonishing, however, if countries with exogenously higher balanced growth paths did not also choose to educate their populations more, to have fewer children per (more educated, higher-wage) female, and perhaps to have a more favorable climate for investment as well. Furthermore, lagging the variables in x_c is unlikely to help because doing so need not attenuate cross-sectional correlation. For example, educational attainments in 1960, 1975, and 1990 are all likely to be well correlated with the exogenous component of the height of the balanced growth path for per capita income between 1960 and 1990. Finally, finding instrumental variables that are well correlated with the variables in x_c but are not themselves affected by per capita income is a daunting task. Simply lagging the determinants, as is often done in the literature, serves no useful purpose.

A second problem arises because countries with exogenously higher balanced growth paths tend also to have higher initial per capita incomes. As a result, y_c^0 is positively correlated with the error term ξ_c even if x_c is not, biasing the estimates of η and β toward zero. For example, I (Evans 1997b) show that even if x_c can account for 90% of the variance in the heights of the balanced growth paths for y_c, the probability limit of the estimator of η is about $\frac{1}{2}\eta$.

A third problem results from the enormous heterogeneity of countries. This heterogeneity makes the assumption that the parameters of Equation (2) are identical across countries simply incredible. In estimating static cross-sectional regressions like those estimated in Section 7.4, it might be reasonable to make this assumption. The reason is that ordinary least squares consistently estimate a weighted average of these parameters under the standard orthogonality restriction on x_t. By contrast, in estimating dynamics, incorrectly assuming identical parameters can result in serious biases and should probably be avoided at all cost (see Im, Pesaran, and Shin 1995).

---

[2] Barro reports that the convergence rate can be a high as 6% a year for countries with highly educated populations.

An alternative to the cross-sectional approach considered earlier emphasizes the time-series implications of the stock-adjustment model (1). Suppose that only cross-sectional data are available on x_c, the vector of variables useful in explaining the height of country c's balanced growth path for per capita income. In that case, model (1) implies that

$$\Delta y_{ct} = d_c - \eta_c(y_{c,t-1} - \tau_{t-1}) + \zeta_{ct} \tag{3}$$

where y_{ct} is the logarithm of per capita income for country c in period t; d_c is a parameter that incorporates the country-specific component of y_{ct}^*, including that explained by x_c; τ_t is the time-specific component of y_{ct}^* (i.e., the common trend of the y^*s); and ζ_{ct} is a stationary error term with a zero mean and finite variance. I give c subscripts to the parameters d_c and η_c in order to allow for cross-country heterogeneity. This unobservable common trend τ_t can be eliminated from Equation (3) by averaging Equation (3) across the countries and subtracting each member of the resulting equation from the corresponding member of Equation (3). The result is

$$\Delta(y_{ct} - \bar{y}_t) = (d_c - \bar{d}) - \eta_c(y_{c,t-1} - \bar{y}_{t-1}) + (\zeta_{ct} - \bar{\zeta}_t) \tag{4}$$

where $\bar{y}_t$, $\bar{d}$, and $\bar{\zeta}_t$ are the cross-country means of y_{ct}, d_c, and ζ_{ct}. Because $\zeta_{ct} - \bar{\zeta}_t$ may be serially correlated, one would implement Equation (4) empirically in the form

$$\Delta(y_{ct} - \bar{y}_t) = \delta_c + \rho_c(y_{c,t-1} - \bar{y}_{t-1}) + \sum_{i=1}^{p} \phi_{ci} \Delta(y_{c,t-1} - \bar{y}_{t-1}) + u_{ct} \tag{5}$$

where ρ_c is a parameter that is zero or negative depending on whether η_c is zero or positive, δ_c is a parameter with the same sign as $d_c - \bar{d}$, $\phi_{c1}, \phi_{c2}, \ldots, \phi_{cp}$ are parameters arising from the serial correlation of $\zeta_{ct} - \bar{\zeta}_t$, and u_{ct} is a serially uncorrelated error term with a zero mean and finite variance. Estimating Equation (5), which takes the form of an augmented Dickey-Fuller regression, then enables one to infer whether the per capita incomes of the countries in the sample converge toward balanced growth paths. Given convergence, one can also estimate how high each country's balanced growth path is and how rapidly convergence toward it occurs.

Andrew Bernard and Steven Durlauf (1995) applied a variant of this approach to data for individual countries, finding little evidence of convergence. Unfortunately, time-series tests based on one or a few countries for sample periods of even 100 years have little power to reject the null hypothesis of no convergence. Substantial power can be obtained if data for a large number C of countries are pooled and the restrictions $\rho_1 = \rho_2 = \cdots = \rho_c \equiv \rho$; $\phi_{11} = \phi_{21} = \cdots = \phi_{c1}, \phi_{12} = \phi_{22} = \cdots = \phi_{c2}, \ldots; \phi_{1p} = \phi_{2p} = \cdots = \phi_{Cp}$

are imposed. Doing so, Nazrul Islam (1995) rejected the null hypothesis that $\rho = 0$ at very small levels and estimates that the convergence rate is nearly 10% a year. Bernard and Jones (1996a,c) also rejected the null hypothesis for the labor and total factor productivities in a panel of 14 OECD countries.

Unfortunately, these restrictions can be easily rejected, and imposing them strongly affects the results (see Lee, Pesaran, and Smith 1998). Following Levine and Lin (1993), Georgios Karras and I (1996a) used a procedure that imposes only the restriction $\rho_1 = \rho_2 = \cdots = \rho_c$, also obtaining a strong rejection of $\rho = 0$. Although this restriction is valid under the null hypothesis that all the ρs are zero, the Monte-Carlo simulations of Maddala and Wu (1997) suggest that appreciable size distortions can result from using this procedure. Finally, application of the procedure of Im et al. (1995), which does not impose any of these restrictions, yields little evidence that the ρs differ from zero (see Lee et al. 1998 and the survey in Maddala and Wu 1997).

The cross-sectional approach has been widely used to test whether the per capita incomes of regions converge toward their balanced growth paths and, if so, to estimate how rapidly the convergence takes place.[3] Some examples are Barro and Sala-i-Martin (1991, 1992a,b, 1995, Ch. 11) for regions of the United States, Europe, and Japan; Neven and Gouyette (1995) and Filip and Van Rompuy (1995) for regions of Europe; Carayannis and Mallick (1996) for regions of Canada; and Hofer and Worgotter (1996) for regions of Austria. This literature typically finds slow convergence not materially faster than that found for countries. This finding is suspect for two reasons, however. First, the estimates may to be severely biased for the reasons discussed earlier. Second, because the theories that motivate the empirical work assume no labor mobility, the estimates may be difficult to interpret if labor is in fact highly mobile across the regions. Although the assumption of no labor mobility may be reasonable for countries, it is clearly inappropriate for the regions within many countries. The next section works out the implications of interregional labor mobility in some simple theoretical models.

7.3   Theoretical implications of labor mobility

Typically, the growth literature assumes closed economies. Although that assumption might be defensible for countries, it is implausible for the regions within a country, especially one like the United States in which many factors are highly mobile and the barriers to trade in goods and transportation costs are low.

---

[3] These questions have also been addressed using panel methods (e.g., Bernard and Jones 1996b; Evans and Karras 1996b). They report strong evidence in favor of convergence. Unfortunately, these findings may be unreliable because parameter homogeneity is imposed.

The purpose of this section is to analyze growth within the regions of a country characterized by a high degree of factor mobility. To that end, I assume that labor and perhaps some other factors are costlessly mobile within a country consisting of S regions. Some or all of the goods produced in these regions may also be costlessly tradable interregionally. Of course, not all factors and goods can be costlessly mobile because regions would then cease to be well defined economically. I further assume that there are more immobile factors than mobile factors and goods in each region. This assumption prevents trade in factors and goods from equalizing the prices of the immobile factors across the regions.

I assume that the value Q_{st} of the output produced in region s during period t is related to the labor input N_{st} and the vector X_{st} of the other mobile inputs as follows:[4]

$$Q_{st} = F(N_{st}, X_{st}; \theta_{st}) \tag{6}$$

where θ_{st} is a vector of region- and time-specific parameters. Differences in the parameters in (6) reflect differences in inputs of immobile factors across regions and over time as well as differences in product mix and the effects of changes in relative product prices. The function $F(\bullet)$ is assumed not only to be increasing in the mobile factor inputs but also to be strictly concave. If it were convex instead, locating all the mobile factors in a single region would generally be optimal because marginal products would then be nondecreasing in scale, and one region would have higher productivity than the rest.[5] Because complete regional specialization is not observed, however, strict concavity must therefore set in at some scale well short of the entire country's supply of mobile factors.[6] For simplicity, I assume strict concavity at every scale. Without loss of generality, I can further assume that, in equilibrium, the labor input in every region is positive.

Labor receives the same remuneration in every region by assumption. If labor is also paid its marginal product, Equation (6) implies that

$$q_{st} \equiv Q_{st}/N_{st} = w_t/\alpha_{st} \tag{7}$$

where w_t is the wage rate and α_{st} is the elasticity of the value of output with respect to the labor input in region s during period t. The elasticity α_{st} should be expected to vary across regions because of differences in product mix and over time because of changes in either relative prices or shifts in technologies. Equation (7) therefore implies that labor productivity is likely to vary across

---

[4] Of course, the vector X_{st} may include physical capital.

[5] Of course, costs of transport for either factors or goods can sustain nonspecialization in the presence of a moderate degree of convexity. (See Krugman 1991 for an example.)

[6] Here I am defining *region* broadly enough for the statement to hold. Agglomeration economies are well known to be important in explaining the existence and size of cities.

regions, even though labor is paid at the same rate everywhere, and to vary over time as well.[7]

Let y_{st} be the logarithm of productivity and $\bar{y}_t$ be the cross-regional mean of the y_{st}s. On the assumption that the elasticities $\alpha_{1t}, \alpha_{2t}, \ldots, \alpha_{St}$ are covariance stationary, the preceding analysis indicates that $y_{1t} - \bar{y}_t, y_{2t} - \bar{y}_t, \ldots, y_{St} - \bar{y}_t$ should also be covariance stationary with nonzero means and positive finite variances.[8] Furthermore, the cross-regional variance of the logarithm of labor productivity, defined by

$$V_t = \frac{1}{S} \sum_{s=1}^{S} (y_{st} - \bar{y}_t)^2 \qquad (8)$$

should fluctuate around a positive mean with a positive finite variance.

Thus far, I have assumed that labor is costlessly and immediately mobile. As a result, labor always receives the same remuneration in every region. Suppose instead that labor moves in response to differences in remuneration but that the response is distributed over time. Rather than modeling the movement of labor as the rational investment activity of households subject to moving costs, I merely posit an ad hoc adjustment equation. Specifically, the labor input in each region adjusts according to[9]

$$\Delta \ln N_{st} = \Delta \ln N_t + v[\ln N_{st}^* - (\ln N_{s,t-1} + \Delta \ln N_t)], \qquad 0 \leq v \leq 1 \qquad (9)$$

where $N_{1t}^*, N_{2t}^*, \ldots, N_{St}^*$ are the efficiency units of labor that would be employed in regions $1, 2, \ldots, S$, were labor instantaneously mobile and N_t is the aggregate labor input. The story underlying Equation (9) is that $N_{st}^\circ \equiv N_{s,t-1} \exp(\Delta \ln N_t)$ workers find themselves in region s at the beginning of t when wage rates are realized. (The growth rate of each region's labor input is assumed to be $\Delta \ln N_t$ in the absence of migration.) N_{st}^* workers would choose to supply labor in region s, were moving costless. The fixed cost of moving differs across workers, leading some workers to move and others to stay. The distribution of costs each

---

[7] These implications are similar to those of Jennifer Roback (1982) in a similar model.

[8] Ventura (1997) has formulated a growth model in which factor prices are equalized across regions. His model implies that their labor productivities can appear to be converging even though growth in each region is endogenous. This result stems in large part from the fact that elasticities $\alpha_1, \alpha_2, \ldots, \alpha_S$ in the model fall toward zero over time if the growth rates of the regions are bounded above zero. As a result, each region's share of wage income in the value of output also approaches zero. Because the wage share has not shown any tendency to vanish in recorded history, this model is not a promising one for interpreting data.

[9] An alternative formulation posits that $\Delta \ln(N_{st}/N_t)$ is proportional to the gap between the logarithm of the wage rate region s during period t and the mean for all regions in the country. Olivier Blanchard and Lawrence Katz (1992) have shown that the implications of this formulation are similar to the one here. I adopt Equation (9) because it is more tractable and less ad hoc than theirs.

period is assumed to be such that it is always optimal to eliminate a fraction v of the gap between $\ln N_{st}^*$ and $\ln N_{st}^\circ$. Consequently, the larger the parameter v is, the more rapidly labor migrates in response to regional shocks. So long as $v > 0$, however, labor is completely mobile in the long run in the sense that the mean of $\ln N_{st} - \ln N_{st}^*$ is zero.

For simplicity, I assume that labor is the only mobile factor and that the elasticity of output with respect to the labor input does not vary across regions or over time. Therefore, the relationship (6) takes the Cobb-Douglas form

$$Q_{st} = N_{st}^\alpha \exp(b_t + a_{st}), \qquad 0 < \alpha < 1 \tag{10}$$

where α is the common value of the elasticity of output with respect to the labor input. The quantity $b_t + a_{st}$ is the total factor productivity of region s during period t. It is decomposed into two terms, the first of which is b_t, the cross-regional mean. By definition, then, $\sum_{s=1}^{S} a_{st} = 0$ every period. The second term a_{st} incorporates at least three effects: the idiosyncratic changes in the supplies of the immobile factors in region s; the idiosyncratic changes in the efficiency of those factors induced by technological change; and the idiosyncratic effects of changes in relative prices, given that regions have different product mixes. I assume that a_{st} is difference stationary at worst.

On the assumption that labor is paid its marginal product,

$$\alpha N_{st}^{\alpha-1} \exp(b_t + a_{st}) = \alpha N_{1t}^{\alpha-1} \exp(b_1 + a_{1t})$$

so that

$$\ln(N_{st}^*/N_{1t}^*) = (a_{st} - a_{1t})/(1 - \alpha) \tag{11}$$

Hence,

$$\ln(N_{st}^*/N_t) = \frac{a_{st}}{1 - \alpha} - \ln \sum_{j=1}^{S} \exp\left(\frac{a_{jt}}{1 - \alpha}\right) \tag{12}$$

since $\sum_{j=1}^{S} N_{jt}^* = N_t$. Substituting Equation (12) into Equation (9) and rearranging produces

$$\ln(N_{st}/N_t) = (1 - v)\ln(N_{s,t-1}/N_{t-1}) + \frac{v a_{st}}{1 - \alpha} - v \ln \sum_{j=1}^{S} \exp\left(\frac{a_{jt}}{1 - \alpha}\right) \tag{13}$$

It then follows from Equations (13) and (10) that

$$y_{st} - \bar{y}_t = (1 - v)(y_{s,t-1} - \bar{y}_{t-1}) + (1 - v)\Delta a_{st} \tag{14}$$

In the complete absence of mobility ($v = 0$), Equation (14) implies that $y_{st} - \bar{y}_t$ moves one-for-one with the idiosyncratic shock to total productivity in region s, exhibiting exactly as much persistence as the shock itself. With some mobility $(0 < v < 1)$, the contemporaneous effect of the idiosyncratic shock is shrunken by the factor $1 - v$, and the persistence of its effect is less than its own. Indeed, even a permanent change in a_{st} affects $y_{st} - \bar{y}_t$ only temporarily. With perfect mobility $(v = 1)$, the idiosyncratic shock ceases to affect $y_{st} - \bar{y}_t$ even temporarily. Finally, so long as labor is perfectly mobile in the long run $(v > 0)$, $y_{st} - \bar{y}_t$ should be mean stationary even if the idiosyncratic shocks to total productivity in region s are difference stationary.

Equation (14) has two other implications worth spelling out. First, the cross-regional variance of the logarithm of output per worker has a constant mean around which it fluctuates. As a result, one should not expect it to drift downward systematically unless the parameters, which are here assumed to be constant, change systematically. Second, the cross-regional variance is lower, the more mobile labor is. For example, if every region's idiosyncratic shock is a first-order autoregression with the autoregressive parameter π and innovation variance ψ^2, the mean of the cross-regional variance is $\psi^2/(1 - \pi^2)$ when labor is completely immobile, and 0 when labor is perfectly mobile.[10] Downward drift in the cross-regional variance therefore suggests increasing mobility of factors over time.

At least since Heckscher and Ohlin, economists have widely appreciated that trade in goods can be a substitute for trade in factors. Paul Samuelson (1953) formalized this intuition in his famous factor-price equalization theorem. It is reasonable, then, to expect a reduction in barriers to trade or in transportation costs to have effects similar to those of an increase in labor mobility. See Dan Ben-David (1993) for evidence supporting this conjecture.

Ideally, one would like to test these theories using measures of labor productivity. In practice, one must typically use measures of per capita income instead. Using the latter, however, raises two issues: households choose the per capita labor supplied to the market; and they choose where to live. The endogeneity of the per capita labor input creates no problem if its long-run supply is vertical. In that case, it fluctuates around a constant mean along the balanced-growth path since the income and substitution effects exactly cancel each other. By contrast, if its supply is not vertical, it diverges across regions. I follow the literature here in assuming that its long-run supply is vertical even though some fairly convincing evidence exists against the assumption (see Evans and Karras 1997b).

The endogeneity of residence may also create problems. For example, suppose that the supply of inputs can be completely divorced from the choice of where to live. In that case, everyone might live in California but own labor and other factors located elsewhere. Dividing the output produced in a given state by the number of individuals residing there would then produce

---

[10] The zero value is an artifact of the assumption that the α's are identical across regions and constant over time as the first example considered here makes clear.

infinite values for every state except California. This problem can be overcome by putting only the income received by the residents in the numerator. The size of the resulting series, however, then partly reflects the effect of income and wealth on the demand for regional amenities. For example, Florida and Arizona, whose winters are warm, might attract relatively wealthy retirees and high-income workers. In practice, however, individuals often live near where their inputs are supplied. Labor, by its very nature, requires the presence of its owner. For the most part, the same is true of human capital. Physical capital may also tend to be supplied locally because it is typically more productive when managed by its owner than when managed by an employee. The evidence reported by Gur Huberman in Chapter 4 in this volume suggests that even marketed claims to capital are overrepresented in the portfolios of households that live near the underlying capital. Finally, if households are life-cycle savers, their asset incomes should be cointegrated with their wage incomes. As a result, if per capita labor income is stationary, per capita asset income is also stationary (see Evans and Karras 1997a for proof). All in all, then, the points made in this section are likely to apply to per capita income as well as labor productivity.

I conclude this section with a discussion of the implications of the accumulation of immobile reproducible factors. Barro, Mankiw, and Sala-i-Martin (1995) have shown that the analysis of such accumulation is similar to its closed-economy counterpart if the mobile factors experience diminishing returns in every region as is assumed here. In particular, accumulation generates additional dynamics in $y_{st} - \bar{y}_t$. The additional dynamics are more persistent, the more elastic the production functions are with respect to these factors. Clearly, the dynamics are likely to be appreciably less persistent for regions than for countries because the class of immobile reproducible factors is smaller for the former than for the latter. Except for this last result, then, allowing for the accumulation of immobile reproducible factors does not alter any of the conclusions of this section.

7.4   Empirical analysis for the U.S. states

Many goods and factors have long been quite mobile across the U.S. states (see Kim 1997). State data on per capita income should therefore prove useful in exploring the ideas developed in Section 7.2.

In carrying out this exploration, I use annual data on per capita factor income (personal income less transfer payments) spanning the period 1929–96 for each of the contiguous U.S. states.[11] I obtained the underlying data from a CD-ROM

---

[11] In an earlier paper, I also considered per capita personal income, per capita wage income, and per capita asset income. The results were similar in all cases to those reported here.

provided by the Bureau of Economic Analysis (RCN-0128) and from the BEA's web page. I have not bothered to deflate the data because state-specific deflators are unavailable. (Deflating by a common national price index would merely subtract the same value from both y_{st} and $\bar{y}_t$ in $y_{st} - \bar{y}_t$.)

7.4.1 Is there convergence?

I first investigate whether the per capita factor incomes of the contiguous U.S. states converge toward parallel balanced growth paths (i.e., whether $y_{st} - \bar{y}_t$ is mean stationary). For this purpose, I employ the procedure formulated by Im et al. (1995). It entails using ordinary least squares to fit Equation (5) to the data for each state s and then calculating the following test statistic

$$\sqrt{S} \sum_{s=1}^{S} (\hat{\tau}_s - \mu_{DF}) / \sigma_{DF} \tag{15}$$

and comparing it to the critical values from the standard normal distribution. In expression (15), $\hat{\tau}_s$ is the t-ratio for the estimate of ρ_s, and μ_{DF} and σ_{DF} are the mean and standard deviation of the appropriate Dickey-Fuller distribution. A sufficiently negative test statistic leads to rejection of the null hypothesis

$$H_0: (\rho_1 = 0 \wedge \rho_2 = 0 \wedge \cdots \wedge \rho_S = 0)$$

$$\wedge (\delta_1 = 0 \wedge \delta_2 = 0 \wedge \cdots \wedge \delta_S = 0)^{12}$$

in favor of the alternative hypothesis

$$H_1: \rho_1 < 0 \wedge \rho_2 < 0 \wedge \cdots \wedge \rho_S < 0^{13}$$

The reason is that if H_0 is true, the t-ratios are independent of each other and each follows a Dickey-Fuller distribution.

Table 7.3 reports summary statistics on the t-ratios obtained by fitting Equation (5) to the logarithm of per capita factor income. For purposes of comparison, the last column of the table reports analogous statistics for the appropriate

[12] I impose the condition that the δs are all zero for two reasons. First, I think that it is highly implausible that states can have endogenously different trend growth rates. Second, the resulting test is more conservative than one that left the δs unrestricted. This restriction still allows per capita incomes to diverge across regions so long as they only wander apart rather than trend apart.

[13] If any ρ is negative, all must be negative, and if any is zero, all must be zero (see Evans 1998 for proof). In other words, H_1 is equivalent to $\rho_1 < 0 \vee \rho_2 < 0 \cdots \vee \rho_S < 0$. Truth of H_0, however, does not rule out the possibility that some proper subsets of the regions have per capita incomes whose pairwise logarithmic differences are stationary. To formulate a test for the presence of such subsets when no evidence for H_1 can be found is a difficult statistical problem, well beyond the scope of this paper. Fortunately, the issue is moot because H_0 can be readily rejected with the data analyzed here.

Table 7.3. *Summary statistics on the t-ratios for the contiguous U.S. states*

Statistic	Sample	Dickey-Fuller distribution
Mean	−2.250	−1.528
Standard deviation	0.837	0.866
5th percentile	−3.994	−2.911
10th percentile	−3.779	−2.597
25th percentile	−2.878	−2.088
50th percentile	−2.286	−1.554
75th percentile	−1.702	−0.992
90th percentile	−1.275	−0.413
95th percentile	−0.903	−0.042

Notes: A common lag length (p) of 3 years was chosen for each state. Pretesting indicated that this choice is adequate. Estimation was by ordinary least squares over the sample period 1933–96. A Monte Carlo simulation with 1,000,000 iterations estimated the values reported in the last column.

Dickey-Fuller distribution. Clearly, the empirical distribution for the t-ratios is shifted considerably to the left relative to the Dickey-Fuller distribution. This result suggests a pronounced tendency of the logarithm of every series to converge toward a common national trend. Formal confirmation is provided by the test statistic, which is −6.64. The null hypothesis of difference stationarity can therefore be rejected at any reasonable significance level.[14]

7.4.2   How rapid is the convergence?

Given the strong evidence for the convergence of the series toward a common trend, it makes sense to estimate how rapidly the convergence takes place. Estimation of convergence rates is complicated by two considerations, however. First, unless $y_{st} - \bar{y}_t$ is a first-order autoregression (i.e., $p = 0$), y_{st}'s convergence rate depends on the horizon considered. I therefore focus on the asymptotic convergence rate, which prevails at arbitrarily long horizons. It is $1 - \lambda_s$, where λ_s is the dominant root of the polynomial

$$Z^{p+1} - (1 + \rho_s)z^p + (1 - z)\sum_{i=1}^{p} \phi_{si} z^{p-i} \tag{16}$$

---

[14] Carlino and Mills (1993) have presented evidence that the parameters in Equation (5) may have shifted between the interwar and postwar period. Because parameter instability biases unit-root tests against rejection of the null hypothesis, the evidence is thus even more resoundingly against the null hypothesis than the analysis in the text would suggest.

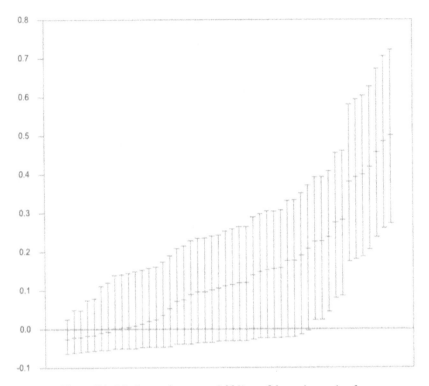

Figure 7.1. Median estimates and 90% confidence intervals of convergence rates for factor income.

In many applications, this measure provides an excellent approximation to the convergence rates prevailing at horizons of more than one or two years because the other dynamics die out quickly. Second, estimating the dominant root λ_s merely by plugging the ordinary least squares estimates of ρ_s and the ϕ_{si}s into (16) and solving for it yields a strongly biased estimate. For example, the median bias is 0.064 for $\lambda_s = 0.97$, $T = 60$, and $p = 0$ (see Andrews 1993, p. 148). One must therefore correct for the bias in some fashion.

Using local-to-unity asymptotic distribution theory, James Stock (1991) formulated a convenient method for doing so and for constructing confidence intervals. Using this method, I calculated unbiased estimates and 90% confidence intervals of the convergence rates for the per capita factor incomes of the contiguous U.S. states. Figure 7.1 plots these convergence rates, which are arranged in ascending order.

The estimated convergence rates average 0.1445 per year with a standard deviation of 0.1472 per year. The confidence intervals are wide, typically including both negative and very large positive values. Drawing strong inferences about the convergence rate of any given state is thus unwarranted. It is nonetheless reasonable to claim that about a quarter of the states have convergence rates of 0.2 or more. Furthermore, the uncertainty about the mean of these convergence rates is considerably less than the uncertainty about each state's convergence rate. The central limit theorem suggests that the confidence interval for the mean of the estimated convergence rates should be about $1/\sqrt{48}$ times as wide as the average of the widths for the 48 individual states. The 90% confidence interval for the mean of the convergence rates is therefore approximately $(0.1248, 0.1660)$.

Using the cross-sectional approach described in Section 7.2, Barro and Sala-i-Martin (1991, 1992b, 1995) estimated convergence rates for the U.S. states of about 2% a year, much smaller than what is reported in the previous paragraph. I obtained similar estimates if I used their approach. For example, fitting Equation (2) to the data and using the same xs as I employ in regression (21) yields

$$D\hat{y}_s = \begin{array}{l} 0.0386 \\ (0.0175) \end{array} - \begin{array}{l} 0.0117 \ y_s^0 \\ (0.0008) \end{array} + \begin{array}{l} 0.000600 \ HEART_s \\ (0.000588) \end{array} - \begin{array}{l} 0.00189 \ MOUNT_s \\ (0.00054) \end{array}$$
$$+ \begin{array}{l} 0.000438 \ COL_s, \\ (0.000090) \end{array} \qquad R^2 = 0.9994, \ SEE = 0.001305 \tag{17}$$

which implies a convergence rate of 2.32% a year.[15] I included the same xs in Equation (17) as I found to be significant in Equation (21).[16] I (Evans 1997b) show that if the parameters of Equation (5) do not vary across states and if $p = 0$, then

$$r = 1 - [1 + 68 \, \text{plim} \, \hat{\eta}/(1 - \omega)]^{1/68} \tag{18}$$

where r is the true convergence rate, 68 is the number of years over which Dy is calculated, $\hat{\eta}$ is the ordinary least squares estimator of η, and $\omega \equiv \text{cov}(y^0, \mu \mid x)/\text{var}(y^0 \mid x)$. A consistent estimate of ω for the data at hand is 0.2018.[17] Plugging this value and the estimate of η in the regression (17) into Equation (18) results in a convergence rate of 8.91% a year. Unfortunately, this estimate of the true convergence rate cannot be statistically distinguished from even 100% a year because plugging 0.2032 into Equation (18) in lieu of 0.2018 would

---

[15] This figure is $1 - (1 - 0.0117 \times 68)^{1/68}$, where 68 is the number of years that the growth rate Dy spans.

[16] HEART is one for states in what I call the *heartland* and zero for the other states; MOUNT is one for mountain states and zero for the other states; and COL is the average fraction of the population 25 years or older with at least four years of college in 1970, 1980, and 1990. The next subsection provides more detail.

[17] Squaring the standard error of estimate of the ordinary least squares regression of y^0 on an intercept, *HEART, MOUNT*, and *COL* produce a consistent estimate of $\text{var}(y^0 \mid x)$. Multiplying the square of the standard error of estimate of Equation (19) by the coefficient on μ in the regression of y^0 on an intercept, *HEART, MOUNT, COL*, and μ produces a consistent estimate of $\text{cov}(y^0, \mu \mid x)$. The arithmetic is $1.251(0.1014/0.2524)^2 = 0.2018$.

result in $r = 1$. (The difference between 0.2032 and 0.2018 is not statistically significant at any conventional significance level.) Therefore, cross-sectional regressions do not rule out even gigantic convergence rates.

7.4.3   What affects convergence rates?

The characteristics of a state may affect its convergence rate. In particular, a state's convergence rate may depend on where it is and how well its population is educated. For example, Jess Benhabib and Mark Spiegel (1994) and Robert Barro (1997) have argued that a more schooled population is more easily able to adopt new technologies from other regions and to transfer physical and human capital from low-return regions to high-return regions.

I therefore regressed the convergence rate on five regional dummy variables (*HEART, SOUTH, PLAIN, MOUNT*, and *PACIF*),[18] the average fractions of the population 25 and older with at least four years of high school (*HS*) and at least four years of college (*COL*) in 1970, 1980, and 1990, and the average number of years of schooling completed by this population (*SCH*) in 1940, 1950, and 1960. After dropping insignificant regressors, I obtained the regression

$$\hat{r}_s = 1.84 - 0.382 \; SOUTH_s - 0.0312 \; HS_s + 0.0314 \; COL_s,$$
$$\phantom{\hat{r}_s = }(0.39) \quad (0.083) \qquad \qquad (0.0064) \qquad (0.0108)$$
$$R^2 = 0.6683, \qquad SEE = 0.1551 \tag{19}$$

where $\hat{r}_s$ is the estimated convergence rate of state s, and the figures in parentheses are heteroskedasticity-consistent standard errors. Not surprisingly, the estimates indicate that Southern states tend to have lower convergence rates than other states. States in which large fractions of the population have four years of high school but not four years of college also tend to have low convergence rates. This result is inconsistent with those reported by Benhabib and Spiegel (1994) and Barro (1997) for samples of countries.

7.4.4   How far apart are state-balanced growth paths?

The relative height of state s's balanced growth path can be measured by the unconditional mean of $y_{st} - \bar{y}_t$. The standard deviation of these means across

---

[18] *HEART* is one for Delaware, Illinois, Indiana, Maryland, Michigan, New Jersey, New York, Ohio, Pennsylvania, and Wisconsin and zero otherwise; *SOUTH* is one for Alabama, Arkansas, Florida, Georgia, Kentucky, Louisiana, Mississippi, North Carolina, Oklahoma, South Carolina, Tennessee, Texas, Virginia, and West Virginia and zero otherwise; *PLAIN* is one for Iowa, Kansas, Minnesota, Missouri, Nebraska, North Dakota, and South Dakota and zero otherwise; *MOUNT* is one for Arizona, Colorado, Idaho, Montana, Nevada, New Mexico, and Utah and zero otherwise; and *PACIF* is one for California, Oregon, and Washington. The excluded states are Connecticut, Maine, Massachusetts, New Hampshire, Rhode Island, and Vermont.

the U.S. states is thus a reasonable measure of how far apart their balanced growth paths are. Equation (5) implies that μ_s, the unconditional mean of $y_{st} - \bar{y}_t$, takes the form

$$\mu_s \equiv -\delta_s/\rho_s \tag{20}$$

It can therefore be estimated by using ordinary least squares to fit Equation (5) to the data for state s and plugging the resulting estimates of δ_s and ρ_s into Equation (20). Carrying out these calculations yields estimated means with a cross-state standard deviation of 0.1580. Thus, the balanced growth paths for factor income are rather far apart.

The μ_ss may depend on the states' characteristics. I therefore regressed the μs on the same variables as I did for the convergence rates. After dropping insignificant regressors, I obtained the following:

$$\hat{\mu}_s = \begin{array}{l} -0.593 + 0.135 \ HEART_s - 0.0811 \ MOUNT_s \\ (0.083) \quad (0.037) \qquad\qquad (0.0417) \\ + \ 0.0381 \ COL_s, \qquad R^2 = 0.6146, \qquad SEE = 0.1014 \\ (0.0055) \end{array} \tag{21}$$

This regression indicates that per capita factor income tends to be higher in the heartland and lower in the mountain states than elsewhere. This finding may reflect the prevalence of manufacturing in the former and extractive industries in the latter. A college-educated population is also associated with higher per capita factor incomes. Each 1% of the population with four years of college adds about 3%. The size of the high-school population and years of schooling do not appear to have a separate effect, however. Interestingly, after adjusting for the size of the college-educated population, the South does not appear to have unusually low values of per capita factor income. Of course, in interpreting this regression, one should realize that the coefficient on COL could just as well reflect causation running from per capita factor income to schooling as the other way.

7.4.5   How does the cross-state variance evolve over time?

Another way of investigating whether the per capita incomes of the contiguous U.S. states converge toward parallel balanced growth paths is to examine how the cross-state variance of y_{st} evolves over time.[19] If $y_{st} - \bar{y}_t$ is covariance

[19] Danny Quah (1996) has used a related approach in which the cross-sectional distribution of per capita income is discretized and the intertemporal transitions between the points of the distribution are modeled as Markovian. This approach permits a richer description of how the cross-sectional distribution evolves over time than can be obtained from examining just the cross-sectional variance. Unfortunately, it presupposes covariance stationary, thereby ruling out the hypothesis testing carried out here.

stationary for every state s,

$$V_t = \frac{1}{S} \sum_{s=1}^{S} (y_{st} - \bar{y}_t)^2 \tag{22}$$

is also covariance stationary. In particular, it fluctuates around a constant positive mean. By contrast, under H_0, V is difference stationary with a positive drift rate (for proof, see Evans 1996). The latter result is most easily seen when $y_{st} - \bar{y}_t$ is a driftless random walk in each region. In that case,

$$V_t = \frac{1}{S} \sum_{s=1}^{S} \sigma_s^2 + V_{t-1} + \frac{1}{S} \sum_{s=1}^{S} \left(u_{st}^2 - \sigma_s^2 \right) \tag{23}$$

where σ_s is the standard deviation of u_{st}. Putting these results together, one can assert that V has the representation[20]

$$\Delta V_t = \kappa + \gamma V_{t-1} + \sum_i \psi_i \Delta V_{t-i} + \varepsilon_t \tag{24}$$

where ε_t is an independently and identically distributed zero-mean error term with a positive finite variance and κ, γ, and the ψs are parameters such that $\kappa > 0$ and $-2 < \gamma \leq 0$. The null hypothesis holds if $\gamma = 0$, and the alternative hypothesis holds if $\gamma < 0$. Note that V cannot fall indefinitely because it must be either stationary around a constant positive mean or nonstationary and upward trending.

Under the null hypothesis, the t-ratio for the least-squares estimator of γ converges in distribution to standard normal since $\kappa > 0$. Furthermore, it diverges to $-\infty$ under the alternative hypothesis. Thus, a sufficiently negative t-ratio permits the null hypothesis to be rejected. For the sample sizes encountered in practice, however, the finite-sample distribution is intermediate between the Dickey-Fuller and standard normal distributions. As the ratio of κ to the standard deviation of ε_t rises from zero to infinity, the finite-sample distribution passes from the former to the latter. For example, the 0.05 critical values of the distribution with $T = 66$ are -2.913, -2.232, -1.882, -1.754, and -1.645 for ratios of 0, .4, 1.0, 2.5, and ∞. Therefore, if this ratio is known, Monte Carlo simulations can be used to obtain appropriate critical values.

Calculating an approximation to the ratio is straightforward. Suppose that u_{st} can be adequately represented as normal with identical variances σ^2 across the regions. In that case, $\kappa = \sigma^2$ and u_{st}^2/σ^2 is distributed as $\chi^2(1)$, which has

---

[20] If the δs differ from zero as they would if the growth rates of states were endogenous, a linear time trend would also appear in Equation (24). Its slope coefficient would be positive under the null hypothesis and zero under the alternative hypothesis. See Evans (1996) for proof.

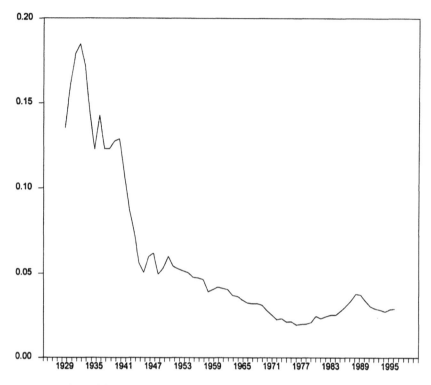

Figure 7.2. Cross-state variance of log per capita factor income (1929–96).

a mean of one and a variance of two. Hence, given independence across the regions, the variance of ε_t is $2\sigma^4/S$, and the ratio in question is $\sqrt{S/2}$.

Figure 7.2 plots the cross-state variance of the logarithm of per capita factor income. Two features of the plot are noteworthy: innovations to the variance appear to dissipate quickly, and the variance has fallen a great deal over the sample period. The first observation suggests strong mean reversion, whereas the latter indicates that factor mobility has increased over time, thereby shifting the data-generating process toward either faster convergence or less regional heterogeneity of immobile factors. If such changes have indeed taken place, assuming that Equations (5) and (24) hold over the entire sample period with unchanged parameters is problematical. Such parameter instability decreases the likelihood of finding evidence of mean reversion, however. For this reason, the evidence for rapid convergence is even stronger than it would appear to be on first blush.[21]

---

[21] A fall in the variance resulting from structural shifts is not "convergence" in the sense that the term is used in this paper. Convergence implies that only about half the changes in V lower

Pretesting revealed that one lag suffices to fit the data. The result from using ordinary least squares to fit Equation (24) is

$$\Delta \hat{V}_t = \underset{(0.00149)}{0.00166} - \underset{(0.0207)}{0.0567} \ V_{t-1} + \underset{(0.105)}{0.278} \ \Delta V_{t-1},$$

$$R^2 = 0.1881, \qquad SEE = 0.007407 \tag{25}$$

The t-ratio for the estimate of γ is -2.74. A Monte Carlo simulation with 100,000 iterations revealed that the 0.01 critical value of this test statistic is approximately -2.427. The evidence for convergence of the factor incomes of the contiguous U.S. states to parallel growth paths is therefore strong. This finding confirms the other results of this section.

7.5   Comparison with countries

It is instructive to compare the results reported in the previous section for U.S. states with those that the literature has obtained for countries. As pointed out in Section 7.2, there is little evidence for convergence across large groups of countries. If convergence is nonetheless accepted as given, Evans (1997b) provides comparable estimates of convergence rates for 48 countries. The estimated convergence rates for most of these countries have wide confidence intervals, extending from somewhat negative values to substantial positive values. The mean of these estimates is 5.89% a year with a 90% confidence interval extending from 3.93% a year to 8.58% a year.[22] The convergence rates for the U.S. states are therefore likely to be much larger than the convergence rates for these countries. A natural interpretation is that factor mobility is much higher across U.S. states than it is across countries. In addition, the relative lack of barriers to trade in goods and the relatively low transportation costs within the United States may play an important role. See the evidence reported in Chapters 6 and 8 in this volume, which indicates that factors are much more mobile and trade barriers are much lower between U.S. states than between countries.

Mean cross-country differences in log per capita income are much larger for countries than for U.S. states. The standard deviation of the μ's for the 48 countries in the sample for Evans (1997b) is 0.9900, which is gigantic compared to 0.1580 for the per capita factor incomes of the contiguous U.S. states. No doubt the low degree of international factor mobility and the high

it unless initial conditions somehow place it far from its mean. De novo, it would be better to use "reversion" to refer to the tendency to approach balanced growth paths and "convergence" to refer to the effects of structural shifts like increasing mobility or decreasing transportation costs and trade barriers. The dead hand of past usage, however, makes this distinction more confusing than clarifying.

[22] Indeed, the evidence that convergence occurs at all is largely confined to rich countries (see Evans 1996, 1998).

degree of interstate factor mobility in the United States are key determinants of this difference.

In order to assess how schooling affects convergence rates and the levels of the balanced growth paths for per capita income, I regressed them on SEC, the average enrollment rate in secondary schools between 1950 and 1990.[23] The resulting regressions are

$$\hat{r}_c = 0.0496 + 0.0231 \; SEC_c, \qquad R^2 = 0.1387, \qquad SEE = 0.1506$$
$$\quad\;\;\; (0.0360) \quad (0.0839) \tag{26}$$

and

$$\hat{\mu}_c = -1.23 + 3.19 \; SEC_c, \qquad R^2 = 0.5569, \qquad SEE = 0.6677$$
$$\quad\;\;\; (0.20) \quad (0.42) \tag{27}$$

Unlike for the states, the convergence rates appear to be insensitive to schooling. By contrast, schooling appears to be an important determinant of the μ's for both countries and states. Interestingly, dummy variables for Latin America, Asia, and Africa, which by themselves are highly significant in a regression for $\hat{\mu}_c$, are completely insignificant after controlling for schooling.

7.6   Conclusions

The per capita factor incomes of the contiguous U.S. states show a pronounced tendency to converge toward parallel balanced growth paths. Furthermore, the convergence is rapid on average, even though the estimated convergence rates are widely dispersed across the states and quite imprecisely estimated for each individual state. Theory suggests that this rapid convergence results from the high factor mobility within the United States, even though the absence of interstate barriers to trade in goods and low transportation costs may also play an important role. Notwithstanding the high factor mobility, differences in per capita income across the states are substantial. This result, however, is not surprising because the economies of the states are quite heterogeneous. With such heterogeneity, per capita incomes would not be equalized even if all factor prices were equalized.

The per capita incomes of broad groups of countries show no pronounced tendency to converge toward balanced growth paths. To the extent that convergence does take place, it is fairly slow on average. As was true for the states,

---

[23] The countries included in the sample are Argentina, Australia, Austria, Belgium, Bolivia, Brazil, Canada, Chile, Colombia, Costa Rica, Denmark, the Dominican Republic, Ecuador, El Salvador, Finland, France, Germany, Greece, Guatemala, Honduras, India, Ireland, Italy, Japan, Kenya, Mexico, Morocco, the Netherlands, New Zealand, Nigeria, Norway, Pakistan, Panama, Paraguay, Peru, the Philippines, Portugal, Spain, South Africa, Sweden, Switzerland, Trinidad and Tobago, Thailand, Turkey, the United Kingdom, the United States, Uruguay, and Venezuela. Evans (1997b) details the sources of the data on real GDP per worker and SEC_c.

the estimated convergence rates are widely dispersed across the countries and estimated with considerable imprecision for each individual country. Theory suggests that this fairly slow, or even nonexistent, convergence results from the virtual absence of labor mobility across national frontiers and perhaps from low capital mobility, barriers to trade in goods, and significant transportation costs. Finally, differences in labor productivity across countries are gigantic, greatly exceeding those across the contiguous U.S. states. No doubt the absence of labor mobility accounts for the lion's share of these differences, even though the heterogeneity of the economies of the countries probably also exceeds that of the states.

These results suggest that the movement toward unified markets in goods and factors in Europe should lead the per capita incomes of the individual countries to converge toward parallel balanced growth paths if they do not already do so. Moreover, to the extent that they do, the rates at which the convergence takes place should increase, the balanced growth paths should be pulled toward each other, and the cross-sectional variance of the logarithms of per capita income should fall.

References

Aghion, P., and Howitt, P. 1992. A model of growth through creative destruction. *Econometrica* 60: 323–51.

Andrews, D. W. K. 1993. Exactly median unbiased estimation of first order autoregressive/unit root models. *Econometrica* 61: 139–66.

Barro, R. J. 1997. *Determinants of Economic Growth*. Cambridge, MA: MIT Press.

Barro, R. J., and X. Sala-i-Martin. 1991. Convergence across states and regions. *Brookings Papers on Economic Activity 1*: 107–82.

Barro, R. J., and X. Sala-i-Martin. 1992a. Convergence. *Journal of Political Economy* 100: 223–51.

Barro, R. J., and X. Sala-i-Martin. 1992b. Regional growth and migration: A Japan–United States comparison. *Journal of the Japanese and International Economies* 6: 312–46.

Barro, R. J., and X. Sala-i-Martin. 1995. *Economic Growth*. New York: McGraw-Hill.

Barro, R. J., N. G. Mankiw, and X. Sala-i-Martin. 1995. Capital mobility in neoclassical models of growth. *American Economic Review* 85: 103–15.

Ben-David, D. 1993. Equalizing exchange: Trade liberalization and income convergence. *Quarterly Journal of Economics* 108: 653–79.

Benhabib, J., and Spiegel, M. M. 1994. The role of human capital in economic development: Evidence from aggregate cross-country data. *Journal of Monetary Economics* 34: 143–73.

Bernard, A. B., and S. N. Durlauf. 1995. Convergence of international output movements. *Journal of Applied Econometrics* 10: 97–108.

Bernard, A. B., and C. I. Jones. 1996a. Productivity across industries and countries. *Review of Economics and Statistics* 78: 135–46.

Bernard, A. B., and C. I. Jones. 1996b. Productivity and convergence across U.S. states and industries. *Empirical Economics* 21 (1): 113–35.

Bernard, A. B., and C. I. Jones. 1996c. Comparing apples to oranges: Productivity convergence and measurement across industries and countries. *American Economic Review* 86: 1216–38.

Blanchard, O. J., and L. F. Katz. 1992. Regional convergence. *Brookings Papers on Economic Activity* 1: 1–61.

Carayannis, E., and R. Mallick. 1996. Regional income disparities in Canada: Implications for theories of regional convergence. *Review of Regional Studies* 26: 55–74.

Carlino, G., and L. Mills. 1993. Are U.S. regional incomes converging? A time series analysis. *Journal of Monetary Economics* 32: 335–46.

Cass, D. 1965. Optimal growth in an aggregative model of capital accumulation. *Review of Economic Studies* 32: 233–40.

Easterly, W., M. Kremer, L. Pritchett, and L. Summers. 1993. Good policy or good luck? Country growth performance and temporary shocks. *Journal of Monetary Economics* 32: 459–84.

Evans, P. 1996. Using cross-country variances to evaluate growth theories. *Journal of Economic Dynamics and Control* 20: 1027–49.

Evans, P. 1997a. Government consumption and growth. *Economic Inquiry* 35: 209–17.

Evans, P. 1997b. How fast do economies converge? *Review of Economics and Statistics* 36: 219–25.

Evans, P. 1998. Using panel data to evaluate growth theories. *International Economic Review* 39: 295–306.

Evans, P., and G. Karras. 1996a. Convergence revisited. *Journal of Monetary Economics* 37: 249–65.

Evans, P., and G. Karras. 1996b. Do economies converge? Evidence from a panel of U.S. states. *Review of Economics and Statistics* 78: 384–8.

Evans, P., and G. Karras. 1997a. International integration of capital markets and the cross-country divergence of per capita consumption. *Journal of International Money and Finance* 16 (5): 681–97.

Evans, P., and G. Karras. 1997b. "Is the Long-Run Labor Supply Vertical?" Unpublished Manuscript, Ohio State University.

Filip, A., and P. Van Rompuy. 1995. Regional convergence in the European Monetary Union. *Papers in Regional Science* 74: 125–42.

Hofer, H., and A. Worgotter. 1997. Regional per capita income convergence in Austria. *Regional Studies* 30: 549–65.

Im, K. S., M. H. Pesaran, and Y. Shin. 1995. "Testing for Unit Roots in Heterogeneous Panels." Working paper 9526. University of Cambridge, Department of Applied Economics.

Islam, N. 1995. Growth empirics: A panel data approach. *Quarterly Journal of Economics* 110: 1127–70.

Jones, C. I. 1995. Time series tests of endogenous growth. *Quarterly Journal of Economics* 110: 495–526.

Kim, S. 1997. "Economic Integration and Convergence: U.S. Regions, 1840–1987." Working paper 6335. NBER.

Kocherlakota, N., and K.-M. Yi. 1997. Is there endogenous long-run growth? Evidence for the United States and United Kingdom. *Journal of Money, Credit, and Banking* 29: 235–62.

Koopmans, T. C. 1965. "On the Concept of Optimal Economic Growth," in *The Econometric Approach to Development Planning*. Amsterdam: North Holland.

Krugman, P. 1991. Increasing returns and economic geography. *Journal of Political Economy* 99: 483–99.

Landes, D. 1998. *The Wealth and Poverty of Nations*. New York: Norton.

Lee, K., M. H. Pesaran, and R. Smith. 1998. Growth empirics: A panel data approach – A comment. *Quarterly Journal of Economics* 113: 319–24.

Levine, A., and C.-F. Lin. 1993. "Unit Root Tests in Panel Data: New Results." Discussion paper 93-56, University of California, San Diego.

Lucas, R. E., Jr. 1988. On the mechanics of economic development. *Journal of Monetary Economy* 22: 3–42.

Maddala, G. S., and S. Wu. 1997. "A Comparative Study of Unit Root Tests with Panel Data and a New Simple Test." Manuscript. Ohio State University.

Maddison, A. 1995. *Monitoring the World Economy, 1820–1992*. Paris: OECD.

Neven, D., and C. Gouyette. 1995. Regional convergence in the European community. *Journal of Common Market Studies* 33: 47–65.

Quah, D. 1996. Empirics for economic growth and convergence. *European Economic Review* 40: 1353–75.

Roback, J. 1982. Wages, rents, and the quality of life. *Journal of Political Economy* 90: 1257–78.

Romer, P. M. 1986. Increasing returns and long-run growth. *Journal of Political Economy* 94: 1002–37.

Romer, P. M. 1990. Endogenous technological change. *Journal of Political Economy* 98: S71–102.

Samuelson, P. A. 1953. Prices of factors and goods in general equilibrium. *Review of Economic Studies* 21: 1–20.

Solow, R. M. 1956. A contribution to the theory of economic growth. *Quarterly Journal of Economics* 70: 65–94.

Stock, J. H. 1991. Confidence intervals for the largest autoregressive root in U.S. macroeconomic time series. *Journal of Monetary Economics* 28: 435–59.

Ventura, J. 1997. Growth and interdependence. *Quarterly Journal of Economics* 113: 57–84.

CHAPTER 8

Intranational labor migration, business cycles, and growth*

Antonio Fatás[†]

8.1   Introduction

Labor markets are a centerpiece of most macroeconomic models. The predictions of models of economic growth depend on the extent to which labor mobility reduces differences in regional income per capita and helps to adjust markets to changes in economic opportunities that require a geographical reallocation of factors of production. At the same time, different assumptions about the labor market have implications on the propagation of business cycles.

Moving away from aggregate data and studying disaggregated units (regional or sectoral) has recently been a fruitful area in the study of macroeconomic phenomena, producing many insights about the behavior of macroeconomic aggregates. There are two advantages to the use of disaggregated data. First, it allows us to test theories for which the standard aggregate data does not provide enough degrees of freedom. Second, the study of geographical units serves as a bridge between closed-economy models of economic fluctuations and international finance models for open economies. This chapter uses regional labor market data for Europe and the United States to understand the adjustment that takes place in response to both long-term evolutions and short-term economic fluctuations.

For Europe, our sample covers 14 current members of the European Union (all except for Luxembourg). We disaggregate the five largest countries in the sample into 45 regions so that the resulting 54 regions are comparable in size to the U.S. states. Our dataset allows us two types of comparisons. First, within Europe, our mixed sample of regions and countries provides information on

* Paper presented at the conference 'Intranational Macroeconomics', New York Fed, June 29–30, 1998. I thank Gregory Hess, Prakash Loungani, Eric van Wincoop, and conference participants for helpful comments.

[†] Mailing address: INSEAD, Boulevard de Constance, Fontainebleau, France. E-mail: *fatas@econ.insead.fr.*

the extent to which national borders are relevant for labor market adjustment. Second, the comparison with the United States, a more integrated area from an economic, political, and cultural point of view, can be used to forecast the future evolution of European regional labor markets. The process of European economic integration, possibly fostered by the creation of a single currency in January 1999, will change, at least in some dimensions, the economic environment of labor markets and will bring them closer to regional labor markets in the United States.

We start our analysis by reviewing some of the long-term trends in regional labor markets. Our results can be summarized in three sets of findings. First, European regions are characterized by a low degree of labor mobility. This degree is not only much lower than in the United States but has also been declining since the mid 1970s. This decline is a general one and affects regions as much as countries. Second, the persistence of regional employment growth rates is higher in U.S. states than in European regions. Third, and related to the lack of labor mobility, regional differences in unemployment rates in European countries are much more persistent than among U.S. states. Interestingly, this persistence is much more pronounced within than across European countries.

In the second part of this chapter, we analyze the adjustment of labor markets in response to region-specific shocks. We find that these shocks cause permanent changes in the employment share of a region both in Europe and the United States. Migration is the main adjustment mechanism in the United States. Inflows of workers to booming regions not only helps the economy to adjust to the initial increase in labor demand, but it also creates additional persistence as there is a build-up effect after the shock. In Europe, changes in regional participation rates bear most of the employment adjustment. Surprisingly, both in Europe and the United States, unemployment rates react very little, and their response is not very persistent.

The chapter is structured as follows. Section 8.2 presents the data and the level of disaggregation chosen. Section 8.3 studies long-term evolutions of regional labor markets. Section 8.4 analyzes the response to region-specific shocks. Section 8.5 discusses the implications of our results for the future evolution of European migration, and Section 8.6 concludes.

8.2   The level of regional disaggregation

The sample contains regions and countries from the European Union and the United States. For the United States, our sample includes 51 regions (the 50 U.S. states plus the District of Columbia). For Europe, our sample covers 14 of the countries that are current members of the European Union (Luxembourg is excluded). For 5 of those countries, we have disaggregated regional data. The regional data include 8 regions for France, 8 for Germany, 7 for Spain, and 11 for Italy and the UK.[1]

Our analysis takes advantage of the mixed composition of our European sample (countries and regions) to better understand how national borders define within- and across-country labor market dynamics. In our analysis, we study four types of samples:

- The United States. The sample of U.S. states, which includes 51 regions.
- *EU54.* The mixed sample of European countries and regions, which includes 54 regions. More precisely, it includes regional data on 45 regions from France, Germany, Spain, Italy, and the UK, plus the remaining 9 countries (Belgium, Denmark, Greece, Ireland, the Netherlands, Portugal, Sweden, Finland, and Austria). Sometimes we will look at a subsample of EU54, namely the one composed of pure regional data. We will refer to this subsample as *EU45.*
- *EU14.* Country data from the 14 EU countries being considered.
- *Germany, Italy, and the United Kingdom.* Regions belonging to each of these countries, to analyze within-country dynamics.[2]

The EU54 sample allows us to compare Europe and the United States at a similar level of disaggregation. These 54 European regions are similar in size to the U.S. states. The average population of a European region (4.1 million) is about 22% larger than that of the average U.S. state (3.4 million). The variation in population size is much smaller across the European regions: the standard deviation equals 1.42 million, whereas the respective value for the U.S. is 3.66 million. The two largest regions in this regional subdivision for Europe have populations which are comparable to those of Texas and New York. Other large regions such as Belgium, Portugal, Greece, the Bassin Parisien, Ile de France, Bavaria, and Baden-Württemberg have populations comparable to those of Pennsylvania, Ohio, Illinois, and Florida and less than half the size of the population of California. In terms of region size, this subdivision not only leaves us with a fairly homogeneous sample but also maximizes the availability of data and should ensure that the results we obtain are comparable to those for the United States.[3]

---

[1] Data descriptions and sources are available in the Data Appendix.

[2] Although regional data is also available from France and Spain, the short duration of the sample does not allow us to extract any robust conclusions from the isolated analysis of those countries.

[3] Regional data for all the countries being treated as single regions in our sample are either unavailable or very incomplete.

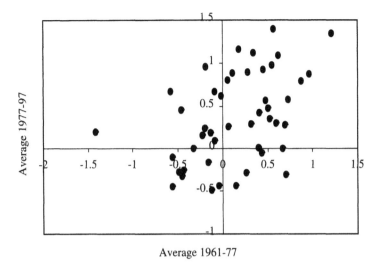

Figure 8.1. Employment growth trends: EU regions.

Before starting our analysis, we should note that regions are defined by political borders and not by economic arguments. Ideally one would like to use information that has been collected based on geographical labor markets. In some cases, the regional units actually used in the analysis are not a good approximation to well-defined geographical labor markets.[4]

8.3   Long-run trends

In this section we look at the long-term evolutions of three labor market variables: employment, unemployment and migration.

8.3.1   Employment

Starting by the sample of 54 EU regions, we can see that there is a significant amount of persistence in the growth rates of regional employment. Regions that grew faster in the first half of the sample continued their faster pace in the second part of the sample. Figure 8.1 summarizes this information by plotting average annual employment growth rates for all the 54 EU regions during the first (1966–77) and second (1977–94) half of the samples.[5] Table 8.1 presents

---

[4] The states of New York and New Jersey are a good example of how the regions used in the analysis might not be good approximations to geographical labor markets.

[5] In order to maximize the available data, we split the sample in different years for France (1971–80 and 1981–90). Berlin and the 8 Spanish regions are excluded from Figure 8.1 because, for different reasons, they are clear outliers.

Table 8.1. *Persistence of employment growth rates*

Sample	β	R^2	Sample	β	R^2
EU54	−0.14 (0.27)	0.01	Germany (**)	1.26 (0.31)	0.76
EU54 (*)	0.41 (0.13)	0.19	Italy	0.62 (0.41)	0.19
EU45	−0.13 (0.29)	0.01	U.K.	0.81 (0.12)	0.83
EU45 (*)	0.56 (0.14)	0.31	U.S.	0.74 (0.07)	0.66
EU14	−0.34 (0.42)	0.05			

$\Delta n_{i,1977-94} = \alpha + \beta \Delta n_{i,1966-77} + \epsilon_i$.
Standard errors in parentheses: (*) Berlin and Spanish regions not included; (**) Berlin not included.

the results of running a cross-sectional regression of the type

$$\Delta n_{i,1977-94} = \alpha + \beta \Delta n_{i,1966-77} + \epsilon_i$$

where Δn_i represents the average regional employment growth during the period considered.

For the EU54 sample, the coefficient is negative and nonsignificant. If one excludes West Berlin and the Spanish regions (which are clear outliers), one obtains a significant coefficient of 0.41 and an R^2 of 0.19.[6] How does this compare to the United States? Figure 8.2 presents the data and the second row of Table 8.1, the results of the regression. The slope is strongly significant, its value is 0.74, and an R^2 is equal to 0.64.

Consequently, at first sight, there is significantly more long-term persistence of employment growth in the United States than in Europe. The persistence of European regional employment growth rates becomes larger if one looks at employment growth rates within countries. If we do a similar analysis for the five countries for which regional data are available, we find a strong persistence that varies across countries. For the EU45 sample (excluding the Spanish regions, which leaves us with a total of 37 regions), the coefficient is highly significant and equal to 0.56 (with an R^2 of 0.29). Stronger results are found if we perform

[6] The limited availability of data for the Spanish regions and the fact that the second half of the sample corresponds to a period of unprecedented destruction of jobs, result in a behavior that is very different from the other European regions. To be able to include them in a meaningful way in a regression such as the one in Table 8.1 we would need to demean the regional variables using the evolution of the national aggregate.

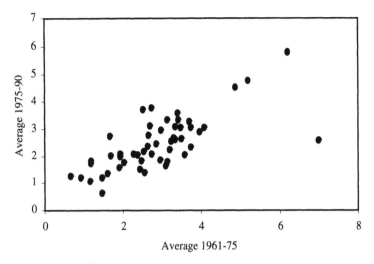

Figure 8.2. Employment growth trends: U.S. states.

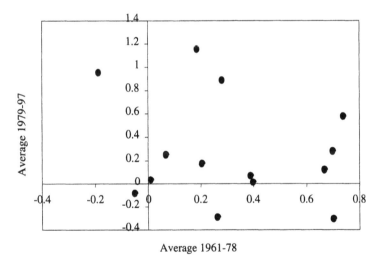

Figure 8.3. Employment growth trends: EU countries.

similar regressions using only regions that belong to the same country. Both the coefficient (the highest in the case of Germany, 1.26) and the R^2 increase (higher than 0.75 for Germany and the United Kingdom).

We can confirm that the persistence of regional employment growth rates is larger within countries than across countries by looking at Figure 8.3, which plots national employment growth rates for the EU14 sample. There is little cross-country persistence, and, as the last row of Table 8.1 indicates, the regression yields a negative coefficient and an R^2 of 0.05.

Table 8.2. *Persistence of unemployment rates*

Sample	β	R^2	Sample	β	R^2
EU54	1.09 (0.29)	0.20	Germany	3.72 (3.11)	0.19
EU45	0.99 (0.30)	0.19	Italy	3.46 (1.69)	0.31
EU45 (*)	0.99 (0.23)	0.33	U.K.	1.68 (0.41)	0.64
EU14	0.71 (0.97)	0.04	U.S.	0.21 (0.08)	0.09

$u_{i,1987} = \alpha + \beta u_{i,1968} + \epsilon_i$.
Standard errors in parentheses: (*) Spanish regions not included.

8.3.2   Unemployment

Figure 8.4 plots regional unemployment rates minus the EU-wide unemployment rate at the beginning and the end of our sample (1968 and 1987).[7] We run a cross-sectional regression of these two variables:

$$u_{i,1987} = \alpha + \beta u_{i,1968} + \epsilon_i$$

where u_i is defined as the difference between regional unemployment rates and the European unemployment rate. Table 8.2 summarizes the results. The regression line has a slope of 1.09 (with a standard deviation of 0.28), and the R^2 equals 0.18.

If we restrict our sample to only regions (EU45), the regression produces a similar coefficient. As was the case with employment growth rates, removing the Spanish regions significantly improves the regression. Country by country, we find not only persistence but in some cases increased dispersion of unemployment rates, as the regression coefficient is larger than 1.

If we use the EU14 country sample, the persistence is less pronounced because both the size of the coefficient and the fit of the regression are smaller.

This may now be compared to Figure 8.5, which shows the same for the United States. The slope of the regression line is 0.20, and the R^2 equals 0.09. Therefore, regional unemployment rates display much more persistence in Europe than in the United States.

The persistence of unemployment rates must be interpreted with great care given that the results are sensitive to the starting and ending years. Despite this, the conclusion seems to be clear; in the U.S. there is very little persistence of

---

[7] For France, the starting year is 1974 and for Spain, 1977.

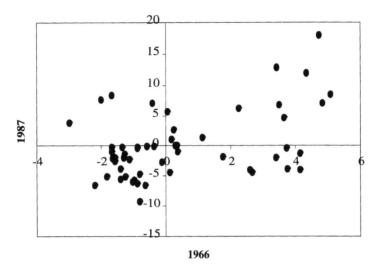

Figure 8.4. Unemployment trends: EU regions.

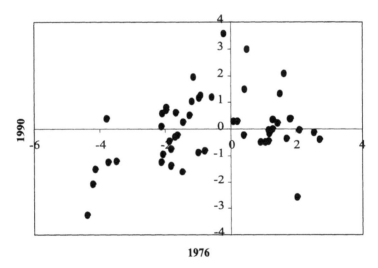

Figure 8.5. Unemployment trends: U.S. states.

regional unemployment rates, while regional unemployment displays significant amount of long-term persistence in Europe. In fact, in some cases, the rising unemployment rate of the 1970s and 1980s has led to growing regional disparities. Surprisingly, this trend is more pronounced within countries than across countries. See Figure 8.6. This seems to be an indication of the lack of internal adjustment mechanisms such as migration at the level of regional labor markets.

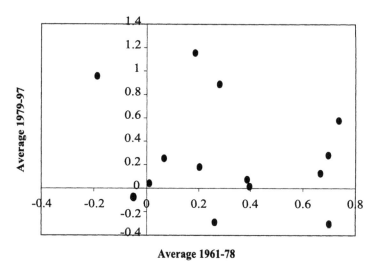

Average 1961-78

Figure 8.6. Unemployment trends: EU countries.

8.3.3 *Migration*

Migration figures are, in general, more difficult to compare both over time and across countries. In addition, international migration responds, in many instances, more to shifts in political attitudes toward migration than to changes in economic conditions. Regarding internal migration data, there are wide cross-country differences with respect to the availability and method of collection of the data. Even though some countries (e.g. Germany) keep reliable figures on gross flows (region of origin and region of destiny), other countries do not have as reliable and detailed figures.

Figures 8.7 and 8.8 look at the average flow of net international migration as a percent of total population for Germany, France, Italy, Japan, and the United States. For all countries, with the exception of Italy and France, there is no clear trend. The case of Italy is interesting because migration switches from emigration to immigration during the sample period.

Interestingly, the observed trend for Italy has also taken place in other southern European countries such as Spain, Portugal, or Greece. For example, even though in the decade 1960–70 there was an average of more than 250,000 migrants leaving Portugal, Spain or Italy every year, in the decade 1984–94 the flow was more than 50,000 in the opposite direction.[8]

---

[8] Country-to-country flows, when available, indicate that this trend is heavily influenced by the changes in the pattern of intra-EU migration. Emigration figures for Italy, Spain, and Portugal in the 1960s are of similar magnitude as the immigration numbers for France and Germany. On the contrary, in the 1990s, migration figures for Italy, France, and Germany are all positive and amount to about two-thirds of the total migration in the EU from non-EU countries. These numbers seem

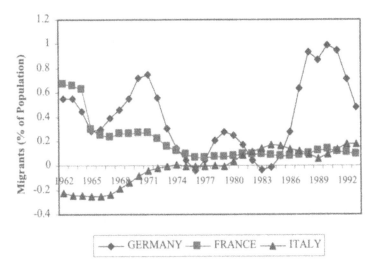

Figure 8.7. Migration trends: European countries.

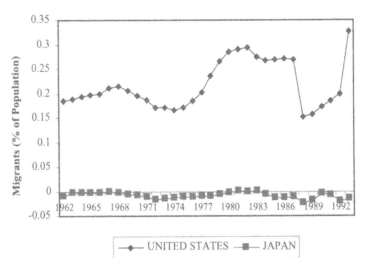

Figure 8.8. Migration trends: U.S. and Japan.

To study within-country migration, we start by looking at data on the proportion of the population who changes region of residence. Table 8.3 summarizes the results of an OECD study.[9]

to indicate that even though in 1960 there were significant flows within the European Union and very little from countries outside of the EU, by the end of the 1980s and early 1990s, most of the flows originated outside of the EU.

[9] Source: OECD (1986).

Table 8.3. *Proportion of population who changed residence*

Annual data	1970	1980
U.S. – states	3.4	3.3
U.S. – counties	6.5	6.2
Germany – Länders (11)	1.8	1.3
England and Wales (8)	1.5	1.1
Norway – counties (19)	3.0	2.3
Multiyear data	1965–70	1975–80
U.S. – States	9.6	9.7
U.S. – counties	17.1	19.5
French regions (21)	6.5	7.9

There are significant cross-country differences. Taking into consideration differences in the sizes of the regional units, the ratio is between two and five times larger in the United States than in Germany. For example, for the comparable units of German Länders and U.S. states, mobility in the United States (3.3) is almost three times higher than in Germany (1.3). Similar differences are found between the United States and other European countries such as France or the United Kingdom.

A second important observation is that there is evidence that interregional mobility has decreased over time in European countries, which confirms the figures for intra-EU migration. The number of people who have changed region of residence has declined over time.[10]

An interesting question is to what extent the decline in migration responds to regional economic disparities. There is evidence that migration responds to differences in regional income. Barro and Sala-i-Martin (1991) document that U.S. states with low income per capita are those with larger population outflows and, moreover, migration is quite persistent over time.[11] In the EU, the migration trends described earlier clearly indicate that during the 1960s and 1970s there was significant migration from poor to rich regions (or countries).

A second relevant factor for migration is disparities in unemployment rates. Here, the decrease in migration is puzzling given the increase in the differential

---

[10] The only exception in Table 8.3 is France. However, the numbers of migration for the period 1970–75 were 8.7, which indicates that migration has declined after 1975.

[11] In fact, this has been one of the mechanisms that explains the observed convergence of income per capita in U.S. states. According to Barro and Sala-i-Martin (1991), without controlling for migrants' human capital, migration could account for as much as a third of the estimated convergence rate. However, after allowing for a reasonable amount of migrants' human capital, the contribution of migration is no more than 10% of the estimated rate of convergence.

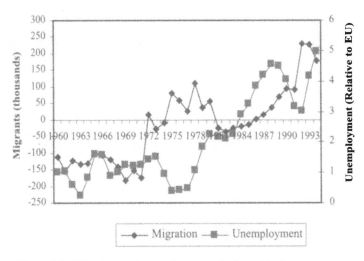

Figure 8.9. Migration and unemployment: Spain and Italy.

of unemployment rates between the receiving and sending countries. Figure 8.9 shows the sum of net migration of Italy and Spain and the difference between their unemployment rate and the average unemployment rate in the EU15.

As is evident in Figure 8.9, the trend toward falling migration coincided with a trend toward larger disparities of regional unemployment rates.

Additional evidence can be found by looking at migration within one of these countries, Spain.[12] If we look at one of the poorest Spanish regions with one of the highest unemployment rates, Andalucia, we can confirm the apparently paradoxical evolution of migration. Migration from Andalucia to richer Spanish regions in Spain or other European countries was large during the 1960s and 1970s. Since then, not only the numbers have decreased but, in recent years, the trend has been reversed, and we observe net migration into Andalucia from other Spanish regions. See Figure 8.10.

Overall, the evidence on migration in Europe across and within countries is consistent. On the average, there is less migration among European regions than among U.S. states. In Europe, migration has decreased over time, and, surprisingly, this fall has coincided with an increase in the relative unemployment of the regions that have been traditional sources of migratory flows.

Why did European interregional migration fall? Several factors have contributed to this trend. The most important factor is the generalized increase in unemployment rates. All empirical studies of migration show a strong negative effect of migration to increases in aggregate unemployment. In addition, the convergence of regional income per capita and the enlargement of the welfare

---

[12] See Bentolila and Dolado (1991) for an analysis of regional migration in Spain.

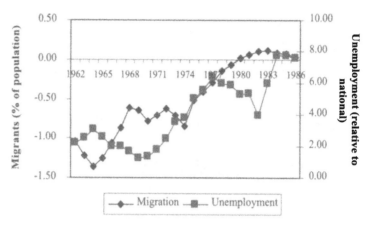

Figure 8.10. Migration and unemployment: Andalucia.

state in some of the relatively poor countries has reduced the incentives to migrate.

8.4   The short run

In previous sections, we have observed that, in both the United States and Europe, there are distinct regional labor market evolutions. How do these variables react to shocks that have a significant region-specific component? How does the response of migration shape the pattern of regional business cycles? These are the questions to which we seek answers in this section.

8.4.1   The framework

Our starting point is to think about the evolution of employment in a region. With substantial specialization of production on a regional level, the dynamics of employment, unemployment, and labor force participation at a regional level will differ from those we observe at a macroeconomic level. In general, the long-term evolution of employment in any region is intimately linked to the trend in demand for the goods produced in that region and the changes in the qualities that potential migrants perceive. In addition to following some kind of trend, employment may be subjected to shocks resulting from changes in demand. The effect of such changes on employment can be more or less permanent, depending on the degree of regional specialization in production and the relative propensities of firms and workers to migrate between regions.[13]

---

[13] One could also think about region-specific shocks that are not related to industry specialization but to regional economic policies. Davis, Loungani, and Mahidhara (1997) and Chapter 9 in this volume analyze separately the effects of regional and industry shocks.

For example, we can think about a region that experiences a positive shock for the goods in which it specializes.[14] Initially one would expect the unemployment rate to fall, the labor force participation rate to rise, and, to the extent real wages are flexible on a regional level, the real wage to rise. The new equilibrium could be achieved in many different ways. First, the higher wage and lower unemployment rates may set off a wave of immigration that would bring wages, unemployment, and labor force participation rates back to their equilibrium levels, while leaving relative employment in the region permanently higher. Second, part of the initial positive shock to employment might be reversed by a rising wage level, a lack of qualified personnel, increasing congestion, and lower investment subsidies, which would induce firms to leave the booming region. Depending on the relative degree of mobility of capital and labor, the flexibility of wages and the response of fiscal incentives, the adjustment can be very different.[15] The persistence and type of labor-market shocks is also relevant for the decision to migrate. Hojvat-Gallin (1998) develops a model where the decision to migrate explicitly depends on current and future labor market conditions.

8.4.2   Unemployment

The starting point of our analysis is to look at the behavior of the unemployment rate. The unemployment rate is an indicator of the adjustment of labor markets to regional shocks. Our variable of study is regional unemployment rates relative to the unemployment rate of the aggregate. We calculate

$$u_{it} = U_{it} - U_{at}$$

where U_i denotes the regional unemployment rate and U_a, the aggregate one (Europe or the United States).

Given our prior that regional unemployment rates display a tendency to return to their mean, we estimate the univariate process followed by unemployment using levels.[16] Allowing for two lags, we run for the EU and the U.S. samples

$$u_{it} = \alpha_i + \beta_1 u_{it-1} + \beta_2 u_{it-2} + v_{it}$$

Table 8.4 shows the results, while the impulse responses caused by a one standard deviation shock in relative unemployment are shown in Figure 8.11.[17] Even though the sizes of the shocks are fairly similar – 0.8% in Europe and

---

[14] This shock could be a sudden change in the demand for the goods in which the region specializes or an improvement in the technology used in the production for those same goods.

[15] For a more formal description of these arguments see Blanchard and Katz (1992).

[16] Notice that, given the observed persistence in regional relative unemployment rates, we also allow for region-specific fixed effects (i.e., different regional natural unemployment rates).

[17] Sample: Europe 1966–87, United States 1970–90.

Table 8.4. *Regional relative unemployment*

Sample	β_1	β_2	Sample	β_1	β_2
EU54	1.1953	−0.3539	Germany	1.1765	−0.1613
	(0.0338)	(0.0336)		(0.0764)	(0.0858)
EU45	1.1488	−0.3298	Italy	1.1243	−0.2112
	(0.0384)	(0.0375)		(0.0809)	(0.0825)
EU14	1.5161	−0.6213	U.K.	1.0740	−0.1221
	(0.0428)	(0.0430)		(0.0705)	(0.0751)
U.S.	0.9194	−0.2387			
	(0.0399)	(0.0368)			

$u_{it} = \alpha_i + \beta_1 u_{it-1} + \beta_2 u_{it-2} + v_{it}.$
Standard errors in parentheses.

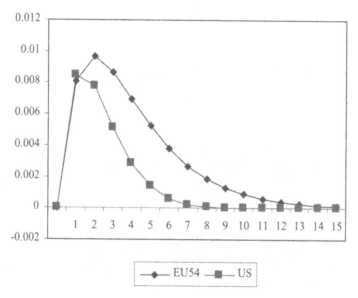

Figure 8.11. Persistence of regional unemployment rates.

0.84% in the United States – its effects are more persistent in European regions. Table 8.4 also displays regressions for regional unemployment rates
at the national level. The results are quite similar to those of the EU54
sample.[18]

In light of the rigidities of European labor markets, the small difference in
persistence between European and U.S. unemployment is surprising. In fact,

---

[18] The only difference is that, given the smaller size of the sample and the documented dispersion
of German and Italian unemployment rates, nonexplosive behavior could only be obtained after
detrending the series.

previous studies of persistence of regional unemployment rates have found even more striking results. Both Eichengreen (1993) and Decressin and Fatás (1995), using different methodologies, show that European regional unemployment rates return to their natural rates faster than those of U.S. states. For example, Decressin and Fatás (1995) construct region-specific unemployment rates by allowing different responses of regions to aggregate shocks. For each of the regional units, they run a regression of the type

$$U_{it} = \alpha_i - \beta_i U_{at}$$

where U_i denotes the regional and U_a the aggregate unemployment rate (Europe or the United States). One can then construct region-specific unemployment rates from the residuals of the regression so that

$$u_{it} = U_{it} - (\hat{\alpha}_i - \hat{\beta}_i U_{at})$$

is the measure of region-specific unemployment. The justification for this adjustment is that the cyclical response to aggregate shocks might be different across regions.[19] Following the procedure of Decressin and Fatás (1995), we construct cyclically adjusted series of regional unemployment and obtained a level of persistence for European regional unemployment that is indeed lower than that of the U.S. states. Results (labeled β-adjusted) are displayed in Figure 8.12.

These results, which confirm those of Eichengreen (1993) using cointegrating techniques, support the existence of natural rates of relative unemployment at the regional level. To shed further light on this issue, we have also run similar regressions using absolute European regional unemployment rates (not measured relative to the aggregate). Now the persistence is much larger and confirms the prior that regional labor markets in Europe are very rigid.

Why is it that the β-adjusted regional unemployment rates display a lower degree of persistence? The preceding procedure might be detrending the series and, thus, eliminating part of its persistence. Given that unemployment in Europe increased in almost all regions during our sample, by allowing the β_is to be different across regions, we allow each of the regional unemployment trends to have a different slope. To illustrate how important this detrending might be, we have detrended both the regional and aggregate unemployment rate and then calculated relative unemployment (as the difference between detrended regional and aggregate unemployment rates). The degree of persistence falls and becomes almost equivalent to when we used cyclically adjusted relative unemployment rates (see Figure 8.12).

[19] The construction of these region-specific variables is similar in spirit to the analysis of Eichengreen (1993) using cointegrating techniques where the cointegration equation, in levels, allows a different coefficient for each of the regional unemployment rates.

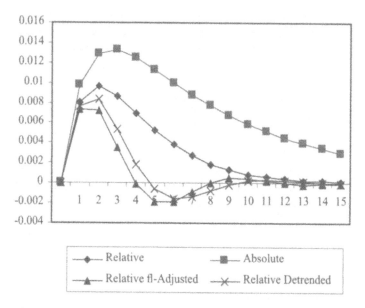

Figure 8.12. Measuring the persistence of regional unemployment (impulse response, annual data).

8.4.3   Employment

We now study the behavior of relative employment. Even though, in the case of unemployment, it was natural to start from the assumption that regional shocks do not have permanent effects on the unemployment rate, in the case of employment we will allow shocks to have permanent effects (i.e., we will model the time series in growth rates).[20]

We estimate the univariate process followed by regional relative employment growth in Europe and the U.S. allowing for two lags; we run

$$\Delta n_{it} = \alpha_i + \beta_1\, \Delta n_{it-1} + \beta_2\, \Delta n_{it-2} + \eta_{it}$$

This regression pools the entire sample and allows for region-specific fixed effects. n_i stands for the logarithm of employment in region i minus the logarithm of employment in Europe (or the United States). Table 8.5 shows the estimates, and Figure 8.13, the impulse response function of employment to a one standard deviation shock for EU54 and the US.[21]

---

[20] We have checked for unit roots and could reject the null for only 2 out of the 54 regions at 5% significance. Also, using levels instead of growth rates does not significantly change most of the results we present, although it has clear implications about long-term responses to regional shocks.

[21] Sample: 1966–87 for the United States and 1966–94 for Europe. Some early years missing for some countries, see Data Appendix.

Table 8.5. *Regional relative employment growth*

Δn_{it}	Δn_{it-1}	Δn_{it-2}	Δn_{it}	Δn_{it-1}	Δn_{it-2}
EU54	0.0756	0.0434	Germany	−0.0267	0.3575
	(0.0366)	(0.0369)		(0.3575)	(0.0963)
EU45	0.0738	0.0617	Italy	0.0176	−0.1501
	(0.0404)	(0.0407)		(0.0750)	(0.0717)
EU14	0.5120	−0.1010	U.K.	−0.3264	0.1397
	(0.0553)	(0.0553)		(0.0727)	(0.0746)
U.S.	0.7404	−0.2349			
	(0.0421)	(0.0412)			

$\Delta n_{it} = \alpha_i + \beta_1 \Delta n_{it-1} + \beta_2 \Delta n_{it-2} + \eta_{it}$.
Standard errors in parentheses.

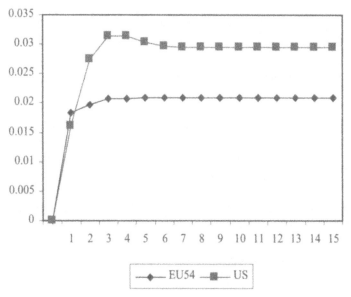

Figure 8.13. Persistence of regional employment (impulse response, annual data).

Although the size of the initial shock in Europe and in the United States is similar (1.8 and 1.5 percentage points, respectively), it has substantially weaker long-run effects in the former than in the latter. This is confirmed by the analysis of Italy, France, the United Kingdom and Germany with n_{it}' being now equal to the logarithm of regional employment minus the logarithm of national employment. The within-country pattern is indeed very similar. Only in the case of Germany does one observe any further increase in employment

after the shock. Both for the United Kingdom and Italy, the permanent effects
of the innovation are equivalent to the initial shock.

Overall, shocks to regional employment have much stronger effects in the
United States than in Europe. Although the impact effect is similar in both areas,
there is a build-up effect in the United States that is not present in Europe. This
could be caused by a stronger response of interregional migrational flows to
regional shocks in the United States. At the root of this finding could also be a
higher degree of regional specialization of production in the United States than
in Europe. To have a more precise answer, we now must study the behavior of
migration.

8.4.4   Migration

Given the evidence on the short-term dynamics of employment and unemployment a natural question to ask is the extent to which migration can explain some
of the observed differences between Europe and the United States.

Because of the lack of homogeneous data on migration, it is very difficult
to establish cross-country comparisons of labor mobility. In general, migration
studies using aggregate data tend to find that the relevant variables have a limited
impact on migratory flows.[22]

Eichengreen (1993), using aggregate data, studies the responsiveness of regional migration to wage and unemployment differences. The results seemed
to confirm previous studies as the size of the elasticities are generally small.
Although higher wages and lower unemployment tend to attract migrants, the
size of the response is too small to favor a quick return to regional balance.
In a comparison between three countries, migration is more responsive in the
United States than in the United Kingdom, whereas migration across Italian
regions is the least responsive to economic conditions.[23]

Studies using gross migrational flows are consistent with these results.
Jackman and Savouri (1992) for the United Kingdom and Decressin (1994)
for Germany find that wage and unemployment differentials can explain gross
migrational flows. Once again, the speed of adjustment is small.

A result that is common to most of the studies that use European data is that
aggregate unemployment significantly reduces migration. For given differences

---

[22] See Greenwood (1975, 1985) for surveys on internal migration in the United States, and Herzog,
Schlottmann, and Boehm (1993) for a review of studies from other countries.

[23] Quantifying these effects is difficult because some of these results are not robust when applied
to different datasets or different methodologies. For example, in a study of net migration across
U.K. regions, Pissarides and McMaster (1990) find that it is differentials in wage growth, not
levels, that influence migration. Differences in regional unemployment rates have an effect on
migration, but the speed of adjustment is very small. Their estimates suggest that even 10 years
after the initial shock, half of the unemployment differential is still present.

in regional unemployment rates or wages, during periods of recession, we observe less geographical mobility.

A second strand of the literature studies microdata on migration with similar conclusions, although, in most cases, migration is more sensitive to economic incentives.[24] The effect of unemployment and wage differential is present in studies for the United States (Herzog and Schlottmann, 1988), the United Kingdom (Hughes and McCormick, 1989), or the Netherlands (Van Dijk, Herzog, and Schlottmann, 1989). In all cases, being unemployed significantly increases the probability of migrating. Interestingly, a direct comparison of the previous three studies suggests that the effect of the unemployment status is the highest in the Netherlands followed by the United Kingdom and then United States. Being unemployed increases labor force migration by 181% in the Netherlands, 93% in the United Kingdom and only 34% in the United States.[25] After controlling for employment status in the period after migration, there is clear evidence that migration in the Netherlands is, in most cases, based on individuals who have already found a job in the region to which they are moving. In the case of the United States, the estimates provide, on the contrary, evidence that there exists a large amount of speculative migration (workers move to booming areas before having found a job in those areas).

An interesting result of microdata, which confirms some of the results of aggregate data, is the influence of the area unemployment in the decision to migrate and the difference between the United States and Europe. Even though high area unemployment increases the probability of migration in the United States, it reduces it in the Netherlands.[26]

In summary, internal migration is responsive to wage and unemployment differences, but the speed of adjustment is too small to allow for a quick reduction in regional imbalances. Across countries, the evidence suggests that migration is more responsive in the United States than in European countries. Beyond the size of the response, two other characteristics emerge: there is more speculative migration in the United States than in Europe, and the conditions of the area from which the migrants move seem to have a perverse effect in some European countries.

8.4.5 *Employment dynamics, unemployment, and migration*

Because of the difficulties in finding a consistent measure of migration, it is difficult to do cross-country studies. At the same time, some of the studies

---

[24] See DaVanzo (1978), or Hughes and McCormick (1989).

[25] See the survey of Herzog et al. (1993) for details on the cross-country comparison of these figures. Also note that it is very difficult to establish accurate international comparisons using these studies because of the differences in methodology and construction of the data.

[26] See Herzog et al. (1993).

discussed earlier do not distinguish properly between long-term trends and short-term dynamics. For that reason, a dynamic analysis of the joint behavior of employment, unemployment, and labor force participation might help our understanding of how labor markets adjust to regional disparities in the short run.

We have in mind the framework described in Section 8.4.1 and, for that reason, we allow for long-term trends in all of our variables. We analyze the joint behavior of regional relative employment, relative unemployment rates and relative participation rates in response to labor demand shocks, which will explain the deviations of the three variables around their long-term trends.[27]

The fact that there is an identity that links participation rates, employment rates, and migration allows us to get an indirect measure of the amount of migration in response to region-specific shocks. The system we estimate for both Europe and the United States follows:

$$\Delta n_{it} = \lambda_{i10} + \lambda_{11}(L)\,\Delta n_{it-1} + \lambda_{12}(L)\,e_{it-1} + \lambda_{13}(L)\,p_{it-1} + \epsilon_{i1t}$$

$$e_{it} = \lambda_{i20} + \lambda_{21}(L)\,\Delta n_{it} + \lambda_{22}(L)\,e_{it-1} + \lambda_{23}(L)\,p_{it-1} + \epsilon_{i2t}$$

$$p_{it} = \lambda_{i30} + \lambda_{31}(L)\,\Delta n_{it} + \lambda_{32}(L)\,e_{it-1} + \lambda_{33}(L)\,p_{it-1} + \epsilon_{i3t}$$

All variables are defined relative to their aggregate (Europe or the United States) counterparts so that n_{it}, e_{it}, and p_{it} are equal to

$$n_{it} = \log(N_{it}) - \log(N_{at})$$

$$e_{it} = \log(E_{it}) - \log(E_{at})$$

$$p_{it} = \log(P_{it}) - \log(P_{at})$$

where E_i and E_a stand for the regional and aggregate employment rate (employment divided by the labor force) and P_i and P_a stand for the regional and aggregate labor force participation rate [labor force divided by the working-age (15–64) population].[28]

Because we are interested in analyzing the effects of exogenous changes in regional labor demand, we need to identify them in some way. Following Blanchard and Katz (1992) and Decressin and Fatás (1995), we associate unexpected changes in regional relative employment within the year with changes

---

[27] Our econometric specification is symmetric and cannot distinguish between the effects of negative and positive demand shocks. Davis, Loungani, and Mahidhara (1997) present evidence of the asymmetric effects of regional shocks.

[28] Equivalently, since $\log(E_{it}) \approx -U_{it}$

$$e_{it} \approx -u_{it} = -(U_{it} - U_{at}).$$

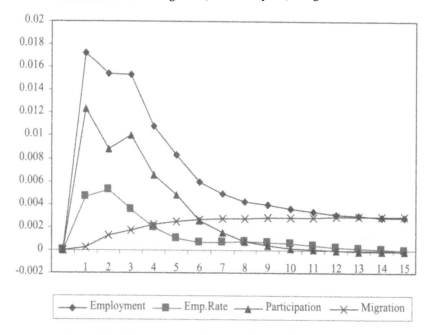

Figure 8.14. Labor market adjustment: Europe (impulse response, annual data).

in labor demand, which is a plausible assumption as long as the largest fraction of these unexpected changes is not due to exogenous changes in labor supply or migration.[29] Consequently, we allow current changes in relative employment to affect unemployment and participation rates but not vice-versa. We then trace the effects of an innovation in relative employment (the effect of ϵ_{i1}) to understand the dynamic effects of an innovation in labor demand on relative employment, employment rates, and participation rates.

Figures 8.14 and 8.15 show the impulse responses of employment, employment rates, and labor force participation rates to a one-standard-deviation innovation in relative employment. We have included migration, which is measured indirectly as the difference between the response of employment and the sum of the employment rate and labor force participation changes.

Essentially, in Europe a one-standard-deviation innovation in regional employment raises relative employment 1.7 percentage points, the relative participation rate by 1.20 points, and the relative employment rate by 0.46 points. In the United States, the respective figures are 1.44 for relative employment, 0.26 for relative participation, and 0.43 for relative employment rates.

---

[29] See Hojvat-Gallin (1998) for an explicit treatment of different types of shocks.

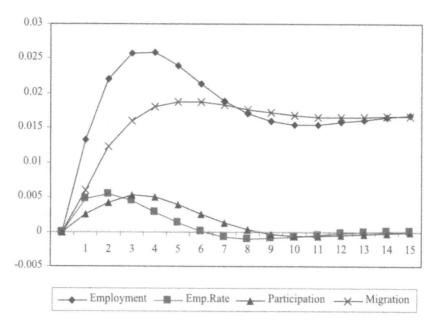

Figure 8.15. Labor market adjustment: United States (impulse response, annual data).

Therefore, although the size of the initial impact on employment is similar in both areas, the adjustment that it triggers is very different. Even though in Europe changes in unemployment rates and labor force participation explain almost 100% of the change in employment, in the United States, a third force, migration, can account for more than 50% of the change in regional employment.[30]

The important role of unemployment and labor force participation in European regions is also present in the years that follow. According to the impulse responses, even after 7 years, these two variables account for 50% of the change in regional employment.

The point that seems to be common to both the United States and Europe is that the rise in the employment rate accounts for a small portion of the gain in employment in response to a positive regional labor demand shock. The main difference arises from the roles played by labor force participation and migration. In the United States, from the first year onward, net immigration

---

[30] Although the results for the United States might seem to contradict some of the evidence, reviewed in Section 8.4.4, on the slow response of migration to regional imbalances, it is important to notice that our analysis allows for permanent regional differences in unemployment. Migration causes a state to return quickly to its natural unemployment rate. Our results do not imply that state unemployment rates are quickly equalized.

accounts for 52% of the increase in regional employment, whereas in Europe it is only after the eighth year that immigration accounts for a similar proportion of the rise in employment. The reverse holds for regional labor force participation. In Europe its increase accounts for more than 70% of the rise in employment in the first year and more than 50% in the second, whereas the respective figures for the United States are 18 and 17%.

Lastly, when we look at the long-run responses to regional shocks, there is a marked difference between Europe and the United States. Once again, in the case of the United States, there is a build up in employment following the shock. The permanent effects on employment are larger than the initial impact. In the case of Europe, there is a clear reversion to the trend by regional employment. There is very little migration even in the long run.[31]

What is the role played by wages in the adjustment to region-specific shocks? Blanchard and Katz (1992) show that, in the United States, there is little change in wages in response to regional labor demand shocks. This suggests the presence of rigidities in the labor market, which do not allow the wage to adjust in response to a fall in the labor demand fall. The fall in labor demand and the lack of job opportunities are, therefore, larger than what the fall in relative regional wages might indicate. In the case of Europe, regional wage rigidities are even larger given that, in most countries, wage bargaining is centralized at the national level.[32]

We have checked whether the European response is due to the fact that people are reluctant to migrate across countries in Europe or whether they are reluctant to migrate even within their countries in response to labor demand shocks. To do so, we have run a similar VAR for Germany, Italy, and the United Kingdom, where variables are all defined relative to their national counterparts. Figures 8.16–8.18 show the results. They confirm that changes in the participation rate are the main adjustment mechanism. Once again, except for Italy, the role played by the employment rate over both the short and long run is negligible. Also, in Italy and Germany we observe a clear reversion of regional employment to the initial level. In the United Kingdom, this reversion is much slower, but, at the same time, labor force participation perfectly follows the evolution of employment. The net result is that, in the three countries, migration plays very little role at any horizon.[33]

---

[31] In both Europe and the United States, the response of employment is less persistent in the three-variable VAR than in the univariate analysis, suggesting that the other two variables can help predict changes in employment. This is consistent with a model where the three variables are jointly determined.

[32] To verify this claim, we have run a four-variable VAR, including wages, for our sample of European regions. There is no response of regional relative wages to labor demand shocks.

[33] Mauro and Spilimbergo (1998) run a similar VAR for Spanish regions distinguishing between

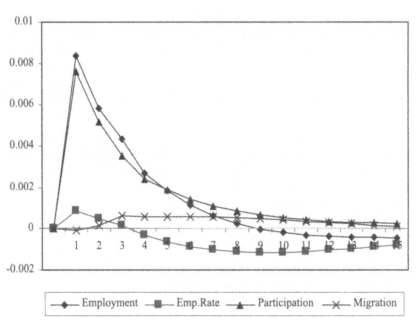

Figure 8.16. Labor market adjustment: Germany (impulse response, annual data).

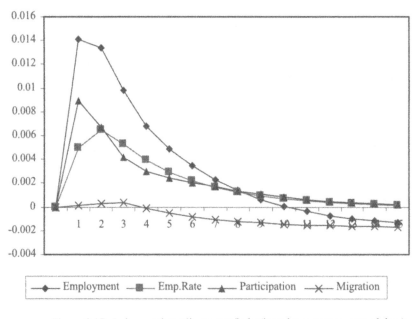

Figure 8.17. Labor market adjustment: Italy (impulse response, annual data).

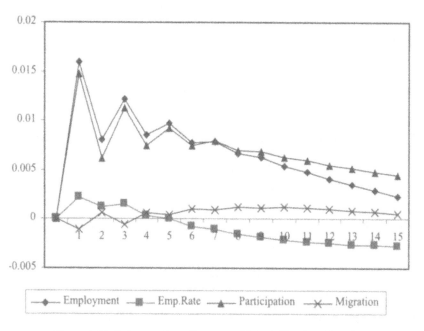

Figure 8.18. Labor market adjustment: United Kingdom (impulse response, annual data).

Here it is important to note that our results do not imply that within countries labor does not move in response to interregional economic disparities. Note that in our trivariate system we have allowed for region-specific fixed effects. Consequently, we are not explaining steady migrational flows between regions (e.g., a steady flow of migrants from Ireland to the United Kingdom or from southern Italy to northern Italy). Such steady flows are driven by structural disparities between regions rather than by labor demand shocks.[34]

These results for European regions clearly show that changes in labor demand are, to a large extent, met by people moving in and out of the labor force. The interpretation of the permanent effects must be taken with great care given that the choice of introducing employment in growth rates and the other two variables in levels conditions the joint response of these three variables in the long run. In fact, if we include participation and unemployment rates in differences, we find that regional shocks have larger permanent effects and are mostly absorbed by changes in labor force participation. Figure 8.19 displays the results.

workers with different skill levels. They found that even though low-skilled workers respond in manner similar to the one we describe here, high-skilled workers are more likely to move in response to regional shocks.

[34] See De Grauwe and Vanhaverbeke (1994) for an analysis of these flows.

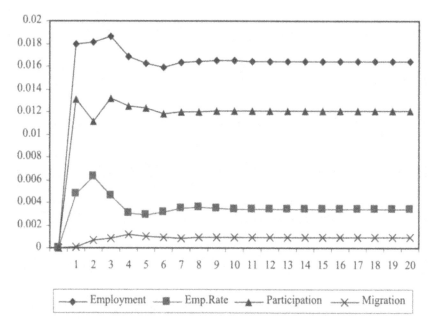

Figure 8.19. Labor market adjustment: Europe (impulse response, annual data; all variables in the VAR in growth rates).

Our results confirm evidence by Burda and Wyplosz (1994) who find that in Germany over the period from 1970 to 1988 the gross flows from out of the labor force to employment often were considerably larger than the gross flows from unemployment to employment. Several mechanisms can explain the empirical relevance of these flows. Moreover, some of them are more likely to operate on the regional rather than the aggregate level. For example, employers in Europe rely considerably on early retirement to adjust the size of the workforce in their firms.[35] Further, in the 1980s, an increasing number of employees qualified for disability pensions. Emerson (1988) noted that during the 1970s and 1980s the number of people on disability pensions in Europe rose enormously and traced this to changes in eligibility criteria. These criteria have become more heavily weighted by social and economic factors rather than strictly medical ones.[36]

[35] In France, around 50% of the 55–64 year old are either unemployed or have left the labor force. Source: *The Economist*, July 25th–31st 1992, p. 57.

[36] The number of people on disability pensions in Germany rose from 1.746 million in 1975 to 2.332 million in 1983, which amounts to 10% of the employed. For the United Kingdom, the numbers are 450,000 and 737,000; for the Netherlands, they are 344,000 and 673,000 (12% of the employed). Apparently in the Mezzogiorno in Italy 2.5 times as many people were on disability insurance than on regular pensions in the early 1980s (see Emerson, 1988). In the United States,

For this reason, it is not surprising that these mechanisms operate more at the regional level than at the national level. Some of these social tensions are the strongest when the restructuring of a specific industrial sector has most of its effects concentrated on a specific geographical area.

8.5   Implications for European migration

Our results for migration show that European labor markets are not well integrated. Do we expect a significant change in these patterns as national borders lose their economic significance and legal barriers to international labor mobility disappear? Are U.S. labor markets a good model of what lies ahead for Europe? The evidence we gathered in this paper seems to suggest that the answer to both of these questions is no. First of all, we have documented a substantial trend toward reduced migration after the mid 1970s. This reduction is also present within countries and goes in the opposite direction of what would be predicted by any migration model given the contemporaneous increase in unemployment differentials. The traditional origins of migration, mainly countries in southern Europe, have experienced a return of previous migrants turning a consistently large emigration flow into net immigration. Within these countries, migration to rich regions and urban and industrial areas has also declined.

At the same time that we have seen a decline in the size of these flows, we have seen a change in their composition. Migration of high-skilled and qualified workers has remained much more stable than the migration of manual low-skilled workers, which has sharply fallen in the last 20 years. In some European regions, or countries, this is a source of concern because migration will then work to increase regional disparities instead of diminish them.[37]

To be able to predict the future evolution of European migration, one must understand the causes of the falling trend in migration in the last two decades. Four factors have contributed to the sharp fall in migration. First of all, there has been a decrease in demand for unskilled labor, one of the main sources of migration during the 1960s and early 1970s. Second, some of the demand for low-skilled workers has been met by migration from countries outside of the European Union. The evidence we presented in Section 8.3 on net migration into the European Union showed increased flows from neighboring countries and some of the traditional sources of low-skilled migrants, Spain

---

the number of people on disability insurance actually declined from 4.129 million in 1975 to 3.865 million in 1983.

[37] See Begg (1995) for a discussion of the case of Ireland.

or Italy, have seen a surge in immigration of this type of workers from North Africa.

The third factor is the generalized increase in European unemployment since 1974. Many empirical studies have shown that an increase in aggregate unemployment reduces overall interregional migration. Not only does migration become less attractive because of the lack of opportunities in other areas, but, in some cases, previous migrants are the first ones to lose their jobs, which generates a flow back to poorer regions.

The last factor is the convergence of regional income per capita, which reduces the incentive to migrate. In addition to the higher income per capita, some of the poor regions benefit from an increase in fiscal and regional transfers as the size of the welfare state has expanded.

These four factors combined with other structural problems that restrict mobility (such as the rigidities in housing markets) are responsible for the current low level of European migration. Will the progressive integration of European economies alter these factors? There is no doubt that the elimination of barriers to labor mobility together with the integration of European economies and the transparency that the creation of a single currency adds will have beneficial effects on labor mobility. However, all these changes will only have minor effects on the four factors that explain the recent evolution of intra-EU migration. The biggest change could come from a general reduction in unemployment rates in EU regions that helped uncover new migration opportunities. If, in addition, this reduction in unemployment originates in the elimination of some of the general rigidities in European labor markets and an increase in competitiveness of labor markets due to increased integration, then we might observe a larger increase in mobility. But even if this change takes place, this increase is very likely to affect mainly high-skilled workers. If this is the case, labor mobility will not work in the direction of reducing regional imbalances, and it might even increase those disparities.[38]

8.6   Conclusions

This chapter has analyzed the evolution and adjustment mechanisms of European and U.S. regional labor markets. The degree of labor mobility is a key element that can explain some of the general differences between both economic areas. In the United States, the high degree of labor mobility creates an

---

[38] The evidence in Faini, Galli, Gennari, and Rossi (1997) suggests that interregional labor mobility in Europe is the highest among high-skilled workers and that increases in household income raises the probability of migration.

environment that allows certain states to consistently grow above the average and where there are no persistent differences in unemployment rates.

European labor markets, on the contrary, are marked by low labor mobility. The first consequence being that employment growth rates are less persistent than in the United States. Although there is evidence that migration responds to regional economic disparities, the speed at which it does is small and has been decreasing since the second half of the 1970s. This trend toward smaller migration, also strong within countries, is more surprising when compared with the evolution of regional unemployment rates. Some of the regions where unemployment rates have increased the most have switched from being a source of migrants to receiving immigration from other regions.

The analysis of the short-term adjustment of labor markets is consistent with these earlier views. In the United States, regional fluctuations are mainly absorbed by migration. This response propagates regional shocks and adds persistence to the initial impact on regional employment. Speculative migration, shown to be much larger in the United States than in Europe, is probably a main factor that explains the quick response of workers to regional business cycles. In Europe, we find that migration is practically absent in the adjustment process. In response to a decrease in regional employment, labor force participation rates fall, and unemployment increases. Surprisingly, it is not the unemployment rate but the fall in participation rates that accounts for the majority of the fall in employment.

Will European labor markets change as a result of further economic integration and the reduction of barriers to international labor mobility? The intranational evidence of European countries suggests that the change, if any, will be minor. Regional migration within countries not only is small but also has decreased, despite an increase in regional unemployment dispersion. This decrease in migration is rooted in the functioning of European labor market institutions, rigid labor markets, and the overall high rate of unemployment, all of which discourage any type of mobility, including geographical mobility. Only if the European unemployment rate is reduced to levels that create tightness on certain regions, can migratory flows reverse their recent trend. However, the composition of these flows is likely to be biased toward qualified workers, which might work in the direction of increasing regional imbalances.

References

Barro, R. J., and X. Sala-i-Martin. 1991. Convergence across states and regions. *Brookings Papers on Economic Activity* 1: 107–98.

Begg, I. 1995. Factor mobility and regional disparities in the European Union. *Oxford Review of Economic Policy* 11(2): 96–112.

Bentolila, S., and J. J. Dolado. 1991. "Mismatch and Internal Migration in Spain, 1962–86," in F. Padoa Schioppa, ed., *Mismatch and Labor Mobility*. Cambridge: Cambridge University Press.

Blanchard, O., and L. Katz. 1992. Regional evolutions. *Brookings Papers on Economic Activity* 1: 1–75.

Burda, M., and C. Wyplosz. 1994. Gross worker and job flows in Europe. *European Economic Review* 38(6): 1287–315.

DaVanzo, J. 1978. Does unemployment affect migration? Evidence from micro data. *Review of Economics and Statistics* 4: 504–14.

Davis, S. J., P. Loungani, and R. Mahidhara. 1997. "Regional Labor Fluctuations: Oil Shocks, Military Spending, and Other Driving Forces. International Finance Discussion Papers, Board of Governors of the Federal Reserve System.

Decressin, J. 1994. Internal migration in West Germany and implications for East-West salary convergence. *Weltwirtschaftliches Archiv* 130(2): 231–57.

Decressin, J., and A. Fatás. 1995. Regional labor market dynamics in Europe. *European Economic Review* 39.

De Grauwe, P., and W. Vanhaverbeke. 1993. "Is Europe an Optimum Currency Area? Evidence from Regional Data," in Paul Masson and Mark Taylor, eds., *Policy Issues in the Operation of Currency Unions*. Cambridge: Cambridge University Press.

Eichengreen, B. 1993. "Labor Markets and European Monetary Unification," in Paul Masson and Mark Taylor, eds., *Policy Issues in the Operation of Currency Unions*. Cambridge: Cambridge University Press.

Emerson, M. 1988. *What Model for Europe?* Cambridge, MA: MIT Press.

Faini, R., G. Galli, P. Gennari, and F. Rossi. 1997. An empirical puzzle: falling migration and growing unemployment differentials among Italian regions. *European Economic Review* 41: 571–79.

Greenwood, M. J. 1975. Research on internal migration: a survey. *Journal of Economic Literature* 13.

Greenwood, M. J. 1985. Human migration: Theory, models, and empirical studies. *Journal of Regional Science* 25(4): 521–44.

Herzog, H. W., A. M. Schlottmann, and T. P. Boehm. 1993. Migration as spatial job-search: A survey of empirical findings. *Regional Studies* 27(4): 327–40.

Hojvat-Gallin, J. 1998. "Regional Labor Market Dynamics and Net Migration." Unpublished doctoral dissertation. University of Chicago.

Hughes, G., and B. McCormick. 1989. "Does Migration Reduce Differentials in Regional Unemployment?" in Van Dijk et al., eds., *Migration and Labor Market Adjustment*. Dordrecht: Kluwer Academic Press.

Jackman, R., and A. Savouri. 1992. Regional migration in Britain: An analysis of gross flows using NHS central register data. *The Economic Journal* 102: 1433–50.

Mauro, P., and A. Spilimbergo. 1998. "How Do the Skilled and the Unskilled Respond to Regional Shocks? The Case of Spain." Mimeo. IMF.

OECD. 1996. *Flexibility in the Labor Market*. Paris: OECD.

Pissarides, C. A., and I. McMaster. 1990. Regional migration, wages and unemployment: Empirical evidence and implications for policy. *Oxford Economic Papers* 42.

Van Dijk, J., F. Herzog, and A. Schlottman, eds. 1989. *Migration and Labor Market Adjustment*. London: Kluwer Academic.

Data appendix

European regions

Country	Region	Country	Region
Germany	Schleswig-Holst./Hamburg	France	Ile de France
	Niedersachsen/Bremen		Bassin Parisien
	Nordrheim-Westfalen		Nord Pas-de-Calais
	Hessen		Est
	Rheinland-Platz/Saarland		Ouest
	Baden-Wurttemberg		Sud-Ouest
	Bayern		Centre-Est
	Berlin		Mediterrane
Italy	Nord-Ovest	U.K.	North
	Lombardia		York and Humberside
	Nord-Est		East Midlands
	Emilia Romagna		East Anglia
	Centro		South-East
	Lazio		South-West
	Campania		West-Midlands
	Abruzzi-Molise		North-West
	Sud		Wales
	Sicilia		Scotland
	Sardegna		Northern Ireland

Data sources

Regional data on unemployment – *OECD, Regional Employment and Unemployment, 1960–87.* Original sources and years. France: 1954, 1962, 1968, 1974–87 (INSEE; Labor Force Survey). Germany: 1960–87 (Stat. Bundesamt; Employment: Microzensus, Unemployment: Registered Unemployed). Italy: 1960–87 (ISTA; Labor Force Survey).[39] Spain: 1977–87 (INE; Labor Force Survey). United Kingdom: 1965–87 (Employment: Establishment Survey, Unemployment: Registered Unemployed). Regional data on employment expanded to 1994 using national sources.

National data on population, labor force, and employment – *OECD economic outlook.*

Regional data on working-age population (15–64 years old) – *EUROSTAT, Regional Databank: REGIO, 1991.* Periods covered by

---

[39] In this dataset, the regional unemployment data for Italy has a considerable statistical break in 1976–77. Before 1977, the national total was considerably larger. We adjusted pre-1977 figures by multiplying them with the ratio of national unemployment to total regional unemployment.

our data are France, 1975–87; Germany, 1975–87; Italy, 1975–87; United Kingdom, 1975–87; Spain, 1981–87.

Migration data on EU countries – *Eurostat, Statistiques sur la Migration, 1996.*

We thank Larry Katz for providing us with the regional data for the United States. The 51 regions for which data are available include the 50 states and the District of Columbia. Employment data come from establishment surveys and comprise nonagricultural employment only. For the trivariate system, the unemployment and population data come from the CPS (last census: 1980). To obtain regional labor force data, CPS unemployment is added to establishment employment, which is normalized so that it is equal to the CPS number in 1976. Working-age population data also comes from the CPS. For a more precise description of the data sources, see the Data Appendix of Blanchard and Katz (1992).

CHAPTER 9

The sources of fluctuations within
and across countries*

Todd E. Clark[†] and Kwanho Shin[‡]

9.1   Introduction

Traditionally, business cycle research has focused on aggregate sources of national business cycles. A recent literature has extended the traditional line of business cycle analysis in two directions. First, recognizing that a nation is comprised of many regions and industries, researchers have examined the importance of national, region-specific, and industry-specific disturbances in the fluctuations experienced by regions within a nation. Second, focusing on international business cycles, researchers have examined the importance of common international, nation-specific, and industry-specific disturbances in the fluctuations experienced by different nations.

The literature on sources of fluctuations within and across countries provides evidence on the importance of borders in business cycle fluctuations. To date, different nations generally determine monetary and fiscal policies independently and restrict migration, trade, and capital flows. Regions within a nation are affected by national monetary and fiscal policies and allow free migration, trade, and capital flows among regions. Comparing the importance of different types of disturbances to regions with the importance of corresponding disturbances to nations around the world provides evidence on the importance of economic borders.

Drawing on the literature, this chapter reviews the evidence on the sources of fluctuations within and across countries and the implications for the role of

* The authors gratefully acknowledge the research assistance of Kevin Wondra and the helpful comments of Andrew Filardo, Atish Ghosh, seminar participants at the Federal Reserve Bank of Kansas City, and participants at the conference on Intranational Macroeconomics. The views expressed herein are solely those of the authors and do not necessarily reflect the views of the Federal Reserve Bank of Kansas City or the Federal Reserve System.

[†] Mailing address: Economic Research Department, Federal Reserve Bank of Kansas City, 925 Grand Boulevard, Kansas City, MO 64198. E-mail: *todd.e.clark@kc.frb.org*.

[‡] Mailing address: Department of Economics, Korea University, Seoul, Korea 136-701. E-mail: *khshin@kuccφ8.korea.ac.kr.*

borders in business cycles.[1] A simple econometric model is presented and applied to within-U.S. and cross-country data in order to provide a framework for examining and interpreting the literature. The chapter then reviews alternative approaches to quantifying sources of comovement. Finally, the chapter discusses the implications of the overall evidence for the role of borders, speculating on what the business cycle would look like in a world without economic borders.

Overall, the evidence yields three general conclusions on the sources of fluctuations within and across countries. First, common shocks are less important in international fluctuations than in within-country fluctuations. Second, region-specific shocks account for a larger share of variation in international data than in within-country data. Finally, industry-specific shocks are a smaller source of variation internationally than within countries. This paper then argues that lowering economic borders among nations should make the sources of international fluctuations look more like the sources of within-country fluctuations. Taking the current integration of within-U.S. business cycles as a benchmark, reducing borders should reduce the importance of country-specific disturbances and boost the importance of common and industry-specific factors.

9.2   A benchmark specification and results from that specification

This section first develops a basic model and then presents benchmark results from that specification. The section concludes by comparing the results to those from previous studies relying on essentially the same model.

9.2.1   The disaggregate VAR/factor model

The benchmark model, referred to henceforth as the *disaggregate VAR/factor model*, takes the essential form laid out by Altonji and Ham (1990) and Norrbin and Schlagenhauf (1988, 1996). Let $X_{r,i,t}$, $X_{r,t}$, $X_{i,t}$, and X_t denote growth in, respectively, industry i in region r; region r; industry i; and either the United States overall or the world. The basic model equations are

$$X_{r,i,t} = \mu_{r,i} + \sum_{p=1}^{P} \alpha_{r,i,p} X_{t-p} + \sum_{p=1}^{P} \beta_{r,i,p} X_{r,t-p}$$

$$+ \sum_{p=1}^{P} \gamma_{r,i,p} X_{i,t-p} + e_{r,i,t} \tag{1}$$

$$e_{r,i,t} = \delta_{r,i} c_t + \theta_{r,i} u_{r,t} + \lambda_{r,i} n_{i,t} + v_{r,i,t} \tag{2}$$

---

[1] Focusing on the sources of regional fluctuations, this study abstracts from the numerous studies, such as Long and Plosser (1987) and Norrbin and Schlagenhauf (1991), that examine only industry fluctuations. In the interest of brevity, this review also abstracts from studies focused on a particular region in the United States, rather than a full set of regions spanning the country. These studies, reviewed in Clark and Shin (1998), include Coulson (1993), Coulson and Rushen (1995), Kuttner and Sbordone (1997), and Shea (1996).

With R regions and I industries, the model includes RI equations of each of the forms (1) and (2).

The set of equations of the form (1) captures the dynamics of fluctuations with a restricted VAR for the set of region-industry variables. The aggregate variables on the right-hand side of (1) are constructed as fixed-weight averages of the region-industry variables:

$$X_t = \sum_{r=1}^{R} \sum_{i=1}^{I} w_{r,i} X_{r,i,t}, \qquad \sum_{r=1}^{R} \sum_{i=1}^{I} w_{r,i} = 1 \tag{3}$$

$$X_{r,t} = \sum_{i=1}^{I} a_{r,i} X_{r,i,t}, \qquad \sum_{i=1}^{I} a_{r,i} = 1 \tag{4}$$

$$X_{i,t} = \sum_{r=1}^{R} b_{r,i} X_{r,i,t}, \qquad \sum_{r=1}^{R} b_{r,i} = 1 \tag{5}$$

Letting Y_t denote the $RI \times 1$ vector of region-industry growth rates, the system of RI equations of the form (1) can then be written as a restricted VAR:

$$Y_t = \sum_{p=1}^{P} \Pi_p Y_{t-p} + e_t \tag{6}$$

$$\Pi_p = \alpha_p W_{RI} + \beta_p W_R + \gamma_p W_I \tag{7}$$

where α_p, β_p, γ_p contain the regression coefficients for lag p and W_{RI}, W_R, and W_I contain, respectively, the appropriate $w_{r,i}$, $a_{r,i}$, and $b_{r,i}$ weights. The lag length P is set at 4 for quarterly data and 1 for annual data.

According to the error model (2), a shock $e_{r,i,t}$ to industry i in region r reflects: a common (national for within-U.S. analysis or world for cross-country analysis) shock c_t; a region r-specific shock $u_{r,t}$; an industry i-specific shock $n_{i,t}$; and a shock idiosyncratic to industry i in region r. Note that, for simplicity, "region" is used to refer to both a region within a nation and to a nation. The variances of the structural shocks c_t, $u_{r,t}$ $(r = 1, \ldots, R)$, and $n_{i,t}$ $(i = 1, \ldots, I)$ are all normalized to 1. The $\phi_{r,i}$, $\theta_{r,i}$, and $\lambda_{r,i}$ parameters are estimated.

The error model (2) is identified by assuming the common, region-specific, and industry-specific shocks to be independent. Although some may view this formulation as overly restrictive, it in fact provides a useful lower bound on the importance of region-specific and industry-specific forces.[2] For example, the

---

[2] Clark (1998) reports corroborating evidence, based on a model augmented to allow separate shocks common to particular groups of regions. Horvath and Verbrugge (1997) also provide evidence for this view. They allow a shock to industry i to have an immediate effect on any industry j that is directly linked by an input-output relationship. This identification produces a larger role for industry shocks than would an identification assuming the shock to i has no contemporaneous effect on j.

model attributes all comovement among regions to the common and industry-specific components. If some of the observed regional comovement in fact stems from correlation among the region-specific shocks or from a shock to region r having contemporaneous effects on region s, the estimates will generally overstate the importance of the common component and understate the importance of the region shocks.

As Altonji and Ham (1990) and Stockman (1988) discuss, the shocks in (2) may be viewed as having a variety of sources. In within-country analysis, the common shock captures innovations in national supply and demand, such as monetary policy changes. The results of Davis, Loungani, and Mihidhara (1997), Hooker and Knetter (1997), and Samolyk (1994) suggest changes in the regional distribution of national military spending or regional financial conditions may be sources of region-specific shocks. Changes in regional fiscal policy may also produce region-specific shocks. In cross-country analysis, the common component reflects international developments such as oil price changes and common movements in monetary policy. In both within-country and cross-country analysis, the industry-specific shocks stem from changes in product demand, input prices, and productivity.

9.2.2   Estimation

The disaggregate VAR/factor model is estimated in two steps. In the first, the regressions (1) are estimated by ordinary least squares (OLS). In the second, the regression residuals are used in estimating the error model (2) by maximum likelihood (ML), as implemented with the estimation-maximization (EM) algorithm. Although computationally simple, this estimation procedure has a drawback, discussed in more detail in Clark and Shin (1998): calculating standard errors for the error model estimates is generally intractable. However, to provide a rough sense of the sampling uncertainty, Monte Carlo-simulated standard errors are reported for the quarterly, within-U.S. employment estimates.[3] The procedure is used for only one specification because the simulations require roughly one week of computing time.

The presented results are limited to shares of innovation and steady-state variance due to common, region-specific, industry-specific, and idiosyncratic shocks. Steady-state shares are calculated using the fitted innovation variance matrix and the restricted VAR structure (6)–(7). Decompositions are reported for both industries within regions and aggregate regions. The decomposition for aggregate regions is based on the fact that the $R \times 1$ vector of growth rates for the region aggregates, $X_{R,t}$, is given by $X_{R,t} = W_R Y_t$, where W_R and Y_t are as defined earlier. The k-step ahead forecast error variance for aggregate regions

---

[3] The Monte Carlo data are generated using the fitted regression equations and draws of normally distributed errors with a covariance matrix equal to the fitted covariance matrix.

can then be calculated as

$$\mathrm{Var}(X_{R,t+k} \mid Y_t) = W_R \cdot \mathrm{Var}(Y_{t+k} \mid Y_t) \cdot W_R' \qquad (8)$$

9.2.3 Data

To ensure the accuracy of the measured importance of region-specific and industry-specific shocks, the benchmark results are based on quarterly data. If shocks propagate across regions and industries, truly region-specific and industry-specific shocks may be identified as common shocks in annual data, causing the estimates to understate the importance of region and industry shocks. Accordingly, the model is estimated using quarterly growth in: (1) employment in eight one-digit industries in the eight aggregate U.S. regions defined by the Bureau of Economic Analysis (the BEA regions) and (2) industrial production in eight two-digit manufacturing industries in ten European nations. However, because results for one-digit employment are not strictly comparable to results for two-digit manufacturing production, the model is also estimated using annual data that are more comparable: employment in six one-digit industries in the eight BEA regions and in eight European nations. Appendix A provides some detail on the data.

In addition to entailing choices with respect to time-series aggregation, the specification of the dataset entails making choices with respect to the business cycle variable, the level of cross-section aggregation, and trend model. In practice, the key consideration in choosing a business cycle measure is data availability. Many economists probably generally prefer gross domestic product (GDP) for examining business cycles, although, for particular questions, other indicators may be preferred.[4] Quarterly GDP, however, is less widely available than employment or industrial production. A second consideration is the comparability of within-country and cross-country data. The only available data comparable within the United States and across countries are annual figures on employment, unemployment, and GDP. As detailed in Clark and Shin (1998), these issues of availability and comparability and still other issues arise in determining the degree of cross-section aggregation and trend model. Ultimately, however, the broad findings emphasized later seem to be robust across data specifications.

9.2.4 Quarterly benchmark results

Table 9.1 presents benchmark results for quarterly, within-U.S. employment growth. For the average region-industry unit within the U.S. – that is, when the

---

[4] The findings of Basu and Fernald (1995) may be seen as suggesting GDP should *not* be preferred. Basu and Fernald argued that value added data can imply large spillovers across sectors even when such spillovers do not truly exist (in gross output), because the assumptions underlying the construction of value added are false.

Table 9.1. *Variance decomposition – quarterly disaggregate VAR/factor model estimates, 1957:2–97:4 (within-U.S. employment, one-digit industries)*

	Fitted innov. var.	Shares of innovation variance				Fitted st-st. var.	Shares of steady-state variance			
		Common	Region	Industry	Idiosyn.		Common	Reg.	Ind.	Idiosyn.
Region-industry level										
Average	49.727	0.130 (0.014)	0.126 (0.007)	0.253 (0.010)	0.491 (0.010)	65.285	0.170	0.159	0.286	0.384
Region level										
New England	1.760	0.213 (0.060)	0.276 (0.059)	0.173 (0.030)	0.338 (0.044)	9.836	0.134	0.336	0.167	0.364
Mideast	1.355	0.355 (0.069)	0.345 (0.055)	0.143 (0.024)	0.157 (0.023)	2.857	0.370	0.267	0.217	0.147
Great Lakes	2.869	0.586 (0.061)	0.096 (0.037)	0.100 (0.025)	0.218 (0.034)	6.436	0.544	0.099	0.202	0.155
Plains	1.308	0.352 (0.068)	0.249 (0.057)	0.149 (0.026)	0.250 (0.032)	3.278	0.424	0.171	0.224	0.181
Southeast	1.620	0.382 (0.066)	0.275 (0.051)	0.206 (0.030)	0.137 (0.020)	4.327	0.352	0.246	0.258	0.145
Southwest	1.603	0.194 (0.061)	0.449 (0.058)	0.076 (0.015)	0.280 (0.038)	4.687	0.185	0.408	0.137	0.270
Rocky Mtn.	2.442	0.191 (0.064)	0.466 (0.061)	0.088 (0.016)	0.255 (0.030)	5.012	0.213	0.389	0.168	0.230
Far West	2.249	0.304 (0.064)	0.417 (0.059)	0.068 (0.014)	0.211 (0.026)	5.470	0.292	0.347	0.162	0.199
Average	1.901	0.322 (0.038)	0.322 (0.023)	0.125 (0.012)	0.231 (0.015)	5.238	0.314	0.283	0.192	0.211

Notes: The table reports estimates of the disaggregate VAR/factor model Equations (1)–(2) obtained from quarterly growth in one-digit industries in BEA regions. The reported share figures are shares of variance attributable to common, region-specific, industry-specific, and idiosyncratic shocks. The innovation estimates correspond to a decomposition of 1-step ahead forecast error variances. The steady-state estimates are based on a decomposition of 251-step ahead forecast error variances, evaluated using the restricted VAR (6)–(7) written in companion form. The "*Average*" row for the region-industry level reports the average, across region-industry units, of the decompositions for each region-industry unit. As described in Section 9.2.2, the "Region Level" estimates are based on an aggregation of the fitted variance-covariance matrix of the set of region-industry units. Average 1982–97 employment shares are used as weights in the aggregation. The figures in parentheses are approximate standard errors, calculated with Monte Carlo simulations.

variance decompositions for each industry i in region r are averaged across all r, i pairs – idiosyncratic shocks are the most important source of innovation variance, accounting for 49.1%. Industry-specific shocks are the second most important source of variation, with a variance share of 25.3%. Common and region-specific shocks are of basically equal importance, with innovation variance shares of 13.0 and 12.6%, respectively. For the average aggregate region – that is, when variance decompositions for each region r, calculated using (8), are averaged across regions – common and region-specific shocks are the leading sources of variation, each accounting for 32.2% of the innovation variance. Idiosyncratic shocks are next in importance, with an innovation variance share of 23.1%. The remaining 12.5% of the average region's innovation variance is due to industry-specific shocks.

Over time, there appears to be little propagation of shocks across regions in the within-U.S. estimates. In results not reported for brevity's sake, when the sources of variation for each region-industry and each aggregate region are decomposed into shares due to own vs. other region shocks and own vs. other idiosyncratic shocks, the "own" and "other" shares are essentially the same in the steady state as at impact. If significant propagation occurred, such that a shock specific – at impact – to region r spread to region s over time, the shares of variance due to "other" region shocks would be higher in the steady state than at impact.[5] Correspondingly, the variance shares of "own" region shocks would be lower in the steady state than at impact. Because no such shifts in shares are evident, there is little net propagation of shocks in the disaggregate model estimates. As discussed in Section 9.3.1, this finding, in conjunction with stronger evidence of propagation from a less restrictive, aggregate model, suggests the disaggregate VAR may overly restrict feedback.

Table 9.2 reports benchmark estimates for quarterly growth in industrial production across Europe. For the average region-industry unit in Europe – that is, averaging the variance decompositions for each industry i in region r across all r, i pairs – idiosyncratic shocks are the leading source of variation, with an innovation variance share of 59.0%. Region-specific shocks are the second most important source of variation, with a variance share of 22.6%. Common and industry-specific shocks are roughly equal in importance, with innovation variance shares of 7.7 and 10.7%, respectively. For the average aggregate region – that is, averaging the variance decompositions for each region r, calculated using (8), across regions – region-specific shocks are the most important source of innovation variance, accounting for 46.4%. The second largest source of variation for the average region is idiosyncratic shocks, with an innovation variance share of 35.0%. Common shocks account for 13.1% of the

---

[5] By construction, the shares of innovation variance due to "other" components equal 0.

Table 9.2. *Variance decomposition – quarterly disaggregate VAR/factor model estimates, 1976:4–97:1 (European industrial production, two-digit manufacturing industries)*

	Fitted innov. var.	Shares of innovation variance				Fitted st.-st. var.	Shares of steady-state variance			
		Common	Region	Industry	Idiosyn.		Common	Reg.	Ind.	Idiosyn.
		Region-industry level								
Average	151.797	0.077	0.226	0.107	0.590	220.060	0.080	0.252	0.129	0.538
		Region level								
Austria	29.299	0.353	0.002	0.032	0.613	41.837	0.279	0.083	0.069	0.569
Finland	55.318	0.005	0.612	0.027	0.355	65.553	0.028	0.582	0.049	0.341
France	22.029	0.214	0.390	0.216	0.181	32.395	0.163	0.447	0.195	0.195
W. Germany	50.428	0.231	0.373	0.092	0.303	64.053	0.198	0.403	0.092	0.307
Ireland	85.070	0.000	0.568	0.006	0.425	96.665	0.005	0.535	0.040	0.420
Italy	52.602	0.001	0.745	0.081	0.172	63.576	0.047	0.685	0.090	0.178
Netherlands	26.401	0.105	0.484	0.047	0.364	42.833	0.078	0.475	0.084	0.362
Spain	44.536	0.162	0.510	0.012	0.316	59.369	0.137	0.480	0.037	0.346
Sweden	72.933	0.231	0.285	0.014	0.470	87.637	0.210	0.299	0.029	0.462
United Kingdom	29.715	0.004	0.668	0.029	0.300	38.318	0.041	0.602	0.065	0.292
Average	46.833	0.131	0.464	0.056	0.350	59.224	0.119	0.459	0.075	0.347

Notes: The table reports estimates of the disaggregate VAR/factor model Equations (1)–(2) obtained from quarterly growth in two-digit manufacturing industries in the listed countries. The reported share figures are shares of variance attributable to common, region-specific, industry-specific, and idiosyncratic shocks. For simplicity, "region" is used to refer to nation. The innovation estimates correspond to a decomposition of 1-step ahead forecast error variances. The steady-state estimates are based on a decomposition of 251-step ahead forecast error variances, evaluated using the restricted VAR (6)–(7) written in companion form. The "*Average*" row for the regional-industrial level reports the average, across region-industry units, of the decompositions for each region-industry unit. As described in Section 9.2.2, the "Region level" estimates are based on an aggregation of the fitted variance-covariance matrix of the set of region-industry units. The fixed weights used in the aggregation are taken from OECD (1997).

innovation variance. Finally, the share of innovation variance attributable to industry-specific shocks is 5.6%.

Over time, there appears to be little propagation of shocks across nations in the disaggregate model estimates for Europe. In results not reported, when the sources of variation are decomposed into shares due to own vs. other region shocks and own vs. other idiosyncratic shocks, the "own" and "other" components are essentially the same in the steady state as at impact. But again, as shown in Section 9.3.1, a more aggregate and less restrictive VAR model implies much richer propagation of shocks, suggesting the disaggregate VAR model may overly restrict feedback.

Even though Table 9.2's estimates assume the sources of variation have been stable over 1975–97, the integration of nations has probably increased, due to forces such as the European Monetary System (EMS). Testing stability, however, requires reducing the scale of the model and using data available for a longer period. Accordingly, industries are dropped, and the model is simplified to a VAR(4) in national growth rates (for the countries in Table 9.2) and the error model

$$e_{r,t} = \delta_r c_t + u_{r,t} \tag{9}$$

Dropping industries should not much affect conclusions on stability because industry-specific shocks are minor sources of variation in the benchmark estimates.[6] Growth in total industrial production, which is available longer, is used in lieu of manufacturing production. The sample is divided into sub-samples of 1962:2–79:4 and 1980:1–97:4, between which the parameters of (9) are allowed to differ. According to these estimates, there has been no significant shift in the average shares of variance.[7] On average, common shocks account for 21.8% (17.4%) of the innovation (steady-state) variance over 1962–79 and 16.4% (14.8%) of the innovation (steady-state) variance over 1980–97; the change in the innovation variance shares has a standard error of 5.4. To the extent this finding may be viewed as suggesting integration has increased only modestly, the benchmark 1975–97 results should accurately reflect the importance of different types of shocks over the period.

Comparing the quarterly within-U.S. and cross-country results reveals three general differences.[8] First, common shocks account for a smaller share of variance in international data than in within-U.S. data. Second, region-specific

---

[6] See Clark and Shin (1998) for more formal evidence.

[7] In contrast, Fatás (1997) finds that cross-Europe correlations of employment growth are higher in the EMS period than in a period preceding the EMS. However, the increases in correlations are probably too small to be statistically significant, especially given that the pre-EMS and EMS periods are each only 14 years long.

[8] For the remaining source of variation, idiosyncratic shocks, the relative importance varies with the set of countries used.

innovations are more important internationally than within the United States. Finally, industry-specific innovations account for less variation internationally than within the United States. Note that, using the Monte Carlo standard errors reported in Table 9.1 as a rough guide to sampling uncertainty, these differences between the within-U.S. and cross-country estimates appear to be statistically significant.

Even though the within-U.S. and cross-country estimates might also be seen as suggesting that the shocks affecting nations are much larger than those affecting U.S. regions, data differences preclude making such a comparison. The variance of the overall reduced-form shock to each region, estimated from the model parameters and reported in the second column of each table, is much larger for European nations than for U.S. regions. But comparing these estimates is problematic because the within-U.S. results are for total employment, whereas the international results are for manufacturing production. The measured international shocks may be bigger simply because manufacturing is more volatile than an overall economy and production is more volatile than employment.

9.2.5   Benchmark results for comparable annual data

The left panel of Table 9.3 presents benchmark results for annual, within-U.S. employment growth. For the average region-industry unit within the United States, common shocks are the leading source of variation, accounting for 42.6%. Industry-specific shocks have the second-largest innovation variance share, at 26.6%. Region-specific and idiosyncratic shocks are of essentially equal importance, with innovation variance shares of 15.2 and 15.5%, respectively. At the aggregate region level, common shocks are an even more important source of fluctuations, with a variance share of 71.5%. Region-specific shocks are second in importance, accounting for 20.4% of the variance. Industry-specific and idiosyncratic shocks are relatively unimportant, with variance shares of 4.6 and 3.4%, respectively. A decomposition of steady-state variance is not reported because, in the annual data, the restricted VAR implied by the disaggregate model regression estimates has explosive autoregressive roots.

The right panel of Table 9.3 presents estimates for annual employment growth in a comparable set of industries within European countries. For the average *region-industry* unit in Europe, idiosyncratic shocks have the largest innovation variance share, at 40.0%. Region-specific shocks are second in importance, accounting for 28.2% of the variance. Common and industry-specific shocks have shares of 13.6 and 18.2%, respectively. At the aggregate region level, the largest share of variation, 36.6%, is due to region-specific shocks. Common, industry-specific, and idiosyncratic shocks are of roughly equal importance, with variance shares of about 20%. However, in the G7 estimates

Table 9.3. *Variance decomposition – annual disaggregate VAR/factor model estimates, 1972–93 (within-U.S. and European employment, one-digit industries)*

	Within-U.S. employment							European employment				
	Fitted innov. var.	Shares of innovation variance						Fitted innov. var.	Shares of innovation variance			
		Common	Reg.	Ind.	Idiosyn.				Common	Reg.	Ind.	Idiosyn.
Region-industry level												
Average	9.232	0.426	0.152	0.266	0.155	**Average**		5.044	0.136	0.282	0.182	0.400
Region level												
New England	2.615	0.576	0.294	0.059	0.071	Belgium		0.867	0.277	0.148	0.203	0.371
Mideast	1.418	0.751	0.137	0.055	0.057	Denmark		0.856	0.017	0.214	0.701	0.069
G. Lakes	2.968	0.825	0.131	0.023	0.020	Finland		0.335	0.249	0.635	0.034	0.082
Plains	2.195	0.781	0.160	0.042	0.017	France		2.453	0.128	0.545	0.114	0.213
Southeast	2.845	0.783	0.149	0.063	0.005	W. Germany		1.152	0.144	0.357	0.243	0.257
Southwest	2.945	0.603	0.341	0.027	0.029	Italy		0.547	0.404	0.221	0.159	0.216
Rocky Mtn.	2.567	0.578	0.360	0.033	0.029	Sweden		1.529	0.342	0.428	0.070	0.160
Far West	2.268	0.826	0.061	0.068	0.044	U.K.		3.301	0.359	0.384	0.017	0.240
Average	2.478	0.715	0.204	0.046	0.034	**Average**		1.380	0.240	0.366	0.193	0.201

Notes: The table reports estimates of the disaggregate VAR/factor model Equations (1)–(2) obtained from annual growth in one-digit industries in the listed regions. For simplicity, in the European estimates "region" is used to refer to nation. For comparability purposes, two of the U.S. industries listed in Appendix A and used in generating the Table 9.1 estimates – (1) mining and (2) finance, insurance, and real estate – are excluded from the estimation. The European industries are listed in Appendix A. The "Region level" estimates are obtained by aggregating the region-industry estimates using average 1970–93 employment shares. For additional details, see the notes to Table 9.1.

reported in Clark and Shin (1998), industry-specific shocks are somewhat less important than either common or idiosyncratic shocks.

These benchmark results for comparable annual data are consistent with the broad conclusions drawn from the quarterly data, except that, in annual data, from the perspective of aggregate regions industry-specific shocks are more important in international variation than in within-U.S. variation.[9] In addition, the annual data estimates suggest that the shocks affecting nations are modestly smaller than those affecting regions within the United States. The fitted variance of the overall reduced-form shock to each region averages 2.478 for U.S. regions and 1.380 for European nations.

9.2.6   Comparison with previous results using same basic approach

Several studies have relied on specifications very similar to the disaggregate VAR/factor model: Altonji and Ham (1990), Helg et al. (1995), Krieger (1989), and Norrbin and Schlagenhauf (1988, 1996). The general conclusions drawn from the benchmark estimates are very much in line with the results of these studies. Note that tables in a longer version of this chapter (Clark and Shin 1998) summarize the estimates obtained in these and other studies in the literature.

Altonji and Ham (1990) use the model to investigate the sources of variation in annual data on employment in one-digit industries in Canadian provinces. Their model is augmented to include current and lagged U.S. GNP growth in (1), to capture the potentially considerable influence of the neighboring United States. In qualitative terms, their estimates are broadly similar to those reported earlier for annual U.S. data. Abstracting from the important effect of the United States on Canada, common shocks are the leading source of variation in the *average region*, accounting for 33% of the innovation variance. Region-specific shocks are also important, although less so than common shocks, with an innovation variance share of 17%. Industry-specific shocks play only a small role in variation in Canadian regions. Altonji and Ham's results are only qualitatively different from the preceding results for annual U.S. employment in that idiosyncratic shocks are a significant source of variation, roughly equal in importance to region-specific shocks.

Helg et al. (1995) examine the sources of fluctuations in European industrial production using a disaggregate VAR and principal components analysis of the residuals. They estimate a slight variant of (1) with quarterly data for two- and three-digit industries in European nations. Rather than fit a formal error model to the residuals, Helg et al. use principal components analysis to gauge the relative importance of region-specific and industry-specific shocks. They compute

---

[9] However, from the perspective of region-industries, industry-specific shocks are less important internationally than within the United States in both quarterly and annual data.

principal components for the set of industries within each country (country PCs) and for the set of countries given a particular industry (industry PCs). The estimates show that, on average, the country PCs explain more of the variation in nation-industry production than the industry PCs do, suggesting nation-specific shocks are more important than industry-specific shocks.

Krieger (1989) relies on a variant of the disaggregate VAR/factor model to examine the sources of variation in annual GNP data for one-digit industries in Canada, West Germany, and Japan. Krieger's specification differs from the benchmark model in that current and lagged U.S. GNP growth is included in (1), and the common shock is excluded from (2). Krieger's basic results are consistent with this paper's benchmark results for annual international data. At the level of the average region-industry, Krieger's estimates show that, abstracting from the important role of U.S. disturbances, idiosyncratic shocks are the most important source of variation, followed by country-specific and in turn by industry-specific shocks. At the level of the average nation, country-specific shocks are the most important source, apart from U.S. shocks, with an innovation variance share of 27%. Industry-specific and idiosyncratic shocks are of lesser and essentially equal importance, accounting for 13 and 11%, respectively, of the innovation variance.

Norrbin and Schlagenhauf (1988) apply a specification like the disaggregate VAR/factor model to quarterly employment in one-digit industries in U.S. Census Regions. Their specification differs somewhat from the benchmark model in that the common, region-specific, and industry-specific components are allowed to follow AR(1) processes. Norrbin and Schlagenhauf's estimates are similar to the benchmark results in some, but not all, respects. Their estimates are comparable in that, in terms of the sources of steady-state variation for the average aggregate region, common shocks are a leading source, with a share of 47%. Norrbin and Schlagenhauf's estimates differ from the benchmark in that region-specific shocks are much less important and industry-specific shocks are more important, with respective variance shares of 11 and 28%.[10] Nonetheless, Norrbin and Schlagenhauf's estimates are consistent with the broad conclusions drawn earlier.

Norrbin and Schlagenhauf (1996) use the basic formulation of Norrbin and Schlagenhauf (1988) to examine the sources of cross-country fluctuations in quarterly industrial production in two-digit industries. Their estimates are broadly similar to the benchmark results for international industrial production discussed earlier. In Norrbin and Schlagenhauf's results, as in the benchmark, region-specific and idiosyncratic shocks are the leading sources of variation for the average country. The exact order of importance, however, differs.

---

[10] Reestimating the benchmark model with lag and sample specifications comparable to Norrbin and Schlagenhauf's produces results quite similar to theirs.

Although the benchmark results indicated that region-specific shocks are more important, Norrbin and Schlagenhauf's estimates indicate that idiosyncratic shocks are more important than region-specific shocks, with shares of 40 and 34%, respectively. The importance of world and industry-specific shocks is roughly the same in the benchmark and Norrbin and Schlagenhauf estimates. Norrbin and Schlagenhauf report world and industry-specific shock shares of 16 and 10%.

9.3   Variations on the disaggregate VAR/factor model approach

This section reviews some closely related alternatives to the disaggregate VAR/ factor model. Like the disaggregate VAR/factor model, these alternative for- mulations include an error model that decomposes innovations into unob- served components that are common, region-specific, etc. More specifically, this section reviews aggregate VAR/factor models, Choleski decomposition- based VARs, and dynamic factor models.

9.3.1   The aggregate VAR/factor model

Clark (1998) uses an aggregate version of the benchmark model (1)–(2). In this specification, henceforth referred to as the aggregate VAR/factor model, the basic variables are region aggregates and industry aggregates. For example, in the cross-country specification considered later, the model variables are the growth rates of total manufacturing production in a set of European nations and "world" production in two-digit manufacturing industries ("world" consists of the included countries). Formally, letting Z_t denote the $(R + I) \times 1$ vector of aggregate region and industry growth rates and $e_{r,t}$ and $e_{i,t}$ represent the region r and industry i error terms, the model is

$$Z_t = \sum_{p=1}^{P} \Psi_p Z_{t-p} + e_t \tag{10}$$

$$e_{r,t} = \delta_r c_t + u_{r,t} + \sum_i a_{r,i} n_{i,t} \tag{11}$$

$$e_{i,t} = \delta_i c_t + \sum_r b_{r,i} u_{r,t} + n_{i,t} \tag{12}$$

c_t, $u_{r,t}$, and $n_{i,t}$ represent unobserved common, region-specific, and industry- specific innovations, respectively. δ_r, δ_i, $a_{r,i}$, and $b_{r,i}$ measure the initial responses of regions and industries to the structural shocks. The δ_r and δ_i co- efficients are parameters to be estimated, whereas the $a_{r,i}$ and $b_{r,i}$ coefficients are treated as known and set equal to employment or output shares.

The aggregate VAR/factor model can be derived from a version of the disaggregate VAR/factor model in which the VAR coefficients in (6) are unrestricted rather than forced to take the form (7). In fact, the aggregate VAR can be shown to impose fewer coefficient restrictions on the unrestricted disaggregate model than the actual disaggregate model does. However, deriving the aggregate error model (11)–(12) from the disaggregate version (2) requires assuming that the law of large numbers applies to the weighted average of the idiosyncratic shocks $v_{r,i,t}$.[11]

Applying the aggregate VAR/factor model to quarterly employment growth in U.S. Census Regions and one-digit industries, Clark (1998) obtains results similar to the benchmark estimates. In Clark's estimates, common and region-specific shocks are the leading sources of variation for aggregate regions, while industry-specific shocks are somewhat less important. Common, region-specific, and industry-specific shocks account for, respectively, 40, 41, and 20% of the average region's innovation variance. In contrast to the benchmark, Clark's estimates reveal significant propagation of region-specific and industry-specific shocks over time. Clark's estimated average shares of steady-state variance attributable to common shocks, own region-specific shocks, other region-specific shocks, and industry-specific shocks are 17, 16, 33, and 34%.

To better compare the disaggregate and aggregate specifications, the aggregate VAR/factor model is estimated with aggregate data corresponding to the disaggregate data underlying the benchmark results. The $a_{r,i}$ and $b_{r,i}$ shares needed to estimate the aggregate model are the same fixed weights used in the disaggregate model analysis. The VAR lag length P is set at 4 for U.S. employment growth but just 2 for growth in international industrial production, in order to conserve degrees of freedom. The aggregate VAR/factor model is estimated with Clark's (1998) two-step procedure. In the first step, the VAR (10) is estimated by OLS. In the second step, the error model Equations (11)–(12) are estimated using the VAR residuals and generalized method of moments (GMM).

Tables 9.4 and 9.5 present estimates of the aggregate VAR/factor model for quarterly growth in within-U.S. employment and European industrial production. These estimates are broadly similar to the corresponding disaggregate model estimates reported in Tables 9.1 and 9.2. In U.S. regions, region-specific shocks are the most important source of innovation variance, accounting for an average of 52.3%. Common shocks and industry-specific shocks are of lesser, but still substantial, importance, with roughly equal shares of 23.2 and 24.5%, respectively. In European nations, nation-specific shocks are the biggest source

---

[11] Clark and Shin (1998) present some evidence that, from the perspective of aggregate regions, variation attributable to idiosyncratic shocks in the disaggregate model is simply attributed to region-specific shocks in the aggregate model.

Table 9.4. *Variance decomposition – quarterly aggregate VAR/factor model estimates, 1948:2–97:4 (within-U.S. employment, one-digit industries)*

	Fitted innov. var.	Shares of innovation variance			Fitted st.-st. var.	Shares of steady-state variance		
		Common (s.e.)	Region (s.e.)	Industry (s.e.)		Common	Region	Industry
New England	2.454	0.038 (0.057)	0.770 (0.052)	0.192 (0.031)	11.952	0.053	0.553	0.394
Mideast	1.346	0.771 (0.271)	−0.055 (0.269)	0.284 (0.046)	7.051	0.196	0.403	0.401
Great Lakes	3.333	0.209 (0.133)	0.629 (0.121)	0.162 (0.022)	18.168	0.096	0.522	0.382
Plains	1.299	0.112 (0.094)	0.559 (0.077)	0.329 (0.048)	7.030	0.069	0.534	0.396
Southeast	1.329	0.443 (0.125)	0.202 (0.108)	0.355 (0.061)	9.098	0.139	0.467	0.393
Southwest	1.259	0.035 (0.050)	0.621 (0.038)	0.345 (0.067)	8.022	0.017	0.671	0.312
Rocky Mtn.	2.454	0.146 (0.106)	0.695 (0.093)	0.160 (0.024)	8.976	0.074	0.681	0.244
Far West	3.060	0.103 (0.085)	0.765 (0.076)	0.132 (0.022)	11.042	0.075	0.621	0.304
Average	2.067	0.232 (0.067)	0.523 (0.047)	0.245 (0.031)	10.167	0.090	0.557	0.353

Notes: The table reports estimates of the aggregate VAR/factor model (10)–(12) obtained from quarterly growth in total employment in BEA regions and U.S. one-digit industries. The reported share figures are shares of variance attributable to common, region-specific, and industry-specific shocks. The innovation estimates correspond to a decomposition of 1-step ahead forecast error variances. The steady-state estimates are based on a decomposition of 251-step ahead forecast error variances, evaluated using the VAR written in companion form. The weights needed for model estimation are fixed at average 1982–97 employment shares.

Table 9.5. *Variance decomposition – quarterly aggregate VAR/factor model estimates, 1976:4–97:1 (European industrial production, two-digit manufacturing industries)*

	Fitted innov. var.	Shares of innovation variance			Fitted st.-st. var.	Shares of steady-state variance		
		Common (s.e.)	Region (s.e.)	Industry (s.e.)		Common	Region	Industry
Austria	26.305	0.385 (.111)	0.572 (0.103)	0.044 (0.020)	50.932	0.232	0.537	0.231
Finland	33.571	0.006 (.017)	0.967 (0.020)	0.027 (0.010)	67.834	0.028	0.823	0.148
France	15.271	0.313 (.093)	0.622 (0.088)	0.065 (0.029)	41.201	0.179	0.510	0.311
W. Germany	35.938	0.244 (.121)	0.722 (0.114)	0.034 (0.026)	66.484	0.183	0.678	0.139
Ireland	56.146	0.032 (.041)	0.952 (0.042)	0.016 (0.010)	100.259	0.032	0.766	0.202
Italy	32.624	0.011 (.028)	0.960 (0.031)	0.029 (0.012)	77.501	0.081	0.731	0.187
Netherlands	21.539	0.469 (.117)	0.491 (0.112)	0.040 (0.018)	47.885	0.252	0.516	0.232
Spain	29.116	0.172 (.122)	0.800 (0.118)	0.028 (0.013)	70.493	0.123	0.734	0.143
Sweden	49.877	0.365 (.114)	0.613 (0.113)	0.023 (0.015)	108.934	0.183	0.586	0.231
United Kingdom	18.779	0.080 (.058)	0.872 (0.058)	0.048 (0.025)	39.528	0.057	0.722	0.221
Average	31.917	0.208 (.045)	0.757 (0.041)	0.035 (0.017)	67.105	0.135	0.660	0.205

Notes: The table reports estimates of the aggregate VAR/factor model (10)–(12) obtained from quarterly growth in manufacturing production in the listed countries and in "world" two-digit industry aggregates, where "world" is defined to consist of just the listed countries. The reported share figures are shares of variance attributable to common, region-specific (or nation-specific), and industry-specific shocks. The innovation estimates correspond to a decomposition of 1-step ahead forecast error variances. The steady-state estimates are based on a decomposition of 25½-step ahead forecast error variances, evaluated using the VAR written in companion form. The weights needed for model estimation are fixed at the weights reported in OECD (1997).

of fluctuations, accounting for an average of 75.7% of the innovation variance. Common shocks are a smaller, but significant, source of variation, with an innovation variance share of 20.8%. Industry-specific shocks have little immediate impact on European nations.

In contrast to the disaggregate estimates, the aggregate VAR/factor model estimates suggest considerable propagation of shocks across regions. For U.S. regions, in the steady state the share of variance due to region-specific shocks edges up to 55.7%, as a decline in the importance of each region's own shock is more than offset by an increase in the importance of other regions' shocks. The share of variance attributable to industry-specific shocks rises to 35.3%. Accordingly, the importance of common shocks declines, to a variance share of 9.0%. For European nations, in the steady state the share of variance due to nation-specific shocks falls modestly, as a decline in the importance of each nation's own shock is less than fully offset by an increase in the importance of other nations' shocks. The share of variance attributable to industry-specific shocks increases to 20.5%. The importance of common shocks declines modestly, to a steady-state variance share of 13.5%. Given that the aggregate VAR imposes fewer restrictions on the disaggregate structure (6) than the disaggregate model does, these findings suggest the disaggregate VAR/factor model may overly restrict feedback among regions and industries.

Overall, comparing the within-U.S. and cross-country estimates of the aggregate VAR/factor model yields conclusions in line with those drawn from the disaggregate model, with one exception.[12] In both the aggregate and disaggregate estimates, region-specific shocks are a larger source of variation in international data than in within-U.S. data, whereas industry-specific shocks are less important in international variation than in within-U.S. variation (in quarterly data). The results differ in that the aggregate estimates indicate common shocks are of roughly equal importance within the United States and internationally, whereas the disaggregate estimates indicate that common shocks are more important within the United States than internationally. The difference in estimates seems to raise some uncertainty about the benchmark conclusion that common shocks are less important internationally than within the United States.

9.3.2   A Choleski decomposition scheme

Viñals and Jimeno (1996) apply a Choleski decomposition to a bivariate VAR to identify common and region-specific shocks. In this approach, VARs in

---

[12] As in the quarterly benchmark results, even though the estimates might also be seen as indicating that the shocks affecting nations are bigger than those affecting U.S. regions, data differences preclude making such a comparison.

aggregate and regional unemployment are specified for each of a set of regions, and a Choleski ordering is used to identify common and region-specific components. In Viñals and Jimeno's European analysis, for example, the VAR variables are EU-wide and national unemployment. As shown by Jimeno (1992), this model can be viewed as a restricted version of the simple VAR/factor model (9). The key restriction is that the law of large numbers applies to sector-specific shocks.

The Choleski decomposition-based model appears to yield estimates broadly consistent with the benchmark results. In Viñals and Jimeno's (1996) estimates for annual unemployment, common shocks are less important in Europe than in the United States, whereas nation-specific shocks are more important in Europe. For example, averaged across states, the share of innovation variance due to common shocks is 79%, compared to an average share of 44% for European nations.

9.3.3 Dynamic factor models

Camen (1989), Forni and Reichlin (1997), Gerlach and Klock (1988), Gregory, Head, and Raynauld (1997), and Lumsdaine and Prasad (1997) use dynamic factor models to disentangle the sources of fluctuations. These studies generally ignore industries and assume that fluctuations in a region are driven by unobserved common and region-specific factors. Compared to a VAR/factor model, the dynamic factor model has both advantages and disadvantages. The dynamic factor approach allows the dynamics of common and region-specific shocks to differ, whereas the VAR/factor model assumes that all shocks are propagated by the same dynamic (VAR) structure. However, even though the dynamic factor model allows no propagation of region-specific shocks across regions, the VAR/factor model allows the disturbances to propagate.

The results of most dynamic factor analyses are broadly in line with the VAR/factor model results presented earlier.[13] Camen (1989) and Lumsdaine and Prasad (1997) find a significant common component in international industrial production. In Gerlach and Klock's (1988) estimates for quarterly GDP growth, most variation in the G7 is due to the country-specific factor (an average of more than 70%), although a significant portion (more than 20%) is due to the common factor. Similarly, the Gregory et al. (1997) estimates show that country-specific components are the leading source of variation in quarterly GDP growth in G7 nations.[14]

---

[13] As detailed in Clark and Shin (1998), estimates for the data used in this study provide further evidence that the dynamic factor model yields conclusions similar to those from the disaggregate VAR/factor model.

[14] Estimated with Hodrick and Prescott (1997) filtered data, however, the common factor is roughly equal in importance to country-specific factors.

Although Forni and Reichlin's (1997) findings differ significantly from those reported earlier, they may do so spuriously. Forni and Reichlin fit dynamic factor models to annual growth in personal income by U.S. counties and to annual growth in GDP by regions within European nations. The U.S. model features common, state, and local components; the European model includes common, national, and local components. According to their estimates, the within-U.S. and cross-country decompositions are very similar. For the United States, the common, state, and local components account for an average of 46, 23, and 31% of the observed variation. Using a six-country sample, the variance shares of European, national, and local components are 47, 24, and 29%. It seems likely, however, that using comparable regional disaggregations for the United States and Europe would produce results more in line with the literature. Forni and Reichlin's U.S. data, for counties, are far more disaggregate than their European data, which are more like U.S. states.

9.4   Alternative error model approaches

The studies and results reviewed above generally treat the shocks of interest as unobservable and estimate the associated error model with what can be viewed as factor model methods. Many studies in the literature, however, rely on alternative approaches to estimating error models. This section reviews two alternatives: using dummy variables to represent components that are common, region-specific, and so on; and using observed aggregate data to represent common components.

9.4.1   The dummy variable approach

Bayoumi and Prasad (1997), Bini Smaghi and Vori (1992), Costello (1993), Davis et al. (1997), Prasad and Thomas (1998), and Stockman (1988) use regressions on dummy variables to quantify the importance of common, region-specific, and industry-specific components.[15] In this approach, a common factor or shock is represented with a set of dummy variables for time, whereas region-specific and industry-specific factors are captured with sets of variables interacting the time dummies with region and industry dummies. Pooled data on growth in industry i in region r, for example, are then regressed on the dummies. As discussed in Clark and Shin (1998), even though this approach offers the advantage of simplicity, it suffers some disadvantages.

---

[15] Rosenbloom and Sundstrom (1999) use the same approach to examine the sources of variation in biennial, Depression-era employment for manufacturing industries in U.S. states. In the interest of brevity, this interwar study of biennial data with no international analog is excluded from the review.

The dummy variable approach seems to produce results broadly in line with the VAR/factor model estimates.[16] Using GDP growth rates for one-digit industries in BEA regions, Bayoumi and Prasad (1997) find that the shares of region-industry variance due to common, region-specific, industry-specific, and idiosyncratic components are 29, 19, 25, and 27%, respectively. Using one-digit data for European nations, Bayoumi and Prasad estimate variance shares of 19, 16, 18, and 47% for common, region-specific, industry-specific, and idiosyncratic shocks. In these estimates, as in the benchmark annual results on the sources of region-industry variation, common and industry-specific shocks are less important internationally than within the United States, while idiosyncratic shocks are more important. Bayoumi and Prasad's results differ from the benchmark only in that region shocks are of roughly equal importance in international and within-U.S. data, rather than of greater importance in international data. This difference may reflect the use of the dummy variable approach. In Clark and Shin's (1998) estimates, the gap between the cross-country and within-U.S. shares for region-specific shocks is somewhat smaller with the dummy variable model than with the disaggregate VAR/factor model.

Using a model that excludes the common component, Bini Smaghi and Vori (1992), Costello (1993), and Stockman (1988) find nation-specific and industry-specific effects to be important sources of international fluctuations. For annual growth in industrial production by manufacturing industries across European nations, Bini Smaghi and Vori estimate that the orthogonal components of nation-specific and industry-specific effects explain 19 and 17%, respectively, of nation-industry variation. In annual Solow residuals for two-digit industries in the G7 excluding France, Costello estimates that the orthogonal component of nation-specific effects accounts for 16% of nation-industry variation, whereas the orthogonal component of industry-specific effects accounts for 18%. Using annual growth in industrial production by two-digit industries across eight nations, Stockman attributes 17 and 19% of region-industry variation to the orthogonal components of nation-specific and industry-specific effects, respectively.[17]

By comparison, Bini Smaghi and Vori (1992) find that, for within-U.S. data, region-specific shocks are much less important than in international data, whereas industry-specific shocks are much more important. Using annual growth in GDP for manufacturing industries in U.S. regions, Bini Smaghi and Vori estimate variance shares of 5 and 58% for the orthogonal components of nation-specific and industry-specific effects, respectively. The very large role of

---

[16] Clark and Shin (1998) corroborate this conclusion, reporting dummy variable estimates for the annual data used in this study.

[17] In these studies, because the mean growth rates are modeled with dummies rather than filtered out, the estimates understate the absolute importance of the nation-specific and industry-specific factors.

industry-specific shocks in the U.S. estimates appears to reflect the absence of a common factor in the model. Using annual unemployment rates for the United States, Davis et al. (1997) conclude that both common and region-specific components are important.[18] Prasad and Thomas (1998) examine the sources of fluctuations in annual employment in one-digit industries in Canadian provinces. According to their estimates, common, province-specific, and industry-specific shocks each account for about 12–14% of region-industry variation, whereas more than 60% of the variation is idiosyncratic.

9.4.2   The observables approach

Blanchard and Katz (1992), Decressin and Fatás (1995), and Hess and Shin (1997) quantify the sources of variation by using observed aggregate variables to represent common components. Blanchard and Katz, for example, regress growth in each U.S. state on U.S. growth. The observables approach can be justified by appealing to the law of large numbers.[19] For example, aggregated across a large number of regions, region-specific shocks should have no effect on an aggregate variable, so the aggregate can be used as a proxy for the common component.

The observables approach yields results broadly consistent with those produced by other approaches. For annual employment growth in U.S. states, Blanchard and Katz (1992) report an average $\bar{R}^2$ of 66%, indicating that most annual variation is due to a national component and a smaller, but significant, portion is due to a region-specific component. Decressin and Fatás (1995) find that regressing employment growth for some small European countries and for regions in France, Germany, Italy, Spain, and the United Kingdom on growth for all of Europe yields an average $\bar{R}^2$ of just 20%. Adding nation-specific effects boosts the average $\bar{R}^2$ to 50%. They conclude that a smaller proportion of movements in employment growth is common to European regions than to U.S. states. Hess and Shin's (1997) estimates indicate that nearly three-quarters of the variation in annual state-industry GDP is idiosyncratic, whereas most of the rest is industry-specific.

9.5   Other approaches to quantifying sources of comovement

Even though most of the literature relies on the three methods just reviewed, a portion uses other approaches to examining the sources of fluctuations. Some

---

[18] The contrast between their full sample estimates and estimates based on just the 1970–78 period suggests that Marston's (1985) findings of a much smaller role for region-specific shocks and low persistence of the shocks is largely the result of Marston's short sample.

[19] The Viñals and Jimeno (1996) specification can also be viewed as observables model.

studies examine correlations across regions and industries, whereas others identify structural economic shocks. This section reviews these alternatives.

9.5.1   Correlation analyses

Many studies use cross-region and cross-industry correlations to gauge the relative importance of common, region-specific, and industry-specific shocks. Christodulakis, Dimelis, and Kollintzas (1995), Fatás (1997), Ghosh and Wolf (1997), Hess and Shin (1998), Kollman (1995), and Wynne and Koo (1997) rely exclusively on correlations in gauging the sources of fluctuations.[20] Altonji and Ham (1990), Bini Smaghi and Vori (1992), Clark (1998), Costello (1993), Engle and Kozicki (1993), Helg et al. (1995), and Hess and Shin (1997), studies principally reliant on other approaches, also use correlations.

The results from correlation analyses are generally consistent with the model-based results discussed in Sections 9.2–9.4. Using country-industry data, Costello (1993), Helg et al. (1995), and Kollman (1995) find that growth is more correlated across industries within a country than across countries within an industry, suggesting nation-specific factors are more important than industry-specific factors. Using data for industries in U.S. regions, Ghosh and Wolf (1997) and Kollman find that growth is more correlated across regions within an industry than across industries within a region, indicating that, at the region-industry level, industry-specific shocks are more important than region-specific factors. When industries are ignored, correlations across regions within a country are generally greater than correlations across countries, suggesting that region-specific factors are more important in international fluctuations than in within-country fluctuations. In Wynne and Koo (1997), for instance, the average correlation of GDP across U.S. regions is 0.79, whereas the average correlation of GDP across EU countries is 0.29.

9.5.2   Models of structural economic shocks

While the studies reviewed in Sections 9.2–9.4 simply decompose fluctuations into common, region-specific, and industry-specific components without formally identifying structural sources of those components, other studies seek to identify structural economic shocks.[21] Bayoumi and Eichengreen (1993)

---

[20] Gerlach (1988) uses coherences, the frequency domain analog of correlations, to examine co-movement in international industrial production.

[21] Using a DYMIMIC approach, Norrbin and Schlagenhauf (1988) link the common, region-specific, and industry-specific components to structural forces such as monetary policy. The specification of these forcing variables, however, does not determine the identification of the common, region-specific, and industry-specific components. Rather, it only serves to potentially yield more efficient estimates.

impose long-run restrictions on a VAR to identify aggregate supply and demand shocks for BEA regions and European nations and then use correlations and principal component analysis to assess the cross-region comovement of the shocks. Extending Bayoumi and Eichengreen, Chamie, DeSerres, and Lalonde (1994) identify supply, real demand, and monetary policy shocks in U.S. Census Regions and European countries. The sources of comovement are quantified by fitting the factor model (9) to the shocks. Working from a dynamic general equilibrium framework, Ahmed et al. (1993) impose long-run restrictions on a VAR to identify worldwide technology and country-specific labor supply shocks. In a similar vein, Kwark (1999) imposes both long-run and short-run restrictions to identify worldwide and country-specific technology shocks.

The results from these more structural studies are broadly consistent with those of the literature surveyed earlier. Bayoumi and Eichengreen's (1993) estimates for annual data indicate that aggregate supply and demand shocks are significantly more idiosyncratic across European nations than across U.S. regions, suggesting a smaller region-specific component in disturbances to U.S. regions than to European nations. The quarterly estimates of Chamie et al. (1994) also indicate that region-specific components are more important in Europe than in the United States.[22] Ahmed et al. (1993) find that, even though the world shock is important, own country-specific supply shocks originating in the labor market are the leading source of quarterly output fluctuations. Similarly, Kwark's (1999) results showed that output fluctuations are primarily due to own country-specific technology shocks.

9.6   A summary and implications for the role of borders in business cycles

Overall, the literature on the sources of business cycle fluctuations within and across countries yields three broad conclusions. First, common shocks are less important in international fluctuations than in within-country fluctuations. Second, region-specific shocks are more important in international fluctuations than in within-country fluctuations. Third and finally, industry-specific shocks, when measured accurately, are less important internationally than within the United States. As indicated in Section 9.2.3, industry-specific shocks would seem to be accurately measured in quarterly, but probably not annual, data.

Accordingly, the evidence on the sources of fluctuations suggests that lowering the economic borders dividing nations will reduce the relative importance

---

[22] Their U.S. results, however, probably underestimate the importance of region-specific components. The U.S. regional industrial production figures used by Chamie et al. (1994) are not truly regional data. Their data are simply aggregates of *national* industrial production indexes by detailed industry.

of country-specific disturbances in international fluctuations, while boosting the importance of common and industry-specific factors. In general, lowering borders should make national economies more integrated, causing international business cycle fluctuations to look more like within-country fluctuations. For example, Bayoumi and Eichengreen (1993) expected the European Monetary Union (EMU) to lead to increased flows of labor, capital, and goods. Increased trade flows should boost the relative importance of common and industry-specific shocks, given Frankel and Rose's (1997, 1998) evidence that the cross-country bilateral correlation of business cycle activity is strongly and positively related to the degree of bilateral trade intensity.

More specifically, lowering borders by coordinating policy should reduce the importance of country-specific shocks and raise the importance of common shocks. The EMU, for instance, will coordinate monetary policy and impose some restrictions on fiscal policy by limiting the allowable deficit-to-GDP and debt-to-GDP ratios.[23] To the extent that policies have been significant sources of nation-specific shocks, such coordination of policy should reduce the role of nation-specific disturbances and boost the importance of common shocks, a point emphasized by Christodulakis et al. (1995). Admittedly, though, if policy shocks have been small and the systematic components of monetary and fiscal policy have been important stabilizers, coordination may increase the importance of nation-specific shocks and exacerbate nation-specific fluctuations because each nation will be giving up the ability to respond to the significant shocks hitting its economy. This interpretation underlies the view of Bayoumi and Eichengreen (1993), among others, that if nation-specific shocks are a major source of variation, monetary union is not desirable. Note, however, that as Bini Smaghi and Vori (1992) and Frankel and Rose (1997, 1998) argued, the suitability of a group of regions for currency union is endogenous. Adopting a common currency will likely change the relative importance of common and region-specific shocks and the efficacy of currency union.

The current integration of within-U.S. business cycles provides a useful bound on the cross-country integration of business cycles. As discussed in Section 9.1, the economic borders among nations are currently considerably greater than those among U.S. regions. Although agreements such as EMU will reduce borders among nations, the borders will likely remain somewhat greater than those among nations. For example, Sala-i-Martin and Sachs' (1992) find that the federal tax and transfer system in the United States is important to the integration of U.S. states, yet the EMU agreement does not create an EMU-wide fiscal authority. Accordingly, the benchmark within-U.S. estimates suggest that, until the borders among nations are lowered to resemble the borders

---

[23] Although monetary policies have at times been linked by fixed exchange rate agreements, policies have been, at most, partly coordinated. Therefore, this discussion assumes pacts like EMU will increase the degree of coordination.

dividing U.S. regions, nation-specific shocks are likely to decline in importance but remain the leading source of fluctuations in nations.

Data appendix

This appendix provides some essential data details. Clark and Shin (1998) provide additional detail.

A.1   U.S. employment

A list of the BEA regions follows:

> *New England*: Connecticut, Maine, Massachusetts, New Hampshire, Rhode Island, Vermont
> *Mideast*: Delaware, District of Columbia, Maryland, New Jersey, New York, Pennsylvania
> *Great Lakes*: Illinois, Indiana, Michigan, Ohio, Wisconsin
> *Plains*: Iowa, Kansas, Minnesota, Missouri, Nebraska, North Dakota, South Dakota
> *Southeast*: Alabama, Arkansas, Florida, Georgia, Kentucky, Louisiana, Mississippi, North Carolina, South Carolina, Tennessee, Virginia, West Virginia
> *Southwest*: Arizona, New Mexico, Oklahoma, Texas
> *Rocky Mountain*: Colorado, Idaho, Montana, Utah, Wyoming
> *Far West*: California, Nevada, Oregon, Washington

The industries are the eight SIC one-digit industries: (1) mining; (2) construction; (3) manufacturing; (4) transportation and public utilities; (5) wholesale and retail trade; (6) finance, insurance, and real estate; (7) services; and (8) government.

A.2   International industrial production

The countries included are listed in Table 9.2. The industries correspond to ISIC two-digit manufacturing industries: (1) food, beverages, and tobacco; (2) textiles, clothing, and footwear; (3) wood and wood products; (4) paper and paper products; (5) chemicals and associated products; (6) nonmetallic mineral products; (7) basic metals; and (8) metal products, machinery, and equipment.

A.3   International employment

The countries included are listed in Table 9.2. The industries generally correspond to ISIC one-digit industries: (1) construction; (2) manufacturing;

(3) transport, storage, communication, electricity, gas, and water; (4) wholesale and retail trade, restaurants, and hotels; (5) community, social, and personal services; and (6) producers of government services. For comparability to the United States, industry (3) is a combination of two ISIC industries.

References

Ahmed, S., B. W. Ickes, P. Wang, and B. S. Yoo. 1993. International business cycles. *American Economic Review* 83: 335–59.

Altonji, J. G., and J. C. Ham. 1990. Variation in employment growth in Canada: The role of external, national, regional, and industrial factors. *Journal of Labor Economics* 8: 198–236.

Basu, S., and J. G. Fernald. 1995. Are apparent productive spillovers a figment of specification error? *Journal of Monetary Economics* 36: 165–88.

Bayoumi, T., and B. Eichengreen. 1993. "Shocking Aspects of European Monetary Integration," in F. Torres and F. Giavazzi, eds., *Adjustment and Growth in the European Monetary Union*, pp. 193–229. Oxford: Cambridge University Press.

Bayoumi, T., and E. Prasad. 1997. Currency unions, economic fluctuations, and adjustment: Some new empirical evidence. *IMF Staff Papers* 44: 36–58.

Bini Smaghi, L., and S. Vori. 1992. "Rating the EC as an Optimal Currency Area: Is It Worse than the U.S.?," in R. O'Brien, ed., *Finance and the World Economy*, vol. 6, pp. 79–104. Oxford: Oxford University Press.

Blanchard, O. J., and L. F. Katz. 1992. Regional evolutions. *Brookings Papers on Economic Activity* 1: 1–75.

Camen, U. 1989. "A European-Wide Business Cycle: Does It Exist?" Discussion paper. Graduate Institute of International Studies.

Chamie, N., A. DeSerres, and R. Lalonde. 1994. "Optimum Currency Areas and Shock Asymmetry: A Comparison of Europe and the United States." Working paper no. 94-1. Bank of Canada.

Christodulakis, N., S. P. Dimelis, and T. Kollintzas. 1995. Comparisons of business cycles in the EC: Idiosyncracies and regularities. *Economica* 62: 1–27.

Clark, T. E. 1998. Employment fluctuations in U.S. regions and industries: The roles of national, region-specific, and industry-specific shocks. *Journal of Labor Economics* 16: 202–29.

Clark, T. E., and K. Shin. 1998. "The Sources of Fluctuations Within and Across Countries." Research working paper 98-4. Federal Reserve Bank of Kansas City.

Costello, D. 1993. A cross-country, cross-industry comparison of productivity growth. *Journal of Political Economy* 101: 207–22.

Coulson, N. E. 1993. The sources of sectoral fluctuations in metropolitan areas. *Journal of Urban Economics* 33: 76–94.

Coulson, N. E., and S. F. Rushen. 1995. The sources of fluctuations in the Boston economy. *Journal of Urban Economics* 38: 74–93.

Davis, S. J., P. Loungani, and R. Mahidhara 1997. "Regional Labor Fluctuations." International Finance Discussion Paper No. 578. Board of Governors of the Federal Reserve System.

Decressin, J., and A. Fatás. 1995. Regional labor market dynamics in Europe. *European Economic Review* 39: 1627–55.

Engle, R. F., and S. Kozicki. 1993. Testing for common features. *Journal of Business and Economic Statistics* 11: 369–80.

Fatás, A. 1997. EMU: Countries or regions? Lessons from the EMS experience. *European Economic Review* 41: 743–51.

Forni, M., and L. Reichlin. 1997. "National Policies and Local Economies: Europe and the U.S." Discussion paper no. 1632. Centre for Economic Policy Research.

Frankel, J. A., and A. K. Rose. 1998. The endogeneity of the optimum currency area criteria. *Economic Journal* 108: 1009–25.

Frankel, J. A., and A. K. Rose. 1997. Is EMU more justifiable ex post than ex ante? *European Economic Review* 41: 753–60.

Gerlach, S. 1988. World business cycles under fixed and flexible exchange rates. *Journal of Money, Credit, and Banking* 20: 621–32.

Gerlach, S., and J. Klock.1988. State-space estimates of international business cycles. *Economics Letters* 28: 231–4.

Ghosh, A., and H. Wolf. 1997. "Geographical and Sectoral Shocks in the U.S. Business Cycle." Working paper no. 6180. National Bureau of Economic Research.

Gregory, A. W., A. C. Head, and J. Raynauld. 1997. Measuring world business cycles. *International Economic Review* 38: 677–701.

Helg, R., P. Manasse, R. Monacelli, and R. Rovelli. 1995. How much (a) symmetry in Europe? *European Economic Review* 39: 1017–41.

Hess, G. D., and K. Shin. 1998. Intranational business cycles in the United States. *Journal of International Economics* 44: 289–314.

Hess, G. D., and K. Shin. 1997. International and intranational business cycles. *Oxford Review of Economic Policy* 13: 93–109.

Hodrick, R. J., and E. C. Prescott. 1997. Postwar U.S. business cycles: An empirical investigation. *Journal of Money, Credit, and Banking* 29: 1–16.

Horvath, M. T. K., and R. Verbrugge. 1997. "Shocks and Sectoral Interactions: An Empirical Investigation." Manuscript. Stanford University.

Hooker, M. A., and M. M. Knetter. 1997. The effects of military spending on economic activity: Evidence from state procurement spending. *Journal of Money, Credit, and Banking* 29: 400–21.

Jimeno, J. 1992. The relative importance of aggregate and sector-specific shocks at explaining aggregate and sectoral fluctuations. *Economics Letters* 39: 381–5.

Kollman, R. 1995. The correlation of productivity growth across regions and industries in the United States. *Economics Letters* 47: 437–43.

Krieger, R. 1989. "Sectoral and Aggregate Demand Shocks to Industrial Output in Germany, Japan, and Canada." Finance and Economics Discussion Paper No. 75. Board of Governors of the Federal Reserve System.

Kuttner, K. N., and A. M. Sbordone.1997. Sources of New York employment fluctuations. *Economic Policy Review*, Federal Reserve Bank of New York 3: 21–35.

Kwark, N.-S. 1999. "Sources of International Business Cycle Fluctuations: Country–Specific Shocks or Worldwide Shocks?" *Journal of International Economics* 48: 367–85.

Long, J. B., Jr., and C. I. Plosser. 1987. Sectoral vs. aggregate shocks in the business cycle. *American Economic Review* 77: 333–6.

Lumsdaine, R. L., and E. S. Prasad. 1997. "Identifying the Common Component in International Economic Fluctuations." Working paper no. 5984. National Bureau of Economic Research.

Marston, S. T. 1985. Two views of the geographic distribution of unemployment. *Quarterly Journal of Economics* 100: 57–79.

Norrbin, S. C., and D. E. Schlagenhauf. 1996. The role of international factors in the business cycle. *Journal of International Economics* 40: 85–104.

Norrbin, S. C., and D. E. Schlagenhauf. 1991. The importance of sectoral and aggregate shocks in business cycles. *Economic Inquiry* 29: 317–35.

Norrbin, S. C., and D. E. Schlagenhauf. 1988. An inquiry into the sources of macroeconomic fluctuations. *Journal of Monetary Economics* 22: 43–70.

OECD. 1997. *Indicators of Industrial Activity*, no. 4.

Prasad, E., and A. Thomas. 1998. A disaggregate analysis of employment growth fluctuations in Canada. *Atlantic Economic Journal* 26: 274–87.

Rosenbloom, J. L., and W. A. Sundstrom. 1999. "The Sources of Regional Variation in the Severity of the Great Depression: Evidence from U.S. Manufacturing, 1919–37." Working paper no. 6288. National Bureau of Economic Research. *Journal of Economic History* 59: 714–47.

Sala-i-Martin, X., and J. Sachs. 1992. "Fiscal Federalism and Optimum Currency Areas: Evidence for Europe from the United States," in M. Canzoneri, P. Masson, and V. Grilli, eds., *Establishing a Central Bank: Issues in Europe and Lessons from the U.S.*, pp. 195–219. Cambridge: Cambridge University Press.

Samolyk, K. A. 1994. Banking conditions and regional economic performance. *Journal of Monetary Economics* 34: 259–78.

Shea, J. 1996. Comovement in cities. *Carnegie–Rochester Conference Series on Public Policy* 44: 169–206.

Stockman, A. C. 1988. Sectoral and national aggregate disturbances to industrial output in seven European countries. *Journal of Monetary Economics* 21: 387–410.

Viñals, J., and J. F. Jimeno. 1996. "Monetary Union and European Unemployment." Discussion paper no. 1485. Centre for Economic Policy Research.

Wynne, M. A., and J. Koo. 1997. "Business Cycles Under Monetary Union: EU and U.S. Business Cycles Compared." Working paper no. 97-7. Federal Reserve Bank of Dallas.

PART III

Fiscal and monetary policy

CHAPTER 10

Regional nonadjustment and fiscal policy: Lessons for EMU*

Maurice Obstfeld[†] and Giovanni Peri[‡]

10.1 Introduction

How will members of the European Monetary Union (EMU) adjust to asymmetric macroeconomic shocks after the single currency is in place? On the eve of the third and final stage of EMU, considerable uncertainty over the answer remains, despite nearly three decades of research.[1] Much of that research has tried to distill lessons for Europe by studying the performance of existing currency unions. In this chapter, we extend this evidence and review some of its main findings, in the process identifying key areas in which definitive conclusions remain elusive. On the basis of our interpretation, we advance some conjectural scenarios for macroeconomic adjustment patterns in the Euro zone.

Given its overall satisfactory economic performance and political stability, the United States has been the natural starting point for research into intranational adjustment mechanisms. Sometimes the United States is taken as a

* We thank Reza Baqir, Ryan Edwards, and Stefan Palmqvist for excellent research assistance. Tamim Bayoumi, Giovanni Favara, Ingo Fender, Larry katz, Paul Masson, Chris Salmon, and Till von Wachter offered valuable help in locating and organizing data. Olivier Blanchard, David Card, Barry Eichengreen, Antonio Fatás, Peter Kenen, Barry McCormick, Jacques Mélitz, Andrew Oswald, Frédéric Zumer, and especially Jürgen von Hagen have made many very helpful suggestions, as did participants in the October 1997 *Economic Policy* panel meeting in Bonn and the Berkeley Labor Lunch. All errors and opinions are our own. Research support was provided by the National Science Foundation (through a grant to the National Bureau of Economic Research), the Alfred P. Sloan Foundation, and the Center for German and European Studies at the University of California, Berkeley.
† University of California, Berkeley, CEPR, and NBER. Mailing address: Department of Economics, University of California, Berkeley, Berkeley, CA 94720. E-mail: *obstfeld@econ. berkeley.edu.*
‡ Mailing address: IGIER, Bocconi University, Milan, Italy. E-mail: *giovanni.peri@uni-bocconi.it.*
1 One of the early academic discussions is Corden (1972), which was inspired by the Werner Report and sets out many of the themes that the subsequent literature explores. Ingram (1973) is another notable early contribution. A recent comprehensive review of issues is contained in Kenen (1995).

model for predicting integrated Europe's evolution. More often, it serves as an exemplar of regional adjustment or insurance mechanisms that at present appear largely absent among prospective EMU members but may need to evolve to ensure the union's success. The key regional adjustment mechanisms are labor mobility and local relative price responses, whereas the main insurance mechanism, alongside private capital markets, is based on interregional transfer payments mediated by the central government.

In this chapter, the focus is instead to compare the internal adjustment patterns European countries display with those of the United States. We also look at Canada, which is closer to Europe in its labor market and fiscal institutions than the United States is. A direct comparison of the United States with other currency unions is revealing. It suggests that Europe's (and to some extent Canada's) model of regional response to idiosyncratic shocks differs from that in the United States. Changes in relative regional real exchange rates are generally small. Outside of the United States, however, there is more reliance on interregional transfer payments and less on interregional labor migration, and the overall pace of regional adjustment appears slower. The large and continuing transfers from western to eastern Germany, where open unemployment still runs around 18%, represent a notably pathological example of this tendency.

Ultimately EMU may lead to changes in the institutions governing economic relations within and between European Union (EU) member states. Given those institutions, however, the subnational economic adjustment patterns of European countries offer a better guide than the United States does to how the Euro currency area is likely to evolve. One goal of the chapter is to ask whether regional response patterns typical of individual European economies are likely to emerge at the EMU level. Another goal is to judge the past performance of the European countries themselves as currency unions. The implication for EMU of this assessment is immediate. Because country-specific shocks often affect subnational regions differently, sluggish regional adjustment, if uncorrected by policy reforms, will worsen the pain they inflict and thereby complicate life under the single currency.

The plan of this chapter is as follows. Section 10.2 reviews the main mechanisms of adjustment and insurance available to a region or country hit by an idiosyncratic economic shock. An overview of data for the United States, Canada, and some EU members is suggestive of national differences in the primary modes of response to shocks. In Section 10.3, we look more closely at regional unemployment data, observing that local unemployment persistence is higher outside the United States and that interregional migration plays a much smaller role in adjustment in Europe than in the United States. Section 10.4 takes up regional relative price adjustment as an element in the return to full employment after a shock. In none of the countries we examine does regional relative price adjustment play a large role when compared with the long-term changes in international relative prices that one commonly observes. The reasons for this contrast are uncertain and surely differ across countries. But the slow adjustment of regional labor markets in European countries suggests that the low variability of their interregional real exchange rates partly reflects price rigidities that impede adjustment, rather than the efficient operation of natural currency areas. By preventing large relative-price changes, such price rigidities may support the political viability of free trade within currency unions.

The extent of regional risk sharing through capital markets and especially through government transfer payments has received considerable attention in research on currency unions, starting with the estimates on fiscal redistribution and stabilization in the influential MacDougall Report (Commission of the European Communities 1977). In Section 10.5, we review this literature and conclude that fiscal transfers play a central role in supporting existing currency unions, albeit less so in the United States, where labor is most mobile, than in Canada and Europe. A main point of our discussion is that transfers tend to be quite persistent and sometimes to respond to shocks with lags. Indeed, though various mechanisms, transfer programs intended to provide social insurance may lengthen the adjustment process and, in extreme cases, induce regional dependence on fiscal inflows. Thus, we argue that sharp distinction the literature has made between the redistribution and stabilization functions of fiscal transfers, while conceptually valid, is overdrawn in practice. Given the central role of fiscal transfer systems in other currency unions, we are led to ask, in Section 10.6, whether the EMU countries will inevitably see a need to augment substantially current EU transfer programs. Our conclusion is that it will become hard to resist pressures for a more extensive "transfer union," especially if the EU wishes to pursue deeper and broader political or economic integration in the face of existing national income disparities. That conclusion leads us to propose a set of alternative measures that could reproduce the benefits of an extended transfer mechanism while avoiding many of its pitfalls.

10.2   Adjustment and insurance: questions and trends

10.2.1   Mechanisms of adjustment and stabilization

A country suffering an unexpected adverse real economic shock has several options for response when domestic market rigidities generate higher unemployment. Options that are attractive in the face of a transitory shock may be less so when the shock is permanent, or highly persistent. In the latter case, the country faces a problem of long-run *adjustment* to a permanently lower standard of living. In the former, it faces a less severe financing problem, that of cushioning employment and output in the face of transitory bad luck.

National fiscal stabilizers, either discretionary or automatic, can be helpful in riding out temporary real shocks, as can private external borrowing. A country with a flexible exchange rate may gain from currency depreciation. However, a temporary disturbance generally warrants a relatively small (and short-lived) depreciation, and a currency participating in an adjustable peg system would not normally realign. For that reason, the prospect of temporary disturbances is of secondary relevance in comparing the merits of outright currency union with those of an adjustable-peg regime such as the European Monetary System.[2]

When a negative real shock is permanent, however, there are no options for cushioning its impact over the long term, simply because a country cannot live outside its long-run budget constraint. Solvency constraints rule out using permanently higher fiscal or external deficits to maintain public or private spending (Corden 1972; Krugman 1993).

Thus, there is no choice but adjustment, and adjustment can occur in one of two ways (absent significant international labor mobility). The first option is to do nothing and rely on deflation and falling real wages to restore full employment, possibly a long and agonizing process marked by persistently high joblessness. The second is to devalue the domestic currency. If there is some nominal stickiness in prices and wages, and room for real wage adjustment as well, a country can devalue its currency, thereby making its goods more competitive internationally and restoring full employment quickly. Importantly, devaluation does not enable a country to escape a long-run real income loss. But although the country's terms of trade worsen permanently and immediately, that loss is widely shared by residents and is widely viewed as preferable to the fiscal drain and social tensions that protracted unemployment causes. Moreover, and quite fundamentally, the currency realignment leads to a more efficient national and international allocation of resources.

As noted, the existence of a devaluation option depends not only on some nominal wage or price stickiness but also on some willingness of domestic price setters to accept an exchange-rate-induced reduction in their real incomes as a fait accompli. Without this prerequisite, devaluation will have only short-lived relative-price effects that are quickly offset by higher domestic inflation (Hinshaw 1951; McKinnon 1963). After this surge of inflation, the price level and real wages will fall as the economy gradually adjusts to its worsened terms of trade. In the case of substantial real wage resistance, there is therefore no shortcut through devaluation: only a lengthy period of high unemployment will bring about the necessary fall in real wages. The real effects of devaluation tend to be weaker in smaller and more open economies.

---

[2] In the specific context of EMU, however, the prospect that the stability pact will hamstring national fiscal policies brings more urgency to the question of temporary shocks. See Eichengreen and Wyplosz (1998) for analysis of the stability pact's possible effects.

A country that can enter private insurance arrangements with foreigners (equity contracts, for example) can partially guard against permanent and transitory shocks alike. In the case of a temporary shock, protection through insurance contracts may be more effective than borrowing, which must be repaid irrespective of the economy's future performance. Even when a permanent adverse national shock occurs, a permanently lower level of real net dividend outflows affords some offset. In practice, however, labor income is vastly less insurable than capital income, so the benefits from cross-border insurance arrangements accrue disproportionately to those who own internationally diversified financial wealth. At best, the resulting dividend payments affect labor incomes and employment indirectly. Exchange-rate adjustments thus remain potentially useful as a way of regaining full employment and redistributing domestically the pain of adjustment to permanent adverse shocks.

Regions within a currency union plainly lack the devaluation option after a permanent region-specific setback but may be able to obtain persistent and even permanent streams of inward net transfer payments from more fortunate regions. To some degree, these transfers represent private intranational insurance payments, but in modern economies government-intermediated redistributions from other regions also bulk large. Public transfers support the incomes of the unemployed and enhance local demand, in theory substituting for outward migration, which is a major adjustment mechanism within national units if not always between them. Short-lived inward transfers, like local fiscal expansion, can play a stabilization role by cushioning the initial impacts of adverse shocks. Open-ended transfers also stabilize, but they are not a mode of regional adjustment to permanent shocks. Instead they finance regional *nonadjustment* indefinitely.

10.2.2   Regional unemployment, inflation, and fiscal flows

An overview of regional unemployment trends in some existing currency unions provides a backdrop for the closer analyses of regional economic adjustment described in the following sections. The data provide hints about both the speed of adjustment and international differences in intranational adjustment patterns.

Several authors have looked at the dispersion of regional unemployment rates to assess both the incidence of regionally asymmetric shocks and the speed of adjustment to them (Eichengreen 1990, 1991; Emerson et al. 1992; De Grauwe and Vanhaverbeke 1993; Masson and Taylor 1993; Viñals and Jimeno 1996). An initial fact important in comparing the behaviors of different currency unions is that the regional divergence in unemployment rates is relatively low in the United States, with little tendency to increase secularly. Figures 10.1 and 10.2 plot, respectively, standard deviations and coefficients of variation (standard deviations divided by means) for regional unemployment rates.

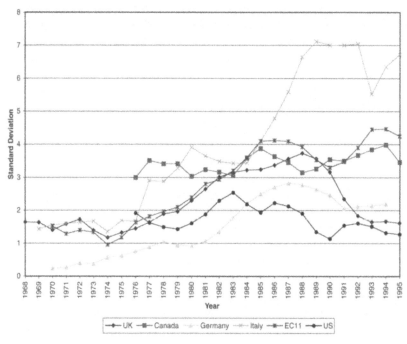

Figure 10.1. Standard deviations of regional unemployment rates (1968–95).

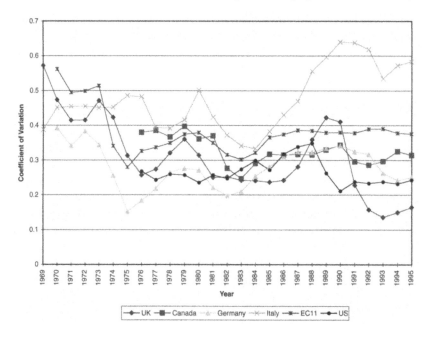

Figure 10.2. Coefficients of variation of regional unemployment rates (1969–95).

Shown for comparison are data from Canada, Germany, Italy, the United Kingdom, the United States, and the "EU11" – the signers of the Maastricht Treaty other than Luxembourg. Italy stands out for its sharply increasing regional unemployment-rate disparities, which are much more severe even than those among the EU11. Dispersion in the United Kingdom also was relatively high until the mid-1980s, and its drop afterward, notwithstanding the recession of the early 1990s, is remarkable.[3] In Canada, unemployment dispersion has been relatively high but steady for many years. In Germany, it has been relatively low among the western Länder included in Figures 10.1 and 10.2 but has risen over time on a simple standard deviation measure; it would appear higher still were eastern Germany included. The coefficient of variation for western Länder remains fairly constant in recent years because overall western unemployment has risen sharply. Overall, Germany's unemployment dispersion seems intermediate between that of the United States and the EU11, and in recent years it looks quite similar to that of the EU11 minus Spain.[4]

Patterns of unemployment dispersion have been *persistent* outside the United States, in the sense that the regions of relatively high unemployment have tended to remain the same over time. This feature is evident in Figures 10.3–10.6, which show the evolution of regional unemployment rates for Canada and the three European countries.

To document the contrast with U.S. regional unemployment behavior, Figures 10.7–10.11 show scatter plots of regional relative unemployment rates in 1995 against 1985 rates. (For Germany the years compared are 1994 and 1984.) The plots in Figures 10.7–10.11 show significantly positively correlated unemployment rates in the two periods. For the case of American states illustrated in Figure 10.11, there is a less strongly significant positive relationship with a much lower R^2 statistic, suggesting less history-dependence in U.S. regional unemployment rates.[5]

---

[3] McCormick (1997) discusses U.K. regional employment trends.

[4] A quick look at two other large European countries confirms the trend toward regional unemployment divergence on the continent. The standard deviation of regional unemployment rates in 19 French départements has increased from 1.1% in 1980 to 3.7% in 1993 (compare with Figure 10.1), whereas the average national unemployment rate has increased from 6 to 11%. For Spain the evolution seems even more unbalanced because the standard deviation of 17 regional unemployment rates has increased from 3% in 1985 to 5.2% in 1993 with little net change in national average unemployment (Spain's unemployment rate stood near 21% in both years; see Eurostat, various years).

[5] The results are: Canada, slope $= 0.78$, t-statistic $= 5.20$, $R^2 = 0.75$; Germany, slope $= 0.77$, t-statistic $= 3.65$, $R^2 = 0.58$; Italy, slope $= 1.35$, t-statistic $= 6.42$, $R^2 = 0.68$; United Kingdom, slope $= 0.60$, t-statistic $= 8.77$, $R^2 = 0.79$; United States, slope $= 0.26$, t-statistic $= 2.50$, $R^2 = 0.15$. Eichengreen (1990, p. 160) finds that unemployment rates in U.S. regions are less serially correlated than the aggregate unemployment rates of European countries. He interprets the finding as evidence of slower labor-market adjustment in Europe. Here, we have shown that the empirical result carries over to regional unemployment rates outside the United States.

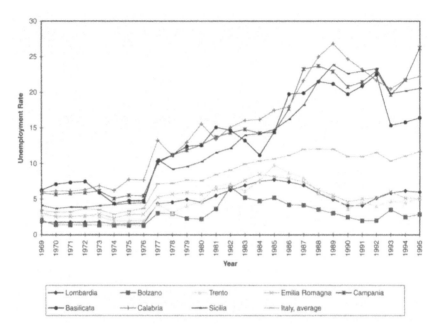

Figure 10.3. Regional unemployment rates in Italy (1969–95).

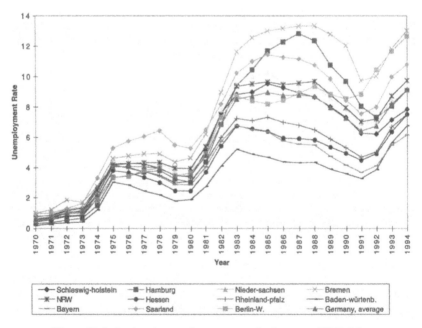

Figure 10.4. Regional unemployment rates in Germany (1970–94).

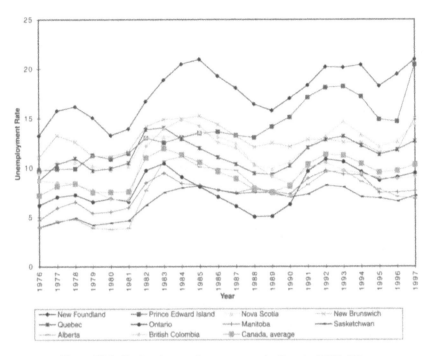

Figure 10.5. Regional unemployment rates in Canada (1976–97).

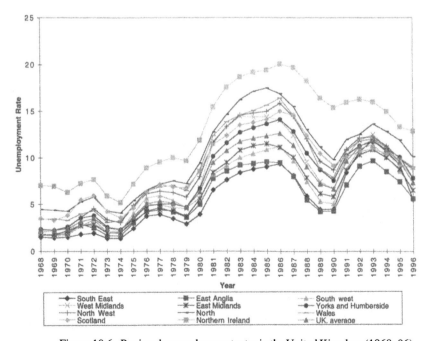

Figure 10.6. Regional unemployment rates in the United Kingdom (1968–96).

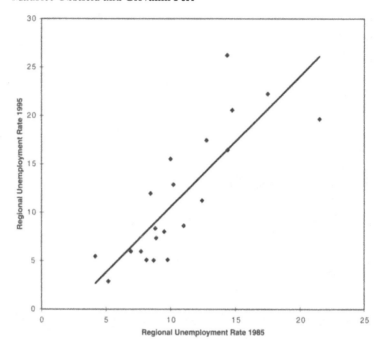

Figure 10.7. Persistence of regional unemployment rates in Italy (1985–95).

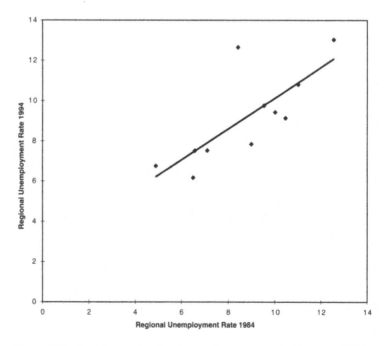

Figure 10.8. Persistence of regional unemployment rates in Germany (1984–94).

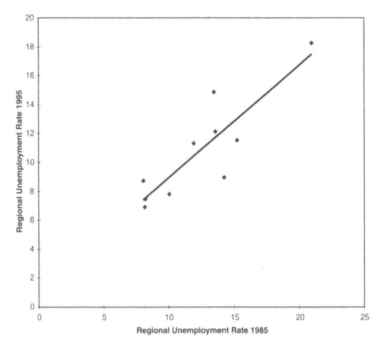

Figure 10.9. Persistence of regional unemployment rates in Canada (1985–95).

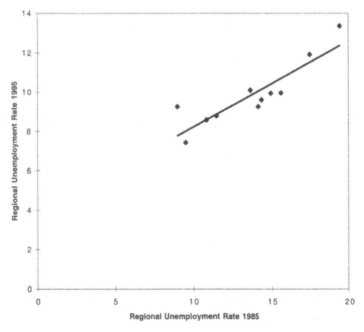

Figure 10.10. Persistence of regional unemployment rates in the United Kingdom (1985–95).

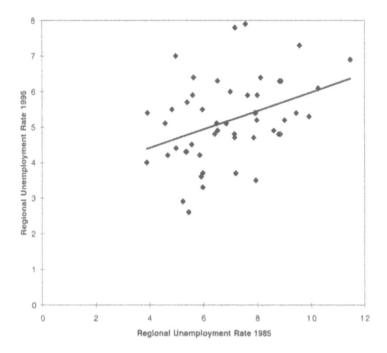

Figure 10.11. Persistence of regional unemployment rates in the United States (1985–95).

The estimated intertemporal correlations in these figures do not allow us, however, to distinguish between two explanations with somewhat different implications for evaluating regional macroeconomic adjustment speeds. A region may have a persistently high "natural" rate of unemployment, resulting from differences in industrial mix, urbanization, unemployment benefit administration, and so on. On the other hand, slow adjustment to regional shocks is reflected in the persistence of unemployment deviations from these regional means. The econometric identification of such deviations, however, requires a specific statistical model. We will argue in the next section that, particularly in Europe, regional shocks with persistent effects play an important role, and that persistence is in part due to a low propensity of workers to migrate away from regions where unemployment exceeds the local natural rate.[6]

According to the model of adjustment sketched at the start of this section, an unemployment rate persistently above the local natural rate should be associated

---

[6] The distinction between means and deviations cannot always be drawn sharply because benefits administration may respond endogenously to local unemployment, with further feedback effects on unemployment duration. In Canada, for example, the duration of unemployment benefits in a province and the minimum prior work requirement to qualify for benefits depend on the level of the provincial unemployment rate. See Green and Riddell (1997).

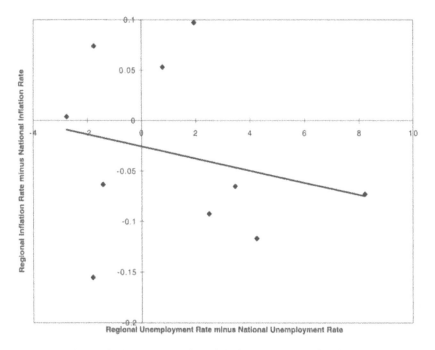

Figure 10.12. Average regional inflation – average regional unemployment in Canada (1976–96).

with downward pressure on regional prices. Eventually, increasing local competitiveness will feed through positively to local labor demand. For Canada and Italy, Figures 10.12 and 10.13 show some negative long-run cross-sectional association between average regional relative inflation (measured by the GDP deflator) and average regional relative unemployment. For Germany, Figure 10.14 shows a positive correlation. Thus, although ongoing unemployment should in theory lead to a regional terms-of-trade loss over time, the tendency for this to occur in practice is tenuous. (For the United Kingdom and the United States, regional/state price indexes are not available.)[7]

Government fiscal stabilizers deliver transfers to depressed regions; furthermore, national fiscal systems typically redistribute revenue from richer to poorer jurisdictions. Figures 10.15 and 10.16 document, for Canada and Italy alike, a significant positive correlation between average regional unemployment and average transfer inflows. Figure 10.17, for the United States, shows a positive but

---

[7] The left-hand variable in the regression is the difference between average annual regional inflation and average annual national inflation (in percent per year). The right-hand variable is the average regional unemployment rate less the national average (in percent). Results are: Canada (1976–95), slope $= -0.07$, t-statistic $= -0.62$, $R^2 = 0.06$; Germany (1976–95), slope $= 0.01$, t-statistic $= 0.35$, $R^2 = 0.01$; Italy (1977–94), slope $= -0.03$, t-statistic $= -2.46$, $R^2 = 0.27$.

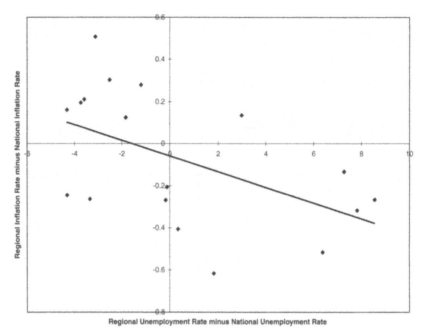

Figure 10.13. Average regional inflation – average regional unemployment in Italy (1977–94).

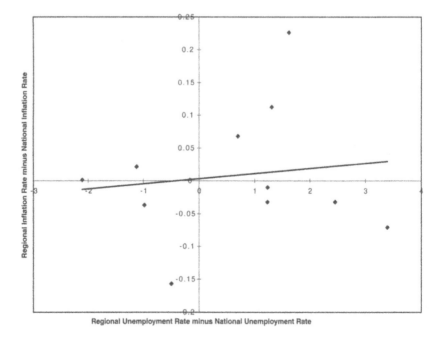

Figure 10.14. Average regional inflation – average regional unemployment in Germany (1974–94).

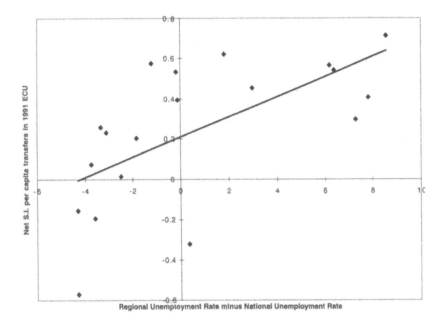

Figure 10.15. Net transfers – relative regional unemployment rates in Italy (1977–94).

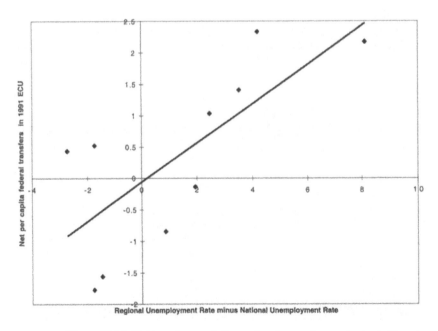

Figure 10.16. Net transfers – relative regional unemployment rates in Canada (1976–95).

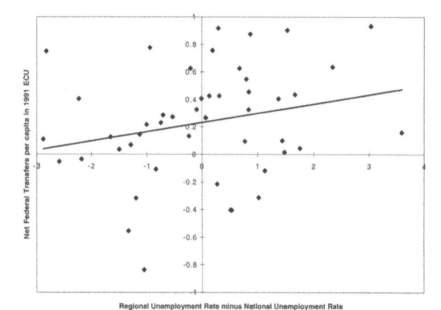

Figure 10.17. Net transfers – relative regional unemployment rates in the United States (1976–85).

only marginally significant correlation.[8] These pictures suggest a potentially important role for fiscal transfers in providing insurance against regional recession.

The persistence of transfers mirrors that of unemployment rates. In both Canada and Italy, the ranking of high unemployment regions is remarkably stable over time and correlates well with ranking by net transfer inflow per population member. Clearly, intranational fiscal flows to Canada's Atlantic provinces and Italy's Mezzogiorno play a significant redistributive role and are not merely responding as short-term automatic stabilizers to temporary regional shocks.[9] Their availability facilitates delayed regional adjustment. An entire

[8] The left-hand variable in the regression is the per capita net transfer inflow in thousands of 1991 ECU. The right-hand variable is the average regional unemployment rate less the national average (in percent). Results are: Canada (1976–95), slope $= 0.03$, t-statistic $= 3.12$, $R^2 = 0.54$; United States (1976–85), slope $= 0.10$, t-statistic $= 2.01$, $R^2 = 0.05$; Italy (1977–94), slope $= 0.05$, t-statistic $= 3.57$, $R^2 = 0.42$. The transfer data for Canada, the United States, and Italy, which we also use in econometric analysis in Section 10.5, are not comparable because those for Italy include social insurance payments only and exclude, for example, flows related to tax payments. See the Data Appendix for details. We do not graph our German data, which are also severely limited.

[9] In Italy the official data on unemployment underestimate its true extent because of the Casa Integrazione Guadagni (CIG) program, which covers part of the wages of workers who otherwise might be laid off (see, for example, Bertola and Ichino 1995). Because CIG payments are quite

national economy could postpone adjustment in the same way only if it could arrange for persistent streams of unrequited transfers from foreigners.

10.2.3   Barriers to regional adjustment

The balance of this chapter contains a critical review and synthesis of earlier studies relevant to a study of regional adjustment within existing currency unions. On the basis of that review and some new evidence, we argue that, in Europe and to some extent in Canada, adjustment to local employment shocks via domestic migration is more limited than in the United States.

In addition, relative regional price adjustments also appear to play a limited role. It could be that interregional real exchange rates are potentially quite flexible, but that in existing currency unions, labor mobility, high interregional trade elasticities, and a paucity of asymmetric real shocks all make for regional relative price stability. To some degree, the United States fits this picture. We argue that, in existing European currency unions, interregional real exchange rates are actually rather rigid and hypothesize that political imperatives underlie the rigidity.

Interregional fiscal transfers, especially long-term redistributive transfers, seem to be used quite heavily in Europe and Canada. Given the absence of prompt and strong internal adjustment mechanisms, fiscal flows therefore appear to play a prominent role – sometimes an uneasy one – in the non-American currency unions.

Two related conclusions for EMU follow. First, limited market flexibility within EMU countries will make it harder for them to cope with nation-specific shocks because the latter generally have heterogeneous regional impacts. Second, if EMU aims to attain the degree of economic cohesion of its constituent nations, limitations on national fiscal policies will eventually make it hard to resist the extension of existing EU mechanisms of income redistribution.

10.3   Adjustment through migration

10.3.1   Data on migration

A comparison of labor mobility in the United States, Canada, and Europe begins with the raw data on interregional labor movements. The OECD reports that in 1986, 1.1% of Britons and Germans changed their region of residence, as

persistent, classifying workers on CIG as unemployed would raise the correlation between social insurance inflows and true unemployment. Of course, many who are officially unemployed work in the underground economy. Notice that by entering the underground economy and evading taxes, officially unemployed workers automatically generate a net fiscal transfer into the region where they operate.

Table 10.1. *Average net interregional migration (percent of regional population)*

Period	Canada	U.S.	Germany	Italy	U.K.
1970–9	0.62	1.20	0.27	0.37	0.47
1980–9	0.63	0.84	0.34	0.33	0.26
1990–5	0.52	0.87	0.31	0.40	0.20

Notes: National figures are population-weighted averages over regions. For the period indicated, each regional figure is calculated as the average absolute value of the change in regional working-age population (measured net of national working-age population growth). German numbers are for western Länder only, leaving out Berlin.

opposed to only 0.6% of Italians but 1.5% of Canadians and 3% of Americans (OECD 1990).[10] These numbers probably understate the Canadian economy's capacity to reallocate labor interregionally because they do not account for foreign migration, which is substantial for Canada. Canada thus would appear to occupy an intermediate position between the European countries and the United States. De Grauwe and Vanhaverbeke (1993) report similar magnitudes for a larger sample of EU countries in 1987, defining a country's mobility index by the regional average of immigration plus emigration as a percent of regional population. Their results indicate lower intranational labor mobility in southern than in northern Europe. Even though *intra*national migration is lower in most of Europe than in the United States or Canada, *inter*national movements of people within Europe are, at present, smaller still.

If the goal is to assess the role of labor migration in reducing large regional employment differentials, net rather than gross migration numbers might be more revealing. Table 10.1 reports such numbers for Canada, the United States, Germany, Italy, and the United Kingdom. Here we approximate net in- or out-migration for a region as the average absolute value of the percentage change in regional working-age population (measured net of the rate of national working-age population growth). National averages are population-weighted averages

[10] A problem with such measurements – indeed, the problem applies to all the subnational evidence discussed in this chapter – is that constitutionally recognized regional units are based on politico-historic rather than economic boundaries, so that the definition of "region" has a substantive effect on one's conclusions. Because the available data correspond to these units, however, not much can be done except to control for obviously anomalous cases. The numbers reported in this paragraph refer to Canadian provinces and territories, Italian regioni, 11 west German Länder, ten U.K. regions (excluding Northern Ireland), and 51 U.S. states (including Washington, D.C., as a "state").

of the regional growth rates. For Germany our sample consists of ten western Länder, Berlin being the omission.

Subject to the caveat that average regional sizes differ across countries, the general impression that emerges is that net migration is substantially higher in North America than in Europe. If these numbers can be taken as a rough indicator of labor mobility, mobility is higher in Canada than in Europe, and higher still in the United States. Mobility, as measured by net flows, seems on the whole to be similar in Germany, Italy, and the United Kingdom. However, a comparison of these numbers with those reported by De Grauwe and Vanhaverbeke (1993) would suggest that "gross" or two-way labor flows are more important in Germany and the United Kingdom than in Italy.

10.3.2   *Interpreting migration data: low barriers or regionally balanced shocks?*

There is a major conceptual problem in accepting migration data as evidence on mobility. Observed net flows reflect the push of asymmetrical shocks as well as the resistance due to migration barriers. Thus, if idiosyncratic regional shocks have not been prominent, then little migration would be observed even with low barriers. As Eichengreen (1991) notes in discussing similar data, "simple tabulations still do not distinguish the disturbance from the response." Indeed, because our basic data all are mostly endogenous economic variables, this identification problem is the central one in reliably assessing regional adjustment patterns. In the present context of migration, the identification problem surfaces in the possibility that labor mobility is (potentially) really quite high even though labor movements are small.

The wide and variable regional unemployment differentials in Europe might be viewed as prima facie evidence of asymmetric localized shocks that should create migratory pressures. Also supportive of the prevalence of such shocks is the finding of De Grauwe and Vanhaverbeke (1993) that, over 1976–90, the variability in long-run average regional employment growth rates *within* European countries tends to exceed that *among* European countries (with less regional divergence in northern than in southern Europe). But as these authors point out, employment levels and unemployment rates are endogenous variables that respond to policies and may convey little information about the incentives to migrate. For example, more liberal administration of unemployment benefits in a region cannot only increase unemployment there but even lead to migration of workers *into* high-unemployment areas, a phenomenon seen in Canada (Courchene 1993, p. 144). It is important to correct for idiosyncrasies in regional institutions or structure in assessing the typical migratory response to a regional shock within a country.

One way to accomplish this end is to postulate a specific statistical model of regional shocks and to gauge their prevalence econometrically. There have been several attempts along these lines. On balance, they point to a potentially important role for asymmetric region-specific disturbances within EU economies. Viñals and Jimeno (1996) estimate a dynamic model of annual regional unemployment in which a region's unemployment rate can be decomposed into a region-specific constant (the region's "natural" rate) and regional, national, and EU-wide random components. These components are identified by the assumption that region-specific shocks do not influence the national data-generating process for unemployment and that nation-specific shocks do not influence the EU-wide unemployment process. Thus, the EU unemployment rate is strongly exogenous with respect to individual EU members' unemployment rates, and both EU and national unemployment are strongly exogenous with respect to regional unemployment. Viñals and Jimeno found that for forecast horizons of up to 5 years, almost two-thirds of the conditional variance of European subnational unemployment rates can be explained by region-specific factors.[11]

Forni and Reichlin (1997) use a dynamic unobserved index model to separate fluctuations in annual regional growth rates of real output into parts due to EU, national, and regional factors. They find that the decomposition for EU regions is quite similar to that for U.S. states. Although regional shocks are found to play a significant role in Europe, they do not appear as important as in the Viñals-Jimeno analysis of unemployment rates. However, the statistical method of Forni and Reichlin allows the EU-wide component of growth and the national components to have divergent regional effects. They also search for a European "core," defined as a group of regions in which at least 70% of the variance of output growth comes from the common Europe-wide shock component. The resulting set of regions does not coincide with a group of EU member states, and all major countries are, to some degree, out of the core. Conversely, Spain and Italy, which usually are identified as "peripheral" in studies of EMU as an optimum currency area, have important regions that belong to the core. These findings again suggest the presence of regional asymmetries within EU countries.

---

[11] The authors also imposed the constraint that the national and EU components of unemployment have identical effects across the regions of a country, an assumption that is necessary to conserve degrees of freedom in estimation but that also makes it impossible to distinguish econometrically between truly idiosyncratic regional shocks and national or EU shocks that have divergent regional effects. For the purpose of thinking about regional adjustment problems, the two are not that different, as we shall argue later, so the numbers Viñals and Jimeno reported are probably a reasonable guide to the frequency of regional shocks that warrant long-run labor reallocation. (They find that country-specific shocks explain much of the variance of EU unemployment when EU shocks are defined so as to have symmetric effects on different countries.)

10.3.3   Structural models of migration response

The studies just summarized contradicted the view that migration barriers within European countries are low and that the low degree of observed migration reflects a scarcity of regionally asymmetric shocks. But even if we accept that asymmetric shocks have occurred, an international comparison of their effects still requires some quantitative standardization of the shocks.

A fairly direct way to compare regional labor mobility across countries is to look at the responsiveness of domestic labor flows to interregional wage differences. Taking this route, Eichengreen (1993a) finds that interregional migration is much more sensitive to lagged changes in wage differentials in the United States (1962–88) than in the United Kingdom (1961–82) or Italy (1962–85). Lagged unemployment also has the largest estimated effect in the United States.[12]

Eichengreen's (1993a) estimates constituted strong evidence of relatively limited labor mobility in Europe. However, the current wage difference alone may be an imperfect indicator of the expected lifetime income difference associated with a job change. Furthermore, given the nationwide wage determination process that prevails throughout much of Europe, regional unemployment differences may find little reflection in regional wage differences. Thus, an alternative framework capturing the dynamic response of regional labor markets to local shocks is a useful complement to Eichengreen's findings.

Such an empirical framework was originated and applied to U.S. states by Blanchard and Katz (1992). Decressin and Fatás (1995) have explored the implications for regions within Europe. Blanchard and Katz proceed by estimating a three-equation vector-autoregressive (VAR) system in which the variables of interest are the change in the log level of regional employment, the log employment rate (ratio of employment to labor force), and the log participation rate (ratio of labor force to working-age population) – all variables being expressed as deviations from respective national means. The motivation for focusing on the *change* in the employment level is that the variable appears to have a unit root component, that is, a random component subject to permanent changes. This result for the United States, which generalizes to European countries as Decressin and Fatás (1995) illustrated, is itself suggestive that permanent (or at least highly persistent) regional shocks are regular occurrences in industrial countries.

In each of Blanchard and Katz's three regression equations, the left-hand variable depends on its own lags and those of the other two variables, as well as a random disturbance. In addition, even though the change in employment

---

[12] Eichengreen (1993a) also documents that energy prices and national real exchange rates, which may be viewed as largely exogenous to regions, have asymmetrical effects on regional labor markets within the United States, the United Kingdom, and Italy.

depends only on lagged variables, the employment and participation rates depend on the current change in employment. This feature reflects Blanchard and Katz's critical identifying assumption that innovations in the employment-change equation are exogenous labor-demand shocks, which affect the other two variables contemporaneously with no immediate reverse feedback. If one buys the identifying assumption, the estimated dynamic system allows one to trace through time the responses of all three variables to an asymmetric regional labor-demand shock.[13] One can also track the effect on migration from the region. Note the identity that regional employment, N, equals the product of the employment rate, E (1 minus the unemployment rate), the participation rate, P, and working-age population, Pop:

$$N = (E)(P)(Pop)$$

In terms of logarithmic changes (which approximate percentage changes), the preceding relationship equates the percent change in total employment to the sum of the corresponding percent changes in the employment rate, the participation rate, and population.

$$\frac{\Delta N}{N} = \frac{\Delta E}{E} + \frac{\Delta P}{P} + \frac{\Delta Pop}{Pop}$$

Because our variables are expressed as deviations from national averages, $\Delta Pop/Pop$ can be interpreted as inward migration provided regional demographic trends are shared by the entire nation, or if those trends evolve independently of labor-demand shocks. In that case, migration can be inferred from the behavior of employment, the employment rate, and the participation rate.

The other key assumption Blanchard and Katz make is that region-specific characteristics creating mean differentials in labor-market variables can be modeled as region-specific constants in the regression equations. To estimate, they pool their data over all U.S. states, thus allowing regional fixed effects to differ but imposing uniform dynamics. Blanchard and Katz thus address the econometric identification problem by identifying regional labor demand shocks as the estimated residuals from relative employment growth equations that assume fixed but possibly distinct unconditional regional mean growth rates.[14]

---

[13] Davis, Loungani, and Mahidhara (1997) and Blanchard and Katz (1992) provided alternative estimates for the United States based on observable exogenous determinants of regional labor demand, for example, defense contracts. These results are broadly consistent with those for the United States that we discuss later. Davis et al. found, however, some sensitivity of the adjustment pattern to the measure of employment used in estimation and suggested a somewhat slower response of migration in response to some shocks.

[14] Because of trends in technology or preferences, agglomeration economies, externalities, and better local institutions, or for social and cultural reasons, some regions tend to attract more workers and firms over the long run, whereas others have a secular tendency to decline in scale.

Table 10.2. *Impulse response profiles for a Blanchard-Katz regional labor-demand shock*

Country	Variable	First year	Five years	Ten years	Fifteen years
Italy	Employment	1.00	0.69	0.55	0.45
	Employment rate	0.23	0.12	0.07	0.04
	Participation rate	0.56	0.36	0.24	0.15
	Migration	0.22	0.21	0.24	0.27
Germany	Employment	1.00	1.03	0.57	0.17
	Employment rate	0.28	0.49	0.10	−0.02
	Participation rate	0.61	0.23	0.34	0.20
	Migration	0.11	0.31	0.13	−0.01
U.K.	Employment	1.00	0.63	0.37	0.36
	Employment rate	0.11	0.04	−0.04	−0.02
	Participation rate	0.85	0.42	0.14	0.04
	Migration	0.04	0.17	0.28	0.33
Canada	Employment	1.00	0.63	0.37	0.34
	Employment rate	0.46	−0.05	−0.12	−0.08
	Participation rate	0.43	0.25	0.12	0.09
	Migration	0.11	0.43	0.37	0.32
U.S.	Employment	1.00	0.74	0.44	0.48
	Employment rate	0.24	−0.01	−0.03	0.00
	Participation rate	0.43	0.16	−0.02	−0.01
	Migration	0.33	0.59	0.49	0.49

Notes: Units are percentage points. The German estimates are based on western Germany, excluding Berlin. Migration, participation rate, and employment rate may not sum to employment because of rounding.

Table 10.2 shows the reactions of the key regional labor-market variables to a 1% positive shock to relative labor demand. The impulse response profiles are based on estimation and simulation of Blanchard-Katz VARs, assuming two lags of each variable. (A variable's impulse response profile simply tracks through time the dynamic effect on the variable of the 1% shock to employment.) We have updated the original Blanchard-Katz U.S. data sample to extend it over 1976–95 (their data ended in 1990). We also report estimates for Canada (1976–96), Italy (1969–95), Germany (1970–93), and the United Kingdom (1969–94). For Germany, we omit West Berlin: only partial data are available, and the city appears to be an outlier in terms of its labor-market behavior.

Although the table offers a rich diversity in responses, a few regularities stand out. Perhaps the most salient feature is the much lower persistence of

Thus, employment trends may arise. (See Peri 1997 for an empirical study relating long-run employment growth in Italian cities and provinces to local sociocultural characteristics.)

the employment rate effect in the United States and Canada compared with the three EU countries. Five years later, the employment rate has returned to its initial level in the United States and Canada, whereas in Europe the half-life of the employment rate response is on the order of 4–7 years. Part of the answer can be found in migration. In the United States, there is a substantial initial migratory inflow to the region, which grows, peaks, and then reverses but remains substantial in the long run. In Canada, initial migration is smaller, but it then follows a pattern similar to that in the United States (albeit with consistently lower migratory flows).

In Italy, in contrast, the adjustment pattern suggests that worker mobility is on the average fairly low, but that there is a part of the labor force (young, skilled, educated workers, and those who live within commuting distance of other "regions") that is rather mobile and thus in a position to respond rapidly to shocks. After these workers have reacted, others find it more difficult to move, even if they experience a long unemployment spell or ultimately move out of the labor force. The very persistent participation changes for Italy (and some other countries) could reflect changes in disability status, early retirements, and movement between the legitimate and underground economies. In 1993, only 32.9% of Italian men aged 55–64 were officially participating in the labor force. (The comparable participation rates were about twice as high in the United States and the United Kingdom, and roughly 85% in Japan and Switzerland.)

Like Italy, Germany displays a small initial migration response and a large initial participation response. Migration subsequently grows but then reverses direction because the long-run permanent component of the labor-demand shock is small. In the United Kingdom, the participation response is an even more dominant equilibration mechanism, with migration appearing to gain in importance only in the very long run.

Two caveats are important in interpreting these long-run results. First, by modeling the participation and employment rates as stationary or mean-reverting rather than unit root processes, the statistical model forces migration to accommodate in full permanent changes in the level of employment. Second, the data series are too short to provide any reliable information about long-run responses. Thus, no long-run predictions of the model can be taken too seriously. The question, really, is whether the modeling assumptions we have made seriously distort estimates of short- and medium-term responses. We therefore estimated a version of the model in which relative employment is stationary, experiencing exclusively temporary fluctuations around a deterministic time trend. Necessarily in this alternative model, the long-run effects of labor-demand shocks on migration is zero. However, the first-year effects and the response 5 years later are very close to those reported in Table 10.2.

Decressin and Fatás (1995) apply the Blanchard-Katz methodology (over the years 1975–87) to European countries and to a pooled sample of European subnational regions and small countries. As in studies already discussed, they find large initial participation effects. They also find that migration, although quite low in the short run, rises in the long run to accommodate a fairly large estimated permanent component of the typical employment shock. Most importantly, their results differ from ours in finding that European employment rate responses are not noticeably more persistent than in the United States. We have already described why the long-run implications of these models should be discounted. We are less certain why Decressin and Fatás find such low employment rate persistence. The discrepancy seems to result from their identification of region-specific variables, not as simple differences from national averages, but as residuals from a regression of the log regional variable on the log national average. Blanchard and Katz (1992) found that using this approach instead of simple differences matters little for the United States. We have found that the choice has only minor effects on the Canadian and U.K. results. But when one applies the "residual" approach to Germany and Italy, the employment rate response indeed appears much less persistent.

We are unpersuaded that the method used by Decressin and Fatás yields an economically meaningful representation of the region-specific component of shocks. The justification for using their method to identify idiosyncratic regional shocks is, presumably, that for each region, the estimated time series of shocks is uncorrelated with the time series of the corresponding national-average variable. But this property is not clearly desirable or reasonable. As the study by Eichengreen (1993a) illustrates, region-specific shocks may be correlated with aggregate unemployment because they are generated by events – real exchange rate shifts, oil shocks, increased competition from low-wage countries – with divergent impacts on different regions (see also Davis, Loungani, and Mahidhara 1997). Furthermore, common shocks may feed into unemployment through distinct regional persistence mechanisms, as in the statistical model of Forni and Reichlin (1997). Our analysis, instead, embodies the simple hypothesis that any gap between the regional unemployment rate and its natural level should set in train pressures for migration. On this assumption, regional labor-demand shocks would seem to have much more persistent effects in Europe than in North America. This finding, consistent with the other evidence, suggests that there is indeed substantially lower labor mobility, not just among, but within, the existing currency unions of Europe.

It is tempting to relate the different unemployment adjustment patterns to differing labor-market institutions, but this is not straightforward. Germany has more open-ended unemployment benefits than Canada or the United States and a higher benefit replacement rate than either of those countries or the United Kingdom (Nickell 1997 presents a convenient OECD comparison; see also Bertola and Ichino 1995). However, Italy's official u.i. entitlement is very modest, and Canada's system can easily be "worked" to allow a high level of income support punctuated only by a short spell of employment each year (Courchene 1993; Green and Riddell 1997). Although unemployment benefits may be paid in disguised forms in Italy (e.g., medical benefits), generous jobless provisions seem at best only part of the reason for persistent regional unemployment. Other factors relevant particularly to continental Europe may be the very high coverage of wages by union contracts, a factor inhibiting regional wage flexibility, and relatively high tax rates, which discourage job creation, increase "wait" unemployment, and make underground activities more attractive. A definitive explanation of sluggish labor reallocation must rest on further microeconometric evidence.

Housing markets are very likely to be part of the story, however. Hughes and McCormick (1987) explain how rent controls, publicly allocated rental housing, and subsidized owner occupation restricted the stock of private rental housing in the United Kingdom, reducing mobility and raising aggregate unemployment. Oswald (1996) demonstrate a negative relationship between the private rental housing stock and unemployment for OECD countries. The United States has low unemployment despite a high rate of home ownership, but U.S. markets for long-term mortgages are relatively efficient and overall transaction costs are low.

10.4   Regional relative price adjustment

Research on the developed currency unions of North America and Europe suggests that, on almost any measure, relative regional prices tend to fluctuate less than international relative prices (Vaubel 1976, 1978; Eichengreen 1991; De Grauwe and Vanhaverbeke 1993; von Hagen and Neumann 1994). This fall in relative price variability is often viewed as one of the advantages of a currency union. At the same time, it raises questions about how the intranational mechanism of adjustment to permanent shocks differs from the international mechanism.[15] For Canada, Germany, and Italy, Table 10.3 shows standard deviations of (log) regional gross domestic product (GDP) deflators relative to

---

[15] In contrast to the general tendency in the literature, Poloz (1990) found relatively high variability in the relative GDP deflators of some Canadian provinces – higher, in some cases, than that between European countries. However, these findings applied mainly to Alberta and Saskatchewan, which are extremely open to trade and are heavy exporters of primary commodities. In such cases, regional real exchange rate movements themselves are largely exogenous shocks, in that they strongly reflect global movements in primary commodity prices. The change in the regional real exchange rate is not primarily the response to some region-specific shock. Also, Poloz's method of normalizing real exchange rate levels over 1980–7 gives an exaggerated appearance of variability for several provinces because the variability measure he calculates apparently is the standard deviation in the level (not logarithm) of relative price. (Poloz chooses a 1971 base year despite the run-up in commodity and especially energy prices since the early 1970s.) Thus, Poloz's volatility figures for the Alberta/Ontario real exchange rate over 1980–7, say, are not readily comparable to those he calculates for the France/Germany rate.

Table 10.3. *Intranational relative price variability: Annual levels (percent)*

Country	Period	Average	High region	Low region
Canada	1970–95	1.4	2.1	0.6
Germany	1970–95	1.2	3.0	0.3
Italy	1970–96	2.5	5.0	1.0

Notes: Regional standard deviations of the log regional GDP deflator less the log national GDP deflator. Regional figures are averaged (with equal weights) to obtain each country's aggregate regional variability measure.

Table 10.4. *Intranational relative price variability: Annual changes (percent)*

Country	Period	Average	High region	Low region
Canada	1970–95	0.8	1.1	0.3
Germany	1970–95	0.9	1.2	0.3
Italy	1970–96	0.8	1.2	0.6

Notes: Regional standard deviations of regional GDP deflator inflation rate less national GDP deflator inflation rate. Regional figures are averaged (with equal weights) to obtain each country's aggregate regional variability measure.

national GDP deflators. Table 10.4 does an analogous calculation of the standard deviation of annual first differences in such real exchange rates. Table 10.3 is meant to illustrate the long-run range of variation in real exchange rates that these currency unions have experienced over a quarter century, while Table 10.4 is meant to illustrate the degree of short-run (year-to-year) variability in real exchange rates around their trends (which are small in these regional data).[16]

Table 10.5 (on 1988–96 national real exchange rate levels vis-à-vis Germany) and Table 10.6 (on changes over that same period) allow a comparison of intranational with international variability in relative prices. Real exchange rate variation within currency unions often is quite low compared to that between countries, as previous research has shown. With more of the European Exchange Rate Mechanism's (ERM) track record available, however, it is clear that fixed exchange rates can induce international real exchange rate volatility levels matching those seen across regions of low-inflation countries. Of

---

[16] The choice of GDP deflators is meant to capture regional export competitiveness. Vaubel (1976, 1978), Eichengreen (1991), and von Hagen and Neumann (1994) studied regional CPI-based real exchange rates. De Grauwe and Vanhaverbeke (1993) used data on regional unit labor costs.

Table 10.5. *International price variability relative to Germany, 1988–96: Annual levels (percent)*

ERM core		Other current ERM		Non-ERM Europe		Non-Europe	
Country	Percent	Country	Percent	Country	Percent	Country	Percent
Austria	0.6	Finland	17.2	Greece	3.5	Australia	12.4
Belgium	1.1	Ireland	9.1	Norway	10.1	Canada	16.6
Denmark	3.9	Italy	12.6	Sweden	13.3	Japan	8.4
France	3.4	Portugal	6.8	U.K.	9.6	New Zealand	11.3
Netherlands	3.2	Spain	9.4			U.S.	8.1

Notes: Standard deviation of the log national GDP deflator less Germany's log national GDP deflator, in national currency.

Table 10.6. *International price variability relative to Germany, 1988–96: Annual changes (percent)*

ERM core		Other current ERM		Non-ERM Europe		Non-Europe	
Country	Percent	Country	Percent	Country	Percent	Country	Percent
Austria	0.7	Finland	10.7	Greece	3.7	Australia	11.4
Belgium	1.2	Ireland	4.2	Norway	4.9	Canada	10.1
Denmark	2.0	Italy	8.8	Sweden	9.8	Japan	10.7
France	1.7	Portugal	5.2	U.K.	6.9	New Zealand	10.1
Netherlands	1.0	Spain	7.3			U.S.	7.7

Notes: Standard deviation of national GDP deflator inflation less inflation in Germany's national GDP deflator, measured in national currency.

Germany's five "ERM core" partners – those that have not realigned against Germany in the last 10 years – all with the possible exceptions of Denmark and France show real exchange rate variability that is closely consistent with that within the three currency unions. Austria, indeed, shows less variability on either measure than the average German Land.

Outside the ERM core, real exchange rate volatility is much higher, but to differing degrees. In this respect there is little difference, on the whole, between the non-core ERM members, which have realigned or floated against Germany in the 1990s, and European countries outside the ERM, which have at times shadowed the deutsche mark (DM) or European currency units (ECU). Finland and Sweden, both reliant on primary product exports, stand out for their wide real exchange rate swings. Greece's low real-rate volatility is remarkable; evidently changes in the drachma's nominal rate have largely offset differential inflation. Real exchange rate variability against Germany tends to rise outside

Europe, but in this respect the U.S. record differs little from that of most other countries who entered EMU in 1999.

For Vaubel (1976, 1978), the amplitude and frequency of real exchange rate movements between two regions is almost a sufficient statistic of their suitability to form a currency union. An absence of asymmetric real shocks, interregional factor mobility, regional proximity, and a high extent of mutual trade all should promote stability in the real exchange rate. Vaubel and the authors who have followed him all recognize that the observed volatility of international real exchange rates may well overstate the macroeconomic disadvantages of forming a currency union. Particularly under floating nominal exchange rates, monetary and portfolio shocks that would be absent in a currency union contribute powerfully to real exchange rate volatility.[17]

The opposite possibility has received less recognition, however. Market distortions and government policies may allow *too little* real exchange rate variation in a currency union, given the asymmetric shocks that occur. On this reading, the stability of interregional real exchange rates could reflect systematic interference with the workings of markets, motivated by distributional or political ends, and reveal little about a currency union's innate desirability.

For Europe, the latter possibility derives credence from the existence of nationwide wage norms and the practice of administered pricing in many sectors, including housing. Thus, the authors of "One Market, One Money" express the hope that under the single currency, competition and wage discipline will enhance price and wage flexibility, facilitating intra-EMU real exchange rate adjustment in the absence of significant international labor mobility (Emerson et al. 1992, p. 136). On this view, EMU optimists should wish to see *more* real exchange rate flexibility between the ERM core and Germany than among German regions (see Tables 10.3–10.6), but there is scant evidence of this. The effect should be all the more pronounced because an internationally asymmetric permanent shock gives rise to a permanent real exchange rate change, whereas the corresponding disturbance should have only a temporary real exchange rate effect within an area of free factor mobility. The counterargument, that there have been no asymmetric shocks, rings rather hollow given that the sample underlying Tables 10.5 and 10.6 includes German reunification. (More formal

---

[17] Using a data sample that includes locations in Europe and an econometric specification that controls for distance and trade barriers, Engel and Rogers (1995) found that higher nominal exchange rate volatility between two markets systematically raises intermarket variability in relative prices. See Obstfeld (1998) for a survey. It is not correct, however, to assert that monetary factors have no effect on interregional real exchange rate volatility within currency unions. The evidence is that interregional relative price variability is higher when mean national inflation is higher. Debelle and Lamont (1997) offered a useful capsule review of the evidence, as well as new evidence that the dispersion of prices within U.S. cities is positively related to the citywide inflation rate.

evidence on the existence of asymmetric national shocks is discussed by Bayoumi and Eichengreen 1996, Forni and Reichlin 1997, Viñals and Jimeno 1996, and Weber 1997.)

For the United States, Blanchard and Katz (1992) find that regional relative wage and price movements play at best a small supporting role in the adjustment to permanent labor-demand shocks. They ascribe this finding to the predominance of migration as a regional adjustment mechanism in the United States. In light of the last section's finding that interregional migration is of more limited importance in Canada and especially in Europe, one might expect to find regional prices playing a bigger role in offsetting regional shocks. Figures 10.12–10.14 suggest that any such tendencies may be small, but these figures do not indicate whether high regional unemployment rates are due to shocks that might warrant price adjustment.[18] To focus on that issue, we attempt to estimate local price responses conditional on asymmetric shocks to employment.

We do this by estimating bivariate VARs in relative regional employment growth and the (log) relative regional GDP deflator. This specification imposes the assumption that relative regional employment is subject to permanent shocks, whereas relative regional prices are not. Eventually, factor inflows within a national economy should eliminate regional price discrepancies due to relative labor-demand shocks, even when those shocks have permanent components.

As in the last section, we impose a common propagation mechanism on all regions in a country but allow for region-specific unconditional mean levels of employment growth and the price of GDP. Our estimated impulse responses incorporate the maintained identifying assumption that employment-growth shocks are labor-demand shifts that can affect local prices within a year, but that respond to local prices only after a year has passed. Again, the German results are based on the ten western German Länder excluding Berlin.

Table 10.7 reports our findings. Only in Germany is their a noticeable short-run local price increase in response to a positive labor-demand shock, and the effect disappears (indeed, becomes slightly negative) immediately after the

---

[18] The relative price decline within Italy shown in Figure 10.13 probably does not represent the operation of market forces as described in textbook accounts of regional adjustment. Attanasio and Padoa Schioppa (1991, p. 260) explained why southern Italian CPIs tend to be relatively low, and most of the reasons carry over to GDP deflators: "The reasons for their low cost of living can probably be found partly in subsidies provided by the Central Government in some services (highways, for instance, are free in the South and not in the North-Centre), partly by cheaper labor in the underground and criminal economy, partly by cheaper rents which are publicly regulated (both for residential and business dwellings) and finally by the lower weight the Southern regions assign to non-agricultural consumption which is everywhere the most expensive and the one whose cost rises more rapidly." Given the convergence between southern and northcentral nominal wages over the last couple of decades or so (a result of the scala mobile along with other features of Italian wage setting), the implication is that relative real wages in the south actually have *risen*.

Table 10.7. *Impulse response of local price level to a labor-demand shock*

Country	Variable	First year	Five years	Ten years	Fifteen years
Italy	Employment	1.00	0.80	0.79	0.79
	GDP deflator	0.02	0.00	0.00	0.00
Germany	Employment	1.00	1.50	1.53	1.53
	GDP deflator	0.30	0.08	0.00	0.00
Canada	Employment	1.00	1.25	1.22	1.22
	GDP deflator	0.06	0.21	0.07	0.02

Notes: Units are percentage points. The German estimates are based on western Germany, excluding Berlin.

period of the shock. This pattern provides very weak support for the idea that in Germany local prices help in regional adjustment because in that country the employment rate remains high long after the initial year of a labor-demand shock (recall Table 10.2). In Canada, local prices eventually show a small tendency to rise after the first period, whereas in Italy they don't seem to move at all. The results for Canada change very little when Alberta and Saskatchewan, both big primary commodity producers, are excluded.

The estimates in Table 10.7 imply larger permanent effects of employment shocks than those in Table 10.2, which are based on a VAR including the participation and employment rates. This discrepancy is puzzling. When we add prices to the larger VAR system underlying Table 10.2, however, the implications for regional real exchange rates are close to those of Table 10.7.[19]

Although the low responsiveness of prices could in principle reflect rapid migratory responses or high interregional trade integration, neither explanation seems plausible for Europe in view of the low migration responses and persistent employment-rate effects documented in Section 10.3.

The analysis thus does not contradict the view that interregional real exchange rate variability is relatively low in Europe in part because of price rigidities and government policies that slow the pace of adjustment. This conclusion is neither surprising nor novel. Governments routinely interfere with the income redistributions relative price changes otherwise would cause – the Common Agricultural Policy and the contorted compensation devices that have supported it being one extreme example. Continental European wage-setting institutions by and large also reflect a philosophy of regional equalization in earnings. It is often argued that intra-EU exchange flexibility is incompatible

[19] We also estimated VARs involving relative per capita GDP as well as relative prices, with results broadly similar to those in Table 10.7.

with the survival of the single market because currency-induced real exchange rate movements would induce strong pressures for protection (see, for example, Eichengreen 1993b). The same argument suggests, however, that large swings in relative regional prices could be politically problematic for economic integration at the national level. Even when domestic labor mobility is low, sharp regional price swings therefore are unlikely to be allowed a big role in adjustment. When interpreted in this light, the low extent of interregional price movement tells us little about the ease with which resources are reallocated in currency unions, or about the need for reallocation.

10.5   Interregional insurance and fiscal transfers

Private insurance markets and government interregional transfer schemes can cushion the effects of temporary and permanent economic shocks. In the case of temporary shocks, they provide more complete protection than borrowing would. In the case of permanent shocks, they reduce the need for a long-run adjustment in regional consumption levels. A key facet of a currency union's performance depends on how well private or public insurance can fulfill these roles. In this section, we compare the roles of private insurance for U.S. states and for EU countries and then examine the operation of public interregional transfer systems in the United States, Canada, and Europe. A major finding is that transfers are quite persistent, reflecting the persistence of unemployment, and thus facilitate slower regional adjustment.

10.5.1   Evidence on private insurance

Some basic evidence on the mechanism of private insurance within currency unions has been developed by Atkeson and Bayoumi (1993), who compare the extent of private risk sharing across U.S. census regions with that across European countries. A starting point for comparison is the relation of gross regional product to personal income, the difference between the two consisting of external capital income, remittances of labor earnings, and government transfers. Even excluding government and labor transfers, the percentage by which GDP differs from personal income in U.S. census regions is one to two orders of magnitude above the percentage difference between French, German, or Italian GDP and gross national product (GNP). Thus, New England's personal income exceeded its GDP by around 9% on average over 1963–86, whereas the corresponding figure for Germany or France is only 0.2%.

Atkeson and Bayoumi also found (in 1966–86 data) that U.S. national capital income is the preponderant determinant of U.S. regional capital income, and that U.S. regional capital income is slightly (but significantly) negatively correlated with regional labor income, suggesting some role of financial wealth in insuring human wealth, albeit a small one. The situation appeared to be quite different in the European Community on 1970–87 data. Capital incomes in Belgium, France, Greece, the Netherlands, and the United Kingdom appeared more weakly correlated with the aggregate capital income of those countries plus Germany. In a more recent study covering the years 1981–90, Sørensen and Yosha (1996) conclude that cross-border asset ownership contributes much more toward smoothing the cross-sectional variability of annual consumption in the United States than in the EU.

The dismantling of EU capital-account restrictions under the Single European Act probably has gone partway to diminish the contrast between the United States and Europe. Furthermore, the introduction of the Euro will greatly enhance the integration and efficiency of the European capital market. But fully catching up to the United States will take time and depends on the further opening of domestic European financial markets. In the meantime, an important private insurance mechanism of the U.S. currency union seems to be less developed in the future EMU. As long as Europe's capital markets lag behind those of the United States, the need for the government to provide substitute insurance is correspondingly greater.

10.5.2   Fiscal transfers in existing currency unions

Since at least the work of Ingram (1959), economists have recognized the role of interregional fiscal transfers in equilibrating regional balances of payments within currency unions. The question was placed squarely on the European agenda by the MacDougall Report (Commission of the European Communities 1977), although the issue had been raised years earlier in the Werner Report. MacDougall and his colleagues argued that in existing industrialized currency unions, both fiscal *redistribution* to offset long-run regional income differentials and *stabilizing* fiscal transfers aimed at providing a short-term cushion against cyclical shocks are substantial. Their report suggested (p. 49) that on average roughly 40% of any long-run regional per capita income disparity is eliminated by equalization policies. They also contended (p. 35) that in the United Kingdom and France, "as much as one-half to two-thirds of a short-term loss of primary income due to, for example, a fall in a region's external sales may be offset through the public finance system, and much the same may be true of regions in other modern integrated economies."

Although the MacDougall Report regarded international fiscal flows at that level as impracticable for the near term, it suggested (pp. 20–1) that a European Community budget on the order of 5–7% of community GNP, providing for net transfers between member states both for equalization and stabilization purposes, might provide sufficient support to allow Europe to proceed to monetary unification: "A federation with these special characteristics would facilitate creation of a monetary union. Existing national federations enjoy such union internally, and its maintenance is powerfully assisted by the largely automatic equalising and stabilising interregional flows through the channels of federal finance." Important to the argument we shall make later, the MacDougall Report regarded redistribution as well as stabilization as vital elements in sustaining a currency union. In the authors' view, a country giving up substantial fiscal as well as monetary autonomy within a single market served by a single money might be running a greater risk of permanent economic decline.

The study of U.S. fiscal federalism by Sala-i-Martin and Sachs (1992) moved the discussion to a more rigorously quantitative level. They regressed log-levels of U.S. census regions' relative transfers and taxes on the log-level of relative personal income in the region. The bottom-line finding is that on average across regions during the years 1970–88, federal taxes and transfers together offset fully 40% of a one-dollar shock to local personal income. Taken at face value, the result would imply that even the U.S. currency union, with its relatively footloose labor force, relies heavily on fiscal transfers to offset regional shocks (although not as heavily as a credulous reader of the MacDougall Report might have predicted).

Von Hagen (1992) argues that the Sala-i-Martin and Sachs (1992) regression of relative tax and transfer levels on relative income levels confounds the stabilization role of transfers with their redistributive role. He proposes to regress year-to-year tax and transfer changes on income changes to get at the stabilization effect, and to regress yearly levels of taxes and transfers on yearly levels of incomes to get at the redistributive effect. Von Hagen's estimates over a 1981–86 sample of U.S. states look at the response of net fiscal inflows to gross state product (GSP) rather than personal income before taxes (the two differing primarily because of asset income from other states). Thus the results are not immediately comparable to those of Sala-i-Martin and Sachs. He finds that short-run stabilizing role of net transfers – their response to a one-year change in GSP – amounts to only ten cents on the dollar. Long-run redistribution in the United States is, however, estimated to be very large, roughly 47 cents on the dollar.

Subsequent researchers have continued to reconsider the U.S. experience but also have added data on other countries. Goodhart and Smith (1993) applied von Hagen's (1992) specifications to U.S., Canadian, and U.K. data, finding stabilization effects similar to his for the United States and Canada, but somewhat larger (21 cents on the dollar) for the United Kingdom. They find, however, that the estimated redistributive effects are quite close to the stabilization effects. They argue that these estimates are likely to underestimate the true effects because von Hagen's measure of taxes omits social security contributions. Pisani-Ferry, Italianer, and Lescure (1993) revisited the United States and introduce France and Germany, using a simulation methodology based on the characteristics of national fiscal systems rather than on regression analysis. They find a 17 cents on the dollar offset to a decline in gross regional product in the United States and offsets roughly twice that size for France and Germany. The huge difference compared with the United States stems in large part from the operation of the French and German unemployment insurance and social security systems, together with the system of interregional grants (Länderfinanzausgleich) in Germany.

Returning to econometrics, Bayoumi and Masson (1995) analyze the United States and Canada. (In Canada, as in Germany, interregional equalization is a constitutional principle.) Using a specification somewhat different from von Hagen's, and pursuing estimation of stabilization via yearly differences but of redistribution via long-run average levels, they find a 31% stabilization effect and a 22% redistribution effect for the United States. These effects refer to percentages of shocks to personal income, not GSP. For Canada, where federal taxes are less important and provinces exercise considerable discretion fiscal policy, the stabilizing effect fiscal flows is only 17%. However, the extensive Canadian equalization system results in a redistributive effect of 39%.[20]

Mélitz and Zumer (1997) try to reconcile these conflicting conclusions by applying uniform accounting procedures and a common econometric methodology to the U.S., Canada, the UK, and France. Their estimated stabilization coefficients with respect to personal income are around 20% for the United States, the United Kingdom, and France, but only 10–14% for Canada. They estimate a 38% long-run equalization of personal incomes in France, an equalization of 26% in the United Kingdom, and equalizations around 17% in Canada and the United States. Their estimate of Canadian redistribution is much lower than the 39% "headline" estimate of Bayoumi-Masson. The explanation is their exclusion of federal grants to provincial governments from their estimates of personal-income stabilization. Mélitz and Zumer argue that such grants belong only in estimates of output stabilization. One might justify the Bayoumi-Masson

---

[20] Even though the modern system of Canadian equalization grants dates from 1957, its current incarnation originates in the Constitution Act of 1982 (section 36[2]), which committed the national government to "the principle of making equalization payments to ensure that provincial governments have sufficient revenues to provide reasonably comparable levels of public services at reasonably comparable levels of taxation." Under the present system, five provinces – British Columbia, Manitoba, Ontario, Quebec, and Saskatchewan – define a "standard" level of per capita revenues from 33 specified revenue sources. The standard refers not to actual revenues but to their hypothetical level at national average tax rates. Provinces with per capita revenues (at national average tax rates) above the standard receive no equalization payments but make none either. Payments to provinces below the five-province standard (again, at national average tax rates) come from the federal government, which is supposed to bring the poorer provinces up to par (see Boadway and Hobson 1993). Although this system might be thought to complicate econometric analysis, it is only part of the total tax and transfer system, which includes also federal taxes, social assistance payments, and unemployment insurance. Indeed, the overall long-run relationship between personal income before and after taxes and transfers appears quite linear for Canada, as Figure 2 of Bayoumi and Masson (1995) shows.

accounting, however, by arguing that direct grants from the center or from other localities allow local governments to lower taxes or increase their provision of public goods and services valued by consumers.

Thus, a considerable range of estimates remains for some countries. Does any consistent pattern emerge? Coming back to the United States, a stabilization coefficient with respect to personal income of 20% – a number not inconsistent with von Hagen's (1992) estimate of 10% with respect to GSP – seems to emerge from the literature as a rough consensus figure. Interestingly, Asdrubali, Sørensen, and Yosha (1996), who explained empirically the cross-sectional correlation of per capita GSP and per capita state consumption, presented estimates that imply a U.S. stabilization coefficient of 21% with respect to personal income. The extent of redistribution among U.S. states appears to be close to that figure as well, although there is less convergence in the literature. For Canada, redistribution seems to be higher, and stabilization lower than in the United States, although the latter result is explained by Canada's more decentralized fiscal system. Such evidence as is available for France, Germany, and the United Kingdom indicates a higher degree of stabilization and/or redistribution compared with the "twenty-twenty" standard of the United States, especially in the two continental countries.[21] The continuing transfer flow from western to eastern Germany is a conspicuous example of interregional redistribution.

In assessing the role of transfers, it is important to remember that their importance in stabilizing labor incomes might be disproportionately large, due to the limited capital-market access of those with little financial wealth. Atkeson and Bayoumi (1993) confirm that in the United States, fiscal transfers play a larger role than asset income in insuring labor income. A related point is that continental European financial markets have provided more limited opportunities for diversification in general than those of the United States, making fiscal transfers more valuable at the margin.

10.5.3   Stabilization, redistribution, and transfer dynamics

The textbook case of complete contingent securities markets – in which all risks can be marketed – provides a useful benchmark from which to assess the roles of government transfers in the realistic case where asset markets are far from complete. In complete markets, any uncertain contingency, whether it has a permanent or temporary effect, can be insured against. Events that are perfectly predictable cannot be insured, although borrowing and lending will be available to smooth their effects over time.

In the absence of complete markets, an omniscient government planner might facilitate regional risk sharing by making the contingent interregional transfers

---

[21] On redistribution in Germany, see Costello (1993).

that might otherwise have been effected privately. In this case, we would view the government as providing insurance services. The government might also make noncontingent transfers based on known structural features of regions – for example, an exogenously fixed payment from an oil-producing region to one without natural resources. These are pure redistributions.

The notion of *stabilization* used in the empirical fiscal federalism literature does not correspond perfectly to that of insurance because elements of the tax-and-transfer system that provide insurance against permanent (or highly persistent) shocks may induce fiscal flows that are indistinguishable from redistributions once a shock has occurred. One might instead view the proper stabilizing function of fiscal transfers as that of partially compensating for missing interregional insurance markets.[22] In that case, however, the redistributive effects as estimated in the literature will also tend to capture the stabilization function in its response to permanent or long-lived shocks. Estimated redistributive coefficients would not be irrelevant to the question of stabilization, although it might be hard to distinguish their stabilization and true redistributive components. At the same time, the stabilization coefficients estimated by standard approaches might fail to capture lags in stabilizing fiscal flows (see, e.g., Eichengreen's 1991 case study of Michigan in the early 1980s).

These factors motivate the search for a dynamic fiscal-flow model in which pure redistribution can be separated empirically from transfers that provide insurance against idiosyncratic shocks.[23] To that end, we propose a bivariate VAR specification based on the same variables that Bayoumi and Masson (1995) and Mélitz and Zumer (1997) analyze. Denote by $y_{i,t}$ region i's relative per capita personal income in period t, that is, the log of regional per capita personal income less that of national personal per capita income. Let $y_{i,t}^{\alpha}$ denote relative *available* per capita income, defined in terms of per capita personal income less tax outflows from the region, plus transfer inflows.[24] The VAR specification we propose is

$$y_{i,t}^{\alpha} = \alpha_i + (1 - y)y_{i,t} + b_{11}(L)y_{i,t-1} + b_{12}(L)y_{i,t-1}^{n} + \varepsilon_{1i,t} \qquad (1)$$

$$y_{i,t} = \beta_i + b_{21}(L)y_{i,t-1} + b_{22}(L)y_{i,t-1} + \varepsilon_{2i,t} \qquad (2)$$

---

[22] This is the approach taken by Persson and Tabellini (1996), who studied the endogenous determination of risk sharing and redistribution within a federal union. Their simplified model is not immediately applicable to making positive predictions about EMU because it omits certain elements, notably potential labor mobility, likely to be important in practice.

[23] Goodhart and Smith (1993) and Mélitz and Zumer (1997) also stressed fiscal dynamics.

[24] We focus on personal income, rather than regional product, to evaluate the extra stabilization transfers provided after private portfolio diversification. In terms of the econometrics, regional personal income will be "more exogenous" than regional product if financial income comes from nationally diversified sources – and simultaneity bias is a potential problem notwithstanding the identifying assumption we make later. For Italy, we have no personal income data, so we use regional product instead.

Table 10.8. *Redistributive and stabilizing effects of transfers, Canada, United States, and Italy*

Country	δ: Long-run redistribution	y: First-year stabilization
Canada	0.53	0.13
(federal taxes, transfers, grants)	(0.03)	(0.02)
United States	0.19	0.10
(federal taxes, transfers, grants)	(0.03)	(0.01)
Italy	0.08	0.03
(social insurance system)	(0.02)	(0.03)

Notes: Standard errors are given in parentheses.

where the lag polynomials $b_{ij}(L)$ imply two lags, that is, all are linear functions of the lag operator L (which assigns to any variable its value the period before). In this setup, we assume that the innovation in the second equation is an exogenous change in regional relative income per head, which affects net transfers, and hence available income, but is not itself affected by the change in transfers in the same period.

We take the ordinary least squares estimate of ã in Equation (1) as measuring the contemporaneous stabilizing effect of the transfer. Here, this coefficient measures the response of fiscal flows to an *unanticipated* relative income shock, whereas the coefficient usually associated with stabilization in the literature applies to any relative income change, expected or not. The VAR setting allows also us to trace the entire dynamic response of income and available income, and hence of transfers (which can be approximated as $y_{i,t}^a - y_{i,t}$). Notice we are assuming that, once correction is made for region-specific means, relative per capita income is a stationary or mean-reverting variable: we do not contemplate long-run regional divergence.

The estimated VAR also allows us to estimate long-run redistribution. In this setting the estimate does not depend on random realizations of per capita regional income. Equations (1) and (2) allow one to calculate the steady-state (unconditional mean) values $\bar{y}_i^a$ and y_i for each region, as functions of the region-specific constants $\hat{a}_i$ and $\hat{a}_i$ and the other equation coefficients. A regression of $\bar{y}_i^a$ on y_i across regions i yields the coefficient $1 - \ddot{a}$, where ä denotes the coefficient of long-run redistribution.

Table 10.8 reports our estimates of the redistribution and stabilization coefficients for Canada (1971–95), Italy (1979–93), and the United States (1969–85), where for the United States we have simply used the same data as Bayoumi and Masson (1995).

For Canada, our stabilization effect is quite similar to the estimates of Mélitz and Zumer (1997) and slightly below that of Bayoumi and Masson (1995). But

Table 10.9. *Dynamic response of transfers to a regional income shock*

Country	Variable	First year	Five years	Ten years	Fifteen years
Canada	Δy	1.00	0.68	0.21	0.05
	$\Delta trans$	−0.13	−0.07	0.00	0.00
United States	Δy	1.00	0.27	0.07	0.02
	$\Delta trans$	−0.10	−0.07	−0.02	0.00
Italy	Δy	1.00	0.17	0.01	0.00
	$\Delta trans$	−0.03	−0.03	−0.01	0.00

Notes: The variable *trans* is defined as the log of available relative regional income per capita less the log of relative regional income per capita. The operator Δ denotes a first difference.

the redistributive effect that our method measures is much higher than those in the literature. For the United States, we find only about half the stabilization effect suggested by recent studies that have used personal income as the regional activity variable. (However, the stabilization effect rises from 10 to 12% the period after the shock first occurs.) The U.S. redistribution coefficient is, however, close to the canonical 20% figure. Finally, for Italy the redistribution coefficient is significant but very small (although the extent of regional income inequality is large). The estimated first-year stabilization effect, at only 3%, is insignificant, statistically and economically. However, as we have noted, our Italian data give a very partial picture of total fiscal flows.

Table 10.9 provides a more complete picture of the dynamic response of relative transfers to a relative regional income shock. The main point to notice is that the transfer effect of the income shock is quite persistent, taking in all cases over 5 years to be reduced by half. In Canada, transfers fall back to their baseline more quickly than output does, whereas the reverse is true in Italy and the United States. Thus, in Canada the stabilizing role of transfers declines over time for a typically persistent output shock.[25]

The high persistence of stabilizing transfers, even in the United States, suggests that their role goes beyond that of temporarily cushioning cyclical shocks. They appear to represent rather long-lived inflows to regions that have suffered macroeconomic reversals, and, as such, facilitate postponement of any necessary adjustment in labor force and relative prices.

[25] We also tried to apply our method to the German fiscal system, but data limitations were particularly severe. The following results, based on total taxes paid by the Länder to the federal government (after correction for Länderfinanzausgleich redistributions), omit transfers and therefore should be interpreted with caution. (See the Data Appendix for more details.) The tendency emerging was a rather large redistributive role for taxes (a 36% coefficient of redistribution). We found a delayed and rather persistent reaction of tax payments to a relative-income shock (negligible in the first period, 12% in the second, 4% in the fifth).

10.6   Lessons for EMU and a proposal

The preceding comparative analysis of North American and European currency unions yields several regularities and contrasts, which might be useful in evaluating the future performance and evolution of EMU.

1   Labor mobility is a weaker aid to regional adjustment in Europe than in the United States or even in Canada. We see a glacial pace of regional labor-market adjustment accompanied by high and persistent regional employment differentials.

2   Despite relatively low interregional labor mobility and despite the absence of independent macro policy options for subnational European regions, regional real exchange rate flexibility is not greater than in currency unions with higher labor mobility.

3   Fiscal transfers from booming to depressed regions, both for redistributive and stabilization purposes, play a significant role in all the currency unions we have examined, although their role seems most modest in the United States. Transfer flows and the economic shocks to which they respond appear to be quite persistent, making it difficult to draw a sharp line between the long-run redistributive and short-run stabilizing roles of transfers. By providing long-lived fiscal inflows from the rest of the country, existing systems of fiscal federalism in Europe ensure that regions experiencing permanent negative idiosyncratic shocks will be relieved of some of the pressure to adjust.

Because EMU is an entirely novel experiment in full monetary unification among major political powers without full political unification or an overarching fiscal authority, it is difficult to predict how EMU might evolve. If EMU develops national adjustment mechanisms similar to those driving regional adjustment within existing currency unions, the preceding list of regularities offers several alternative templates.

At least in the foreseeable future, EMU is unlikely to rely on international labor mobility to any great extent. In post-Schengen Europe as within its constituent states, workers theoretically have full freedom of movement. But the factors that nonetheless limit intranational migration curb international migration even more, and there is the additional barrier of language and custom. Workers in potential source countries reluctant not only to migrate but also to welcome foreign competitors in potential host countries. As "One Market, One Money" puts it, "large-scale labor mobility in the Community is neither feasible, at least not across language barriers, nor perhaps desirable" (Emerson et al. 1992, p. 151). Because intra-European migration on a large scale would be perceived as socially disruptive, EMU is likely to put in place incentives to remain at home – a point we elaborate later.

Does this mean that national price and wage levels in EMU will become more flexible to accommodate needed national adjustments in real exchange rates? The experiences of existing continental currency unions provide no supporting evidence, nor do those of countries that have long pegged to the Deutsche mark. The heightened perception of a single market that the Euro will bring could even promote a greater tendency toward EMU-wide wage bargaining or coverage. As Eichengreen (1992) noted, desires to limit cross-border migration might also contribute to this outcome. The labor-market experience of East Germany after unification is an extreme one that does not fully apply across different European countries, but it carries a relevant warning.

From a political viewpoint, sharp movements in intra-EMU wages or competitiveness levels would undermine support for the single market as surely as sharp exchange rate movements between member states. Workers in countries that had lost competitiveness would allege unfair competition, especially in the face of plant closures and shifts of capital to low-wage EMU countries. Relatively immobile firms might call for protection. Such developments, like the threat of migration, would sharpen EMU leaders' interest in promoting wage convergence – even at the cost of economic efficiency. For all of these reasons, we doubt that EMU will display substantially greater flexibility in internal real exchange rates than its constituent members currently do.

Laboring under these constraints on adjustment, the EU will eventually face strong pressures to expand its centralized fiscal functions in the direction of intercountry stabilization transfers. Given the generally high persistence of macroeconomic shocks in Europe, especially shocks at the national level, stabilization payments are likely to play a substantial ex post redistributive role as well. There are several reasons to expect this development.

A country that joins a currency union provides its partners with a public good by expanding the domain over which the single currency is used. Correspondingly, its claim on community protection against persistent or even permanent shocks can be legitimized. The Werner Report took it for granted that "an increase in financial intervention effected at Community level" would be a necessary adjunct to monetary union, and the MacDougall Report argued the point in detail 7 years later.[26] Van Rompuy, Abraham, and Heremans (1991, p. 119) contended that "States agree on the centralization of competences and on the discipline implied by the adherence to the EMU in exchange for redistributive mechanisms."

Indeed, this has been the pattern already: the Maastricht Treaty's Protocol on Economic and Social Cohesion, which set up the Cohesion Fund, and the consequent 1992 increase in Structural Funds, were essential components in sealing the final agreement on EMU. Countries that run into severe economic

---

[26] The Werner Report is reproduced in Steinherr (1994, p. 25).

difficulties under EMU may well be able to lobby successfully for additional side-payments. To the extent that the stability pact limits national fiscal responses and social safety nets, pressures on Brussels will be heightened further, as argued by von Hagen and Eichengreen (1996). Attempts to extend EU political or economic integration will provide ample further opportunities for bargaining over transfers.

Large intra-EMU unemployment and income differentials, coupled with some scale-back of existing support systems for the unemployed and indigent, would create incentives for substantial migrations – migrations which, as we have argued, EMU leaders could perceive as politically unacceptable. Incipient migratory pressures, and the consequent fear of social strife, would in practice be the most compelling reason for EU leaders to extend the transfer system. Examples from existing currency unions abound. Courchene (1993) describes the role of the Canadian transfer system in keeping unemployed workers in the poorer Atlantic provinces. Within Italy, northward migration flows out of the Mezzogiorno have declined sharply since the early 1970s as a result of higher transfers to the south (as well as enforced real wage convergence and housing shortages due to rent controls; see Attanasio and Padoa Schioppa 1991). In the United States, welfare programs starting in the Depression have slowed migration out of Appalachia. In Germany, wage and fiscal policies have discouraged east-to-west movements of workers. (The prospect that the EU will be enlarged toward the labor-abundant east has already brought into contention the question of redirecting versus enlarging existing transfer facilities.)

There would naturally be serious political resistance to the enlargement of EU transfer programs. As von Hagen (1993, p. 281) observes, an enhanced international transfer facility would not draw political support from sentiments of national solidarity. Indeed, the existing regional support programs of Belgium, Canada, Italy, and other countries plainly strain the national solidarity that remains. Even if a pure insurance system could be designed, the persistence of shocks and transfers might leave the current payers unclear as to their expected future benefits from continuing the arrangement. Such tensions would make an enlarged transfer program politically destabilizing ex post, but might well fail to prevent its creation.

Would an expanded European Transfer Union (ETU) be good or bad for Europe? Obviously the development would be advantageous to the extent that it provided otherwise unavailable risk pooling among EMU countries. Van der Ploeg (1991), Wyplosz (1991), and Goodhart and Smith (1993), among many others, have spelled out that advantage, but also draw attention to the considerable moral hazards such intercountry insurance would involve. Workers might view an ETU as a backstop for high wage demands (as occurred in East Germany after unification). Governments might give in more easily to demands for anticompetitive labor-market measures. (Courchene, 1993, p. 140, relates how Quebec during the 1970s maintained a higher minimum wage than other provinces, successfully shifting the costs of its policy onto the federal budget.) In addition, individual incentives for job search at the EU level would be curbed (as intended by some of those who would support setting up an ETU).

The scope for moral hazard could be reduced in several ways, but probably not eliminated. Goodhart and Smith (1993) suggest that adverse incentive effects could be minimized by ensuring that the transfers were temporary.[27] Because shocks in Europe tend to have persistent effects, however, such transfers would provide only a small degree of risk sharing. If the goal is to provide a meaningful amount of additional insurance against asymmetric shocks, it will be difficult in practice to avoid transfer payments that look, ex-post, like long-term redistributions. Even if inward transfers are initially motivated by factors that are believed to be transitory, they will inherit persistence from the persistence of unemployment and are likely themselves to induce even greater persistence in unemployment, with further positive feedback to transfers (Lindbeck 1995 discusses some plausible mechanisms).

Further dangers come with an ETU. To the extent that financing and administering the plan concentrates greater fiscal authority in Brussels, an ETU would create a more effective political counterweight to the European Central Bank (ECB; von Hagen and Eichengreen 1996; McKinnon 1997). That evolution could make the ECB more accountable, as the French hope, but in the process it could lead to accommodation and other inflationary errors, as the Germans fear.

If one views the prospect of a European transfer union with alarm, what measures might make it less attractive to its proponents? We see four complementary avenues of approach, all subject to some political or technical difficulties, but none unsurmountably problematic.

First, we can rethink and relax the excessive deficits procedure and the stability pact as soon as possible after EMU starts. Because these provisions of the EMU constitution reduce local fiscal powers while providing no substitute at the center, countries encountering difficulties have a natural opening to press for a central fiscal institution. Greater fiscal latitude at the national level would equip countries only to cushion temporary asymmetric shocks, but that in itself would reduce the pressure for an ETU.

Do the costs of giving up the fiscal restraints outweigh these advantages? A positive side-effect of the Maastricht Treaty's fiscal norms is that they may in the long run promote internal economic reform. However, there is scant evidence that such reforms will go beyond the limited extent they have attained in 1997–98; Eichengreen and Wyplosz (1998) argue that the constant threat of excessive deficits sanctions could even retard reforms. Might not public deficit biases

[27] Von Hagen and Hammond (1997) illustrated some of the perils in trying to follow this route.

reemerge if there are no fiscal restraints? That is a possibility, but deficit bias would be even less constrained by the capital market if practiced at the EU level. On other issues, the rationale for the fiscal criteria is weak, as argued by Buiter, Corsetti, and Roubini (1993), von Hagen and Eichengreen (1996), and many others. Once an EMU of 11 countries is a fait accompli, much of the original political motivation for the criteria will be gone, and the prospect of amending the pertinent sections of the Maastricht Treaty may appear less daunting.

As a second measure, the EU's total borrowing power could be limited – a guarantee against fiscal pulls on the center à la Canada. If EMU member states can borrow, there is little justification, for example, for giving the European Investment Bank an expanded role, along the lines feared by von Hagen and Eichengreen (1996).

A third and very essential task is vigorous internal restructuring – including further reductions in the generosity of pension and other support programs, lower taxes on employment, more hiring and firing flexibility, vigilant financial liberalization, and housing market reform. Such measures would increase each member state's capacity to adjust rapidly to shocks and to deploy fiscal policy when necessary. They would also reduce moral hazards at the individual level. As always, this part of the agenda remains the most difficult to implement in view of the political realities on the ground. In Europe, there is extra resistance because policies that open labor markets to domestic "outsiders" also allow foreign workers in. However, any resulting migratory pressures would be less problematic in the setting of growth and job creation that these policies would bring about, especially if reform is pursued throughout the EU.

A fourth suggestion comes from the observation the missing markets for human capital insurance provide much of the theoretical basis for beliefs that an ETU might be beneficial. In principle each individual national government could act as a capital-market intermediary for its residents, making insurance payouts to them in the form of higher transfers or lower taxes. To accomplish that end, governments would issue perpetual Euro-denominated liabilities indexed to domestic nominal per capita GDP growth.[28] The proceeds would be invested in an internationally diversified portfolio of assets. In this way, each government could lay off some of its GDP risk; its net cash flow would tend to go up when GDP growth was unexpectedly low, just as under an ETU. Permanent and transitory shocks alike could be handled. But no central EU institution is needed to carry out the plan.

An advantage of the setup is that each country would need to strive for good macroeconomic performance to maintain favorable terms for marketing its GDP-linked securities. The price of the securities would plummet if a

---

[28] Closely related securities have been proposed and studied by Shiller (1993). Nominal rather than real GDP indexing would protect buyers of the securities against inflation.

country ever tried to issue enough to make deliberate macroeconomic policy failure attractive. Given its independence, it is unlikely the ECB would ever be tempted in that direction either. Some technicalities would need to be worked out (e.g., safeguards against deliberate misreporting of GDP). Finally, the plan's feasibility probably would require a weakening of the Maastricht deficit norms because the government deficit might become more vulnerable to wide temporary fluctuations.

The alternative scenario we have outlined raises significant challenges for the European Union. The EMU is about to be born, however, only because Europe has shown the creativity and determination to meet such challenges in the past. The same qualities will be needed in abundance now to make EMU work.

Data appendix

All data are at the annual frequency.

A.1   Italy

The regional division adopted for Italy is the standard classification into regioni adopted by the Italian government and by the EU. This definition divides the Italian territory into 20 regions: Piemonte, Valle d'Aosta, Lombardia, Trentino, Veneto, Friuli, Liguria, Emilia, Toscana, Umbria, Lazio, Marche, Abruzzo, Molise, Campania, Puglia, Basilicata, Calabria, Sicilia, and Sardegna. We have divided the region Trentino into its two provinces (Trento and Bolzano), given that the province of Bolzano, being a bilingual province (provincia autonoma), enjoys somewhat greater autonomy.

Labor markets: The regional data on employment, unemployment, total population, and population of working age for the period 1969–95 were collected from the Italian statistical yearbooks (ISTAT, *Annuario Statistico Italiano*, yearly issues); from ISTAT, *Bollettino Mensile di Stastistica*; various issues; and from ISTAT, *Annuali di Statistiche del Lavoro*, yearly issues. Data on CIG, available only for the period 1984–94, were collected from ISTAT, *Annuario Statistico Italiano*.

Prices and GDP: Data on regional prices are the GDP deflators reported in *Annuario Statistico Italiano* (1969–95). Data on regional GDP (1977–92) were collected from the ISTAT publication *Le Regioni in Cifre* (1994).

Social insurance: Data on transfers to persons and on contributions to the social insurance system are taken from the *Annuario Statistico*. For the period 1977–94, the variable is defined as the value in billions of 1991 lire of the contributi e prestazioni degli enti previdenziali, covering all social welfare spending (pensions, unemployment insurance, health care). The definition of the variable "net transfers" is the value (in millions of 1991 lire per capita) of the transfers received by a region for social insurance minus the contributions paid by the region to the central government.

A.2   Germany

The regional unit for the analysis of German data is the Land. Although we have considered only the western Länder, our analysis includes the following 11 regions: Schleswig-Holstein, Hamburg, Niedersachsen, Bremen, Nordrhein-Westfalen, Hessen, Rheinland-Pfalz, Baden-Württemberg, Bayern, Saarland, and West Berlin.

Labor market: Data on employment and unemployment over 1970–94 for each Land were collected from the *Bundesanstalt fur Arbeit*, data on working-age population (1970–93) come from the *Statistisches Jahrbuch*, various issues, and from the *Statistisches Bundesamt*.

Prices and GDP: GDP deflators and nominal GDP at the Land level for 1970–94 were provided by the Finanzamt Baden-Württemberg. Total population data also come from this source.

Fiscal variables: The data on total direct and indirect taxes collected by the federal government in each Land are from the *Statistisches Jahrbuch*, various issues. The data on net transfers occurring across Länder under the Länderfinanzausgleich (LFA or "round of tax redistribution") are used to calculate the net tax "payments" from each Land to the federal government. In particular, we subtracted from the taxes any net amount that the Land receives from other Länder during the LFA, while we add any negative amount. These data were taken from the *Statistisches Bundesamt*, various issues.

A.3   Canada

The ten provinces constituting the Canadian Federation are the geographical units of our regional analysis. They are Newfoundland, Prince Edward Island, Nova Scotia, New Brunswick, Quebec, Ontario, Manitoba, Saskatchewan, Alberta, and British Columbia.

All data for the Canadian provinces as well as for the entire country were obtained from the "Cansim" database at the following World Wide Web address: *http://www.statcan.ca/cpi-bin/Cansim*.

Labor market: Data on employment and the labor force were taken from the directory Socio-Economic Statistics. We used the yearly series for total population, "population older than 15," "labor force older than 15," and "employment older than 15." These series are available for 1976–96 for each province and for the country as a whole.

Prices and personal income: Data on prices are the yearly implicit GDP deflator for each province, available for 1971–96. The data on personal income for the period 1971–96 were also purchased from the "Cansim" web site. Tamim Bayoumi and Paul Masson kindly made available to us the dataset that they used in their 1995 paper. Data on personal income, personal transfers, taxes, and federal grants to local government are available in this dataset for the period 1965–85. For a more detailed description of these data see the data appendix of Bayoumi and Masson (1995).

Fiscal variables: Total federal taxes for each province have been calculated as the total of direct federal taxes from persons. The total federal transfers are the sum of the transfer payments to persons and to local government. These, valued in thousands of 1991 Canadian dollars per capita, have been used to calculate the "net transfers" to a province as the difference between the transfers received from the federal government and the taxes paid.

A.4 United Kingdom

The eight regions into which England is divided plus Wales, Scotland, and Northern Ireland are the geographical regional units considered for the United Kingdom. The following is the complete list: South East, East Anglia, South West, West Midlands, East Midlands, York and Humberside, North West, North, Wales, Scotland, and Northern Ireland.

Labor market: Data on employment, unemployment, and working-age population for each region for the period 1969–94 come from the *Yearly Statistical Abstract* (yearly issues) and from the *Employment Gazette* (various issues) and *Historical Supplement of the Employment Gazette* (various issues), London, Employment Department.

A.5 United States

The geographical regional units for the analysis of U.S. labor markets are the 50 states plus the District of Columbia.

Labor market: Data on employment, unemployment and working-age population for the period 1976–90 have been taken from the data set used by Olivier Blanchard and Larry Katz in their 1992 paper. We thank them for providing these data, which we have updated for 1991–95 using information from the Geographic Profile Data Set.

Personal income and transfers: Total taxes paid to the federal government are defined as the sum of personal taxes and social insurance payments. Total transfers from the federal government are the sum of personal transfers and transfers to local governments. The data on personal income, taxes, and transfers for the period 1969–85 were taken from the dataset provided by Tamim Bayoumi and Paul Masson. For a more detailed description of these data see the appendix to Bayoumi and Masson (1995).

A.6   International GDP deflator and exchange rate data

Year-average figures from OECD, *Fiscal Positions and Business Cycles on Diskette, 77/1.* European cross-rates were derived from dollar exchange rates using triangular arbitrage.

References

Asdrubali, P., B. E. Sørensen, and O. Yosha. 1996. Channels of interstate risk sharing: United States 1963–90. *Quarterly Journal of Economics.*

Atkeson, A., and T. Bayoumi. 1993. Do private capital markets insure regional risk? Evidence from the United States and Europe. *Open Economies Review.*

Attanasio, O. P., and F. P. Schioppa. 1991. "Regional Inequalities, Migration and Mismatch in Italy, 1960–86," in F. P. Schioppa, ed., *Mismatch and Labor Mobility.* Cambridge: Cambridge University Press.

Bayoumi, T., and B. Eichengreen. 1996. "Operationalizing the Theory of Optimum Currency Areas." Discussion Paper Series No. 1484. Centre for Economic Policy Research.

Bayoumi, T., and P. R. Masson. 1995. Fiscal flows in the United States and Canada: Lessons for Monetary Union in Europe. *European Economic Review.*

Bertola, G., and A. Ichino. 1995. Crossing the river. *Economic Policy.*

Blanchard, O. J., and L. F. Katz. 1992. Regional evolutions. *Brookings Papers on Economic Activity.*

Boadway, R. W., and P. A. R. Hobson. 1993. *Intergovernmental Fiscal Relations in Canada.* Canadian Tax Foundation/L'Association Canadienne d'Études Fiscales.

Buiter, W., G. Corsetti, and N. Roubini. 1993. Excessive deficits: Sense and nonsense in the Treaty of Maastricht. *Economic Policy.*

Commission of the European Communities. 1977. "Report of the Study Group on the Role of Public Finance in European Integration." Economic and Financial Series No. A13. Brussels.

Corden, W. M. 1972. *Monetary Integration.* Princeton Essays in International Finance No. 93 (April).

Costello, D. 1993. The redistributive effects of interregional transfers: A comparison of the European community and Germany. *European Economy*, Reports and Studies No. 5.

Courchene, T. J. 1993. Reflections on Canadian federalism: Are there implications for the European economic and monetary union? *European Economy*, Reports and Studies No. 5.

Davis, S. J., P. Loungani, and R. Mahidhara. 1997. "Regional Labor Fluctuations: Oil Shocks, Military Spending, and Other Driving Forces." International Finance Discussion Papers No. 578. Board of Governors of the Federal Reserve System.

Debelle, G., and O. Lamont. 1997. Relative price variability and inflation: Evidence from U.S. cities. *Journal of Political Economy.*

Decressin, J., and A. Fatás. 1995. Regional labor market dynamics in Europe. *European Economic Review.*

De Grauwe, P., and W. Vanhaverbeke. 1993. "Is Europe an Optimum Currency Area? Evidence from Regional Data," in P. R. Masson and M. P. Taylor, eds., *Policy Issues in the Operation of Currency Unions.* Cambridge: Cambridge University Press.

Eichengreen, B. 1990. One money for Europe? Lessons from the US currency union. *Economic Policy.*

Eichengreen, B. 1991. "Is Europe an Optimum Currency Area?" Working paper no. 3579. National Bureau of Economic Research.

Eichengreen, B. 1992. Comment. *Brookings Papers on Economic Activity.*

Eichengreen, B. 1993a. "Labor Markets and European Monetary Unification," in P. R. Masson and M. P. Taylor, eds., *Policy Issues in the Operation of Currency Unions.* Cambridge: Cambridge University Press.

Eichengreen, B. 1993b. European monetary unification. *Journal of Economic Literature.*

Eichengreen, B., and C. Wyplosz. 1998. The stability pact: Minor nuisance, major diversion. *Economic Policy.*

Emerson, M., et al. 1992. *One Market, One Money: An Evaluation of the Potential Benefits and Costs of Forming an Economic and Monetary Union.* Oxford University Press.

Engel, C., and J. H. Rogers. 1995. "Regional Patterns in the Law of One Price: The Roles of Geography vs. Currencies." Working Paper 5395. National Bureau of Economic Research.

Eurostat. Various years. *Regional Statistical Handbook.*

Forni, M., and L. Reichlin. 1997. "National Forces and Local Economies: Europe and the United States." Discussion Paper 1632. Centre for Economic Policy Research.

Goodhart, C. A. E., and S. Smith. 1993. "Stabilization." *European Economy*, Reports and Studies No. 5.

Green, D. A., and W. C. Riddell. 1997. Qualifying for unemployment insurance: An empirical analysis. *Economic Journal.*

Hinshaw, R. 1951. Currency appreciation as an anti-inflationary device. *Quarterly Journal of Economics.*

Hughes, G., and B. McCormick. 1987. Housing markets, unemployment and labor market flexibility. *European Economic Review.*

Ingram, J. C. 1959. State and regional payments mechanisms. *Quarterly Journal of Economics.*

Ingram, J. C. 1973. *The Case for European Monetary Integration*, Princeton Essays in International Finance No. 98.

Kenen, P. B. 1995. *Economic and Monetary Union in Europe: Moving beyond Maastricht.* Cambridge: Cambridge University Press.

Krugman, P. 1993. "Lessons of Massachusetts for EMU," in F. Torres and F. Giavazzi, eds., *Adjustment and Growth in the European Monetary Union.* Cambridge: Cambridge University Press.

Lindbeck, A. 1995. "Hazardous Welfare-State Dynamics." *American Economic Review, Papers and Proceedings.*

McCormick, B. 1997. Regional unemployment and labor mobility in the UK. *European Economic Review.*

McKinnon, R. I. 1963. Optimum currency areas. *American Economic Review.*

McKinnon, R. I. 1997. "Market-Preserving Fiscal Federalism in the American Monetary Union," in M. I. Blejer and T. Ter-Minassian, eds., *Macroeconomic Dimensions of Public Finance: Essays in Honour of Vito Tanzi.* Routledge.

Masson, P. R., and M. P. Taylor. 1993. "Currency Unions: A Survey of the Issues," in P. R. Masson and M. P. Taylor, eds., *Policy Issues in the Operation of Currency Unions.* Cambridge: Cambridge University Press.

Mélitz, J., and F. Zumer. 1997. "Regional Redistribution and Stabilization by the Center in Canada, France, the UK and the US." Mimeo. CREST-INSEE and OFCE.

Nickell, S. 1997. Unemployment and labor market rigidities: Europe versus North America. *Journal of Economic Perspectives.*

Obstfeld, M. 1998. Open-economy macroeconomics: Developments in theory and policy. *Scandinavian Journal of Economics.*

OECD 1990. *OECD Employment Outlook,* Paris.

Oswald, A. 1996. "A Conjecture on the Explanation for High Unemployment in Industrialised Nations: Part I." Mimeo. University of Warwick.

Peri, G. 1997. "Do Civic Spirit and Economic Diversity Help Growth? Evidence from Italian Cities and Provinces, 1961–1991." Mimeo. University of California, Berkeley.

Persson, T., and G. Tabellini. 1996. Federal fiscal constitutions: Risk sharing and redistribution. *Journal of Political Economy.*

Pisani-Ferry, J., A. Italianer, and R. Lescure. 1993. "Stabilization Properties of Budgetary Systems: A Simulation Analysis." *European Economy,* Reports and Studies No. 5.

Poloz, S. 1990. "Real Exchange Rate Adjustment between Regions in a Common Currency Area." Bank of Canada, Mimeo (February).

Sala-i-Martin, X., and J. Sachs. 1992. "Fiscal Federalism and Optimum Currency Areas: Evidence for Europe from the United States," in M. B. Canzoneri, V. Grilli, and P. R. Masson, eds., *Establishing a Central Bank: Issues in Europe and Lessons from the US.* Cambridge: Cambridge University Press.

Shiller, R. J. 1993. *Macro Markets: Creating Institutions for Managing Society's Largest Economic Risks.* Oxford University Press.

Sørensen, B. E., and O. Yosha. 1996. "International Risk Sharing and European Monetary Unification." Working Paper 40-96. Foerder Institute, Tel Aviv University.

Steinherr, A., ed. 1994. *30 Years of European Monetary Integration from the Werner Plan to EMU.* Longman.

van der Ploeg, F. 1991. Macroeconomic policy coordination issues during the various phases of economic and monetary integration in Europe. *European Economy,* Special Edition No. 1.

van Rompuy, P., F. Abraham, and D. Heremans. 1991. Economic federalism and the EMU. *European Economy,* Special Edition No. 1.

Vaubel, R. 1976. Real exchange-rate changes in the European Community: The empirical evidence and its implications for European currency unification. *Weltwirtschaftliches Archiv.*

Vaubel, R. 1978. Real exchange-rate changes in the European Community: A new approach to the determination of optimum currency areas. *Journal of International Economics.*

Viñals, J., and J. F. Jimeno. 1996. "Monetary Union and European Unemployment." Documento de Trabajo 9624. Banco de España, Servicio de Estudios.

von Hagen, J. 1992. "Fiscal Arrangements in a Monetary Union: Evidence from the US," in D. E. Fair and C. de Boissieu, eds., *Fiscal Policy, Taxes, and the Financial System in an Increasingly Integrated Europe.* Dordrecht: Kluwer.

von Hagen, J. 1993. "Monetary Union and Fiscal Union: A Perspective from Fiscal Federalism," in P. R. Masson and M. P. Taylor, eds., *Policy Issues in the Operation of Currency Unions.* Cambridge: Cambridge University Press.

von Hagen, J., and B. Eichengreen. 1996. Federalism, fiscal constraints, and European Monetary Union. *American Economic Review, Papers and Proceedings.*

von Hagen, J., and G. W. Hammond. 1997. "Insurance against asymmetric shocks in a European Monetary Union," in J.-O. Hairault, P.-Y. Hénin, and F. Portier, eds.,

Business Cycles and Macroeconomic Stability: Should We Rebuild Built-in Stabilizers? Dordrecht: Kluwer.

von Hagen, J., and M. J. M. Neumann. 1994. Real exchange rates within and between currency areas: How far away is EMU? *Review of Economics and Statistics.*

Weber, A. 1997. "Sources of Purchasing Power Parity Disparities: Europe versus the United States." Mimeo. Universität Bonn.

Wyplosz, C. 1991. Monetary Union and fiscal policy discipline. *European Economy,* Special Edition No. 1.

CHAPTER 11

Fiscal policy and intranational risk sharing[*]

Jürgen von Hagen[†]

11.1   Introduction

A fundamental feature of the modern state is to provide risk-sharing arrangements for its citizens. In this chapter, we focus on the state as a provider of intranational risk sharing, defined as sharing income risk among the inhabitants of the different regions of a state. State-provided intranational risk sharing occurs when a nation's fiscal system redistributes income across regions in response to unforeseen economic developments. This can take a variety of forms in practice. Often, it is simply a by-product of general welfare and tax-transfer systems. In some federal states (e.g., Australia, Germany, and Canada), intranational risk sharing is provided by fiscal mechanisms designed for the horizontal redistribution of income among subcentral governments. In the United States and elsewhere, intranational risk sharing is the product of budgetary transfers from the central government to regional or local governments. Such mechanisms are generally based on equity considerations: protecting the individual against economic hardship is part of the solidarity defining a society. As Delors (1989, p. 89) put it in his plea for a fiscal risk-sharing mechanism among the members of the European Monetary Union (EMU)

> ". . . in all federations the different combinations of federal budgetary mechanisms have powerful "shock-absorber" effects dampening the amplitude either of economic difficulties or of surges in prosperity of individual states. This is both the product of, and the source of the sense of national solidarity which all relevant economic and monetary unions share."

Furthermore, intranational risk sharing has an obvious aspect of intranational economic stabilization. Channeling income from prospering regions to regions

[*]   This paper was published in *Economic Policy* 26 (April 1998): 205–47. Reprinted with permission of Blackwell. I thank Oved Yosha, Gregory Hess, and Eric van Wincoop for helpful comments and suggestions.

[†]   Zentrum für Europäische Integrationsforschung, University of Bonn, Indiana University, and CEPR. Mailing address: ZEI, Walter Flex Str. 3, 53113 Bonn, Germany. E-mail: *vonhagen @united.econ.uni-bonn.de*

in distress can help attenuate asymmetries in the cyclical fluctuations of different regions belonging to the same country and produce a more even economic development across all regions. This aspect has gained particular attention in the context of EMU in the past 25 years. Starting with the MacDougall Report (European Commission, 1977a,b), many economists have argued that a viable EMU requires a fiscal transfer mechanism to deal effectively with "asymmetric" shocks (i.e., economic disturbances that affect its different regions in different ways). More recently, Sala-i-Martin and Sachs (1991) claimed that a successful EMU must be vested with instruments for regional redistribution comparable to those existing in the United States. Although their empirical analysis has been the subject of a large debate, the basic argument, that the loss of the exchange rate channel for adjustment to asymmetric shocks must be compensated by an appropriate fiscal policy tool to avoid large and protracted regional swings in economic growth and unemployment, has received wide acceptance (e.g., Wyplosz, 1991; Frenkel and Goldstein, 1991; Pisani–Ferry, Italianer, and Lescure 1993).

Section 11.2 discusses the principles of intranational risk sharing, including the moral hazard problems involved and some aspects of political economy. Section 11.3 reviews the empirical evidence of intranational risk sharing provided by fiscal mechanisms in the United States and other countries. In contrast to the general acceptance of the claim that viable monetary unions need such mechanisms, the empirical literature suggests that fiscal policy contributes relatively little to the stabilization of asymmetric shocks in most federal systems. Section 11.4 develops an argument to resolve that puzzle. We show that regional asymmetries in the propagation mechanisms of fiscal and monetary policy may lead to a conflict between stabilizing regional income fluctuations around average national income and stabilizing regional incomes over time, and a conflict between stabilizing asymmetric shocks and stabilizing aggregate shocks at the national level. If such asymmetries are large, large-scale fiscal mechanisms for intranational risk sharing may not be desirable.

11.2 Principles of intranational risk sharing

Economists have approached intranational risk sharing from two ends. One strand of the literature considers risk sharing among consumers inhabiting different regions as a special case of consumption smoothing (e.g., Asdrubali, Sørensen, and Yosha, 1996; Atkeson and Bayoumi, 1993; van Wincoop, 1995; Athanasoulis and van Wincoop, 1998). The basic question is, to what extent consumers of a given country are able to diversify regional risk. The other strand of the literature starts from optimum-currency area considerations and regards intranational transfer mechanisms as an alternative to flexible exchange rates and other market mechanisms for regional economic stabilization of output and employment (e.g., Mundell, 1961; Kenen, 1969; Wyplosz, 1991; Goodhart and Smith 1993; von Hagen and Hammond, 1998).

11.2.1   Consumption smoothing

In a world of complete capital markets, all risk sharing would be provided by capital markets.[1] Consumers would insure themselves against region-specific shocks by holding portfolios that pay higher returns when their incomes out of economic activities in their own region are low. As a result, consumption would be highly correlated across regions, and interregional consumption correlations would be stronger than interregional income correlations.[2]

When capital markets are incomplete, however, consumption smoothing can be provided by fiscal transfers of income across regions. Consider a country composed $i = 1, \ldots, n$ regions.[3] The representative consumer in each region receives an income y_{it}, which is a random variable with fixed expectation and a fixed variance. We abstract from private sector saving, for simplicity.[4] Thus, in the absence of a central government fiscal policy, the representative consumer's budget constraint in each region is $c_{it} = y_{it}$.

If the representative consumers are risk averse, a central government can make them better off by using fiscal policy to pool income risk across the regions. Assume that the central government can employ two instruments for this purpose, a set of state-dependent taxes $\tau_i(y_i)$, and a set of state-dependent transfers $g_i(y_i)$. Assume, further, that interregional equity considerations constrain tax policies such that the income tax rate is the same in all regions. Budget balance for the central government requires

$$\sum_{i=1}^{n} \tau y_{it} = \sum_{i=1}^{n} g_{it} \tag{1}$$

Finally, let the transfers paid to all regions be the same, $g_{it} = \tau y_t$, where y_t denotes average national income. The consumer's budget constraint then is $c_{it} = (1 - \tau)y_{it} + g_{it}$.

Consider, first, the case of purely state-dependent taxes and transfers, so that fiscal policy has no element of pure redistribution. Optimal intranational risk sharing is obtained by choosing τ minimizing the variance of consumption c_{it}.

---

[1] Asdrubali et al. (1996) distinguishes between capital markets and credit markets. Although this distinction is useful in their analysis for statistical reasons, we use the term "capital markets" in the common, more general sense of financial markets.

[2] There is an obvious analogy here with models of international risk sharing tested in the context of tests of international capital mobility (e.g., Backus, Kehoe, and Kydland, 1992).

[3] See Fatás (1998) for a similar exposition.

[4] Alternatively, one might assume that y_{it} contains asset incomes and is defined net of saving.

Under these assumptions, region i would choose the tax rate

$$\tau^{*i} = \frac{w_i(w_i - \rho_i)}{1 + w_i(w_i - 2\rho_i)}, \quad \text{where } w_i = \sqrt{\frac{\text{var}(y_{it})}{\text{var}(y_t)}} \tag{2}$$

Here, ρ_i is the correlation between region i's income and the country's average income.

Equation (2) bears a number of insights. Region i's optimal tax rate depends on the correlation of its income with the country's average income, and on the relative variance of its income compared to average income. If all shocks are uncorrelated and identically distributed, optimal intranational insurance amounts to full equalization of all stochastic incomes, $c_{it} = y_t$. More generally, however, this is not true. For high-risk regions ($w_i > 1$), the optimal tax rate increases with the correlation of its income with average income. For $\rho_i < 2w_i/(1 + w_i^2)$, the optimal tax rate increases as the variance ratio increases (i.e., high-risk regions desire more insurance). In general, regions with different risk characteristics desire different tax rates.

Thus, each region would like to choose a different tax rate, which is not possible by assumption. A single state-contingent tax rate that is optimal for all regions cannot be chosen. To make consumers in all regions agree on the same rate nevertheless, the central government could use state-independent taxes and transfers to implement side payments between regions, compensating those that are further off from their welfare-maximizing tax rate (Persson and Tabellini, 1996b). In such a scenario, high-risk regions would pay a risk premium to low-risk regions to compensate the latter for providing more insurance than they would themselves desire.

11.2.2 Regional stabilization

The other approach to intranational risk sharing derives from the theory of optimum currency areas (Kenen, 1969; Mundell, 1961) and considers the consequences of losing the exchange rate channel of adjustment to asymmetric shocks between regions sharing the same currency for the stability of these regional economies (e.g., Wyplosz, 1991; Goodhart and Smith, 1993; von Hagen and Hammond, 1998). The macroeconomic perspective brings a broader range of alternative adjustment mechanisms into the picture. Apart from capital markets, these are wage and price adjustment to regional shocks and migration of labor between regions. Ingram (1959) first noted the potential usefulness of interregional fiscal transfers to achieve a greater degree of regional income and employment stability, if market mechanisms do not provide sufficient regional stabilization. The macroeconomic perspective allows to consider fiscal transfers paid to regional governments instead of individual consumers.

The classical case under this approach was first presented by Mundell (1961). Consider an autonomous shift in aggregate demand which reduces the demand for the products of one region and raises the demand for the products of another region. If each region had its own currency and the exchange rate was flexible, the decline in income in the first region would cause its currency to depreciate. Sticky prices imply that this would cause the relative price of its products to fall both at home and in the other region. The result would be an increase in domestic and export demand, which would partly offset the initial demand shock. Thus, exchange rate adjustment contributes to stabilizing the economies in both regions.

If the two regions share the same currency, other mechanisms for adjustment must play this role. Although the required relative price adjustment could still work through output price and wage adjustments, prices and wages do not seem sufficiently flexible in practice.[5] This leaves factor movements, and movements of labor in particular, as alternative market adjustment mechanisms.[6] As workers move from the first to the second region, full-employment output would adjust to the shift in demand.

If labor markets do not provide sufficient adjustments either, fiscal transfers between the two regions can do the job. Specifically, taxing the prosperous region and paying the proceeds to the region in distress restores aggregate demand there and reduces aggregate demand in the former region. The same result can be obtained by increasing central government spending in the depressed region and reducing it in the prospering region.

Regarding fiscal transfers as a substitute for nominal exchange rate adjustment has an important implication. The literature generally agrees that nominal exchange rate flexibility accelerates economic adjustment to asymmetric shocks, but it is not a necessary condition for adjustment in the long run. Even if prices and wages are sticky and labor migration is slow, regional markets sharing the same currency should eventually adjust to asymmetric shocks. This suggests that fiscal transfers offsetting temporary asymmetric shocks are more important to secure the viability of a monetary union than transfers tied to permanent shocks. The resulting limitation of intranational risk sharing to temporary shocks seems much less natural under the consumption-smoothing approach where insurance against both temporary and permanent shocks is considered.

Fiscal transfers offsetting temporary asymmetric shocks between regions can obviously be carried out in a fully discretionary, case-by-case manner. Mundell's

---

[5] Hochreiter and Winckler (1995) present empirical evidence suggesting that real wage flexibility increased under the "hard" peg of the Austrian schilling to the Deutsche mark. Nevertheless, the role of price and wage flexibility in adjusting to regional shocks seems very limited in practice as observed by Obstfeld and Peri (1998) for the United States, Canada, and European countries.

[6] The importance of labor mobility for the operation of a common currency was first stressed by Mundell (1961).

analysis bears little relation to intranational insurance per se, if insurance is understood to imply an ex-ante guarantee that transfers be paid when asymmetric shocks occur. However, constitutional rules ensuring transfer payments between regions or the existence of a central budget providing for appropriate transfers can give assurance to all regions involved that payments will be executed should they be hit by adverse shocks in the future. Such assurance may be important to make the promise of paying transfers to regions in distress credible. The literature on EMU (Delors, 1989; Wyplosz, 1991; Pisani-Ferry et al., 1993) has emphasized the importance of credible promises of fiscal transfers for a country's willingness to surrender its monetary autonomy.

11.2.3 Mutual insurance versus self-insurance

In principle, regional governments can self-insure their regions against transitory shocks by borrowing and lending in the national or international capital market. In the preceding example, the depressed region's government could borrow and spend the proceeds on domestic output, whereas the prospering region's government would invest its higher tax revenues in national or international assets. Because the issue is insurance against transitory shocks, a region's borrowing and lending would be zero on average over long time horizons. Thus, no fiscal mechanism spanning across regions would be required.

However, self-insurance of this kind requires that regions in distress have access to the capital market. In the presence of credit rationing, this may not be the case. Self-insurance then requires that a region's net position in the capital market is never negative, which demands the accumulation of a sufficiently large capital fund over time. The cost of this fund in terms of consumption forgone makes self-insurance less attractive than intranational insurance. Regions, particularly if they are small, may also face higher borrowing rates than lending rates in the market. If so, the average cost of self-insurance is positive even if the average level of borrowing is zero, and the cost is larger, the larger the variance of the shocks insured. Capital market imperfections are thus important to justify the preference for intranational insurance.

Bayoumi and Masson (1997, 1998) point to another advantage of intranational insurance. Self-insurance implies that increased government spending during a recession is matched by a future tax liability. Rational, forward-looking consumers anticipate the future tax payments and reduce consumption accordingly. Under intranational insurance, in contrast, transfers paid to a depressed region do not increase that region's expected future tax liabilities, if the expected value of future asymmetric shocks is zero and the insurance scheme is balanced across regions. Under these assumptions, intranational insurance is a more effective tool of regional stabilization. Interestingly, Bayoumi and Masson report evidence from Canada suggesting that the demand effect of payments to provinces resulting from intranational insurance is positive and significant, whereas debt-financed central government transfers to the provinces have no significant demand effects.

11.2.4 Moral hazard problems

Like all kinds of insurance, intranational insurance is plagued with moral hazard problems.[7] Moral hazard problems arising in the context of unemployment insurance and other welfare programs are well understood and need no elaboration in our context, although intranational insurance based on such mechanisms obviously suffers from the same problems. In our more special context, two specific aspects of moral hazard deserve attention.

One regards the incentive of regional governments participating in intranational insurance to invest in risk-avoidance strategies. Persson and Tabellini (1996a) show that a government's incentive to raise local taxes and spend the proceeds on projects that make negative asymmetric shocks less likely in the home region is reduced by the prospect of transfers from other regions when such shocks hit. With decentralized policies geared at risk-avoidance, local governments invest too little in such activities. The implication is that investment in risk-avoidance strategies should not be left uncoordinated between the regional governments. A central government providing intranational insurance will find it preferable to centralize policies aiming at risk-avoidance or to subsidize investment in such strategies by the regional governments in order to increase the level of their investment. Thus, moral hazard creates an "incentive complementarity" (Persson and Tabellini, 1996b) in the sense that making intranational insurance a central government program raises the incentive to create further central government programs related to regional risk.

The other moral hazard problem regards the effectiveness of market mechanisms for adjustment to transitory, asymmetric shocks. Migué (1993) argues that, because taxes and transfers are generally distortive in practice, redistributive policies reduce the incentive for private individuals to adjust to regional shocks. Here, it is particularly important to go beyond Mundell's example and consider supply shocks. Individuals who receive transfer incomes from the central government when their region fares badly may see less reason to accept wage cuts, to move into other industries, or to move into other regions. The implication is that central-government-provided intranational insurance can reduce the effectiveness of market mechanisms for adjustment.

---

[7] von Hagen (1993), van der Ploeg (1991), Wyplosz (1991), and Goodhart and Smith (1993) all warn of the potential moral hazard risk involved in interregional insurance in a European Monetary Union. Courchene (1993) points to the example of Quebec, which maintained a higher minimum wage than other Canadian provinces in the 1970s and was able to shift the cost of higher unemployment in bad times on to the federal budget.

Obstfeld and Peri (1998) discuss one important example of this, namely labor market adjustment to regional, asymmetric shocks. They show that regional differences in unemployment rates are much more persistent within European states than within the United States, and that interregional migration within European states contributes much less to the adjustment to asymmetric shocks than it does in the United States. Because cultural and language barriers, which are often referred to, to explain the slow labor market adjustment across European states, do not exist within these states, and fiscal transfers paid in response to asymmetric shocks are much larger in European states than in the United States, Obstfeld and Peri interpret this observation as showing that the generous welfare programs in Europe reduce the incentive for workers to move in response to economic shocks. In doing so, European transfer programs reduce the effectiveness of labor market adjustment.

Although the logic of the argument is compelling, interpreting the evidence is difficult because the causality might be reversed. Countries where markets adjust sluggishly for whatever reason would likely choose higher levels of intranational insurance. Still, the theoretical arguments and the empirical evidence suggest that full intranational insurance is unlikely to be desirable, and that the choice of an efficient level of intranational insurance is a complicated matter, even more so when intranational insurance is a by-product of a central government budget or welfare system.

11.2.5 Political economy aspects

Existing mechanisms of intranational risk sharing are the product of political choices. The design and size of such programs are, therefore, likely to depend on the political processes by which they are chosen. Persson and Tabellini (1996a,b) present models of federations and federal states analyzing this dependence. In their analysis, federations rely on intergovernmental transfers, whereas federations implement intranational insurance on the basis of federal government programs.

In Persson and Tabellini's analysis, regions are exposed to uncorrelated regional income shocks, which give rise to risk pooling, but which have different risk characteristics. In particular, a region can be "riskier" than others in the sense that it is more often hit by adverse economic shocks. As explained in Section 11.2.1, efficient intranational risk sharing under such circumstances involves full insurance but requires that a "riskier" region pays a risk premium to the less risky ones. To facilitate this, the insurance must combine state-dependent with state-independent transfer payments, where the latter represent the risk premium. But the existence of state-independent transfers implies a scope for permanent redistribution between regions and creates a source of conflict between citizens of the different regions.

Persson and Tabellini (1996b) show that full insurance combined with the efficient risk premium can be obtained when the intergovernmental transfers are the result of a Nash bargain (or unanimity vote) among the representative agents from each region. In contrast, majority voting in each region separately does not sustain a voting equilibrium with efficient intranational insurance. Moreover, a voting equilibrium in which all regions decide separately on the same combination of state-dependent and state-independent transfers does not exist because voters in each region will try to exploit the state-independent tax to extract permanent redistribution in their favor from the other regions. With separate votes in all regions, a voting equilibrium can only be reached if the insurance mechanism is limited to state-dependent transfers, and this produces an undersupply of intranational insurance. One interpretation of this is that intranational insurance should be decided at the constitutional design stage of a federation (i.e., be the result of negotiations between the representatives of the regions and subject to a ratification requirement in each region).

If intranational risk sharing is provided by a federal program targeting individuals rather than regions and voted in federal referenda in which citizens of all regions take part, Persson and Tabellini show that the efficient intranational insurance can be obtained in a majority vote if all regions have the same risk properties. With different degrees of riskiness, majority voting leads again to inefficiencies. If voters are subject to other kinds of risk in addition to regional income risk, the federal referendum can facilitate the formation coalitions across regional borders allowing voters to exploit intranational insurance against the latter to insure themselves against other types of risk. As intranational risk sharing becomes intertwined with other purposes, such coalitions will vote for too much of it.

11.3   Empirical evidence

11.3.1   Market adjustment to asymmetric shocks in the United States

The debate over European monetary integration in the last decade has produced numerous empirical studies of intranational insurance in the United States and elsewhere. Most of these studies have focused on the fiscal transfer mechanisms involved. Intranational insurance provided through capital markets is much harder to estimate due to data problems. Only a few studies exist for the United States. Atkeson and Bayoumi (1993) use state data from 1966 to 1986 to estimate the extent to which state incomes are insured against state-specific risks through U.S. capital markets. They do this by regressing changes in per capita incomes earned from capital located in a state on changes in per capita incomes earned from capital located in the rest of the country, state labor incomes, and state capital products. Their estimate suggested that state capital incomes are mainly driven by incomes earned from capital located in the rest of the country and that a decline in state labor incomes is offset by a small but significant increase in capital incomes. Thus, asset markets provide significant but little intranational insurance. The strong correlation between state consumption (proxied by retail sales) and state incomes suggests also that intranational insurance is far from perfect.

Asdrubali et al. (1996) provide a more elaborate study of income smoothing across states. The model they estimate is directly derived from accounting relations and, therefore, involves no further assumptions about consumer choices as Atkeson and Bayoumi's analysis does. Using data from 1964 to 1990, their estimates suggest that capital markets smooth 39% of cross-state fluctuations in gross state product, and that credit markets smooth another 23% of these fluctuations. This gives financial markets a much larger role in consumption smoothing than Atkeson and Bayoumi's results do. The more direct method of estimation lends more credibility to their results. Athanasoulis and van Wincoop (1998), who estimate the reduction of the standard deviation of state income due to financial markets at different time horizons, found that financial markets smooth about 30% of shocks to gross state products at horizons of 1–2 years, and 35% on average over up to 26 years.

11.3.2   Intranational insurance through the U.S. federal fiscal system

Turning to intranational insurance provided by the federal fiscal system, recent literature has provided a large number of estimates, summarized in Table 11.1. The numbers indicate the estimated increase, measured in cents, in the net transfers received by a state or region in response to a one-dollar decline of the state's or region's income relative to the U.S. average.

The MacDougall Report looks at the issue of intranational insurance by asking to what extent the federal fiscal system reduces income differences between U.S. states. The same question is asked in Sachs and Sala-i-Martin, who consider the following regression for an answer:

$$\ln\left(\frac{tax_{it}}{tax_t}\right) = \alpha + \beta \ln\left(\frac{Y_{it}}{Y_t}\right) + trend + residual \tag{3}$$

where tax_{it} denotes the taxes paid by region i to the federal government in period t, tax_t is the national aggregate of tax_{it}, Y_{it} is personal income in region i and year t, and Y_t is the national aggregate of Y_t. Sachs and Sala-i-Martin run a similar regression with transfers as the dependent variable. They consider the nine U.S. census regions as geographical units.

Sachs and Sala-i-Martin interpret the coefficient β as a measure of the offsetting effect of the federal fiscal system to region-specific income shocks. Estimating the combined effect of taxes and transfers at 33–40 cents to the

Table 11.1. *Estimates of federal
intranational redistribution and insurance
in the United States*

	Type of Transfer	
Author	Redistribution	Insurance
MacDougall Report		28
Sachs, Sala-i-Martin		33–40
von Hagen	47	10
Atkeson & Bayoumi		7
Goodhart & Smith	15	13
Pisani-Ferry et al.		17
Gros & Jones		4–14
Bayoumi & Masson	7–22	7–30
Mélitz & Zumer	16	12–20
Asdrubali et al.		13
Sørensen & Yosha		15
Fatas		11
Obstfeld & Peri	19	10
Athanasoulis & van Wincoop	20	10

Note: Entries indicate the estimated (range of) net federal transfers received by a region in response to a one-dollar difference in the level or change in state income or product compared to U.S. average income or product.

dollar, they conclude that the federal fiscal system provides very substantial insurance against asymmetric regional shocks, a conclusion that conforms with the MacDougall Report.

But this conclusion is unwarranted. As von Hagen (1992) first pointed out, equation (3) shows by how much the tax liabilities and transfer benefits of a region are reduced or increased relative to the national average, if its income is larger or smaller than the national average by a given amount, without making a distinction between permanent and transitory income differences. Thus, equation (3), like the MacDougall Report, lumps together two very different things provided by a federal fiscal system, namely permanent redistribution to reduce secular income differences between regions and insurance against asymmetric shocks. von Hagen (1992) proposes to get a better estimate of the second issue by running Sachs' and Sala-i-Martin's regression in first differences:

$$\Delta \ln(tax_{it}) = \alpha_t + \beta \, \Delta \ln(Y_{it}) + dummies + residual \tag{4}$$

Rather than estimating a trend, von Hagen allows the intercepts of his panel regression to vary and account for the U.S. business cycle. The dummies are for the oil-producing states. von Hagen uses state gross products as the explanatory variable. As Table 11.1 shows, the *insurance* effect thus obtained is substantially lower than the Sachs and Sala-i-Martin estimate, whereas the redistributive effect is about the same.

Subsequent papers have generally accepted the distinction between redistribution and insurance or regional stabilization and come out with estimates that are closer to von Hagen's (1992) results. Bayoumi and Masson's (1995) estimate the insurance effect based on the following regression:

$$\Delta \left(\frac{Y_{it} - tax_{it} + transfer_{it}}{Y_t - tax_t + transfer_t} \right) = \alpha_i + \beta \, \Delta \frac{Y_{it}}{Y_t} + residual \tag{5}$$

Their study stands out among the later estimates for a relatively high insurance coefficient (see Table 11.1). But this may be due to a second distinction between this and Sachs and Sala-i-Martin's regression and von Hagen's, discussed more elaborately by Fatás (1998). This distinction is that an increase in the net transfers received by a state may be financed either by a reduction of the net transfers received by all others, which corresponds to intranational insurance, or by an increase in the federal budget deficit, in which case the federal government implicitly undertakes the borrowing on behalf of that state. Neither Sachs and Sala-i-Martin nor Bayoumi and Masson (1995) distinguish between these two possibilities, although the time-varying intercepts in von Hagen's regression can be interpreted to do just that implicitly.[8] Fatás (1998) shows that accounting for this distinction properly reduces the insurance effect implied by the Sachs and Sala-i-Martin estimate to about 10 cents on a dollar change in relative income.

Mélitz and Zumer (1998) compare estimates based on state income and estimates based on gross state products as the measure of regional economic activity. They find that the insurance effect associated with gross-state-product estimates tend to be lower than the effect associated with state-income estimates. Conceptually this raises the difficulty that state incomes include incomes earned from economic activities outside the state. Athanasoulis and van Wincoop (1998) estimate the stabilizing role of the federal fiscal system at time horizons of different lengths. They find that the federal fiscal system reduced the standard deviation of changes in state incomes by about 10% at a horizon of 1–2 years and by 15% on average over all horizons.

The study of Pisani-Ferry et al. (1993) stands out in this group for its very different methodology. These authors use a macroeconomic simulation model

---

[8] More specifically, Fatás (1998) notes that a necessary condition for intranational insurance is that the correlation between shocks at the state level and shocks at the national level be less than one. Empirically, he finds that the average correlation coefficient between state and aggregate U.S. annual real income growth rates is 0.72.

augmented by a model of budgetary flows within a country based on government accounting relations to assess the tax and transfer effects of asymmetric regional shocks. Despite their different methodology, however, their estimate for the United States is similar to most of the post-Sachs and Sala-i-Martin literature.

In sum, the empirical studies of the 1990s confirm that there is a significant intranational insurance provided by the federal fiscal system in the United States. Even though there is still some disagreement about the size of the insurance, the empirical evidence clearly suggests that such insurance is of much smaller magnitude than the redistributive effect of the federal fiscal system, and that the insurance does not offset much more than 10 cents on a dollar change in state income caused by an asymmetric shock.

11.3.3   Intranational insurance in other states

Several studies have presented similar estimates for countries other than the United States. Table 11.2 summarizes these results. Canada is an obvious study object in the context of EMU; it was included also in the MacDougall Report. It is of particular interest because Canada has an explicit, constitutionally grounded mechanism for horizontal transfers among the provinces, the Canadian Equalization System. Equalization aims at reducing differences in the standards of living between Canadian provinces by compensating the poorer provinces for their less prosperous tax bases. According to Canadian legal tradition, equalization is an outflow of the principle of equality of all citizens before the law.

The MacDougall Report estimated that the Canadian federal system reduces income differences between provinces by 32 cents per dollar. Bayoumi and Masson, based on the regression equation (5), estimate an insurance of 14 cents to the dollar, less than their estimate for the United States, and put the redistributive effect of the Canadian system at 39 cents to the dollar. Other studies agree with the magnitude of the intranational insurance in Canada but provide more different estimates of the redistributive effect.

One difficulty with the Canadian equalization system is that it is designed to bring relatively poor provinces up to a standard defined by the average per capita revenues of Ontario, British Columbia, Saskatchewan, Manitoba, and Quebec (Courchene, 1997). Under the rules of the system, Alberta, British Columbia, and Ontario do not receive equalization payments at all, the remaining provinces that are included in the standard receive a partial offset for a revenue short fall, and those not included in the standard receive full offset for a decline in revenues. At the same time, a poor province receives a transfer when revenues in the provinces included in the standard increase, even if the economy of that province performs like the Canadian average. This shows the emphasis on redistribution rather than intranational insurance and implies that regressions

Table 11.2. *Estimates of central
government intranational redistribution
and insurance in other countries*

Country/Author	Redistribution	Insurance
Canada		
MacDougall		32
Bayoumi & Masson	39	14
Goodhart & Smith		12–19
Mélitz & Zumer	18	14
Obstfeld & Peri	53	13
France		
MacDougall		54
Pisani-Ferry et al.		37
Mélitz & Zumer	38	17–19
Germany		
MacDougall		29
Pisani-Ferry et al.		34–42
Italy		
MacDougall		47
Obstfeld & Peri	8	3
U.K.		
Goodhart & Smith		21
Mélitz & Zumer	29	21

Note: Entries indicate the estimated (range of) net federal transfers received by a region in response to a 1-
dollar difference in the level or change in state income
or product compared to U.S. average income or product.

like equation (5) employed by Bayoumi and Masson (1995) and Mélitz and
Zumer (1998) are likely to misrepresent the working of the system.

Recent literature has also evaluated intranational insurance in France,
Germany, Italy, and the United Kingdom. The results show a surprising degree of variation across countries. Mélitz and Zumer and Goodhart and Smith
obtain similar estimates for the United Kingdom, where intranational insurance seems somewhat larger than in Canada and the United States. Mélitz and
Zumer also find that intranational insurance is small in France. Their result is
much different from the estimate of Pisani-Ferry et al. (1993), who use a very
different and less standard methodology, one that relies more heavily on modeling legal rules than on estimating empirical relations. Importantly, Mélitz and
Zumer's result implies that there is no reason to assume that regional insurance
is larger in unitary states than in federations. Similarly, Obstfeld and Peri (1998)
estimate that intranational insurance is tiny in Italy. Pisani-Ferry et al. (1993)
find that intranational insurance in Germany is large, but this is again based on

their idiosyncratic methodology. The fact that fiscal flows through the German equalization system were rather small in preunification Germany makes their result quite unlikely.

In sum, the empirical evidence shows that intranational insurance is a significant part of intranational macroeconomics. But the size of the insurance can be very different in different countries, and there is no empirical evidence to answer the question how important it is in practice for the stabilization of the regional economies.

11.3.4   Intranational insurance in Europe?

Several studies have recently explored the prospects for fiscal insurance among the countries participating in the future European Monetary Union. Mélitz and Vori (1993) explore the insurability of shocks to the national economies of the European states by estimating their correlations across states. For real incomes, they find that the correlations are positive and large for all EU states except the United Kingdom, Denmark, and Ireland. Because only the latter will be a member of the monetary union, the scope for intra-EMU insurance would be small. Even less scope for insurance is found when the transfers are tied to unemployment rather than real income figures. Fatás (1998) reports a similar result and concludes that nothing much is lost if the European Monetary Union operates without a fiscal insurance mechanism.

von Hagen and Hammond (1998) evaluate the hypothetical performance of intra-EMU insurance mechanisms against regional shocks. They construct time series of asymmetric shocks from historical data and simulate the transfer mechanism under various assumptions about the properties of the shocks and the design of the system. Their main focus is on the robustness of the system against changes in the simulation parameters. The results suggest that a satisfactory insurance mechanism against asymmetric shocks can be designed, but that the system would have to be based on very complicated and hence unrealistic formulas to compute the appropriate transfers. Importantly, von Hagen and Hammond find that the quality of the system's performance deteriorates radically with even small changes in the assumptions about the properties of the shocks. Given the complexity of the design, the implication is that the probability of a misdesign is high and the resulting damage considerable.

11.4   The Macroeconomics of intranational risk sharing

The literature discussed so far takes the desirability of intranational risk sharing for the stabilization of regional economies for granted and assumes that there is no conflict between intranational risk sharing and stabilizing a nation's aggregate economy. In this section, we turn to the macroeconomics of intranational risk sharing and look at these questions more closely. Conforming with the literature, we assume that intranational risk sharing is a rules-based approach aimed at reducing income differences between regions through interregional taxes and transfers.

In the appendix, we develop a model of regional macroeconomic stabilization for a country consisting of two regions. A central ingredient of this model is its neo-Keynesian flavor (i.e., the assumption that prices and wages are sticky, which allows aggregate demand to have short-run real effects). Although one may debate the validity of these Keynesian assumptions in principle, they are clearly appropriate for discussing the issue of regional stabilization policy, which is void if aggregate demand policies have no real effects at all. Furthermore, we assume that the two regions have heterogeneous economic structures in the sense that the aggregate demand effect of government spending and the real interest rate elasticities of aggregate demand are different in the two regions. This structural heterogeneity is of key importance for the analysis. Empirically, it is validated by the fact that structural parameters can vary substantially across countries in structural multicountry models, and the observation that monetary policy shocks affect different regions in different ways in existing monetary unions.[9] The two regions in our model produce outputs that are imperfect substitutes in demand. Both are affected by demand and supply (wage and productivity) shocks.

Regional fiscal policy, represented in the model by regional government spending, is able, in principle, to offset the effects of relative demand and supply shocks perfectly in this economy. This, however, requires that the individual shocks can be identified and observed as they occur, and that the regional governments coordinate their fiscal policies very closely. Both requirements seem unrealistic in practice, making discretionary fiscal policy unfit for regional insurance against relative income shocks.

11.4.1   Intranational risk sharing and regional stabilization

We consider a transfer mechanism between the two regions that aims at reducing income differentials between the two regions,

$$g = -g^* = -\frac{\alpha}{2}(y - y^*) \tag{6}$$

The parameter α indicates the degree of insurance: the larger it is, the more closely the regional incomes are tied to national average income. We ask how such a mechanism affects output and prices in the home region in the presence of purely asymmetric shocks. Equations (A5) and (A6) in the appendix provide the basis for an answer.

[9] For empirical evidence on these issues see von Hagen and Waller (1999).

Consider, first, the case of a relative demand shock that shifts demand from the home region to the foreign region. Home output falls and so does the regional output price. In the absence of fiscal transfers, this real exchange rate depreciation helps the home region recover partly from the initial shock, the more so, the larger the relative price elasticity of demand. If the latter is taken as a measure of economic integration, asymmetric shocks matter less when the regions are highly integrated.

With symmetric output effects of a fiscal impulse in the two regions, the transfer from the foreign to the home region unambiguously stabilizes both output and prices in the home region. However, if the output effect of a fiscal impulse is larger in the foreign region than in the home region, the transfer scheme can be counterproductive in the sense that it weakens the economy's self-stabilizing capacity. The reason is that the transfer paid by the foreign region reduces demand there by more than the initial shift in autonomous demand increased it, thus lowering the foreign region's import demand for domestic output. In this case, therefore, home output would be more stable in the absence of a fiscal transfer mechanism.

Consider next the case of a negative relative wage or productivity shock. As before, the fiscal transfer mechanism stabilizes home output unless the impact of government spending of foreign aggregate demand is too large. However, the transfer scheme amplifies the response of the home output price. The reason is straightforward. The transfer increases demand for the home product in a situation where output is down and prices are already rising due to the supply shock. The desirability of a fiscal stabilization mechanism depends, therefore, on the relative size of the price effect and the relative weight of regional price stability in the utility function of the residents of the region. Clearly, when output is inelastic to price changes, the transfer mechanism only raises inflation in the home region and is entirely undesirable.[10]

11.4.2   Intranational risk sharing and national stabilization

Next, we turn to the implications of the regional stabilization mechanism for aggregate output and price level fluctuations. Equation (A7) in the appendix demonstrates that regional asymmetries in the response of aggregate demand to a fiscal impulse imply that the fiscal transfer mechanism translates purely relative into aggregate fluctuations. The reason is that the transfer lowers (raises) demand in one region by less than it raises (lowers) demand in the other, raising national aggregate demand as a result. In the presence of such asymmetries, the transfer scheme can, therefore, create a conflict between stabilization policy at

[10] See Herve and Holzmann (1998), who discuss this case in the context of the classical "transfer problem" of international economics.

the national level and stabilization of the regional economies. For example, a central bank firmly committed to price stability would be enticed to raise interest rates, if the regional stabilization scheme causes aggregate demand to rise following a relative demand or supply shock between the two regions. The monetary restriction would obviously aggravate the recession in the region affected by a negative shock. Thus, in the presence of asymmetric regional responses to fiscal stimuli, the regional transfer mechanism can intensify conflicts between the national monetary and fiscal authorities.

These results were derived assuming equal interest rate elasticities of aggregate demand in the two regions. Releasing that restriction turns the attention to asymmetric reactions to the aggregate shock in the two regions, including asymmetric responses to the common monetary policy. Because the income differential now depends on the size of the aggregate shock [see equation (A8)], the transfer mechanism triggers income flows between the regions in response to aggregate shocks. For example, if a monetary contraction affects output demand in the home region more than elsewhere, the impact effect will be a greater recession in this area, which makes the home region receive transfers from the other region. As shown in the appendix, the regional stabilization mechanism can increase or reduce the effect of an aggregate shock on aggregate income, depending on the relative size of the regional responses to a fiscal impulse. Thus, in the presence of asymmetries in the regional propagation mechanisms of aggregate shocks and fiscal policy, intranational risk sharing can reduce or improve the effectiveness of monetary policy.

11.5   Conclusions

Intranational risk sharing through a nation's tax and transfer system is a fundamental aspect of the fiscal systems of developed economies. It can be justified generally by the desire of consumers to smooth consumption over time and by the desire to stabilize regional output and employment in the absence of exchange rate flexibility between regions. Moral hazard problems and political economy considerations, however, suggest that full risk sharing among regions of asymmetric shocks is not optimal.

The empirical evidence available for a number of countries shows that intranational risk sharing through the fiscal system is significant in all countries. However, there is a large degree of variation in the size of the intranational insurance provided by the tax and transfer system. In the United States, as in most countries for which empirical evidence exists, the actual risk sharing seems to be rather modest. The empirical literature shows that the distinction between redistribution and insurance or stabilization is crucial in the proper estimation. Surprisingly perhaps, there is no clear evidence that intranational risk sharing is larger in unitary than in federal states. Existing research gives no basis for explaining why countries chose the degree of intranational risk sharing they have, and for judging whether the observed degree of risk sharing is close to the optimal one.

An important aspect of tax and transfer-based intranational risk sharing is that payments cannot be implemented to offset regional shocks directly because the shocks are not directly observed in practice. Thus, practical implementation of intranational risk sharing must rely on rules tying payments to income differentials. Such transfers, however, can increase the variability of regional output and prices and interfere with the stabilization of the national economy. Interference between regional and national stabilization may be one reason why we do not observe more intranational risk sharing through the fiscal system in large federations such as Canada and the United States.

References

Asdrubali, P., B. Sørensen, and O. Yosha. 1996. Channels of interstate risk sharing: United States 1963–1990. *Quarterly Journal of Economics* 111: 1081–110.

Athanasoulis, S., and E. van Wincoop. 1998. "Risksharing Within the United States: What Have Financial Markets and Fiscal Federalism Accomplished?" Research Paper 9808. Federal Reserve Bank of New York.

Atkeson, A., and T. Bayoumi. 1993. Do private capital markets insure regional risk? Evidence for the US and Europe. *Open Economies Review* 4: 303–24.

Backus, D. K., P. J. Kehoe, and F. E. Kydland. 1992. International real business cycles. *Journal of Political Economy* 100: 745–75.

Bayoumi, T., and P. Masson. 1995. Fiscal flows in the United States and Canada: Lessons for monetary union in Europe. *European Economic Review* 39: 253–74.

Bayoumi, T., and P. R. Masson. 1997. " The Efficiency of National and Regional Stabilization Policies," in J.-O. Hairault, P.-Y. Hénin, and F. Portier, eds., *Business Cycles and Macroeconomic Stability*. Boston: Kluwer Academic Publishers.

Bayoumi, T., and P. R. Masson. 1998. Liability-creating versus non-liability-creating fiscal stabilization policies: Ricaridan equivalence, fiscal stabilization, and EMU. *Economic Journal* 108: 1026–45.

Courchene, T. 1993. "Reflections on Canadian Federalism: Are There Implications for European Economic and Monetary Union?" in European Commission, *The Economics of Community Public Finance*, European Economy Reports and Studies 5. Brussels.

Courchene, T. 1997. "Subnational Budgetary and Stabilization Policies in Canada and Australia." Mimeo. Queens University.

Delors, J. 1989. "Regional Implications of Economic and Monetary Integration," in Committee for the Study of Economic and Monetary Union, ed., *Report on Economic and Monetary Union in the European Community*. Luxembourg: Office for Official Publications of the EC.

European Commission. 1977a. *Report of the Study Group on the Role of Public Finance in European Integration*, vol. I, Studies: Economic and Financial Series A13. Brussels.

European Commission (1977b). *Report of the Study Group on the Role of Public Finance in European Integration*, vol. II, Studies: Economic and Financial Series B13. Brussels.

Fatás, A. 1998. Does EMU need a fiscal federation? *Economic Policy* 26: 163–92.

Frenkel, J., and M. Goldstein. 1991. Monetary policy in an emerging European economic and monetary union. *IMF Staff Papers* 38: 356–73.

Goodhart, C. E. A., and S. Smith. 1993. "Stabilization," in *European Commission, The Economics of Community Public Finance*, European Economy Reports and Studies 5, pp. 417–55.

Hervé, Y., and R. Holzmann. 1998. *Fiscal Transfers and Economic Convergence in the EU: An Analysis of Absorption Problems and an Evaluation of the Literature.* Baden-Baden: Nomos.

Hochreiter, E., and G. Winckler, 1995. The advantages of tying Austria's hands: The success of a hard-currency strategy. *European Journal of Political Economy* 11: 83–111.

Ingram, J. C. 1959. State and regional payments mechanisms. *Quarterly Journal of Economics.*

Kenen, P. B. 1969. "The Theory of Optimum Currency Areas: An Eclectic View," in R. Mundell and A. Swoboda, eds., *Monetary Problems of the World Economy.* Chicago: University of Chicago Press.

Mélitz, J., and S. Vori. 1993. National insurance against unevenly distributed shocks in a European monetary union. *Recherches Économiques de Louvain* 59, 81–104.

Mélitz, J., and F. Zumer. 1998. "Regional Redistribution and Stabilization by the Center in Canada, France, the United Kingdom, and the United States: New Estimates Based on Panel Data Econometrics." Discussion Paper 1829. CEPR.

Migué, J.-L. 1993. *Federalism and Free Trade*, Hobart Paper. London: Institute of Economic Affairs.

Mundell, R. 1961. A theory of optimal currency areas. *American Economic Review* 51: 205–47.

Obstfeld, M., and G. Peri. 1998. Regional non-adjustment and fiscal policy. *Economic Policy* 26.

Persson, T., and G. Tabellini. 1996a. Federal fiscal constitutions: Risk sharing and moral hazard. *Econometrica* 64: 623–46.

Persson, T., and G. Tabellini. 1996b. Federal fiscal constitutions: Risk sharing and redistribution. *Journal of Political Economy* 104: 979–1009.

Pisani-Ferry, J., A. Italianer, and R. Lescure. 1993. "Stabilization Properties of Budgetary Systems: A Simulation Analysis," in *European Commission, The Economics of Community Public Finance*, European Economy Reports and Studies 5, pp. 417–55.

Sala-i-Martin, X., and J. Sachs. 1991. "Fiscal Federalism and Optimum Currency Areas: Evidence for Europe from the United States," in M. Canzoneri, V. Grilli, and P. Masson, eds., *Establishing a Central Bank: Issues in Europe and Lessons from the U.S.* Cambridge: Cambridge University Press.

Sørensen, B. E., and O. Yosha. 1997. "Federal Insurance of U.S. States: An Empirical Investigation," in A. Razin and E. Sadka, eds., *Globalization: Public Economics Policy Perspectives.* Cambridge University Press.

van der Ploeg, F. 1991. Macroeconomic policy coordination issues during the various phases of economic and monetary integration in Europe. *European Economy* Special Edition 1: 136–64.

von Hagen. J. 1992. "Fiscal Arrangements in a Monetary Union – Some Evidence from the US," in D. Fair and C. de Boissieux, eds., *Fiscal Policy, Taxes, and the Financial System in an Increasingly Integrated Europe*. Deventer: Kluwer Academic Publishers.

von Hagen J. 1993. "Monetary Union and Fiscal Union: A Perspective from Fiscal Federalism," in P. R. Masson and M. P. Taylor, eds., *Policy Issue in the Operation of Currency Unions*. Cambridge: Cambridge University Press.

von Hagen, J., and G. W. Hammond. 1998. Regional insurance against asymmetric shocks: An empirical study for the European community. *The Manchester School* 66: 331–53.

von Hagen, J., and C. J. Waller. (1999). *Regional Aspects of Monetary Policy in Europe*. Boston: Kluwer Academic Publishers.

van Wincoop, E. 1995. Regional risksharing. *European Economic Review* 39: 1545–68.

Wyplosz, C. 1991. Monetary Union and fiscal policy discipline. *European Economy* Special Edition 1: 165–84.

Appendix: A neo-Keynesian model of regional stabilization and risk sharing

We consider a "country" consisting of two regions, the home region and the foreign region. An asterisk (*) denotes variables of the foreign region. Let y be output, p the output price, r the nominal interest rate (which is common to both regions), m the country's money supply, and g the fiscal impulse. All variables denote relative deviations from steady state. Output demand in the two regions is

$$y^d = a - c(r - \pi^e) + d(p^* - p) + g$$
$$y^{d*} = a^* - c^*(r - \pi^e) - d(p^* - p) + f^*g^* \tag{A1}$$

Here, π^e denotes the expected national rate of inflation, a and a^* are shocks to the levels of demand, and $p^* - p$ is the real exchange rate of the home region. With $c^* \neq c$ and $f^* \neq 1$, we allow for some asymmetry in the propagation mechanisms of the two regions. Output supply is characterized by price-setting functions

$$p = w + \theta + \gamma y, \qquad p^* = w^* + \theta^* + \gamma y^* \tag{A2}$$

where w is a nominal wage shock and θ is a productivity shock. Money market equilibrium is given by the condition

$$m + \tfrac{1}{2}(p + p^*) = y + y^* - \tfrac{1}{2}br \tag{A3}$$

For now, we assume that $c^* = c$. Assuming that all current shocks are transitory, we have inflation expectations $\pi^e = -E - 0.5\gamma(y + y^*)$. Taking this into account yields the equilibrium solutions

$$y = \frac{1}{\Delta}[a + g + (2 + \gamma)bc(g - f^*g^*) + \phi(f^* - 1)g^* + E + D]$$

$$y^* = \frac{1}{\Delta}[a^* + f^*g^* - (2 + \gamma)bg(g - f^*g^*) + \phi(f^* - 1)g^* + E - D]$$

(A4)

where $\phi = (d + 0.5c)\gamma$ and $\kappa = c(b - 0.5)$, and where E is the aggregate shock common to both regions and D is the differential shock.[11]

Consider now the transfer mechanism defined in Equation (6). Calculating the equilibrium solutions yields

$$y = \frac{2 - \frac{\alpha(1-f^*)}{\Gamma}}{2(1 + 2\phi) + \alpha(1 + f^*)}\left[a + \frac{1 + (2 + \gamma)bc + 2\phi}{(1 + 2\phi)\Gamma}D\right] \quad (A5)$$

where $\Gamma = 1 + 2(2 + \gamma)bc$. The equilibrium solution for the home region's output price level is

$$p = \frac{1 - \frac{\alpha(1-f^*)}{\Gamma}}{2(1 + 2\phi) + \alpha(1 + f^*)}\gamma a$$

$$+ \left[1 - \frac{2 - \frac{\alpha(1-f^*)}{\Gamma}}{2(1 + 2\phi) + \alpha(1 + f^*)}\frac{1 + bc(2 + \gamma) + 2\phi}{(1 + 2\phi)\Gamma}2\gamma\right)\right](w + \theta)$$

(A6)

Consider first the case of a relative demand shock, $a < 0$. With $0 < f^* \leq 1$, the fiscal transfer mechanism is unambiguously stabilizing both output and prices in the home region. However, if $f^* > 1$, a fiscal transfer scheme weakens the economy's self-stabilizing capacity.[12]

Consider next the case of a negative relative supply shock to the home region, $w > 0$ or $\theta > 0$. Output is stabilized unless f^* is again too large. The response of the output price of the home region, however, is increased by such a mechanism. Aggregate, national output and prices are

$$y + y^* = \frac{\alpha}{\Delta}(f^* - 1)(y - y^*), \qquad \frac{1}{2}(p + p^*) = \frac{\alpha\gamma}{4\Delta}(f^* - 1)(y - y^*) \quad (A7)$$

With $f^* \neq 1$, the fiscal transfer mechanism translates purely relative into aggregate fluctuations.

[11] The aggregate shock is $E = \phi(a + a^* + g + g^* - \kappa(1 + 2\phi)(w + w^* + \theta + \theta^* - 2m)$ and the differential shock $D = (2 + \gamma)bc(a - a^*) + [1 + 2\phi + (2 + \gamma)bc](w^* - w + \theta^* - \theta)$
[12] This is the case, if $f^* > [1 + \phi + bc(2 + \gamma)]/[\phi - bc(2 + \gamma)] > 1$.

To study the implications of asymmetric interest elasticities of aggregate demand, we simplify the analysis and set all asymmetric shocks to zero (i.e., $a = a^*$, $w = w^*$, and $\theta = \theta^*$), implying that $D = 0$. Furthermore, we let $d = 0$. Assuming $f^* = 1$, this yields

$$y - y^* = -\frac{\left(b - \frac{1}{2}\right)(c - c^*)E}{\Delta' + \alpha[1 + b(2 + \gamma)(c + c^*)]} \tag{A8}$$

$$\Delta' = 1 + (c + c^*)[0.5\gamma + b(2 + \gamma)] + 2bcc^*(2 + \gamma)$$

for the income differential. Thus, aggregate shocks, including monetary policy shocks, affect income in the two regions in different ways. With asymmetric effects of fiscal policy in the two regions, the transfer scheme can reduce or amplify the impact of aggregate shocks on the two region's combined incomes, which, in this case, is

$$y + y^* = \frac{-\left(b - \frac{1}{2}\right)c^*}{\Delta'}\left\{1 + \zeta + c\gamma - \frac{\alpha}{2}[1 - f^* + \gamma(1 - \zeta f^*)]\right.$$

$$\left. \times \frac{1 - \zeta}{\Delta' + \alpha[1 + c^*(1 + \zeta)(2 + \gamma)]}\right\}E \tag{A9}$$

where $\zeta = c/c^*$.

CHAPTER 12

Do local banks matter for the local economy? In search of a regional credit channel

Sandra Hanson McPherson[†] *and Christopher J. Waller*[‡]

12.1   Introduction

The role of banks in the transmission mechanism of monetary policy has become an important and hotly debated issue. Although economists have long given banks a special place in the monetary transmission mechanism, monetary policy conducted via open market operations does not require any interaction between the central bank and commercial banks. Observations of this type have raised the question, are banks "special" for the conduct of monetary policy? Traditionally, economists have answered yes to this question.[1] The typical story economists tell undergraduates goes something like this: the Fed uses open market operations to contract the reserves of banks, which reduces the banks' ability to make loans. This reduces investment in capital goods and consumer durable goods, thereby reducing aggregate output and employment. Researchers in the credit channel literature have attempted to explain why this story is accurate and whether or not it is empirically significant for the conduct of monetary policy. This literature refers to the preceding chain of events as the bank-lending channel of monetary policy.[2]

Although this story certainly sounds plausible, it implicitly assumes a significant amount of "incompleteness" or "segregation" of financial markets. First, banks must be unable to offset the loss of reserves by raising funds (increasing their liabilities) from other sources such as international capital markets or the corporate debt market.[3] Second, firms must rely on banks for financing

[†] Mailing address: Department of Finance and Economics, Georgia Southern University, Statesboro, GA 30460. E-mail: *sjhanson@gasou.edu.*
[‡] Mailing address: Department of Economics, University of Kentucky, Lexington, KY 40506. E-mail: *cjwall@pop.uky.edu.*

[1] Why else do we teach a course on money and banking as opposed to money and the auto industry?
[2] The credit channel is really composed of two parts, the balance sheet channel and the bank lending channel. For an excellent review of the credit channel literature, see Bernanke and Gertler (1995).
[3] In short, the Modigliani-Miller theorem does not hold for banks.

investment and cannot replace lost bank loans with financing from alternative sources (debt/equity markets, commercial paper market). If banks are not an important source of lending for the economy, then the whole issue of a bank-lending channel is moot.

Carlino and DeFina (1998, 1999) suggest that monetary policy can have differential effects based on differences in: (1) the interest sensitivity of a region's industrial mix, (2) the share of small firms in the local economy, and (3) the share of small banks in the economy. They refer to the industrial mix as the "interest rate channel" and the size of firms and banks as the "credit channel." They find that regions do respond differently to monetary shocks, particularly the Great Lakes region of the United States, and the region's industrial mix (interest rate channel) is an important cause of the differential responses.[4] However, their results on the importance of the bank-lending channel for transmitting monetary shocks at the regional level are mixed.[5]

Our focus is deeper. We want to know if local banks are "important" for the local economy. A decrease in bank lending in the region (caused by a monetary contraction, weak health of the local banking sector) will cause a decrease in regional investment and a decline in regional output and employment. Samolyk (1994) and Neely and Wheelock (1997) try to determine whether this story is accurate by testing whether or not local bank lending and measures of local bank "health" affect the local economy. They find that regional banking conditions do affect regional economic activity.

However, this relationship between local banks and the local economy is affected by the degree of financial integration. Financial integration implies that financial intermediaries can acquire deposits from savers in any region of the country and firms in a region can borrow from any financial intermediary in the country. As a result, controlling for aggregate shocks, lending by a region's banks and regional economic performance (regional income) should be uncorrelated if financial markets are integrated at the national level.[6] This implies that regional income should not "Granger-cause" regional bank lending and vice versa. Any evidence of Granger causality suggests that banks are important for the local economy and vice versa.[7]

---

[4] Horvath (1999) also finds evidence from regional VAR analysis that regions respond very differently to common aggregate and region specific shocks.

[5] In their (1998) paper, Carlino and DeFina find evidence supporting the idea that the share of small firms matters for explaining the response or regional income to a monetary shock. In their (1997) paper, they find that the share of small firms and small banks does not have any explanatory power. However, they present arguments for why their measure of bank size may not accurately capture the credit channel effect.

[6] Bank lending is measured as the loans originated by banks in a region regardless of where the borrower is located. It does not measure loans to the region by banks in the region.

[7] This argument is essentially the same made by Feldstein and Horioka (1980) regarding the correlation between saving and investment and the extent of international financial market integration.

If empirical analysis reveals that banks play a more important role in the local economy in particular regions of the country and not in others, then monetary policy will have a greater impact on those regions via the bank-lending channel. Hence, by identifying regions of the United States that exhibit Granger causality from local bank lending to local economic activity, we are able to say something about where monetary policy will have its largest effects. Furthermore, if markets are not fully integrated, then banks will be important to the local economy and the health of the regional banking sector will be an important determinant of regional economic performance.

In this chapter, we follow the work of Samolyk (1994) and Neely and Whee-lock (1997) to study the importance of regional banks for the regional economy and vice versa. We do so in order to shed some light on whether or not it is even sensible to consider whether a regional bank-lending channel exists. What we do *not* do is directly test for the existence of a regional bank-lending channel. For example, we do not follow Carlino and DeFina in our empirical work by studying the implications for U.S. monetary policy on different regions. Section 12.5 discusses how our findings are related to the existence of a regional credit channel. Finally, Section 12.6 contains final observations and suggestions for future research.

12.2   A simple regional economic model

In this section, we present a simple regional economic model that is solved under the assumption of complete financial integration (interest rate parity) and then no financial integration. We then calculate various covariances to ascertain when regional income will "cause" regional bank lending or vice versa.

In our simple model, there are three actors in the economy: firms, households, and banks. Firms produce output using capital and finance capital acquisitions by borrowing from banks. Households receive income from the firm and save part of their income, which is deposited in banks. Banks serve as financial intermediaries that accept deposits from households and make loans to firms. We assume that the economy is composed of n regions and that there are a continuum of firms, households, and banks in each region distributed over the unit interval.[8] In the following equations, all variables can be thought of as deviations from steady-state values.

12.2.1   Firms

Firms use capital to produce output according to a production function characterized by diminishing productivity. Production is subject to an exogenous

---

[8] This implies symmetric regions. Our basic results would be unaffected if regions were allowed to vary in size as long as one region did not completely dominate the economy. In that case, we would essentially have the equivalent of one closed economy and one small open economy.

shock that is composed of a common shock and a region specific shock. Production is given by (in logs)

$$y_{it} = \alpha k_{it} + e_{it} \qquad 0 < \alpha < 1 \tag{1}$$

$$e_{it} = \rho e_{it-1} + u_{it} \qquad 0 \leq \rho < 1 \tag{2}$$

$$u_{it} = \eta_t + \mu_{it} \tag{3}$$

where y_{it} denotes output of firms in region i, k_{it} is capital used by region i firms, and e_{it} is the productivity shock to output in region i. We assume that the shock to output is serially correlated and persistent but not permanent. We assume that $E(u_{it}) = 0$, $E(u_{it})^2 = \sigma_\eta^2 + \sigma_\mu^2$, $\text{Cov}(\mu_{it}, \mu_{jt+m}) = 0$ for all $i, j = 1, \ldots, n$, and $m > 0$. Capital is assumed to depreciate fully in one period.

We assume that firms must finance the investment in capital by borrowing from banks. At the beginning of period t, firms borrow to finance capital k_{t+1}, which is used to produce output available at the beginning of period $t + 1$. Firms sell output in competitive markets. Profits are distributed back to banks to repay loans and to owners of capital (households). Consequently, the demand for capital, or demand for loans, by firms in region i is given by

$$I_{it} = k_{it+1} = -\gamma r_{Lt} + \gamma E_t(e_{it+1}) = -\gamma r_{Lt} + \gamma \rho e_{it}$$

$$\gamma = 1/(1-\alpha) \quad (4)$$

where r_{Lt} is the loan rate charged by banks.

Firms' loan demand depends negatively on the real interest rate on loans and the expected value of the next period's productivity shock, ρe_{it}. If the persistence of the shock is high ($\rho \approx 1$), firms expect the current shock to productivity to persist into the future, and so their demand for capital next period will also be high. Contrarily, if the shock is expected to be transitory ($\rho = 0$), then today's shock will not affect future productivity, and so today's loan demand is unaffected. Thus, investment demand by firms is positively related to the persistence of the shock.

12.2.2   Households

Households receive part of the firms' output as income at the beginning of the period when output is realized and sold in the market. Permanent income considerations suggest that if the shock to output is highly persistent, then households simply consume the additional income, and saving is unaffected. On the other hand, if the shock to income is transitory, then households will save almost all the shock to income. As a result, saving is inversely related to the persistence of the income shock. A simple description of household saving in a region is given by

$$S_{it} = (1 - \rho)e_{it} \tag{5}$$

For simplicity, we have abstracted from interest rate effects on region saving.[9] However, this does not mean that households are indifferent to the value of interest rates in the economy because interest rates still affect the allocation of savings across different financial instruments. We assume that households can hold savings in the form of bank deposits or in the form of a nonbank-issued asset (bonds). Bank deposits pay r_{Dt}, whereas bonds pay r_{Bt}. In order to maximize the value of their portfolio, they will deposit their savings in the market that offers the highest rate of return. Thus, while deposit and bond rates do not affect the *level* of household saving, they do affect the *allocation* of savings across banks and across financial markets.

12.2.3 Banks

Banks transform deposits into loans, earn interest on loans, and pay interest on deposits. Implicitly, we assume that banks have some informational advantage that makes it worthwhile to households to have banks lend to firms rather than doing it themselves. The banks' balance-sheet identities require

$$L_{it} = D_{it} + z_{it} \tag{6}$$

where L_{it} are loans to firms by banks in region i and D_{it} are held by banks in region i. The term z_{it} is a shock to bank lending in region i, which is of mean zero with variance σ_z^2. We also assume that it is serially uncorrelated and, most importantly, uncorrelated with the productivity shock. Our intent is to have z_{it} capture all disturbances to regional bank lending that are unrelated to the state of the local economy. For example, it may reflect disintermediation shocks or shocks to bank health such as unexpected loan losses and shocks to bank capital. Alternatively, one could think of z_{it} as the region-specific effects of a monetary-policy-induced shock to bank reserves. We ignore reserve requirements and other outside assets such as government securities for simplicity. It is important to stress at this point that $D_{it} \neq S_{it}$, unless savers in region i only deposit funds in region i banks and region i banks only obtain deposits from savers in region i. Furthermore, L_{it} denotes loans made by banks in region i regardless of where the firm is located – it does not denote the loans by banks in region i to firms in region i.

It is assumed that the banking market is perfectly competitive, which ensures that interest rates on deposits are equalized within a region. Financially integrated markets imply that the loan rate and deposit rates will be equalized across regions as well as with the differential between the loan and the deposit rate reflecting the cost of financial intermediation. For simplicity we set the cost of intermediation to zero which implies that $r_L^j = r_D^j = r^j$ for region j. Financial integration would imply that $r^j = r$ for all j. Finally, perfect capital mobility would imply that households can move their savings freely between

---

[9] This would be the result obtained in a two-period model with log utility.

the banking market and the bond market. Costless intermediation in the bond market then implies $r_{Lt} = r_{Dt} = r_{Bt}$. Given interest rate parity across financial instruments, the households portfolio allocation is indeterminate. Thus, we assume that households put a constant share δ of their savings into deposits and $1 - \delta$ into the bond market.

In order to capture the idea of geographical diversification of the banks' balance sheets, we can write the bank's asset and liabilities as follows:

$$D_{it} = \delta \sum_{j=1}^{n} \theta_{ij}(1 - \rho)e_{jt} \qquad \sum_{i=1}^{n} \theta_{ij} = 1 \tag{7}$$

$$L_{it} = \sum_{j=1}^{n} \lambda_{ij} I_{jt} \qquad \sum_{i=1}^{n} \lambda_{ij} = 1 \tag{8}$$

The parameter θ_{ij} denotes the share of region j's savings/deposits obtained by region i banks, whereas λ_{ij} denotes the share of investment in region j financed by banks in region i. Even though the banks' shares of loans to a region and the sum of bank shares of a region's savings must sum to one, the sum of region i's deposits from all regions and its loans to all regions need not sum to one (i.e., $\sum_{j=1}^{n} \theta_{ij} \neq 1$ and $\sum_{j=1}^{n} \lambda_{ij} \neq 1$). In short, we cannot say anything a priori about the "size" of a region's banks or its market share. If $\theta_{ij} = \lambda_{ij}$, then banks in region i have the equivalent of a zero current account balance with region j (i.e., the amount of borrowing by region i banks from region j households is equal to the lending of region i banks to region j firms). However, if we assume that banks are roughly the same size, then summing the weights over j will add to one.

12.2.4   Full financial integration

12.2.4.1 Geographical diversification and lending-income correlations
In a fully integrated banking system, banks could acquire deposits from and make loans to any region in the economy, and portfolio diversification would entice them to do so. In our model, perfect geographical diversification would correspond to $\theta_{ij} = \lambda_{ij} = 1/n$ for all j in Equations (7) and (8). In this case, all banks are the same size and have the same share of the deposit and loan markets. Correspondingly, region i's deposits would be

$$D_{it} = \delta(1 - \rho)\bar{e}_t \qquad \bar{e}_t = \frac{1}{n}\sum_{i=1}^{n} e_{it} = \rho\bar{e}_{t-1} + \bar{u}_t \qquad \bar{u}_t = \frac{1}{n}\sum_{j=1}^{n} u_{jt}$$

$$\tag{9}$$

If banks had perfectly diversified liabilities, their total deposits would simply be the average amount of deposits occurring in the economy.

Financial integration would imply that there would be equalization of interest rates across regions, and r_{Lt} would be determined as if there were one aggregate loan market. Aggregating across regions implies that equilibrium in the loan market must satisfy

$$\sum_{i=1}^{n} I_{it} = \sum_{i=1}^{n} S_{it} \tag{10}$$

The solution for r_{Lt} is

$$r_{Lt} = + \frac{1}{\gamma n} \left[(\rho + \rho\gamma - 1) \sum_{i=1}^{n} e_{it} - \sum_{i=1}^{n} z_{it} \right] \tag{11}$$

Investment in region i in time t and output in period $t + 1$ are given by

$$I_{it} = \bar{z}_t + (1 - \rho)\bar{e}_t + \gamma\rho(e_{it} - \bar{e}_t) = \bar{I}_t + \gamma\rho(e_{it} - \bar{e}_t)$$

$$\text{where } \bar{z}_t = \frac{1}{n} \sum_{i=1}^{n} z_{it} \tag{12}$$

$$y_{it+1} = \alpha\bar{z}_t + \alpha(1 - \rho)\bar{e}_t + \alpha\rho\gamma(e_{it} - \bar{e}_t) + e_{it+1} \tag{13}$$

From Equation (12), full financial integration implies firms in region i receive the average loan plus an adjustment for the differential between their productivity shock and the average productivity shock (i.e., if region i receives a shock that is above average, it receives an above average loan). Equation (13) shows how output is determined next period as a result of the loans received by region i firms in period t.

12.2.4.2 Controlling for aggregate shocks

Now suppose that the only shocks to the economy were common shocks, $\mu_{it} = z_{it} = 0$ for all i. Then the economy is essentially identical, and effective portfolio diversification is not possible.[10] Using Equations (9), (12), and (13) yields the following conditional sample covariances based on information through $t - 1$:[11]

$$\text{Cov}(L_{it}, y_{it}) = \delta^2(1 - \rho)^2\sigma_\eta^2 \tag{14}$$

$$\text{Cov}(L_{it}, y_{it+1}) = \delta[\alpha(1 - \rho)^2 + \rho(1 - \rho)]\sigma_u^2 \tag{15}$$

$$\text{Cov}(L_{it+1}, y_{it}) = \delta\rho(1 - \rho)\sigma_u^2 \tag{16}$$

---

[10] Regional diversification is occurring; it simply does nothing with respect to reducing the variance of the banks assets and liability base.

[11] These conditional covariances are calculated as $E_{t-1}[(x_{i+m,t} - E_{t-1}(x_{i+m,t}))(z_{i,t} - E_{t-1}(z_{i,t}))]$ for $m \geq 0$.

Not surprisingly, common shocks cause current bank lending and income to exhibit positive contemporaneous correlation but this correlation is affected by the magnitude of δ, which captures the relative share of aggregate saving going into the banking sector. For small values of δ, the correlation between bank lending by regional banks and regional income will be essentially zero. With regards to Granger causality, current lending will Granger-cause future income and current income will Granger-cause future lending. Because common shocks do not produce an incentive to diversify portfolios, capital flows do not occur. Furthermore, diversification of bank portfolios is irrelevant, as is relative bank "size" and bank health. Hence, estimating correlations between bank lending and regional income do not reveal any information regarding financial integration or regional differences unless we control for common shocks. Thus, from here on, we net out common shocks from all variables leaving only regional shocks to influence variables.

In order to control for common shocks, we measure all variables as deviations from the sample average. This nets out the effects of common shocks and leaves only the regional shocks in the covariance calculations. Thus let

$$\hat{L}_{it} = L_{it} - \bar{L}_t \qquad \bar{L}_t = \frac{1}{n} \sum_{i=1}^{n} L_{it} \tag{17}$$

$$\hat{y}_{it} = y_{it} - \bar{y}_t \qquad \bar{y}_t = \frac{1}{n} \sum_{i=1}^{n} y_{it} \tag{18}$$

$$\hat{I}_{it} = I_{it} - \bar{I}_t \qquad \bar{I}_t = \frac{1}{n} \sum_{i=1}^{n} I_{it} \tag{19}$$

measure the deviations of regional values from the national average.

12.2.4.3 Theoretical results on causality
We can use our model to study a variety of different diversification scenarios for each region, controlling for aggregate shocks. A summary of our theoretical results follows:[12]

> *Full financial integration.* Banks geographically diversify their deposit base; firms borrow freely across regions. In this case, $\theta_{ij} = 1/n$, and the lending by regional banks will be uncorrelated with regional income and vice versa. Hence, no Granger causality will be present between these two variables. However, current lending will Granger-cause future lending, and current income will Granger-cause future income.

---

[12] Our early working paper (Hanson-McPherson and Waller 1999) contains the formal expressions for the covariances in all these cases. We describe the general findings here for brevity.

Partial financial integration. Banks do not diversify their deposit base; firms borrow freely across regions. In this case, $\theta_{ij} = 0$ for $j \neq i$ with $\theta_{ii} = 1$, implying banks only acquire deposits from households in their region. Here, lending by regional banks will be correlated with regional economic performance, even though there is interest rate parity across regions due to firm mobility. Correlation between bank lending and economic performance will lead us to conclude that shocks to lending by regional banks will Granger-cause regional economic performance and vice versa. However, there is no economic causation in this situation.

No financial integration. Banks do not diversify their deposit base; firms borrow only from local banks. In this case, $\theta_{ij} = 0$ for $j \neq i$ with $\theta_{ii} = 1$ and $\lambda_{ij} = 0$ for $i \neq j$ and $\lambda_{ii} = 1$. Here, interest rate parity does not exist, and the economy is a collection of closed regional economies. Regional income will be correlated with regional bank lending, and we will find evidence of Granger causality between the two variables. Correlation implies economic causality.

If banks fully diversify their deposit portfolios and have approximately the same share of the deposit market $\theta_{ij} = 1/n$, then no correlation will exist between lending by regional banks and regional economic performance.[13] This result is reminiscent of Feldstein and Horioka's (1980) result on the correlation between saving and investment that arises under perfect capital mobility. Consequently, if the data reveal a strong positive correlation between bank lending and regional income, it would suggest that financial markets are not well integrated at the intranational level.

The second case is one in which banks can only attract deposits from their own region. This corresponds to the U.S. case where bank branching restrictions prevented the creation of a geographically diversified deposit base for U.S. banks. Even though branching restrictions have slowly fallen in the United States since 1982, we still do not observe nationwide banking such as is observed in Canada, for example. Hence, although our empirical dataset covers the years 1985–95, it may still be reasonable to assume that banks have regionally concentrated deposit bases. It may also be the case that small banks may not be able to attract deposits from other regions either directly or through other sources such as issuing large-denomination certificates of deposit.[14] Thus, if a region has a large number of small banks, it may tend to have a nondiversified deposit base. Easing branching restrictions will not necessarily eliminate this source of nondiversification.

---

[13] Diversification of loan portfolios does not affect the covariance because total lending by banks in a region is a function of its deposit base, regardless of where the loans are made.

[14] See Kashyap and Stein (1995).

If banks do not diversify their deposit bases, we obtain a positive correlation between bank lending and income *even though there is interest rate parity!* In short, a shock to regional income increases the deposit base of the regions banks, and thus total lending by the region's banks will be correlated with income today.[15] This is true regardless of where the banks make the loans. For example, we get this positive correlation even if $\lambda_{ii} = 0$, which implies local banks make *no* loans to local firms and thus have absolutely no impact on the performance of the regional economy. The key point of this exercise is to emphasize that the regional concentration of banks' deposit base can lead to a Type 1 error (rejection of the null hypothesis that banks are not important for local economic performance) if a positive correlation between bank lending and income is obtained. Consequently, this is a case where evidence of Granger causality does not imply economic causality. Hence, in the empirical work that follows, one must be mindful of this problem.

Now consider the case where there is no financial integration across regions. In this extreme version of the model, households again deposit all their savings in the local banks as in the preceding section, so $\theta_{ij} = 0$ for $j \neq i$ and $\theta_{ii} = 1$. Now, however, firms are constrained to borrow only from local banks. In this case, $\lambda_{ij} = 0$ for $i \neq j$ and $\lambda_{ii} = 1$. In this extreme case, regions are essentially "islands" of economy activity. Equations (4)–(6) imply that

$$I_{it} = L_{it} = (1 - \rho)e_{it} + z_{it} \tag{20}$$

$$r_{iLt} = -\{[1 - \rho(1 - \gamma)]/\gamma\}e_{it} - (1/\gamma)\,z_{it} \tag{21}$$

The lack of "mobility" on the part of firms to borrow from other regions means that the local shock to lending, z_{it}, now affects the local economy. If banks in region i suffer a negative shock to their lending (say, due to a need to build up loan loss reserves, disintermediation, or a reduction in bank health in the region), then lending to local firms declines, current investment falls, and next period's output decreases. The point of this exercise is to show that if regions are characterized by a disproportionate number of firms who are constrained to borrow from local banks (i.e., small firms), and banks acquire deposits locally (small banks), then shocks to regional bank lending and bank health will have a greater effect on future output in these regions. Consequently, shocks to local bank lending are more likely to "cause" local economic activity and vice versa. Here, evidence of Granger causality corresponds to economic causality.

---

[15] The strength of this correlation is maximized when the income shock is sufficiently persistent but not too much. If the shock is too persistent, households simply consume the additional income, and saving does not increase even though investment and future income increases significantly. If the shock is not very persistent, households save the income, deposits and bank lending rise, but firms do not change investment in response to the current shock because it does not have much impact on future productivity. Thus, future output does not respond to current lending.

Furthermore, if we interpret the shock to bank lending as an idiosyncratic response to a monetary policy reserve shock, then we get the following result. In regions that are well integrated financially (firms borrow across regions and banks acquire deposits across regions), the monetary shock will not affect the correlation between bank lending and regional economic activity. However, in regions that tend to be isolated, the monetary policy shock to reserves will have a much stronger impact on these regions and will appear as a stronger correlation between regional bank lending and regional income. This suggests that a regional bank lending channel exists – regions that are financially isolated will exhibit a greater correlation between regional bank lending and regional income than regions that are financially integrated.

12.3   Data

The model described earlier shows that with financial integration and sufficient geographical diversification of the deposit base, lending by a region's banks will not be correlated with current or future income and vice versa. Consequently, relative bank lending should not cause the economic performance of the local economy and vice versa.

We employ a bivariate VAR to test for Granger causality between lending by regional banks and regional income. In order to test this hypothesis, we need to break down the data by regions; consequently, we break down the data by U.S. Bureau of the Census regions, and run VARs for each region.

The banking data were obtained from the Federal Financial Institutions Examination Council's Reports of Condition and Income (Call Reports). Total domestic deposits and various measures of bank lending are used in the estimations: total domestic loans, domestic commercial and industrial loans, and a proxy for small business loans. The proxy that we use for small business loans is the addition of construction loans with agricultural loans. The dataset contains quarterly data for 51 states (all 50 states plus Washington, D.C.), for the time period 1985–95.[16] For the VAR analysis, the data are aggregated into larger regions. The aggregation that we use to define regions is the U.S. Bureau of the Census definition for regions. In the end, we have nine regions of the United States.

The data used to represent the local economy are personal income data. The personal income data were obtained from the Bureau of Economic Analysis (BEA). The dataset contains quarterly data available from 1985 to 1995 for 51

---

[16] We did not use data earlier than 1985 because we were told that in the early 1980s the methods for calculating the data used in the Call Reports changed significantly enough that comparisons across periods would be meaningless. In order to avoid the problems associated with legal branching restrictions, we chose to focus on the latter period, which occurs after the 1980 and 1982 Money Decontrol Acts.

states. Again, this dataset was also aggregated into the larger Census Bureau regions for the VAR analysis. All the variables in the estimations are transformed into real terms using the Gross Domestic Product Deflator. The variables are then transformed into relative terms, where each variable is a regional measure relative to the national measure. For instance, real relative personal income is calculated by subtracting the log of national real personal income from the log of state real personal income for each state. The transformation is performed in order to ensure that only regional movements in the variables are relevant in the estimation.

12.4   Empirical analysis

In order to examine the correlations between the local banking sector and local economic activity, we examine the reduced-form relation between real relative bank loans and real relative income (and real relative bank deposits in the case of the three-variable vector autoregression). Consequently, we estimate a vector autoregression for each region of the form:

$$A(L)y_{it} = \varepsilon_{it} \tag{22}$$

where $A(L)$ is a matrix of polynomials in the lag operator L and y_t is the vector of variables used in the regression. In our estimation, y_t is a vector containing real relative real loans to businesses and real relative real personal income (and real relative bank deposits). Lastly, ε_{it} is the i.i.d. error. We estimate Equation (22), assuming no contemporaneous variables appear on the right-hand side of the equation. Granger-causality tests are performed to examine the correlations between local bank lending and local economic activity. The correlations are further examined by estimating impulse response functions. Impulse response functions are obtained by inverting the estimated lag polynomial

$$\hat{B}(L) = \hat{A}^{-1}(L) \tag{23}$$

Corresponding confidence bands for the impulse response functions are calculated using Monte Carlo integration.

Two-variable and three-variable vector autoregressions (VARs) are estimated for each of the loan measures. The two-variable VARs consist of real relative personal income and real relative loans. The three-variable VARs consist of real relative personal income, real relative loans, and real relative deposits. Real relative loans are represented by three measures, each creating a new VAR to be estimated. The measures of real relative loans include total domestic loans, domestic commercial and industrial loans, and our proxy of small business loans (agricultural plus construction loans).[17]

---

[17] Our diagnostics of our relative loan and income variables showed that the series did not contain unit roots.

Table 12.1. *Granger-causality quarterly*
data

	$a(L)Y_{t-1}$	$b(L)L_{t-1}$
VAR1		
Y_t	(1) 9/9 (2)	(1) 3/9 (2)
L_t	(1) 4/9 (2)	(1) 9/9 (2)
VAR2		
Y_t	(1) 9/9 (2)	(1) 4/9 (2)
L_t	(1) 4/9 (2)	(1) 9/9 (2)
VAR3		
Y_t	(1) 8/9 (2)	(1) 4/9 (2)
L_t	(1) 5/9 (2)	(1) 9/9 (2)

Notes: Variables measured in number of regions out of
total in which evidence of Granger causality is VAR1:
Loans = total domestic; VAR2: Loans = domestic commercial; and VAR3: Loans = agricultural and construction. (1) Granger-causality tests evaluated at the 0.05.
(2) Granger-causality tests evaluated at the 0.10.

We divide the country into Census regions and run separate VARs for each
region individually. One advantage of this demarcation of the data in conjunction with the simple bivariate VARs is that it allows regions to have different
relationships between bank lending and income. Plus it allows us to pinpoint
which regions of the country differ from one another.

Summaries of the Granger-causality tests are illustrated in the Tables 12.1
and 12.2. The procedure used to conduct the tests is the same for each region
and in each case. Thus, we will present an outline of the procedure used in all
cases by using the East South Central region as an example. Table 12.3 contains the results of the two-variable VAR Granger-causality tests for the East
South Central region. First, the VAR is estimated, and the appropriate lag length
is determined. In order to determine the appropriate lag length, an initial lag
length must be chosen. We chose a lag length of 8 quarters. The lag length is
then tested against shorter lag lengths. In this case, the appropriate lag length
is found to be a lag of three quarters. Given a lag length of three quarters, we
use Granger-causality tests to determine if there are correlations between bank
lending and economic activity. In the income equation, the null hypothesis that
past income does not Granger-cause future income is tested. As shown in Table
12.3, the test statistic is 20.77 and is distributed $F(3,34)$. At the 0.05 significance level, $F(3,34) = 2.92$. Therefore, the null hypothesis that income does
not Granger-cause income is rejected. The null hypothesis that past loans do
not Granger-cause future income is also tested. The test statistic is 4.04 and is
also distributed $F(3,34)$. Thus, we reject the null hypothesis that loans do not

Table 12.2. *Granger-causality quarterly data*

	$a(L)Y_{t-1}$	$b(L)D_{t-1}$	$c(L)L_{t-1}$
VAR1			
Y_t	(1) 9/9 (2)	(1) 3/9 (2)	(1) 2/9 (2)
D_t	(1) 1/9 (2)	(1) 9/9 (2)	(1) 2/9 (2)
L_t	(1) 3/9 (2)	(1) 2/9 (2)	(1) 9/9 (2)
VAR2			
Y_t	(1) 9/9 (2)	(1) 2/9 (2)	(1) 2/9 (2)
D_t	(1) 2/9 (2)	(1) 9/9 (2)	(1) 5/9 (2)
L_t	(1) 2/9 (2)	(1) 2/9 (2)	(1) 9/9 (2)
VAR3			
Y_t	(1) 9/9 (2)	(1) 4/9 (2)	(1) 2/9 (2)
D_t	(1) 5/9 (2)	(1) 9/9 (2)	(1) 1/9 (2)
L_t	(1) 5/9 (2)	(1) 6/9 (2)	(1) 9/9 (2)

Notes: Variables measured in relative number of regions out of total in which evidence of Granger causality is VAR1: Loans = total domestic; VAR2: Loans = domestic commercial and industrial; and VAR3: Loans = agricultural and construction. (1) Granger-causality tests evaluated at the 0.05 significance. (2) Granger-causality tests evaluated at the 0.10 significance.

Table 12.3. *Granger-causality in the East South Central region quarterly data (real relative loans measured as construction and agricultural)*

	Test	Degrees of freedom	F^*
Income			
(i) exclude (given lag)	20.77	(3,34)	2.92
(ii) exclude (given lag)	4.04	(3,34)	2.92
Loan			
(i) exclude (given lag)	9.49	(3,34)	2.92
(ii) exclude (given lag)	80.31	(3,34)	2.92

*Measured at the 0.05 significance.

Granger-cause income. The results of the estimation of the loan equation reveal that we reject the null that loans do not Granger-cause loans as well as reject the null that income does not Granger-cause loans. All the estimations for each region are conducted in a similar manner.

The results of the two-variable VARs are illustrated in Table 12.1, while the results of the three-variable VARs are illustrated in Table 12.2. The tables summarize the number of regions out of the total in which evidence of Granger-causality is found, both at the 0.05 significance level and the 0.10 significance level. Evidence suggesting that past income Granger-causes future income in all regions, and in all cases, is found. Moreover, past loans Granger-cause future loans in all regions and in all cases. However, what we are interested in determining is if loans Granger-cause income and vice versa.

The VARs suggest that roughly one-third to one-half of the regions display Granger causality between bank lending and income, when bank lending is represented by Total Domestic Loans. However, the problem with using total loans is that it includes consumer loans, mortgage loans, and other forms of "nonproduction" loans. The model we used focused on lending to firms for investment purposes rather than consumption smoothing by households. Consequently, we chose to narrow our definition of lending to loans that can be more properly viewed as production loans.

As a result, we used Domestic Commercial and Industrial Loans as the second measure of bank lending. Using this measure, the results of the two-variable VAR now suggest that at least half of the regions display Granger causality between bank lending and income. The results of the three-variable VAR indicate that less than half of the regions exhibit Granger causality.

Finally, we narrow our bank lending measure further by estimating the VARs when bank lending is measured using our proxy of small business loans (construction plus agricultural loans). A stylized fact about bank borrowing is that small firms are the ones most likely to rely on banks for financing production.[18] If banks play a major role in financing small business production, and small businesses make up a significant fraction of total firms, then we might expect to find a strong positive correlation between regional bank lending and regional economic performance. However, it should be pointed out that these small firm-bank relationships do not depend on the *location* of the banks or the firms; banks in one region should be just as able to lend to small businesses in another region as the local bank if financial integration exists. The results of the estimations using our proxy of small business loans suggest that at least half of the regions display evidence of Granger causality between bank lending and income. The evidence found in the Granger-causality tests reveals that there are correlations between the local banking sector and local economic activity in the United States. The strongest evidence for correlations between the two sectors is found in the estimations where real relative loans are represented by the sum of construction and agricultural loans.

It is interesting to note that the regions for which we reject the null of no Granger causality are clustered together in the central United States. This is illustrated in Tables 12.4–12.5 and suggests that there may not be much financial

---

[18] See Gertler and Gilchrist (1994) for example.

Table 12.4. *Regions that display evidence of Granger causality – two-variable VAR*

Loans – Granger causality	Income – Granger causality
New England	New England
East North	East North
East South	East South
West North	West North
West South	West South
Mountain	Mountain
	Pacific

Table 12.5. *Regions that display evidence of Granger causality – three-variable VAR*

Loans – Granger causality	Income – Granger causality
East South	New
West North	East North
West South	East South
	West South
	South
	Mountain
	Pacific

integration of the financial sector in this part of the country; firms, households and banks in the region tend to interact only with each other. On the other hand, this is also the largest agricultural region of the United States, and our measure of small business lending (construction plus agriculture loans) may be inducing a bias against the null hypothesis. Nevertheless, at the 10% significance level, income tends to Granger-cause loans in all but the Mid and South Atlantic regions, whereas lending Granger-causes income everywhere except along the eastern seaboard and the West Coast. Consequently, the evidence suggests that a relative shock to income in most regions of the country is likely to stimulate an increase in lending by the region's banks. As a result we conclude that (1) the deposit base of banks in most of the country is not geographically diversified for the period of study, or (2) financial markets are not well integrated in the center of the country.

Whether or not this is a "hangover" effect of branching restrictions, the prevalence of small banks in the United States, or something more fundamental is unclear. One way to test whether or not branching restrictions are responsible for this correlation is to conduct the same tests for countries that have never

Table 12.6. *Regional distribution of banks*

Assets (A)	#	Total assets (in thousands)	Percent of total	Total loans (in thousands)	Percent of total
Nationwide					
$A < \$3$ million	10,112	752,582,656	15	431,708,336	15
$\$3$ million $< A < \$1$ billion	913	473,344,029	9	282,666,582	10
$A > \$1$ billion	582	3,786,863,513	76	2,091,228,133	75
East South Central					
$A < \$3$ million	790	63,037,483	34	36,761,150	31
$\$3$ million $< A < \$1$ billion	41	20,797,634	11	13,326,011	11
$A > \$1$ billion	26	102,962,203	55	66,734,380	57
Mid Atlantic					
$A < \$3$ million	539	67,212,310	4	36,440,946	4
$\$3$ million $< A < \$1$ billion	913	100,198,708	5	44,339,669	5
$A > \$1$ billion	582	1,654,948,913	91	740,199,100	90

Note: Sums are taken over all banks with nonmissing, nonzero assets and loans in 1994: Q4 Call Report data.

had branching restrictions and see if they look different than they do for the U.S. regions. In another paper (Hanson and Waller 1999), we applied the same Granger-causality tests to Canada, which has had nationwide banking for nearly a century. We find that the null of no Granger causality is almost never rejected for Canada. From that analysis and the work presented here, we conclude that the lingering effects of branching restrictions are probably the source of the positive correlations between lending and income in the United States.

As a check on whether bank size has anything to do with our empirical results, in Table 12.6 we present data on bank size, total bank assets, and total bank loans.[19] In particular, we look at the East South Central region, which consistently displayed Granger causality between regional income and lending by regional banks, and the Mid-Atlantic region, which consistently displayed an absence of Granger causality. What is interesting about Table 12.6 is the fact that in the East South Central region, 34% (55%) of total assets and 31% (57%) of total loans are made by small banks (large banks), whereas in the Mid-Atlantic region 4% (91%) of total assets and 4% (90%) of total loans are made by small banks (large banks). Because small banks are the ones most likely to have nondiversified portfolios and to be tied to local firms and depositors, it is not surprising then that regions with a heavy percentage of small banks display a significant correlation between bank lending and economic performance. This evidence is very consistent with that found by Kashyap and Stein (1997b) who

[19] We thank Cara Lown for giving us this data in her discussion of our paper at the conference.

show that, in a panel of over 1 million commercial banks, the impact of monetary policy is more pronounced for banks with relatively illiquid balance sheets, and this result is driven almost solely by the set of small banks in the panel.

In summary, we believe that the combination of branching restrictions and the proliferation of small banks in the central and western regions of the United States is largely responsible for the empirical correlations uncovered in this paper. We suspect that as the full effect of branching restrictions fades away and nationwide banking emerges on a more prominent scale, the United States will eventually display correlations between regional income and lending by regional banks very similar to Canada.

The impulse response functions reflect the evidence that is found in the Granger-causality tests. We calculated impulse response functions for each case, but only include one of the interesting cases here, the three-variable VAR for East South Central. One of the criticisms of impulse response functions is that the results are dependent upon the ordering of the variables in the decomposition. The determination of the appropriate ordering requires the imposition of a priori restrictions on the reduced form equation. The theory outlined in the first section of the paper indicates that the appropriate ordering of the variables is income, deposits, and then loans. However, in order to address the problem of placing a priori restrictions on the data via the ordering, we estimate impulse response functions with both the ordering described earlier, and the ordering where loans are first, deposits are second, and income is last. It is found that the reverse ordering causes no significant changes in the results.

Figures 12.1 and 12.2 illustrate the impulse response function described previously. Both graphs provide evidence suggesting that there are significant correlations between loans and income in the East South Central region of the United States. Similar exercises for other regions matched the Granger-causality results.

12.5   Monetary policy effects with regional financial market segregation

The preceding theoretical and empirical analysis suggests that monetary policy will have different effects on regions depending on the health of the banking sector in a region, the relative proportion of small firms in a region, and the degree of financial market integration. There are a couple of ways in which a common policy shock can lead to uncommon responses to the regional economy.

The easiest case to study is to assume that some regions are characterized as having large banks and large firms, which are financially "mobile," whereas small banks and small firms characterize other regions. The first group of regions would be able to move across regions and asset markets to borrow and lend while the latter group cannot. Consequently, in the event of a monetary contraction

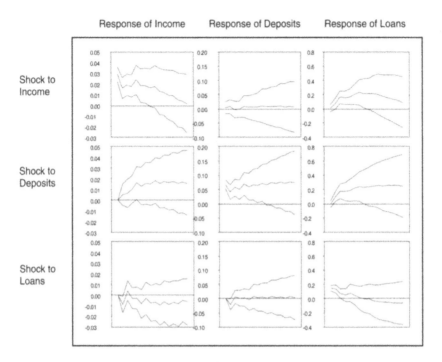

Figure 12.1. Impulse response function for East South Central using first-ordering quarterly data (loans represented by construction and agricultural loans).

that reduces the banks' reserves, these two groups of states will display different responses to the monetary shock. Banks in the first group of regions will be able to replace the lost reserves by borrowing in other markets, and firms in this group will simply substitute out of bank financing of investment into other forms of investment financing. Consequently, the response of output in the regions to the monetary contraction will be small. However, for the small bank/small firm regions, the loss of reserves cannot be replaced, and the firms cannot go outside the local economy to obtain financing for investment. Consequently, these financially segregated regions will suffer a much larger output response to the monetary contraction. Consequently, the impulse response functions for output in the two groups of regions will diverge, with the financially segregated regions of the country bearing the greatest burden of the monetary contraction. The preceding VAR analysis suggests that the Midwestern states of the United States are more segregated financially than those on the East Coast. As a result, the Midwest will bear a greater share of the cost associated with a monetary contraction.

Such a result is not surprising given the history of the Federal Reserve in the United States. Conflict between small banks and farmers in the Midwest

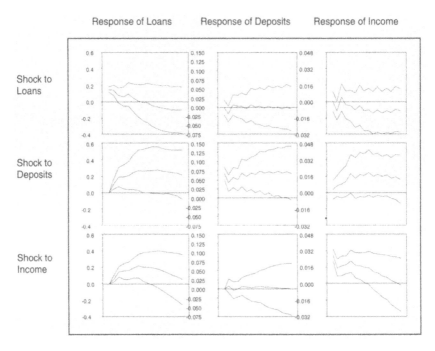

Figure 12.2. Impulse response function for East South Central region using second-ordering quarterly data (loans represented by construction and agricultural loans).

and the large money center banks in New York was a significant factor in the institutional design of the Federal Reserve and in the bimetallism debates in the late 19th century (see Wheelock 1999). Midwestern states almost always argued against contractions in the supply of credit because they felt they bore a disproportionate share of the costs associated with such a contraction. Hence, they typically argued for easy monetary policies rather than tight monetary policies, whereas the East Coast banks worried about inflation and gold flows. The VAR analysis suggests that over a hundred years later, things may not have changed much.

An alternative manner in which the degree of financial integration will affect a region's response to a monetary shock is in how the financial system dampens or magnifies any asymmetric effects of the monetary policy shock. For example, suppose the monetary contraction caused a larger contraction of reserves and loan supply in one region relative to another. If funds do not flow freely across regions and firms cannot move across regions to find financing, then the region with the larger loan supply contraction will experience a larger reduction in investment and output. However, if funds flow freely, then funds will flow from the lesser-hit region to the harder-hit region in order to arbitrage interest rate differentials. The net result is a dampening of the decline in reserves in the hard-hit region (and a subsequent softening of the decline in investment and output) and a lessening of loan supply and a worsening of output in the region experiencing the smaller initial contraction of reserves. The key point is that the impulse response functions would converge over time rather than diverge. Thus, even if the monetary shock hits unequally across regions, the degree of financial integration will lead to a convergence of output responses to the differing shocks.

12.6   Conclusions

We began our study asking the simple question, are local banks important for the local economy? Our theoretical analysis illustrated that the answer to this question is strongly tied to the degree of intranational financial integration. In a well-integrated financial system, the answer to our question is no. In an economy characterized by financial isolation, the answer, not surprisingly, is yes. Our empirical results provided clear evidence that local banks do seem to matter for the performance of the local economy at least in major parts of the country. However, we also are led to believe that this importance will diminish over time, as nationwide banking becomes the norm in the United States as it is in Canada.

What are the implications of our results for U.S. financial and monetary policy? The slow breakdown in branching restrictions over the last 15 years may eventually lead to a breakdown in the positive relationship that we have found between bank lending and regional income. As nationwide banking becomes the norm and mergers swallow up small banks, the U.S. banking system will eventually acquire the geographical diversification necessary for perfect capital mobility. On the other hand, if for other reasons (information, convenience, and cultural) firms, households, and banks in a region continue interacting only amongst themselves, then this positive relationship will continue long after branching restrictions have disappeared.

With regard to monetary policy, our results suggest that a regional credit channel may exist. By contracting the money supply, bank lending may contract differentially across the country. On the coasts, bank lending may not be affected much by a tightening of reserves because banks in these regions can acquire funds elsewhere. In the middle of the country, banks would have to curtail loans to firms who appear to rely on banks for financing, which reduces investment and production, thereby engendering a recession. The issue of regional effects of monetary contractions also has implications for the new European Monetary Union should banking systems differ significantly across Europe.[20]

[20] See Kashyap and Stein (1997a).

Our work should be considered a first step in attempting to understand the extent of banking market integration within the United States and its relationship to the debate on the credit channel of monetary policy. Furthermore, it should be viewed as a complement to other related lines of research, such as the risk-sharing literature, which examines the nature of inter- and intranational capital mobility.

References

Bernanke, B., and M. Gertler. 1995. Inside the black box: The credit channel of monetary policy transmission. *Journal of Economic Perspectives* 9(4): 27–48.

Carlino, G., and R. DeFina. 1998. "The Differential Effects of Monetary Policy Shocks on Regional Economic Activity," *Review of Economics and Statistics* 80: 572–87.

Carlino, G., and R. DeFina. 1999. "Monetary Policy and the U.S. States and Regions: Some Implications for European Monetary Union," in J. von Hagen and C. J. Waller, eds., *Regional Aspects of Monetary Union*. Boston: Kluwer Academic Publishers.

Carlino, G., and R. DeFina. 1997. "The Differential Effects of Monetary Policy Shocks: Evidence from the U.S. States." Working paper 97-12. Federal Reserve Bank of Philadelphia.

Feldstein, M., and C. Horioka. 1980. Domestic saving and international capital flows. *Economic Journal* 90: 314–29.

Hanson McPherson, S., and C. Waller. 1998. "Do Local Banks Matter for the Local Economy?" Unpublished working paper. University of Kentucky.

Hanson McPherson, S., and C. Waller. 1999. "Intranational Financial Integration: Evidence from the Canadian Banking Industry," in J. von Hagen and C. J. Waller, eds., *Regional Aspects of Monetary Union*. Boston: Kluwer Academic Publishers.

Horvath, M. 1999. "Empirical Evidence on Common Money and Uncommon Regions in the United States," in J. von Hagen and C. J. Waller, eds., *Regional Aspects of Monetary Union*. Boston: Kluwer Academic Publishers.

Gertler, M., and S. Gilchrist. 1994. Monetary policy, business cycles and the behavior of small manufacturing firms. *Quarterly Journal of Economics* 109: 309–40.

Kashyap, A., and J. Stein. 1995. The impact of monetary policy on bank balance sheets. *Carnegie-Rochester Conference Series on Public Policy* 42: 151–95.

Kashyap, A., and J. Stein. 1997a. "The Role of Banks in Monetary Policy: A Survey with Implications for European Monetary Union," *Economic Perspectives*, pp. 2–18. Federal Reserve Bank of Chicago.

Kashyap, A., and J. Stein. 1997b. "What Do a Million Banks Have to Say about the Transmission of Monetary Policy?" Working paper no. 6056. NBER.

Neely, M., and D. Wheelock. 1997. Why does bank performance vary across states? Federal Reserve Bank of St. Louis *Review* 79(2): 27–41.

Samolyk, K. 1994. Banking conditions and regional economic performance, evidence of a regional credit channel. *Journal of Monetary Economics* 34: 259–78.

Wheelock, D. 1999. "National Monetary Policy by Regional Design: The Evolving Role of the Federal Reserve Banks in the Federal Reserve System Policy," in J. von Hagen and C. J. Waller, eds., *Regional Aspects of Monetary Union*. Boston: Kluwer Academic Publishers.

Index

www.ingramcontent.com/pod-product-compliance
Ingram Content Group UK Ltd.
Pitfield, Milton Keynes, MK11 3LW, UK
UKHW042211180425
457623UK00011B/157